ESSENTIALS OF MANAGEMENT

Visit the *Essentials of Management* Companion Website at **www.pearsoned.co.uk/boddy** to find valuable **student** learning material including:

- Self assessment multiple choice questions for each chapter
- Links to relevant websites
- An online glossary to explain key terms
- Flashcards to test your knowledge of key terms and definitions

PEARSON

ESSENTIALS OF MANAGEMENT
A Concise Introduction

David Boddy

SELECT CHAPTER: Welcome ▾ GO   SITE SEARCH _____ GO ?

Welcome to the Companion Website for Essentials of Management: A Concise Introduction.

Students - select from the links in the drop-down menu above or the resource links below to access the student study materials.

David Boddy
ESSENTIALS OF
MANAGEMENT
A Concise Introduction

- **Student resources** including:
  - Self assessment multiple choice questions for each chapter
  - Links to relevant websites
  - An online glossary to explain key terms
  - Flashcards to test your knowledge of key terms and definitions

Instructors - visit the <u>Instructor Resource Centre</u> to access password-protected resources accompanying this title.

PEARSON Copyright © 1995 - 2012 <u>Pearson Education</u>. All rights reserved.
<u>Legal Notice</u> | <u>Privacy Policy</u> | <u>Permissions</u>

David Boddy University of Glasgow

ESSENTIALS OF MANAGEMENT
A Concise Introduction

PEARSON

Harlow, England • London • New York • Boston • San Francisco • Toronto • Sydney • Auckland • Singapore • Hong Kong
Tokyo • Seoul • Taipei • New Delhi • Cape Town • São Paulo • Mexico City • Madrid • Amsterdam • Munich • Paris • Milan

Pearson Education Limited
Edinburgh Gate
Harlow
Essex CM20 2JE
England

and Associated Companies around the world

Visit us on the World Wide Web at:
www.pearson.com/uk

First published 2012
© Pearson Education Limited 2012

ISBN 978-0-273-73928-9

British Library Cataloguing-in-Publication Data
A catalogue record for this book can be obtained from the British Library.

Library of Congress Cataloging-in-Publication Data
A catalog record for this book is available from the Library of Congress.

10 9 8 7 6 5 4 3 2 1

15 14 13 12 11

Typeset in 10.5/12.5pt Minion by 73
Printed by Rotolito Lombarda, Italy

The publisher's policy is to use paper manufactured from sustainable forests.

BRIEF CONTENTS

PART 5 LEADING

PART 6 CONTROLLING

CONTENTS

PART 1 AN INTRODUCTION TO MANAGEMENT

PART 2 THE ENVIRONMENT OF MANAGEMENT

PART 3 PLANNING

PART 4
ORGANISING

PART 5 LEADING

PART 6
CONTROLLING

CHAPTER 16
MANAGING OPERATIONS AND QUALITY

CHAPTER 17
CONTROLLING AND MEASURING PERFORMANCE

SUPPORTING RESOURCES

Visit **www.pearsoned.co.uk/boddy** to find valuable online resources

Companion Website for students

- Self assessment multiple choice questions for each chapter
- Links to relevant websites
- An online glossary to explain key terms
- Flashcards to test your knowledge of key terms and definitions

For instructors

- Customisable PowerPoint slides which are downloadable and available to use for teaching
- Complete downloadable Instructor's Manual

Also: The Companion Website provides the following features:

- Search tool to help locate specific items of content
- E-mail results and profile tools to send results of quizzes to instructors
- Online help and support to assist with website usage and troubleshooting

For more information please contact your local Pearson Education sales representative or visit **www.pearsoned.co.uk/boddy**

PREFACE

This book is intended for students who are taking their first course in management. Most will be undergraduates taking the subject as part of a qualification in another discipline (such as engineering, accountancy, law, information technology, science, nursing or social work). Others will be following a course in management as an element in their professional association's examination schemes. The book should also be useful to readers with a first degree or equivalent qualification in a non-management subject who are taking further studies leading to Certificate, Diploma or MBA qualifications.

The book has the following three main objectives:

- to provide those new to the formal study of management with a clear introduction;
- to show that ideas on management apply to most areas of human activity, not just to commercial enterprises; and
- to make the topic attractive to students from many backgrounds and with diverse career intentions.

European context

While many management concepts have developed in the United States, the text encourages readers to consider how their particular context shapes management practice. National and cultural differences influence practice – not only as part of an increasingly integrated Europe but as part of a wider international management community. The cases and Management in Practice features should build an awareness of cultural diversity and the implications of this for working in organisations with different managerial styles and backgrounds.

Integrated perspective

To help the reader see management as a coherent whole, the material is presented within an integrative model of management and demonstrates the relationships between the many academic perspectives. The central integrating theme is of managers interacting with their contexts – which they interpret and shape as they do their work. This should help students to develop the practice of contextual awareness, which should give valuable support in whatever career they follow.

Relating to personal experience

The text assumes that many readers will have little if any experience of managing in conventional organisations, and equally little prior knowledge of relevant evidence and theory. However, all will have experience of being managed and all will have managed activities in their domestic and social lives. The activities in each chapter encourage readers to use and share such experiences from everyday life to explore the ideas presented. In this way, the book tries to show that management is not a remote activity performed by others, but a process in which all are engaged in some way.

Most readers' careers are likely to be fragmented and uncertain, and many will work for medium-sized and smaller enterprises. They will probably be working close to customers and in organisations that incorporate diverse cultures, values and interests. The activities may also help to develop their skills of gathering data, comparing evidence and generally enhancing self-awareness and confidence.

GUIDED TOUR OF THE BOOK

PART 3
PLANNING

Introduction

This part examines the generic management activities of planning and decision-making, and then looks at their application to the task of managing strategy. This depends on understanding the environment of the business and on building an internal capability to deliver whatever strategy management decides upon.

Chapter 6 provides an overview of planning in organisations, setting out the purposes of planning, the types of plan and the tasks of planning. While all these tasks are likely to be part of the process, their shape will always depend on the circumstances for which a plan is being made.

Decision-making is closely linked to planning, made necessary by finite resources and infinite demands. People in organisations continually decide on inputs, transformation processes and outputs – and the quality of those decisions affects organisational performance. Chapter 7 therefore introduces the main decision-making processes, and contrasts several theories of decision-making in organisations.

Chapter 8 outlines the strategy process, and introduces techniques that managers use to analyse the options facing businesses of all kinds. This analysis can then lead to clearer choices about future direction.

The book has 17 **chapters**, in six **parts**.

Chapter openers set out **learning outcomes**. These are usually 5 or 6 in number, and the sections in the chapter match closely these learning outcomes, giving each chapter a strong and consistent structure.

These are followed by the first part of a two-part chapter **Activity**. This is designed to encourage students to reflect at the outset on what they think or know about the topic: it also encourages them to identify one or two people (family or friends) with some experience of organisations, who may be willing to discuss the topic with them. There is a second part to the activity at the end of the main material in the chapter, containing questions which help them to make close connections between what they have found and the topics covered in the chapter.

CHAPTER 1
MANAGING IN ORGANISATIONS

Learning outcomes

When you have read this chapter you should be able to:

1. Explain that the role of management is to add value to resources in diverse settings
2. Give examples of management as a universal human activity and as a distinct role
3. Compare the roles of general, functional, line, staff and project managers, and of entrepreneurs
4. Compare how managers influence others to add value
5. Use ideas from the chapter to comment on the management issues in the Ryanair case study

INTRODUCTION   5

Activity 1.1   What is 'management'?

Before reading this chapter, write some notes on what you understand 'management' to mean.

Choose the organisation or people who may be able to help you learn about the topic. You may find it helpful to discuss the topic with a manager you know, or reflect on an activity you have managed.

- Identify a situation in which someone has been 'managing' an activity, and describe it briefly.
- How did they go about achieving the task?
- Can they identify the types of activities they worked on?
- What clues does that give you about what 'management' may mean in the organisation?
- Keep these notes as you will be able to use them later.

1.1   Introduction

Ryanair (the Chapter case study) illustrates several aspects of management. A group of entrepreneurs saw an opportunity in the market for air travel, and created an organisation to take advantage of it. They bring resources together and transform them into a service which they sell to customers. They differ from their competitors by using different resources (e.g. secondary airports) and different ways to transform these into outputs (e.g. short turnrounds). They have been innovative in the way they run the business, such as in identifying what some customers valued in a flight – cost rather than luxury – and carried a record 74 million passengers in the year to April 2011.

Entrepreneurs like Michael O'Leary of Ryanair are always looking for ways to innovate to create new products, services and ways of working, to make the most of new opportunities. Other managers face a different challenge – more demand with fewer resources. Those managing the United Nations World Food Programme struggle to raise funds from donor countries – aid is falling while hunger is increasing. In almost every public healthcare organisation managers face a growing demand for treatment, but fewer resources with which to provide it.

Organisations of all kinds – from rapidly growing operations like Facebook to established businesses like Shell UK or Marks & Spencer – depend on people at all levels who can run the things efficiently now, and make changes to prepare for the future. This book is about the knowledge and skills that enable people to meet these expectations, and so build a satisfying and rewarding management career.

Figure 1.1 illustrates the themes of this chapter. It represents the fact that people in organisations bring resources from the external environment and transform them into outputs that they hope are of greater value. They pass these back to the environment, and the value they obtain in return (money, reputation, goodwill etc.) enables them to attract new resources to continue in business (shown by the feedback arrow from output to input). If the outputs do not attract sufficient resources, the enterprise will fail.

The chapter begins by examining the significance of managed organisations in our world. It then outlines what management means and introduces theories about the nature of managerial work.

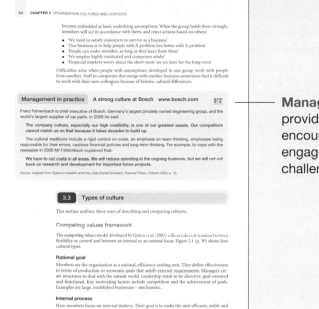

Management in practice boxes provide real-world examples and encourage students to identify and engage with managerial issues and challenges.

Cases: Each chapter ends with a case, which illustrates themes from the chapter. With one exception (Chapter 2 – Robert Owen) students should recognise these contemporary and up-to-date accounts, and gain insights into the management of these enterprises, and the connections between theory and current practice.

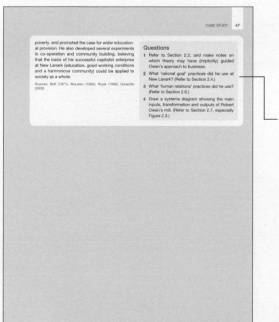

Case questions (in a structured form) encourage students to connect issues in the case with specified Sections in the chapter.

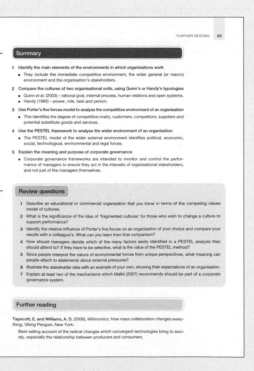

Activity 1.2   Understanding management

Recall the organisation you used in Activity 1.1.

Having read the chapter, make brief notes summarising what you now think 'managing' involves in this company:

- Describe what resources it uses and how it adds value to them. (Refer to Section 1.2.)
- List examples of some of the specialist roles of management (such as a functional or a line manager) and describe what they do in this company. (Refer to Section 1.4.)
- Can you identify examples of managers performing one or more of Mintzberg's roles? (Refer to Section 1.5.)
- What have you been able to find out about how they perform ONE of the management tasks (planning, organising, leading, controlling)? (Refer to Section 1.6.)

Compare what you have found with other students on your course.

Summary

1   Explain that the role of management is to add value to resources in diverse settings
- Managers create value by transforming inputs into outputs of greater value: they do this by developing competences within the organisation which, by constantly adding value (however measured) to resources is able to survive and prosper. The concept of creating value is subjective and open to different interpretations. Managers work in an infinite variety of settings, and Table 1.1 suggested how each setting raises relatively unique challenges.

2   Give examples of management as a universal human activity and as a distinct role
- Management is an activity that everyone undertakes as they manage their daily lives. In another sense management is an activity which many people conduct, not just those called 'managers'. People create the distinct role when they separate the management of work from the work itself and allocate the tasks. The distinction between management and non-management work is fluid and the result of human action.

3   Compare the roles of general, functional, line, staff and project managers and of entrepreneurs
- General managers are responsible for a complete business or a unit within it. They depend on functional managers who can be either in charge of line departments meeting customer needs, such as manufacturing and sales, or in staff departments such as finance which provide advice or services to line managers. Project managers are in charge of temporary activities usually directed at implementing change. Entrepreneurs are those who create new businesses to exploit opportunities.

4   Explain how managers influence others to add value to resources through
- The processes of managing. Henry Mintzberg identified ten management roles in three groups which he labelled informational, interpersonal and decisional. Luthans and, more recently, Wolff and Moser observed that successful managers were likely to be those who networked with people inside and outside the organisation.

'Before and after' Activities enable students to engage with the material by connecting ideas in the chapter to a management situation they have identified.

Chapter **Summaries** aid revision by supplying a concise synopsis of the main chapter topics.

Review questions enable students to check their understanding of the main themes and concepts.

Summary

1   Identify the main elements of the environments in which organisations work
- They include the immediate competitive environment, the wider general (or macro) environment and the organisation's stakeholders.

2   Compare the cultures of two organisational units, using Quinn's or Handy's typologies
- Quinn et al. (2003) – rational goal, internal process, human relations and open systems.
- Handy (1993) – power, role, task and person.

3   Use Porter's five forces model to analyse the competitive environment of an organisation
- This identifies the degree of competitive rivalry, customers, competitors, suppliers and potential substitute goods and services.

4   Use the PESTEL framework to analyse the wider environment of an organisation
- The PESTEL model of the wider external environment identifies political, economic, social, technological, environmental and legal forces.

5   Explain the meaning and purpose of corporate governance
- Corporate governance frameworks are intended to monitor and control the performance of managers to ensure they act in the interests of organisational stakeholders, and not just of the managers themselves.

Review questions

1   Describe an educational or commercial organisation that you know in terms of the competing values model of cultures.
2   What is the significance of the idea of 'fragmented cultures' for those who wish to change a culture to support performance?
3   Identify the relative influence of Porter's five forces on an organisation of your choice and compare your results with a colleague's. What can you learn from that comparison?
4   How should managers decide which of the many factors easily identified in a PESTEL analysis they should attend to? If they have to be selective, what is the value of the PESTEL method?
5   Since people interpret the nature of environmental forces from unique perspectives, what meaning can people attach to statements about external pressures?
6   Illustrate the stakeholder idea with an example of your own, showing their expectations of an organisation.
7   Explain at least two of the mechanisms which Mallin (2007) recommends should be part of a corporate governance system.

Further reading

Tapscott, E. and Williams, A. D. (2006), *Wikinomics: How mass collaboration changes everything*, Viking Penguin, New York.

Best-selling account of the radical changes which convergent technologies bring to society, especially the relationship between producers and consumers.

ACKNOWLEDGEMENTS

This book has benefited from the comments, criticisms and suggestions of many colleagues and reviewers. It also reflects the reactions and comments of students who have used the material on their courses. Their advice and feedback have been of immense help.

Finally, I gratefully acknowledge the support and help that my wife, Cynthia, has provided throughout this project.

David Boddy
University of Glasgow
May 2011

Publisher's acknowledgements

We are grateful to the following for permission to reproduce copyright material:

Figures

Figure 2.1 from *Becoming a Master Manager* 3ed, (Quinn et al 2003) p.13 Copyright © 2003 John Wiley & Sons, Inc. Reproduced with permission of John Wiley & Sons, Inc.; Fig 3.2 Reprinted with the permission of Free Press, a Division of Simon & Schuster, Inc., from COMPETITIVE STRATEGY: Techniques for Analyzing Industries and Competitors by Michael E. Porter, 5e, Simon & Schuster (Inc) (Porter, M.E. 1980) Copyright © 1980, 1988 by The Free Press. All rights reserved; Figure 4.2 from *Clustering Countries on Attitudinal Dimensions*, vol. 10 no. 3, Academy of Management Review (Ronen, S. & Shenkar, O. 1985) pp. 435–454 The Academy of Management review by ACADEMY OF MANAGEMENT. Copyright 1985. Reproduced with permission of ACADEMY OF MANAGEMENT (NY) in the format Textbook via Copyright Clearance Center.; Figure 5.1 from *Management*, 5ed., South-Western (Daft 2000) 135, From Daft. Management, 5E.© 2000 South-Western, a part of Cengage Learning, Inc. Reproduced by permission. www.cengage.com/permissions; Figure 5.2 adapted from *Business & Society*, South-Western Publishers (Carroll, A.B. 1989) 84, From CARROLL. BUSINESS AND SOCIETY. Ethics and Stakeholders, 1E. © 1989 South-Western, a part of Cengage Learning, Inc. Reproduced by permission. www.cengage.com/permissions; Figure 8.1 from Closing the gap between strategy and execution, *MIT Sloan Management Review*, 48 (4), pp. 30–38 (Sull, D.N. 2010); Figures 8.2, 8.4 Reprinted with the permission of Free Press, a Division of Simon & Schuster, Inc., from COMPETITIVE ADVANTAGE: Creating and Sustaining Superior Performance by Michael E. Porter, 5e, Simon & Schuster (Inc) (Porter, M.E. 1980) Copyright © 1985, 1988 by Michael E. Porter. All rights reserved; Figure 8.3 adapted from *Corporate Strategy*, Penguin (Ansoff, H. 1988); Figure 10.1 from *Managing information systems: An organisational perspective*, 2ed., (Boddy, D., Boonstra, A. & Kennedy, G. 2005) FT/Prentice Hall © Pearson Education Ltd 2005; Figures 10.2, 10.3 from *Managing Information Systems: Strategy and Organisation*, 3cd., (Boddy, D., Boonstra, A. & Kennedy, G. 2009) FT/Prentice Hall © Pearson Education Ltd 2009; Figure 12.3 Reprinted by permission of *Harvard Business Review* from How to choose a leadership pattern: should a manager be democratic or autocratic – or something in between?, by Tannenbaum, R. and Schmidt, W.H. 37 (2) 1973, pp. 95–102 Copyright © 1973 by the Harvard Business School Publishing Corporation; all rights reserved; Figure 14.3 from The selection of communication media as an executive skill, 11 (3), pp. 225–232 (Lengel, R.H. and Daft, R.L. 1988) The Academy of Management perspectives by ACADEMY OF MANAGEMENT. Copyright 1988. Reproduced with permission of ACADEMY OF MANAGEMENT (NY) in the format Textbook via Copyright Clearance Center.; Figure 15.3 adapted from *The Human Organization: Its Management and Value*, McGraw-Hill New York (Likert, R. 1967), © The McGraw-Hill Companies Inc.; Figure 16.3 Reprinted by permission of *Harvard Business Review* adapted from Link Manufacturing Process and Product Lifecycles, Hayes, R.H. and Wheelwright, S.C. 57 (1) 1979, pp. 133–140 Copyright © 1979 by the Harvard Business School Publishing Corporation; all rights reserved

Tables

Table 17.4 adapted from *Operations Management*, 6th ed., (Slack, N., Chambers, S. and Johnston, R. 2010) Financial Times Prentice Hall © Pearson Education Ltd 2010

Text

Box on page 225 Reprinted by permission of *Harvard Business Review* from How Pixar Fosters Collective Creativity, by Catmull, E. 86 (9), 2008, pp. 64-72 Copyright © 2008 by the Harvard Business School Publishing Corporation; all rights reserved; Box on page 258 from www.IKEA.com

The Financial Times

Box on page 7 adapted from Turnaround ace shows his metal, *Financial Times*, 27/05/2009 (Peter Marsh and Andrew Bounds), Financial Times; Box on page 29 adapted from Secrets of the maverick cobbler, *The Financial Times*, Copyright © The Financial Times Ltd.; Box on page 54 adapted from Space to breathe amid the crisis, *FT*, 02/03/2009, 16 (Daniel Schaefer); Box on page 77 after Insurgency in India—how the Maoist threat reaches beyond Nepal, *FT*, 26/04/2006, p.13 (Jo Johnson); Box on page 100 adapted from Lobbyist driving a hard bargain, *The Financial Times*, 16/06/2009 (Joshua Chaffin), Copyright © The Financial Times Ltd.; Box on page 113 adapted from BA cuts costs as it anticipates two years of recession, *The Financial Times*, 06/03/2009 (Kevin Done), Copyright © The Financial Times Ltd.; Box on page 115 adapted from The Man who has to shake up Merck, *The Financial Times*, 27/03/2006, p.10 (Christopher Bowe), Copyright © The Financial Times Ltd.; Box on page 155 adapted from 3G wrong number forces change of strategy, *The Financial Times*, 02/03/2009 (Andrew Parker and Paul Taylor), Copyright © The Financial Times Ltd.; Box on page 160 adapted from M&S brand value, *The Financial Times*, 10/11/2010 (Emiko Terazono), Copyright © The Financial Times Ltd.; Box on page 179 adapted from A healthy attitude to risk-taking, *The Financial Times*, 04/08/2008 (Andrew Jack and Haig Simonian), Copyright © The Financial Times Ltd.; Box on page 186 adapted from Prepared to wait for a bigger yield, *The Financial Times*, 15/06/2009 (Hal Weitzman), Copyright © The Financial Times Ltd.; Box on page 199 from Bringing business technology out into the open, *The Financial Times*, 17/09/2003 (Fiona Harvey), Copyright © The Financial Times Ltd.; Box on page 248 adapted from News Corp's wooing of Beijing pays off, *The Financial Times*, 09/01/2003 (James Kynge), Copyright © The Financial Times Ltd.; Box on page 248 adapted from Chairman knows the value of a little help from his friends, *The Financial Times*, 21/02/2003 (Mure Dickie and Kathrin Hille), Copyright © The Financial Times Ltd.; Box on page 287 adapted from 'Catastrophic safety risks' remain for BP, *The Financial Times*, 31/10/2006 (Sheila McNulty), Copyright © The Financial Times Ltd.

Photographs

23 Corbis: Thierry Tronnel/Sygma; 46 Reproduced by kind permission of New Lanark Trust www.newlanark.org; 67 Courtesy of Nokia; 87 Alamy Images: Purestock. 106 Corbis: Bettmann. 124 By kind permission, Crossrail; 146 IKEA Ltd; 192 Alamy Images: Roger Bamber; 210 Alamy Images: M4OS Photos; 252 Corbis: KIMBERLEY WHITE/Reuters; 274 Eden Project; 294 Corbis: Kim Komenich/San Francisco Chronicle; 351 Getty Images.

Cover image: Front: Getty Images

In some instances we have been unable to trace the owners of copyright material, and we would appreciate any information that would enable us to do so.

PART 1

AN INTRODUCTION TO MANAGEMENT

Introduction

This part considers why management exists and what it contributes to human wealth and well-being. Management is both a universal human activity and a distinct occupation. We all manage in the first sense, as we organise our lives and deal with family and other relationships. As employees and customers we experience the activities of those who manage in the second sense, as members of an organisation with which we deal. This part offers some ways of making sense of the complex and contradictory activity of managing.

Chapter 1 clarifies the nature and emergence of management and the different ways in which people describe the role. It explains how management is both a universal human activity and a specialist occupation. Its purpose is to create wealth by adding value to resources, which managers do by influencing others – the chapter shows how they do this. It concludes with some ideas about managing your study of the topic. You are likely to benefit most by actively linking your work on this book to events in real organisations, and the chapter includes a two-part activity which helps you to do this.

Chapter 2 sets out the main theoretical perspectives on management and shows how these can complement each other despite the apparently competing values about the nature of the management task. Be active in relating these theoretical perspectives to real events as this will help you to understand and test the theory.

CHAPTER 1
MANAGING IN ORGANISATIONS

Learning outcomes

When you have read this chapter you should be able to:

1 Explain that the role of management is to add value to resources in diverse settings

2 Give examples of management as a universal human activity and as a distinct role

3 Compare the roles of general, functional, line, staff and project managers, and of entrepreneurs

4 Compare how managers influence others to add value

5 Use ideas from the chapter to comment on the management issues in the Ryanair case study

Activity 1.1   What is 'management'?

Before reading this chapter, write some notes on what you understand 'management' to mean.

Choose the organisation or people who may be able to help you learn about the topic. You may find it helpful to discuss the topic with a manager you know, or reflect on an activity you have managed.

- Identify a situation in which someone has been 'managing' an activity, and describe it briefly.
- How did they go about achieving the task?
- Can they identify the types of activities they worked on?
- What clues does that give you about what 'management' may mean in the organisation?
- Keep these notes as you will be able to use them later.

1.1   Introduction

Ryanair (the Chapter case study) illustrates several aspects of management. A group of entrepreneurs saw an opportunity in the market for air travel, and created an organisation to take advantage of it. They bring resources together and transform them into a service which they sell to customers. They differ from their competitors by using different resources (e.g. secondary airports) and different ways to transform these into outputs (e.g. short turnrounds). They have been innovative in the way they run the business, such as in identifying what some customers valued in a flight – cost rather than luxury – and carried a record 74 million passengers in the year to April 2011.

Entrepreneurs like Michael O'Leary of Ryanair are always looking for ways to innovate to create new products, services and ways of working, to make the most of new opportunities. Other managers face a different challenge – more demand with fewer resources. Those managing the United Nations World Food Programme struggle to raise funds from donor countries – aid is falling while hunger is increasing. In almost every public healthcare organisation managers face a growing demand for treatment, but fewer resources with which to provide it.

Organisations of all kinds – from rapidly growing operations like Facebook to established businesses like Shell UK or Marks & Spencer – depend on people at all levels who can run the things efficiently now, and make changes to prepare for the future. This book is about the knowledge and skills that enable people to meet these expectations, and so build a satisfying and rewarding management career.

Figure 1.1 illustrates the themes of this chapter. It represents the fact that people in organisations bring resources from the external environment and transform them into outputs that they hope are of greater value. They pass these back to the environment, and the value they obtain in return (money, reputation, goodwill etc.) enables them to attract new resources to continue in business (shown by the feedback arrow from output to input). If the outputs do not attract sufficient resources, the enterprise will fail.

The chapter begins by examining the significance of managed organisations in our world. It then outlines what management means and introduces theories about the nature of managerial work.

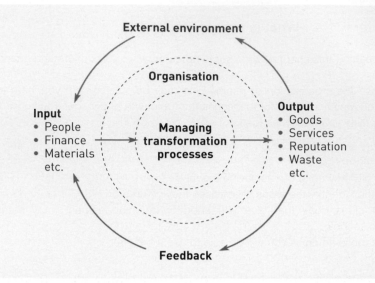

Figure 1.1
Managing
organisation
and environment

1.2 **Managing to add value to resources**

An **organisation** is a
social arrangement for
achieving controlled per-
formance towards goals
that create value.

We live in a world of managed **organisations**. We experience many every day – domestic arrangements (family or flatmates), large public organisations (the postal service), small businesses (the newsagent), well-known private companies (the jar of coffee) or a voluntary group (the club we attend). They affect us and we judge their performance. Did the transaction work smoothly or was it chaotic? Was the service good, reasonable or poor? Will you go there again?

As human societies become more specialised, we depend more on others to satisfy our needs. We meet some of these by acting individually or within family and social groups: organisations provide the rest. Good managers make things work – so that aid is delivered, roads are safe, shops have stock, hospitals function and all the rest. They don't do the work themselves, but build an organisation with the resources *and* competences to deliver what people need. **Tangible resources** are physical assets such as plant, people and finance – things you can see and touch. **Intangible resources** are non-physical assets such as information, reputation and knowledge.

Tangible resources
are the physical assets
of an organisation such
as plant, people and
finance.

Intangible resources
are non-physical assets
such as information, rep-
utation and knowledge.

Competences are the
skills and abilities by
which resources are
deployed effectively –
systems, procedures
and ways of working.

Value is added to
resources when they are
transformed into goods
or services that are worth
more than their original
cost plus the cost of
transformation.

To transform these resources into valuable goods and services people need to work together. They need to know what to do, understand their customers, deal with enquiries properly and generally make the transaction work well. Beyond that they look for opportunities to improve, be innovative and learn from experience. Good managers bring out the best in their staff so that they willingly 'go the extra mile': together they develop effective ways of working that become second nature. These 'ways of working' are **competences** – skills, procedures or systems which enable people to use resources productively. A manager's role is to secure and retain resources and competences so that the organisation adds **value** – it is producing an output that is more valuable than the resources it has used.

Well-managed organisations create value in many ways. If you buy a ticket from Ryanair, you can easily measure the tangible value of a cheap flight. In other purchases the value is intangible, as people judge a product by its appearance, what it feels or smells like, how trendy it is, or whether it fits their image. Others value good service, or a clear set of instructions. Good managers understand what customers value and build an organisation to satisfy them.

| Management in practice | Creating value at DavyMarkham | FT |

www.davymarkham.com

Kevin Parkin is Managing Director (and part-owner) of DavyMarkham, a small engineering company. Although the company has a long history, by the mid-1990s it was making regular losses, and its survival was in doubt. Since Mr Parkin joined the company he has returned it to profit, and in 2009 was predicting a 10 per cent increase in sales the following year. He has concentrated on identifying what the company is good at, and then using tough management and financial discipline to make sure staff follow the recipe for success. Mr Parkin has removed poor managers, walks the shop floor twice a day to check on progress, and engages with the workforce.

> It has been essential to tell people the truth about the business, whether it's good or bad, and giving them the enthusiasm they require to make them want to succeed . . . I also ask [my 'mentors' – people I have known in previous jobs] about key strategic decisions, people issues, market penetration, capital spending and general business solutions.

Source: Adapted from Turnaround ace shows his metal (Peter Marsh and Andrew Bounds), *Financial Times*, 27 May 2009.

Commercial organisations of all kinds (business start-ups, small and medium-sized enterprises, on-line firms and international enterprises) aim to add value and create wealth. So do voluntary and not-for-profit organisations – by educating people, counselling the troubled or caring for the sick.

There are over 160,000 charities in England and Wales, with annual incoming resources of over £52 billion (equal to about 3 per cent of Gross Domestic Product), and employing over 660,000 staff (Charities Commission Annual Report for 2009–10, at **www.charitycommission.gov.uk**). Managing a large charity is at least as demanding a job as managing a commercial business, facing similar challenges of adding value to limited resources. Donors and recipients expect them to manage resources well so that they add value to them.

Theatres, orchestras, museums and art galleries create value by offering inspiration, new perspectives or unexpected insights – and often do so in situations of great complexity (imagine the complexity in staging an opera, concert or major exhibition). Others add value by creating businesses or challenging projects through which people develop new skills or insights, and build long-term friendships.

While organisations aim to add value, many do not do so. If people work inefficiently they will use more resources than customers will pay for. They may create pollution and waste, and so destroy wealth. Motorway builders create value for drivers, residents of by-passed villages and shareholders – but destroy value for some people if the route damages an ancient woodland rich in history and wildlife. The idea of creating value is subjective and relative.

Managers face some issues that are unique to the setting in which they operate (charities need to maintain the support of donors) and others which arise in most organisations (business planning or ensuring quality). Table 1.1 illustrates some of these diverse settings, and their (relatively) unique management challenges – which are in addition to challenges that are common to all.

Whatever its nature, the value an organisation creates depends on how well those who work there obtain resources and develop their competences.

1.3   Meanings of management

Management as a universal human activity

Management is both a **universal human activity** and a distinct occupation. In the first sense, people manage an infinite range of activities:

> When human beings 'manage' their work, they take responsibility for its purpose, progress and outcome by exercising the quintessentially human capacity to stand back

Management as a universal human activity occurs whenever people take responsibility for an activity and consciously try to shape its progress and outcome.

Table 1.1 Where people manage

Setting – industry or type	Examples in this book	'Unique' challenges
Business start-ups	Inamo Restaurant – see Chapter 6, **p. 116** and Chapter 7, **p. 130**	Securing funding to launch, creating good internal systems, selling enough to bring in enough cash to continue.
Small and medium-sized enterprises (SMEs)	DavyMarkham – MIP feature above	Generating enough funds to survive, innovate and enter new markets.
Professional business services	Iris (advertising) – MIP feature in Chapter 7, **p. 130**	Managing highly qualified staff delivering customised, innovative services.
Voluntary, not-for-profit organisations and charities	Eden Project – Chapter 13 case study, **pp. 274–5**	Providing visitors with visit to encourage return visit, raising funds for educational work, fulfilling mission.
Public sector organisations	Crossrail – Chapter 6 case study, **pp. 124–5** A Foundation Hospital – Chapter 17 case study, **pp. 351–2**	Managing high-profile political and commercial interests. Establishing suitable control systems to ensure quality.
Large private businesses	Ryanair – Chapter 1 case study, **pp. 23–4**	Responding to changing economic and political environments, managing diverse activities.
High-tech businesses	Google – Chapter 11 case study, **pp. 229–30** Apple – Chapter 12 case study, **pp. 252–3**	Maintaining constant innovation in rapidly changing markets.
International businesses	Starbucks – Chapter 4 case study, **pp. 87–8** Zara – Chapter 16 case study, **pp. 334–5**	Managing diverse activities across many cultures; balancing central control and local initiative.

Note: MIP = management in practice

from experience and to regard it prospectively, in terms of what will happen; reflectively, in terms of what is happening; and retrospectively, in terms of what has happened. Thus management is an expression of human agency, the capacity actively to shape and direct the world, rather than simply react to it. (Hales, 2001, p. 2)

A **manager** is someone who gets things done with the aid of people and other resources.

Management is the activity of getting things done with the aid of people and other resources.

Rosemary Stewart (1967) expressed this idea when she described a **manager** as someone who gets things done with the aid of people and other resources, so defining **management** as the activity of getting things done with the aid of people and other resources. So described, it is a universal human activity – domestic, social and political – as well as in formally established organisations.

In pre-industrial societies people typically work alone or in family units, controlling their time and resources. They decide what to make, how to make it and where to sell it, combining work and management to create value. Self-employed craftworkers, professionals in small practices and those in a one-person business do this every day.

As individuals we run our lives and careers: in this respect we are managing. Family members manage children, elderly dependants and household tasks. We do it in voluntary or charity activities where we do the work (planting trees or selling raffle tickets) and the management activities (planning the winter programme).

Management as a distinct role

Human action can separate the 'management' element of a task from the 'work' element, thus creating 'managers' who are in some degree apart from those doing the work. **Management as a distinct role** emerges when external parties, usually private or public owners of capital, gain control of a work process that people used to complete themselves. The owners are likely to specify what to make, how to make it and where to sell it – controlling the time, behaviour and skills of their employees. The latter now sell their labour, not their products.

This happens when someone starts an enterprise, initially performing the *technical* aspects of the work itself – writing software, designing clothes – and also more *conceptual* tasks such as planning which markets to serve, or deciding how to raise money. If the business grows and the entrepreneur engages staff, they will need to spend time on *interpersonal* tasks such as training and supervising their work. The founder progressively takes on more management roles – a **role** being the expectations that others have of someone occupying a position. It expresses the specific responsibilities and requirements of the job, and what someone holding it should do (or not do).

This separation of management and non-management work is not inevitable or permanent. People deliberately separate the roles, and can also bring them together. As Henri Fayol (1949) (of whom you will read more in Chapter 2) observed:

> Management . . . is neither an exclusive privilege nor a particular responsibility of the head or senior members of a business; it is an activity spread, like all other activities, between head and members of the body corporate. (p. 6)

Someone in charge of part of, say, a production department will usually be treated as a manager, and referred to as one. The people who operate the machines will be called something else. In a growing business like Ryanair, the boundary between 'managers' and 'non-managers' is likely to be very fluid, with all being ready to perform a range of tasks, irrespective of their title. Hales' (2006) research shows how first-line managers now hold some responsibilities traditionally associated with middle managers. They are still responsible for supervising subordinates, but often also have to deal with costs and customer satisfaction – previously a middle manager's job.

Management as a distinct role develops when activities previously embedded in the work itself become the responsibility not of the employee, but of owners or their agents.

A **role** is the sum of the expectations that other people have of a person occupying a position.

1.4   Specialisation between areas of management

As an organisation grows, senior managers usually create separate functions and a hierarchy, so that management itself becomes divided.

Functional specialisation

General managers typically head a complete unit of the organisation, such as a division or subsidiary, within which there will be several functions. The general manager is responsible for the unit's performance, and relies on the managers in charge of each function. A small organisation will have just one or two general managers, who will also manage the functions.

General managers are responsible for the performance of a distinct unit of the organisation.

Functional managers are responsible for the performance of an area of technical or professional work.

Line managers are responsible for the performance of activities that directly meet customers' needs.

Functional managers are responsible for an area of work – either as line managers or staff managers. **Line managers** are in charge of a function that creates value directly by supplying products or services to customers: they could be in charge of a retail store, a group of nurses, a social work department or a manufacturing area. Their performance significantly affects business performance and image, as they and their staff are in direct contact with customers or clients. At Shell, Mike Hogg was (in 2011) the General Manager of Shell Gas Direct, while Melanie Lane was General Manager, UK Retail.

Management in practice   The store manager – fundamental to success

A manager with extensive experience of retailing commented:

> The store manager's job is far more complex that it may at first appear. Staff management is an important element and financial skills are required to manage a budget and the costs involved in running a store. Managers must understand what is going on behind the scenes – in terms of logistics and the supply chain – as well as what is happening on the shop floor. They must also be good with customers and increasingly they need outward-looking skills as they are encouraged to take high-profile roles in the community.

Source: Private communication from the manager.

Staff managers are responsible for the performance of activities that support line managers.

Staff managers are in charge of activities like finance, personnel, purchasing or legal affairs which support the line managers, who are their customers. Staff in support departments are not usually in direct contact with external customers, and so do not earn income directly for the organisation. Managers of staff departments operate as line managers within their unit. At Shell, Bob Henderson was Head of Legal and Kate Smith was Head of UK Government Relations.

Project managers are responsible for managing a project, usually intended to change some element of an organisation or its context.

Project managers are responsible for a temporary team created to plan and implement a change, such as a new product or system. Mike Buckingham, an engineer, managed a project to implement a new manufacturing system in a van plant. He still had line responsibilities for aspects of manufacturing, but worked for most of the time on the project, helped by a team of technical specialists. When the change was complete he returned to full-time work on his line job.

Entrepreneurs are people who see opportunities in a market, and quickly mobilise the resources to deliver the product or service profitably.

Entrepreneurs are people who are able to see opportunities in a market which others have overlooked. They quickly secure the resources they need, and use them to build a profitable business. John Scott (Managing Director of Scott Timber, now the UK's largest manufacturer of wooden pallets – **www.scott-timber.co.uk**) recalls the early days:

> I went from not really knowing what I wanted to do . . . to getting thrown into having to make a plant work, employ men, lead by example. We didn't have an office – it was in my mum's house, and she did the invoicing. The house was at the top of the yard, and the saw mill was at the bottom. (*Financial Times*, 11 July 2007, p. 18)

Management hierarchies

As organisations grow, senior managers usually create a hierarchy of positions. The amount of 'management' and 'non-management' work within these positions varies, and the boundaries between them are fluid.

Performing direct operations

People who perform direct operations do the manual and mental work to make and deliver products or services. These range from low paid cleaners or shop workers to highly paid pilots or lawyers. The activity is likely to contain some aspects of management work, though in lower-level jobs this will be limited. People running a small business combine management work with direct work to meet customer requirements.

Supervising staff on direct operations

Supervisors (sometimes called first-line managers) typically direct and control the daily work of a group or process. They ensure that front-line staff perform the essential, basic activities correctly – by paying attention to their job, noticing detail, keeping things moving efficiently and courteously to provide the quality of goods or services the customer expects. Supervisors are responsible for monitoring and reporting on work performance in an area, and working to improve it. They allocate and co-ordinate work, monitor the pace and help with problems. Sometimes they work with middle managers to making operational decisions on staff or work methods. Examples include the supervisor of a production team, the head chef in a hotel, or a nurse in charge of a hospital ward. They may continue to perform some direct operations, but will spend less time on them than subordinates.

Managing supervisors and first-line managers

Usually referred to as middle managers, they – such as an engineering manager at Ryanair – are expected to ensure that first-line managers work in line with company policies. They translate strategy into operational tasks, mediating between senior management vision and operational reality. They may help to develop strategy by presenting information about customer expectations, or suggesting alternative strategies to senior managers (Currie and Proctor, 2005). They provide a communication link – telling first-line managers what they expect, and briefing senior managers about current issues – one of the reasons banks got into difficulty in 2008 was because senior managers had no idea of the risks being taken by their traders and loan officers: good middle managers ensure that their bosses know what is going on.

Others face the challenge of managing volunteers. Charities depend on their time and effort, yet commonly face problems when they don't turn up, or work ineffectively – but cannot draw on the systems commonly used to reward and retain paid staff.

Managing the managers

The most senior employee is usually called the 'managing director' or 'chief executive'. Their main responsibility is to ensure that the middle managers work in ways that add value to their resources. In smaller organisations they will deal directly with middle managers, but in larger ones they will work through a team of senior executives in charge of functional areas like marketing or manufacturing. Chief executives influence performance largely by deciding who to appoint to executive positions, and by how they manage this top team. They report to the board of directors about developments in the business, and about issues which require board approval.

Managing the business

Managing the business is the work of a small group, usually called the board of directors. They establish policy and have a particular responsibility for managing relations with people and institutions in the world outside, such as shareholders, national media or government ministers. They need to know broadly about internal matters, but spend most of their time looking to the future or dealing with external affairs. Depending on local company law, the board usually includes non-executive directors – senior managers from other companies who should bring a wider, independent view to discussions. Such non-executive directors can enhance the effectiveness of the board, and give investors confidence that the board is acting in their interests. The board will not consider operational issues.

Stakeholders are individuals, groups or organisations with an interest in, or who are affected by, what the organisation does.

Whatever their role, people add value to resources by influencing others, including internal and external **stakeholders** – who affect, or who are affected by, an organisation's actions and policies. Some stakeholders have different priorities from the managers, so the latter need to influence them to act in ways they believe will add value.

They do this directly and indirectly. Direct methods are the interpersonal skills (see Chapter 12) which managers use – persuading a boss to support a proposal, a subordinate to do more work, or a customer to change a delivery date. Managers also influence others indirectly through:

- the process of managing;
- the tasks of managing (Section 1.6); and
- shaping the context (Section 1.7).

Rosemary Stewart (1967) was one of the first to study the process of management – how managers work. She asked 160 senior and middle managers to keep a diary for four weeks, which showed that they typically worked in a fragmented, interrupted way – with very little time for thinking and working on their own. More recently, Henry Mintzberg found that within that fragmented pattern of work, managers focus on one or more distinct roles.

Henry Mintzberg – ten management roles

Mintzberg (1973) observed how (five) chief executives spent their time, and used this data to identify ten management roles, in three categories – informational, interpersonal and decisional. Managers use one or more of these roles as they try to influence other people. Table 1.2 describes them, and illustrates each with a contemporary example provided by the manager of a school nutrition project.

Informational roles

Managing depends on obtaining information about external and internal events, and passing it to others. The *monitor role* involves seeking out, receiving and screening information to understand the organisation and its context. It comes from websites and reports, and especially from chance conversations – such as with customers or new contacts at conferences and exhibitions. Much of this information is oral (gossip as well as formal meetings), building on personal contacts. In the *disseminator role* the manager shares information by forwarding reports, passing on rumours or briefing staff. As a *spokesperson* the manager transmits information to people outside the organisation – speaking at a conference, briefing the media or giving the department's view at a company meeting. Michael O'Leary at Ryanair is renowned for flamboyant statements to the media about competitors or officials in the European Commission when he disagrees with their policies.

Interpersonal roles

Interpersonal roles arise directly from a manager's formal authority and status, and shape relationships with people within and beyond the organisation. In the *figurehead role* the manager is a symbol, representing the unit in legal and ceremonial duties such as greeting a visitor, signing legal documents, presenting retirement gifts or receiving a quality award. The *leader role* defines the manager's relationship with other people (not just subordinates), including motivating, communicating and developing their skills and confidence – as one commented:

> I am conscious that I am unable to spend as much time interacting with staff members as I would like. I try to overcome this by leaving my door open whenever I am alone as an invitation to staff to come in and interrupt me, and encourage them to discuss any problems. (private communication)

Table 1.2 Mintzberg's ten management roles

Category	Role	Activity	Examples from a school nutrition project
Informational	Monitor	Seek and receive information, scan reports, maintain interpersonal contacts	Collect and review funding applications; set up database to monitor application process
	Disseminator	Forward information to others, send memos, make phone calls	Share content of applications with team members by email
	Spokesperson	Represent the unit to outsiders in speeches and reports	Present application process at internal and external events
Interpersonal	Figurehead	Perform ceremonial and symbolic duties, receive visitors	Sign letters of award to successful applicants
	Leader	Direct and motivate subordinates, train, advise and influence	Design and co-ordinate process with team and other managers
	Liaison	Maintain information links in and beyond the organisation	Become link person for government bodies to contact for progress reports
Decisional	Entrepreneur	Initiate new projects, spot opportunities, identify areas of business development	Use initiative to revise application process and to introduce electronic communication
	Disturbance handler	Take corrective action during crises, resolve conflicts amongst staff, adapt to changes	Holding face-to-face meetings with applicants when the outcome was negative; handling staff grievances
	Resource allocator	Decide who gets resources, schedule, budget, set priorities	Ensure fair distribution of grants nationally
	Negotiator	Represent unit during negotiations with unions, suppliers, and generally defend interests	Working with sponsors and government to ensure consensus during decision-making

Source: Based on Mintzberg (1973), and private communication from the project manager.

The *liaison role* focuses on contacts with people outside the immediate unit. Managers maintain a network in which they trade information and favours for mutual benefit with clients, government officials, customers and suppliers. Some managers, such as chief executives and sales managers, spend a high proportion of their time and energy on the liaison role.

Decisional roles

In the *entrepreneurial role* managers demonstrate **creativity** and initiate change. They see opportunities and create projects to deal with them. The three friends who created Innocent Drinks in 1998 have faced many such choices – such as whether to widen the range of products beyond the original 'smoothie' drinks (and if so, which products), and/or whether to expand into continental Europe (and if so, into which countries). Managers play the *disturbance-handler role* when they deal with problems and changes that are unexpected.

Creativity is the ability to combine ideas in a unique way or to make unusual associations between ideas.

| Management in practice | Handling disturbance www.bt.com | FT |

In early 2009, Ian Livingston, BT's chief executive, surprised financial markets by reporting a pre-tax loss for the first quarter. The main cause was Global Services, which supplies telecoms networks to international companies and public bodies, but also severe competition and the recession – the share price had fallen by 60 per cent in the previous year. To recover, Global Services was split into three units, each focused on one market; capital spending was cut; and 15,000 jobs would go by the end of the next financial year.

Source: *Financial Times*, 30 April 2009.

The *resource-allocator role* involves choosing among competing demands for money, equipment, personnel and other resources. In early 2011 Marks and Spencer (**www. marksandspencer.com**) announced a new strategy, which reflected decisions by the chief executive (and the board) on where to invest funds available for capital projects (such as how much to spend on refurbishing the physical stores, and how much to spend on upgrading the website). In another business a manager has to decide whether to pay overtime to staff to replace an absent team member, or let service quality decline until a new shift starts. This is close to the *negotiator role*, in which managers seek agreement with other parties on whom they depend. Managers at Ryanair regularly negotiate with airport owners to agree on services and fees for a subsequent period.

Mintzberg proposed that every manager's job combines these roles, with their relative importance depending on the manager's level and type of business. Managers usually combine several of these roles as they try to influence others.

They sometimes note two omissions from Mintzberg's list – manager as subordinate and manager as worker. Most managers have subordinates but, except for those at the very top, they are subordinates themselves. Part of their role is to advise, assist and influence their boss – over whom they have no formal authority. Managers often need to persuade people higher up the organisation of a proposal's value or urgency. A project manager:

> This is the second time we have been back to the management team, to propose how we wish to move forward, and to try and get the resources that are required. It is worth taking the time up front to get all members fully supportive of what we are trying to do. Although it takes a bit longer we should, by pressure and by other individuals demonstrating the benefits of what we are proposing, eventually move the [top team] forward. (private communication)

Many managers spend time doing the work of the organisation. A director of a small property company helps with sales visits, or an engineering director helps with difficult technical problems. A lawyer running a small practice performs both professional and managerial roles.

Managers as networkers

Does the focus of a manager's influencing activities affect performance? Mintzberg's study gave no evidence on this point, but work by Luthans (1988) showed that the relative amount of time spent on specific roles did affect outcomes. The team observed 292 managers in four organisations for two weeks, recording their behaviours in four categories – communicating, 'traditional management', networking and human resource management. They also distinguished between levels of 'success' (relatively rapid promotion) and 'effectiveness' (work-unit performance and subordinates' satisfaction). They concluded that *successful* managers spent much more time networking (socialising, politicking, interacting with outsiders) than the less successful. *Effective* managers spent most time on communication and human resource management.

Wolff and Moser (2009) confirmed the link between **networking** and career success, showing building, maintaining and using internal and external contacts was associated with current salary, and with salary growth. Effective networkers seek out useful connections and contacts, and use the information and ideas they gather to create something valuable.

Networking refers to behaviours that aim to build, maintain and use informal relationships (internal and external) that may help work-related activities.

| **1.6** | **Influencing through the tasks of managing** |

A second way in which managers influence others is when they manage the transformation of resources into more valuable outputs. Building on Figure 1.1, this involves the **management tasks** of planning, organising, leading and controlling the transformation of resources. The amount of each varies with the job and the person, and they do not perform them in sequence: they do them simultaneously, switching as the situation requires.

Figure 1.2 illustrates the definition. It expands the central 'transforming' circle of Figure 1.1 by showing that people draw inputs (resources) from the environment and transform them into outputs by planning, organising, leading and controlling. They pass the resulting outputs back into the environment – the feedback loop indicates that this is the source of future resources.

Management tasks are those of planning, organising, leading and controlling the use of resources to add value to them.

External environment

Organisations depend on the external environment for the tangible and intangible resources they need, so they also depend on people in that environment being willing to buy or otherwise value their outputs. Commercial firms sell goods and services and use the revenue to buy resources. Public bodies depend on their sponsors being sufficiently satisfied with their

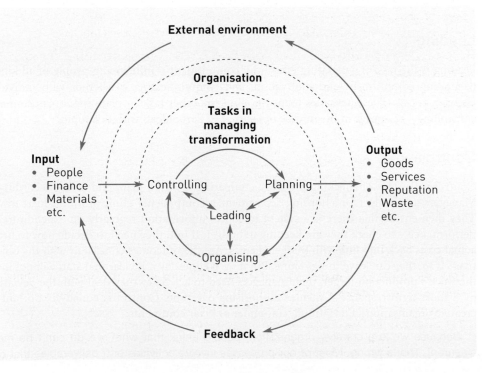

Figure 1.2
The tasks of managing

performance to provide their budget. Most managers are now facing the challenge of how they manage their organisations to ensure that they use natural resources not just efficiently, but sustainably. Part 2 of the book deals with the external environment.

Planning

Planning sets out the overall direction of the work to be done. It includes forecasting future trends, assessing resources and developing performance objectives. It means deciding on the scope and direction of the business, the areas of work in which to engage and how to use resources. Managers invest time and effort in developing a sense of direction for the organisation, or their part of it, and express this in a set of objectives. Part 3 deals with planning.

Management in practice   **Planning major rail projects** www.networkrail.co.uk

More than most civil engineering projects, rail projects depend on extensive and detailed advance planning. In 2010 the UK government announced the preferred route for the first stage of a high speed West Coast railway line. The first stage will run from London to Birmingham, but construction is not expected to begin unto 2015 at the earliest, with completion about four years later. The Crossrail project in London (see Chapter 6 case study, **p. 124**) also illustrates the scale and complexity of the planning required to build a large railway through (and below) the centre of London.

Source: Company website.

Organising

This is the task of moving abstract plans closer to reality by deciding how to allocate time and effort. It includes creating a structure for the enterprise, developing policies for finance and people, deciding what equipment people need and how to implement change. Part 4 deals with organising.

Leading

Leading is the task of generating effort and commitment – influencing people of all kinds, generating commitment and motivation, and communicating – whether with individuals or in teams. These activities focus on all of the other tasks – planning, organising and controlling – so appear in the middle of Figure 1.2. Part 5 deals with this topic.

Controlling

Control is the task of checking progress, comparing it with a plan, and acting accordingly. Managers set a budget for a housing department, an outpatients' clinic or for business travel. They then ensure that there is a system to collect information regularly on expenditure or performance – to check they are keeping to budget. If not, they need to decide how to bring actual costs back into line with budgeted costs. Are the outcomes consistent with the objectives? If so, they can leave things alone. But if by Wednesday it is clear that staff will not meet the week's production target, then managers need to act. They may deal with the deviation by a short-term response – such as authorising overtime. Control is equally important in creative organisations. Ed Catmull, cofounder of Pixar comments:

> Because we're a creative organization, people [think that what we do can't be measured]. That's wrong. Most of our processes involve activities and deliverables that can

be quantified. We keep track of the rates at which things happen, how often something had to be reworked, whether a piece of work was completely finished or not when it was sent to another department . . . Data can show things in a neutral way, which can stimulate discussion. (Catmull, 2008, p. 72)

That discussion to which Catmull refers is the way to learn from experience – an essential contributor to performance – so good managers create and use opportunities to learn from what they are doing. Part 6 deals with control.

The tasks in practice

Managers typically switch between tasks many times each day. They deal with them intermittently and in parallel, touching on many different parts of the job, as this manager in a not-for-profit housing association explains:

My role involves each of these functions. Planning is an important element as I am part of a team with a budget of £8 million to spend on promoting particular forms of housing. So planning where we will spend the money is very important. Organising and leading are important too, as staff have to be clear on which projects to take forward, clear on objectives and deadlines. Controlling is also there – I have to compare the actual money spent with the planned budget and take corrective action as necessary. (private communication from the manager)

And a manager in a professional services firm:

As a manager in a professional firm, each assignment involves all the elements to ensure we carry it out properly. For example, I have to set clear objectives for the assignment, organise the necessary staff and information to perform the work, supervise staff and counsel them if necessary, and evaluate the results. All the roles interrelate and there are no clear stages for each one. (private communication from the manager)

1.7   Influencing through shaping the context

A third way in which managers influence others is through changing aspects of the context in which they work. Changing an office layout, a person's reporting relationships, or the rewards they obtain, alter their context and perhaps their actions. The context is both an influence on the manager and a tool with which to influence others:

It is impossible to understand human intentions by ignoring the settings in which they make sense. Such settings may be institutions, sets of practices, or some other contexts created by humans – contexts which have a history, within which both particular deeds and whole histories of individual actors can and have to be situated in order to be intelligible. (Czarniawska, 2004, p. 4)

Managers aim to create contexts to influence others to act in ways that meet their objectives.

Dimensions of context

Internal context

Figures 1.1 and 1.2 showed the links between managers, their organisation and the external context. Figure 1.3 enlarges the 'organisation' circle to show more fully the elements that make up the internal context (or environment) – the immediate context within which people

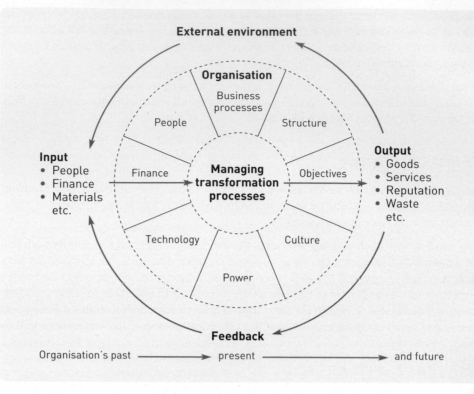

Figure 1.3
The internal and
external contexts
of management

work. As Mark Zuckerberg built Facebook into the world's largest social networking site, he and his team would have dealt with all of the elements shown in the figure:

- **Culture** (Chapter 3) – distinctive norms, beliefs and underlying values;
- **Objectives** (Chapters 6 and 8) – a desired future state of a business or unit;
- **Structure** (Chapter 9) – how to divide and co-ordinate tasks to meet objectives;
- **Technology** (Chapter 10) – facilities and equipment to turn inputs into outputs;
- **Power** (Chapter 12) – the amount and distribution of power with which to influence others;
- **People** (Chapter 13) – their knowledge, skills, attitudes and goals;
- **Business processes** – activities to transform materials and information; and
- **Finance** – financial resources available and how best to use them.

Figure 1.3 also implies that managers work within constraints – some of the elements will help, while others will hinder them. Effective managers do not accept their context passively – they try to change these elements so that they support their objectives (Chapter 11).

Historical context

Managing takes place within the flow of history as what people do now reflects past events and future uncertainties. Managers typically focus on current issues, ensuring that things run properly and that the organisation works. At the same time, history influences them through the structure and culture within which they work, and by affecting how people respond to proposals.

Effective managers also look to the future, questioning present systems and observing external changes. The arrow at the foot of the figure represents the historical context.

External context

Chapter 3 shows that the external context includes an immediate competitive (micro) environment and a general (or macro) environment. These affect performance and part of the manager's work is to identify, and adapt to, external changes. Managers in the public sector are expected to deliver improved services with fewer resources, so they seek to influence people to change the internal context (such as how staff work) to meet external expectations. They also seek to influence those in the external context about both expectations and resources.

1.8 Critical thinking

Brookfield (1987) stresses the benefits of thinking critically, in that it:

> involves our recognizing the assumptions underlying our beliefs and behaviors. It means we can give justifications for our ideas and actions. Most important, perhaps, it means we try to judge the rationality of these justifications . . . by comparing them to a range of varying interpretations and perspectives. (p. 13)

Critical thinking is positive activity that enables people to see more possibilities, rather than a single path. Critical thinkers 'are self-confident about their potential for changing aspects of their worlds, both as individuals and through collective action' (p. 5). He identifies four components of critical thinking.

> **Critical thinking** identifies the assumptions behind ideas, relates them to their context, imagines alternatives and recognises limitations.

Identifying and challenging assumptions

Critical thinkers look for the assumptions that underlie taken-for-granted ideas, beliefs and values, and question their accuracy and validity. They are ready to discard those that no longer seem valid guides to action, in favour of more suitable ones. A manager who presents a well-supported challenge to a strategy that seems unsuitable to their business, or who questions the need for a new structure, is using this aspect of critical thinking.

Recognising the importance of context

Critical thinkers are aware that context influences thought and action. Thinking uncritically means assuming that ideas and methods that work in one context will work equally well in others. What we regard as an appropriate way to deal with staff reflects a specific culture: people in another culture – working in another place or at a different time – will have other expectations. Critical thinkers look for such approaches suitable for the relevant context.

Imagining and exploring alternatives

Critical thinkers develop the skill of imagining and exploring alternative ways of managing. They ask how others have dealt with a situation, and seek evidence about the effectiveness of different approaches. This makes them aware of realistic alternatives, and so increases the range of ideas which they can adapt and use.

Seeing limitations

Critical thinking alerts people to the limitations of knowledge and proposals. They recognise that because a practice works well in one situation does not ensure it will work in another. They are sceptical about research whose claims seem over-sold, asking about the sample or the analysis. They are open to new ideas, but only when supported by convincing evidence and reasoning.

Thinking critically will deepen your understanding of management. It does *not* imply a 'do-nothing' cynicism, 'treating everything and everyone with suspicion and doubt' (Thomas, 2003, p. 7). Critical thinking lays the foundation for a successful career, as it helps to ensure that proposals are supported by convincing evidence and reasoning.

Managing your studies

Studying management is itself a task to manage. Each chapter specifies learning outcomes. The text, the case study and the 'before and after' activities should help you to achieve these, and you can check your progress with the review questions at the end of each chapter. Working on these will help develop your confidence to think critically in your studies and in your career.

Activity 1.2   Understanding management

Recall the organisation you used in Activity 1.1.

Having read the chapter, make brief notes summarising what you now think 'managing' involves in this company:

● Describe what resources it uses and how it adds value to them. (Refer to Section 1.2.)
● List examples of some of the specialist roles of management (such as a functional or a line manager) and describe what they do in this company. (Refer to Section 1.4.)
● Can you identify examples of managers performing one or more of Mintzberg's roles? (Refer to Section 1.5.)
● What have you been able to find out about how they perform ONE of the management tasks (planning, organising, leading, controlling)? (Refer to Section 1.6.)

Compare what you have found with other students on your course.

Summary

1 **Explain that the role of management is to add value to resources in diverse settings**

● Managers create value by transforming inputs into outputs of greater value: they do this by developing competences within the organisation which, by constantly adding value (however measured) to resources is able to survive and prosper. The concept of creating value is subjective and open to different interpretations. Managers work in an infinite variety of settings, and Table 1.1 suggested how each setting raises relatively unique challenges.

2 **Give examples of management as a universal human activity and as a distinct role**

● Management is an activity that everyone undertakes as they manage their daily lives. In another sense management is an activity which many people conduct, not just those called 'managers'. People create the distinct role when they separate the management of work from the work itself and allocate the tasks. The distinction between management and non-management work is fluid and the result of human action.

3 **Compare the roles of general, functional, line, staff and project managers and of entrepreneurs**

● General managers are responsible for a complete business or a unit within it. They depend on functional managers who can be either in charge of line departments meeting customer needs, such as manufacturing and sales, or in staff departments such as finance which provide advice or services to line managers. Project managers are in charge of temporary activities usually directed at implementing change. Entrepreneurs are those who create new businesses to exploit opportunities.

4 **Explain how managers influence others to add value to resources through**

● The processes of managing. Henry Mintzberg identified ten management roles in three groups which he labelled informational, interpersonal and decisional. Luthans and, more recently, Wolff and Moser observed that successful managers were likely to be those who networked with people inside and outside the organisation.

- The tasks of managing. Planning develops the broad direction of an organisation's work, to meet customer expectations, taking into account internal capabilities. Organising sets out how to deploy resources to meet plans, while leading seeks to ensure that people work with commitment to achieve plans. Control checks activity and results against plans, so that people can adjust either if required.
- The contexts of managing. The internal (organisational) context consists of eight elements which help or hinder the manager's work – objectives, technology, business processes, finance, structure, culture, power and people. The historical context also influences events, as does the external context, which consists of competitive and general environments.

Review questions

1 How do non-commercial organisations add value to resources?

2 What is the difference between management as a general human activity and management as a specialised occupation? How has this division happened?

3 Describe, with examples, the differences between general, functional, line, staff and project managers.

4 How does Mintzberg's theory of management roles complement that which identifies the tasks of management?

5 Give examples from your experience or observation of each of the four tasks of management.

6 What is the significance to someone starting a career in management of Luthans' theory about roles and performance?

7 How can thinking critically help managers do their job more effectively?

8 Review and revise the definition of management that you gave in Activity 1.1.

Further reading

Birkinshaw, J. (2010), *Reinventing Management: Smarter choices for getting work done*, Jossey-Bass, San Fancisco, CA.

A small book by a leading management academic gives a short account of the work of general management.

Handy, C. (1988), *Understanding Voluntary Organisations*, Penguin, Harmondsworth.

A valuable perspective on management in the voluntary sector.

Drucker, P. (1999), *Management Challenges for the 21st Century*, Butterworth/Heinemann, London.

Valuable observations from the enquiring mind of this great management theorist.

Scott, D. M. and Halligan, B. (2010), *Marketing Lessons from the Grateful Dead: What every business can learn from the most iconic band in history*, Wiley, Hoboken, NJ.

Practical insights into management generally from two authors with deep insights into how the legendary band achieved its success.

Weblinks

These websites have appeared in, or are relevant to, the chapter:

www.davymarkham.com
www.charitycommission.gov.uk
www.scott-timber.co.uk
www.bt.com
www.marksandspencer.com
www.networkrail.co.uk
www.facebook.com/facebook
www.ryanair.com

Visit two of the business sites in the list above, or those of other organisations in which you are interested, and navigate to the pages dealing with recent news, press or investor relations.

- What are the main issues which the organisation appears to be facing?
- Compare and contrast the issues you identify on the two sites.
- What challenges may they imply for those working in, and managing, these organisations?

Annotated weblinks, multiple choice questions and other useful resources can be found on **www.pearsoned.co.uk/boddy**

Case study Ryanair www.ryanair.com

In 2011 Ryanair, based in Dublin, was Europe's largest low fare airline, and despite the recession, it had carried over 74 million passengers in the 12 months to the end of April, a record for that period. In 1985, the company began offering services between Dublin and London, in competition with the established national carrier, Aer Lingus. In the early years the airline changed its business several times – initially a conventional competitor for Aer Lingus, then a charter company, at times offering a cargo service. The Gulf War in 1990 discouraged air travel and deepened the company's financial problems. In 1991, senior managers decided to focus the airline as a 'no-frills' operator, in which many traditional features of air travel (free food, drink, newspapers and allocated seats) were no longer available. It aimed to serve a group of flyers who wanted a functional and efficient service, not luxury.

In 1997 changes in European Union regulations enabled new airlines to enter markets previously dominated by established national carriers such as Air France and British Airways. Ryanair quickly took advantage of this, opening new routes between Dublin and continental Europe. Although based in Ireland, 80 per cent of its routes are between airports in other countries – in contrast to established carriers which depend heavily for passengers travelling to and from the airline's home country (Barrett, 2009, p. 80).

Managers were quick to spot the potential of the internet, and in 2000 opened **Ryanair.com**, a booking site. Within a year it sold 75 per cent of seats online and now sells almost all seats this way. It also made a long-term deal with Boeing to purchase 150 new aircraft over the next eight years.

Several factors enable Ryanair to offer low fares:

- Simple fleet – using a single aircraft type (Boeing 737 – most of which are quite new) simplifies maintenance, training and crew scheduling.
- Secondary airports – using airports away from major cities keeps landing charges low, sometimes as little as £1 per passenger against £10 at a major airport; it also avoids the delays and costs caused by congestion at major airports.
- Fast turnarounds – staff typically turn an aircraft round between flights in 25 minutes, compared to an hour for older airlines. This enables aircraft to spend more time in the air, earning revenue (11 hours compared to 7 at British Airways).

© Thierry Tronnel/Sygma/Corbis.

- Simplified operations – not assigning seats at check-in simplifies ticketing and administrative processes, and also ensures that passengers arrive early to get their preferred seat.
- Flying directly between cities avoids transferring passengers and baggage between flights, where mistakes and delays are common.
- Cabin staff collect rubbish before and after landing, saving the cost of cleaning crews which established carriers choose to use.

The company has continued to grow rapidly, regularly opening new routes to destinations it thinks will be popular. It now refers to itself as 'the world's largest international scheduled airline', and continues to seek new bases from which to operate its network.

The airline's success depends on balancing low costs, fare levels and load factors. Airline seats are what is known as a perishable good – they have no value if they are not used on the flight, so companies aim to maximise the proportion of seats sold on a flight. Ryanair use a technique known as dynamic pricing, which means that prices change with circumstances. Typically fares rise the nearer the passenger is to the departure date, though if a flight is under-booked, the company encourages sales by lowering fares.

They also earn a growing proportion of revenue from charges and services such as refreshments, and in 2009 sharply increased the cost of checked in bags: it prefers customers to carry hand baggage into the cabin. Each time a passenger rents a car or books a hotel room on the Ryanair website, it earns a commission. It sells scratch cards on board, offers in-flight gambling and on-line gaming over its website: the chief executive thinks that gambling could double Ryanair's profits over the next decade. The company expects revenue from ancillary activities will continue to grow more rapidly than passenger revenue.

Sources: *The Economist*, 10 July 2004; *Independent*, 7 October 2006; *Financial Times*, 7 June 2006; Barrett (2009); Kumar (2006); O'Connell and Williams (2005); Doganis (2006); and company website.

Questions

1 Identify examples of the resources that Ryanair uses, and of the competences that have enabled managers to add value to them. (Refer to Section 1.2.)

2 Refer to Section 1.4 and note what those occupying the specialist roles are likely to be doing in Ryanair.

3 Refer to Section 1.5 and write down which of Mintzberg's management roles can you identify in the Ryanair case? Support your answer with specific examples.

4 Which aspects of the external general environment have affected the company? (Refer to Section 1.6.)

5 Go to the Ryanair website and look for evidence of the work that managers have been doing to help the company continue to grow.

CHAPTER 2
THEORIES OF MANAGEMENT

Learning outcomes

When you have read this chapter you should be able to:

1 Explain why understanding a good theory helps people to make better choices

2 State the structure of the competing values framework, which relates theories to each other

3 Summarise the:
- rational goal
- internal process
- human relations and
- open systems perspectives

4 Use ideas from the chapter to comment on the management issues in the Robert Owen case study

Activity 2.1   What are 'theories of management'?

Before reading this chapter, write some notes on what you understand by the term 'theories of management'.

Choose the organisation or people who may be able to help you learn about the topic. You may find it helpful to discuss the topic with a manager you know, or reflect on an activity you have managed.

- Identify a situation in which someone had to make a decision or deal with a problem, and describe it briefly.
- What ideas seem to have guided the way they dealt with the task?
- Did they think consciously about why they did it that way?
- Keep these notes, as you will be able to use them later.

2.1   Introduction

Robert Owen was an entrepreneur. His attempts to change worker behaviour were innovative, and he was equally creative in devising management systems and new ways of working. The story of his time at New Lanark illustrates three aspects of management. First, he devised systems to help manage the people he employed and to improve mill performance. Second, Owen engaged with the wider social context, such as when he tried to influence Parliament to prohibit employers from using children in their mills and factories. Third, he was managing at a time of transition from an agricultural to an industrial economy, and many of his innovations tried to resolve the tensions between those systems – as we now face tensions between industrial and post-industrial systems.

Managers today cope with similar issues. HMV need to recruit willing and capable people to work in their stores, and ensure that they add value. Co-operative Financial Services (CFS) try (like Owen) to follow ethical principles throughout their business and still earn profits. Managers know that working conditions affect family life – and try to balance the two by subsidising childcare and offering flexible hours to those with family responsibilities. They also operate in a world experiencing changes equal to those facing Owen. The internet is enabling people to organise economic activity in new ways, sustainability is now on the agendas of most management teams, as is the move to a more connected international economy.

Facing such changes, managers continue to search for new ways to manage their business so that they add value to their resources. They make assumptions about the best way to do things – and through trial and error develop methods of working which seem to work reasonably well, and which they tend to repeat. Although they probably do not use the term, they gradually develop their theory of management – their ideas about the relationship between cause and effect, how a change in (say) working methods will affect (say) staff commitment. The more accurate their theory (the better the evidence and experience they use), the more likely they are to obtain the results they want. A manager using inaccurate theory to guide their actions is likely to have less success.

The next section introduces the idea of theories of management, and why they are useful. Section 2.3 presents the 'competing values' framework, which is a convenient way of seeing the relationship between theories, which the following sections outline.

<table><tr><td>

| 2.2 | Why study management theory? |

</td></tr></table>

A **theory (or model)** represents a complex phenomenon by identifying the major elements and relationships

A **theory (or model)** represents a more complex reality. Focusing on the essential elements and their relationship helps to understand that complexity, and how change may affect it. Most management problems can only be understood by examining them from several points of view, so no theory offers a complete solution. The management task is to choose those most likely to work, and combine them into an acceptable solution.

Theories support purpose and values

Managers have different views about the purpose of their role in society, and this affects the theories they use. A feature of many societies is that they have established a balance of power between governments, companies and the 'social sector' – co-operatives, social entrepreneurs, voluntary organisations. Each reflects a different set of challenges, and has encouraged the development of theories about how best to manage in those circumstances.

The theory (or mental model) which a person uses reflects their view of the purpose of their particular job – ranging from serving shareholder interests at one extreme to serving society at the other (Chapter 5, Section 5.4). Their personal values also influence this – some see their job as a technical or financial task, whereas others see that being a manager brings wider responsibilities, including those of dealing fairly and ethically with other people.

Theories identify variables

Whichever broad model of management a person is using, they will use (implicitly) one or more theories, as these help to identify the main variables in a situation, and the relationships between them. The more accurately they do so, the more useful they are. Since every situation is unique, many experienced managers doubt the value of theory. Magretta's answer is that:

> without a theory of some sort it's hard to make sense of what's happening in the world around you. If you want to know whether you work for a well-managed organization – as opposed to whether you like your boss – you need a working theory of management. (Magretta, 2002, p. 10)

We all use theory, acting on (perhaps implicit) assumptions about the relationships between cause and effect. Good theories help to identify variables and relationships, providing a mental toolkit to deal consciously with a situation. The perspective we take reflects the assumptions we use to interpret, organise and make sense of events. As managers influence others to add value they use their mental model (theory) of the situation to decide where to focus effort. The Management in Practice feature below contrasts two managers' mental models.

Management in practice   **Practice reflects theory**   FT

These examples illustrate contrasting theories about managing staff.

Motivating managers: Tim O'Toole, who became chief executive of London Underground in 2003, put in a new management structure, appointing a general manager for each line to improve accountability.

> Now there's a human being who is judged on how that line is performing and I want them to feel that kind of intense anxiety in the stomach that comes when there's a stalled train and they realise that it's their stalled train.

Source: From an article by Simon London, *Financial Times*, 20 February 2004.

Supporting staff: John Timpson, chairman of the shoe repair and key cutting chain, believes the most important people in the company are those who cut customers' keys and re-heel their shoes:

> You come back for the service you get from the people in the shops. They are the stars . . . we need to do everything to help them to look after you as well as possible. [A bonus based on shop takings] is fundamental to the service culture I want. It creates the adrenalin. That is the reason why people are keen to serve you if you go into one of our shops. And why they don't take long lunch breaks.

Source: Adapted from Secrets of the maverick cobbler, *Financial Times*, 3 August 2006.

Models reflect their context

People look for models to deal with the most pressing issues they face. In the nineteenth century, skilled labour was scarce and unskilled labour plentiful: managers were hiring workers unfamiliar with factories to meet growing demand, so wanted ideas on how to produce more efficiently. They looked for ways to simplify tasks so that they could use less-skilled employees, and early management theories gave priority to these issues. This focus on efficiency reflects a manufacturing mindset, which is still highly relevant in many situations. In other situations, the main challenge facing a manager is how to meet changing customer needs quickly and cheaply – so they seek theories about how to create a system that produces frequent innovations and that can change quickly. As business becomes international, they seek theories about managing across the world.

An even bigger contextual challenge to managers is presented by the world's growing population, rising temperatures and sea levels, and probable shortages in many parts of the world of land, water and energy to cope with this. Most countries face a conflict between the rising cost of health care for an ageing population, and their ability to provide it. Theories about how to manage in societies facing these challenges are in short supply.

Critical thinking helps improve our mental models

The ideas on critical thinking in Chapter 1 suggest that working effectively depends on being able and willing to test the validity of any theory, and to revise it in the light of experience by:

- identifying and challenging assumptions;
- recognising the importance of context;
- imagining and exploring alternatives; and
- seeing limitations.

As you work through this chapter, look for opportunities to practise these components of critical thinking.

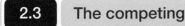

2.3   The competing values framework

Quinn *et al.* (2003) believe that successive theories of management (which they group according to four underlying philosophies – 'rational goal', 'internal process', 'human relations' and 'open systems') complement, rather than contradict, each other. They are all:

> symptoms of a larger problem – the need to achieve organizational effectiveness in a highly dynamic environment. In such a complex and fast-changing world, simple solutions become suspect . . . Sometimes we needed stability, sometimes we needed change. Often we needed both at the same time. (p. 11)

While each adds to our knowledge, none is sufficient. The 'competing values' framework integrates them by highlighting their underlying values – see Figure 2.1.

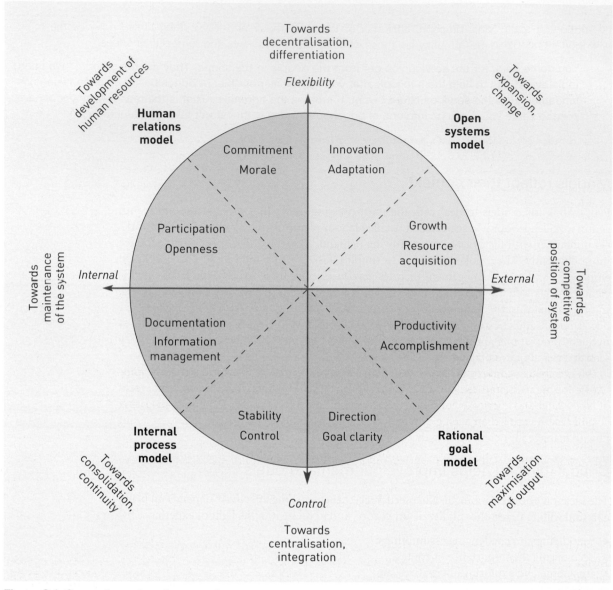

Figure 2.1 Competing values framework

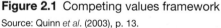

Source: Quinn *et al.* (2003), p. 13.

The vertical axis represents the tension between flexibility and control. Managers seek flexibility to cope with rapid change. Others try to increase control – apparently the opposite of flexibility. The horizontal axis distinguishes an internal focus from an external one. Some managers focus on internal issues, while others focus on the world outside. Successive models of management relate to the four segments.

The labels within the circle indicate the criteria of effectiveness which are the focus of models in that segment, shown around the outside. The human relations model, upper left in the figure, stresses the human criteria of commitment, participation and openness. The open systems model (upper right) stresses criteria of innovation, adaptation and growth. The rational goal model in the lower right focuses on productivity, direction and goal clarity. The internal process model stresses stability, documentation and control, within a hierarchical structure. Finally, the outer ring indicates the values associated with each model – the dominant value in the rational goal model is that of maximising output, while in human relations it is developing people. Successive sections of this chapter outline theories associated with each segment.

2.4   Rational goal models

Adam Smith (1776), the Scottish economist, recorded how pin manufacturers in Glasgow had broken a job previously done by one man into small steps. A single worker now performed one of these repetitively, and this specialisation greatly increased their output. Smith believed this was one of the main ways in which the new industrial system was increasing the wealth of the nation.

The availability of powered machinery during the Industrial Revolution enabled business owners to transform manufacturing and mining processes. These technical innovations encouraged, but were not the only reason for, the growth of the factory system. The earlier 'putting-out' system of manufacture, in which people worked at home on materials supplied and collected by entrepreneurs and their agents, allowed great freedom over hours, pace and methods of work; agents had little control over the quantity and quality of output. Capitalist entrepreneurs found that they could secure more control if they brought workers together in a factory, as this meant that:

> coercive authority could be more easily applied, including systems of fines, supervision . . . the paraphernalia of bells and clocks, and incentive payments. The employer could dictate the general conditions of work, time and space; including the division of labour, overall organisational layout and design, rules governing movement, shouting, singing and other forms of disobedience. (Thompson and McHugh 2002, p. 22)

This still left entrepreneurs with the problem of how to manage these new factories profitably. Although domestic and export demand for manufactured goods was high, so was the risk of business failure.

Frederick Taylor

The fullest answer to the problems of factory organisation came in the work of Frederick W. Taylor (1856–1915), always associated with the ideas of **scientific management**. An American mechanical engineer, Taylor focused on the relationship between the worker and the machine-based production systems that were in widespread use:

Scientific management
The school of management called 'scientific' attempted to create a science of factory production.

> the principal object of management should be to secure the maximum prosperity for the employer, coupled with the maximum prosperity for each employee. The words 'maximum prosperity' . . . mean the development of every branch of the business to its highest state of excellence, so that the prosperity may be permanent. (Taylor, 1917, p. 9)

He believed the way to achieve this was to ensure that each worker reached their state of maximum efficiency, so that each was doing 'the highest grade of work for which his natural abilities fit him' (p. 9). This would follow from detailed control of the process, which would become the managers' primary responsibility: they should concentrate on understanding the production systems, and use this to specify every aspect of the operation. Taylor advocated five principles:

- use scientific methods to determine the one best way of doing a task, rather than rely on the older 'rule of thumb' methods;
- select the best person to do the job so defined, ensuring that their physical and mental qualities were appropriate for the task;
- train, teach and develop the worker to follow the defined procedures precisely;

- provide financial incentives to ensure people work to the prescribed method; and
- move responsibility for planning and organising from the worker to the manager.

Taylor's underlying philosophy was that scientific analysis and fact, not guesswork, should inform management. Like Smith and Babbage before him, he believed that efficiency rose if tasks were routine and predictable. He advocated techniques such as time and motion study, standardised tools and individual incentives. Breaking work into small, specific tasks would increase control. Specialist staff would design these tasks and organise the workers:

> The work of every workman is fully planned out by the management at least one day in advance, and each man receives in most cases complete written instructions, describing in detail the task which he is to accomplish, as well as the means to be used in doing the work . . . This task specifies not only what is to be done but how it is to be done and the exact time allowed for doing it. (Taylor, 1917, p. 39)

Taylor also influenced the development of administrative systems such as record keeping and stock control to support manufacturing.

Management in practice   Using work study in the 1990s

Oswald Jones recalls his experience as a work study engineer in the 1990s, where he and his colleagues were deeply committed to the principles of scientific management:

> Jobs were designed to be done in a mechanical fashion by removing opportunities for worker discretion. This had dual benefits: very simple jobs could be measured accurately (so causing less disputes) and meant that operators were much more interchangeable which was an important feature in improving overall efficiency levels.

Source: Jones (2000, p. 647).

Managers in industrialised economies adopted Taylor's ideas widely: Henry Ford was an enthusiastic advocate. When he introduced the assembly line in 1914, the time taken to assemble a car fell from over 700 hours to 93 minutes. Ford also developed systems of materials flow and plant layout, a significant contribution to scientific management.

Increased productivity often came at human cost (Thompson and McHugh, 2002). Trade unions believed Taylor's methods increased unemployment, and vigorously opposed them. Many people find work on an assembly line is boring and alienating, devoid of much meaning. In extreme cases, the time taken to complete an operation is less than a minute and uses few human abilities.

Frank and Lillian Gilbreth

Frank and Lillian Gilbreth (1868–1924 and 1878–1972) worked together to encourage employers to use scientific management principles. Frank Gilbreth had been a bricklayer, and knew why work was slow and output unpredictable. He filmed men laying bricks and used this to set out the most economical movements for each task. He specified exactly what the employer should provide, such as trestles at the right height and materials at the right time. Supplies of mortar and bricks (arranged the right way up) should arrive at a time which did not interrupt work. An influential book (Gilbreth, 1911) gave precise guidance on how to reduce unnecessary actions (from 18 to 5), and hence fatigue. The rules and charts would help apprentices:

> (They) will enable the apprentice to earn large wages immediately, because he has . . . a series of instructions that show each and every motion in the proper sequence. They eliminate the 'wrong' way [and] all experimenting. (Quoted in Spriegel and Myers, 1953, p. 57)

Lillian Gilbreth focused on the psychological aspects of management, and on the welfare of workers. In *The Psychology of Management* (1914) she proposed, like Taylor, that scientific management would enable individuals to reach their full potential. Careful development of suitable working processes, careful selection, planned training and proper equipment, would help them to build their self-respect. If they did something well, and that was made public, they would develop pride in their work and in themselves. She believed workers had enquiring minds, and that management should explain the reasons for work processes:

> Unless the man knows why he is doing the thing, his judgment will never reinforce his work . . . His work will not enlist his zeal unless he knows exactly why he is made to work in the particular manner prescribed. (Quoted in Spriegel and Myers, 1953, p. 431)

Operational research

Another practice within the rational goal model is **operational research** (OR). This originated in the early 1940s, when the UK War Department faced severe management problems – such as the most effective distribution of radar-linked anti-aircraft gun emplacements, or the safest speed at which convoys of merchant ships should cross the Atlantic. To solve these it formed operational research teams, which pooled the expertise of scientific disciplines such as mathematics and physics and produced significant results. Kirby (2003) notes that while at the start of the London Blitz 20,000 rounds of ammunition were fired for each enemy aircraft destroyed:

Operational research is a scientific method of providing managers with a quantitative basis for decisions regarding the operations under their control.

> by the summer of 1941 the number had fallen . . . to 4,000 as a result of the operational research (teams) improving the accuracy of radar-based gun-laying. (Kirby 2003, p. 94)

In the late 1940s managers in industry and government saw that OR techniques could help managers running civil organisations. The scale and complexity of business was increasing, and required new techniques to analyse the many interrelated variables: developments in computing supported increasingly sophisticated mathematical models. In the 1950s the steel industry needed to cut the cost of transporting iron ore: staff used OR techniques to analyse the most efficient procedures for shipping, unloading and transferring it to steelworks.

The method is widely used in both business and public sectors, where it helps planning in areas as diverse as maintenance, cash flow, inventory, staff scheduling in call centres and allocating students to seminar groups.

OR cannot take into account human and social uncertainties, and the assumptions built into the models may be invalid, especially if they involve political interests. The technique clearly contributes to the analysis of management problems, but is only part of the solution.

Current status

Table 2.1 summarises principles common to rational goal models and their modern application.

Table 2.1 Modern applications of the rational goal model

Principles of the rational goal model	Current applications
Systematic work methods	Work study and process engineering departments develop precise specifications for processes
Detailed division of labour	Where staff focus on one type of work or customer in manufacturing or service operations
Centralised planning and control	Modern information systems increase the scope for central control of worldwide operations
Low-involvement employment relationship	Using temporary staff as required, rather than permanent employees

Examples of rational goal approaches are common in manufacturing and services – but a company will often use just one of the principles that suits their business. The Management in Practice feature below gives an example from a successful service business with committed and involved employees. It aims to give customers the same high-quality experience wherever they are, and uses the principle of systematic work methods to achieve this.

Management in practice   **Making a sandwich at Pret A Manger**   www.pret.com

It is very important to make sure the same standards are adhered to in every single shop, whether you're in Crown Passage in London, Sauchiehall Street in Glasgow or in New York. The way we do that is very, very detailed training. So, for example, how to make an egg mayonnaise sandwich is all written down on a card that has to be followed, and that is absolutely non-negotiable.

When somebody joins Pret they have a ten-day training plan, and on every single day there is a list of things that they have to be shown, from how to spread the filling of a sandwich right to the edges (that is key to us), how to cut a sandwich from corner to corner, how to make sure that the sandwiches look great in the box and on the shelves. So every single detail is covered on a ten-day training plan. At the end of that ten days the new team member has to pass a quiz, it's called the big scary quiz, it is quite big and it is quite scary, and they have to achieve 90 per cent on that in order to progress.

Source: Interview with a senior manager at the company.

The methods are also widely used in the mass production industries of newly industrialised economies such as China and Malaysia. Gamble *et al.* (2004) found that in such plants:

> Work organization tended to be fragmented (on Taylorist lines) and routinised, with considerable surveillance and control over production volumes and quality. (p. 403)

Human resource management policies were consistent with this approach – the recruitment of operators in Chinese electronics plants was:

> often of young workers, generally female and from rural areas. One firm said its operators had to be '. . . young farmers within cycling distance of the factory, with good eyesight. Education is not important.' (p. 404)

2.5   Internal process models

Max Weber

Max Weber (1864–1920) was a German social historian who drew attention to the significance of large organisations, noting that as societies became more complex, they concentrated responsibility for core activities in large, specialised units. These government departments and large industrial or transport businesses were hard to manage, a difficulty which those in charge overcame by creating rules and regulations, hierarchy, precise division of labour and detailed procedures. Weber observed that **bureaucracy** brought routine to office operations just as machines had to production.

Bureaucratic management has these characteristics:

- **Rules and regulations**   The formal guidelines that define and control the behaviour of employees. Following these ensures uniform procedures and operations, regardless of an individual's wishes. They enable top managers to co-ordinate middle managers

Bureaucracy is a system in which people are expected to follow precisely defined rules and procedures rather than to use personal judgement.

and, through them, first-line managers and employees. Managers leave, so rules bring stability.

- **Impersonality**   Rules lead to impersonality, which protects employees from the whims of managers. Although the term has negative connotations, Weber believed it ensured fairness, by evaluating subordinates objectively on performance rather than subjectively on personal considerations. It limits favouritism.
- **Division of labour**   Managers and employees work on specialised tasks, with the benefits originally noted by Adam Smith – such as that jobs are relatively easy to learn and control.
- **Hierarchical structure**   Weber advocated a clear hierarchy in which jobs were arranged by the amount of authority to make decisions. Each lower position is under the control of a higher position.
- **Authority structure**   A system of rules, impersonality, division of labour and hierarchy forms an authority structure – the right to make decisions of varying importance at different levels within the organisation.
- **Rationality**   This refers to using the most efficient means to achieve objectives. Managers should run their organisations logically and 'scientifically' so that all decisions help to achieve the objectives.

Weber was aware that, as well as creating bureaucratic structures, managers were using scientific management techniques to control production and impose discipline on factory work. The two systems complemented each other. Formal structures of management centralise power, and hierarchical organisation aids functional specialisation. Fragmenting tasks, imposing close discipline on employees and minimising their discretion ensures that staff within a function perform in a controlled and predictable way (Thompson and McHugh, 2002).

Weber stressed the importance of a career structure clearly linked to a person's position. This allowed them to move up the hierarchy in a predictable and open way, which would increase their commitment to the organisation. Rules about selection and promotion brought fairness at a time when favouritism was common. He also believed that officials should work within a framework of rules. The right to give instructions was based on a person's position in the hierarchy, and a rational analysis of how staff should work. This worked well in large public and private organisations, such as government departments and banks.

Henri Fayol

Managers were also able to draw on the ideas of **administrative management** developed by Henri Fayol (1841–1925). While Taylor focused on production systems, Fayol devised management principles that would apply to the whole organisation. Like Taylor, Fayol was an engineer who, in 1860, joined a coal mining and iron foundry company combine: he became managing director in 1888. When he retired in 1918 it was one of the success stories of French industry. Throughout his career he kept detailed diaries and notes, which, in retirement, he used to stimulate debate about management in both private and public sectors. His book *Administration, industrielle et générale* became available in English in 1949 (Fayol, 1949).

Administrative management is the use of institutions and order rather than relying on personal qualities to get things done.

Fayol credited his success to the methods he used, not to his personal qualities. He believed that managers should use certain principles in their work – see below. The term 'principles' did not imply they were rigid or absolute:

> It is all a question of proportion . . . allowance must be made for different changing circumstances . . . the principles are flexible and capable of adaptation to every need; it is a matter of knowing how to make use of them, which is a difficult art requiring intelligence, experience, decision and proportion. (Fayol, 1949, p. 14)

Fayol's principles were:

- **Division of work**   If people specialise, they improve their skill and accuracy, which increases output. However, 'it has its limits which experience teaches us may not be exceeded'. (p. 20)
- **Authority and responsibility**   The right to give orders derived from a manager's official authority or their personal authority. '[Wherever] authority is exercised, responsibility arises.' (p. 21)
- **Discipline**   'Essential for the smooth running of business . . . without discipline no enterprise could prosper.' (p. 22)
- **Unity of command**   'For any action whatsoever, an employee should receive orders from one superior only' (p. 24) – to avoid conflicting instructions and resulting confusion.
- **Unity of direction**   'One head and one plan for a group of activities having the same objective . . . essential to unity of action, co-ordination of strength and focusing of effort.' (p. 25)
- **Subordination of individual interest to general interest**   'The interests of one employee or group of employees should not prevail over that of the concern.' (p. 26)
- **Remuneration of personnel**   'Should be fair and, as far as possible, afford satisfaction both to personnel and firm.' (p. 26)
- **Centralisation**   'The question of centralisation or decentralisation is a simple question of proportion . . . [the] share of initiative to be left to [subordinates] depends on the character of the manager, the reliability of the subordinates and the condition of the business. The degree of centralisation must vary according to different cases.' (p. 33)
- **Scalar chain**   'The chain of superiors from the ultimate authority to the lowest ranks . . . is at times disastrously lengthy in large concerns, especially governmental ones.' If a speedy decision was needed it was appropriate for people at the same level of the chain to communicate directly. 'It provides for the usual exercise of some measure of initiative at all levels of authority.' (pp. 34–5)
- **Order**   Materials should be in the right place to avoid loss, and the posts essential for the smooth running of the business filled by capable people.
- **Equity**   Managers should be both friendly and fair to their subordinates – 'equity requires much good sense, experience and good nature'. (p. 38)
- **Stability of tenure of personnel**   A high employee turnover is not efficient – 'Instability of tenure is at one and the same time cause and effect of bad running.' (p. 39)
- **Initiative**   'The initiative of all represents a great source of strength for businesses . . . and . . . it is essential to encourage and develop this capacity to the full. The manager must be able to sacrifice some personal vanity in order to grant this satisfaction to subordinates . . . a manager able to do so is infinitely superior to one who cannot.' (pp. 39–40)
- **Esprit de corps**   'Harmony, union among the personnel of a concern is a great strength in that concern. Effort, then, should be made to establish it.' (p. 40) Fayol suggested doing so by avoiding sowing dissension amongst subordinates, and using verbal rather than written communication when appropriate.

Current status

Table 2.2 summarises some principles common to the internal process models of management and indicates their modern application.

'Bureaucracy' has many critics, who believe that it stifles creativity, fosters dissatisfaction and lowers motivation. Others believe it brings fairness and certainty to the workplace, where it clarifies roles and responsibilities, makes work effective – and raises motivation.

Bureaucratic methods are widely used especially in the public sector, and in commercial businesses with geographically dispersed outlets – such as hotels, stores and banks. Customers expect a predictable service wherever they are, so management design centrally controlled procedures and manuals – how to recruit and train staff, what the premises must look like and how to treat customers. If managers work in situations that require a degree of change and innovation, they need other theories of management.

Table 2.2 Modern applications of the internal process model

Some principles of the internal process model	Current applications
Rules and regulations	All organisations have these, covering areas such as expenditure, safety, recruitment and confidentiality
Impersonality	Appraisal processes based on objective criteria or team assessments, not personal preference
Division of labour	Setting narrow limits to employees' areas of responsibility – found in many organisations
Hierarchical structure	Most company organisation charts show managers in a hierarchy – with subordinates below them
Authority structure	Holders of a particular post have authority over matters relating to that post, but not over other matters
Centralisation	Organisations balance central control of (say) finance or online services with local control of (say) pricing or recruitment
Initiative	Current practice in many firms to increase the responsibility of operating staff
Rationality	Managers are expected to assess issues on the basis of evidence, not personal preference

2.6 Human relations models

In the early twentieth century, several writers such as Follett and Mayo recognised the limitations of scientific management and suggested new methods.

Mary Parker Follett

Mary Parker Follett (1868–1933) graduated with distinction from Radcliffe College (now part of Harvard University) in 1898, having studied economics, law and philosophy. She became a social worker and quickly acquired a reputation as an imaginative and effective professional. She realised the creativity of the group process, and the potential it offered for truly democratic government – which people themselves would have to create.

She advocated replacing bureaucratic institutions with networks in which people themselves analysed their problems and implemented their solutions. True democracy depended on tapping the potential of all members of society by enabling individuals to take part in groups organised to solve particular problems and accepting personal responsibility for the result. Such ideas are still relevant – as shown by some flourishing community-trading groups, and by tenants' groups helping to manage social housing.

In the 1920s, business managers invited her to investigate some industrial problems. She again advocated the self-governing principle that would facilitate the growth of individuals and the groups to which they belonged. Since people bring valuable differences of view to a problem, conflict is inevitable, which the group must resolve – and in doing so they would create what she called an 'integrative unity' among the members.

She acknowledged that organisations had to optimise production, but did not accept that the strict division of labour was the right way to achieve this (Follett, 1920), as it devalued human creativity. The human side should not be separated from the mechanical side, as the two are bound together. She believed that people, whether managers or workers, behave as they do because of the reciprocal responses in their relationship. If managers tell people to behave as if they are extensions of a machine, they will do so. She believed that group working had the power to release human potential:

> The potentialities of the individual remain potentialities until they are released by group life. (Follett, 1920, p. 6.)

Elton Mayo

Elton Mayo (1880–1949) was an Australian who taught logic, psychology and ethics at the University of Queensland. In 1922 he moved to the United States, and in 1926 became Professor of Industrial Research at Harvard Business School, applying psychological methods to industrial conflict.

In 1924, managers of the Western Electric Company began some experiments at their Hawthorne plant in Chicago to discover the effect on output of changing aspects of the physical environment. The first experiments studied the effect of lighting. The researchers established a control and an experimental group, varied the level of illumination and measured the output. As light rose, so did output. More surprisingly, as light fell, output continued to rise: it also rose in the control group, where conditions had not changed. The team concluded that physical conditions had little effect, so they set up a more comprehensive experiment to identify other factors.

They assembled a small number of workers in a separate room and altered variables in turn, including working hours, length of breaks and providing refreshments. The experienced workers were assembling small components to make telephone equipment. A supervisor was in charge and there was also an observer to record how workers reacted. They took care to prevent external factors disrupting the effects of the variables under investigation. The researchers also explained what was happening and ensured that the workers understood what they were expected to do. They also listened to employees' views of working conditions. The researchers varied conditions every two or three weeks, while the supervisor measured output regularly. This showed a gradual, if erratic, increase – even when the researchers returned conditions to those prevailing at an earlier stage – see Figure 2.2.

In 1928, senior managers invited Mayo to present the research to a wider audience (Mayo, 1949). They concluded from the relay assembly test room experiments that the increase in

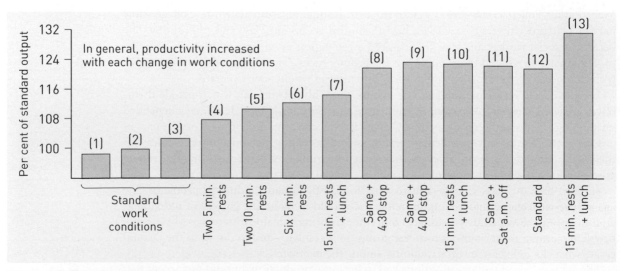

Figure 2.2 The relay assembly test room

Source: After Baron and Greenberg, 1997, p. 13. Reprinted by permission of Pearson Education, Inc., Upper Saddle River, NJ.

output was not related to the physical changes, but to the change in the social situation of the group:

> the major experimental change was introduced when those in charge sought to hold the situation humanly steady (in the interests of critical changes to be introduced) by getting the co-operation of the workers. What actually happened was that 6 individuals became a team and the team gave itself wholeheartedly and spontaneously to co-operation in the environment. (Mayo, 1949, p. 64)

The group felt special: managers asked for their views, were involved with them, paid attention to them and they had the chance to influence some aspects of the work.

The research team also observed another part of the factory, the bank wiring room, which revealed a different aspect of group working. Workers here were paid according to a piece-rate system, in which management pays workers a set amount for each item, or piece, that they produce. Such schemes reflect the assumption that financial incentives will encourage staff to work. The researchers observed that employees regularly produced less than they could have done. They had developed a sense of a normal rate of output, and ensured that all adhered to this rate, believing that if they produced, and earned, too much, management would reduce the piece-rate. Group members exercised informal sanctions against colleagues who worked too hard (or too slowly), until they came into line. Members who did too much were known as 'rate-busters' while those who did too little were 'chisellers'. Anyone who told the supervisor about this was a 'squealer'. Sanctions included being 'binged' – tapped on the shoulder to let them know that what they were doing was wrong. Managers had little or no control over these groups.

Finally, the research team conducted an extensive interview programme. They began by asking employees about the working environment and how they felt about their job, and then some questions about their life in general. The responses showed that there were often close links between work and domestic life. Work affected people's wider life more than the researchers had expected, and domestic circumstances affected their feelings about work. This implied that supervisors needed to think of a subordinate as a complete person, not just as a worker.

Mayo's reflections on the Hawthorne studies drew attention to aspects of human behaviour that practitioners of scientific management had neglected. He introduced the idea of 'social man', in contrast to the 'economic man' who was at the centre of earlier theories. While financial rewards would influence the latter, group relationships and loyalties would influence the former, and may outweigh management pressure.

On financial incentives, Mayo wrote:

> Man's desire to be continuously associated in work with his fellows is a strong, if not the strongest, human characteristic. Any disregard of it by management or any ill-advised attempt to defeat this human impulse leads instantly to some form of defeat for management itself. In [a study] the efficiency experts had assumed the primacy of financial incentive; in this they were wrong; not until the conditions of working group formation were satisfied did the financial incentives come into operation. (Mayo, 1949, p. 99)

People had social needs that they sought to satisfy – and how they did so may support or oppose management interests.

Further analysis of the experimental data has suggested that the team underestimated the influence of financial incentives. Becoming a member of the experimental group in itself increased the worker's income.

Despite possibly inaccurate interpretations, the findings stimulated interest in social factors in the workplace. Scientific management stressed the technical aspects of work. The Hawthorne studies implied that management should pay at least as much attention to human factors, leading to the **human relations approach**. This advocates that employees will work more effectively if management shows interest in their welfare, for instance, through more humane supervision.

Peters and Waterman (1982) published an influential book in which they tried to explain the success of what they regarded as 43 excellently managed US companies. One conclusion

Human relations approach is a school of management which emphasises the importance of social processes at work.

was that they had a distinctive set of philosophies about human nature and the way people interact in organisations. They did not see people as rational beings, motivated by fear and willing to accept a low-involvement employment relationship. Instead, excellent companies regarded people as emotional, intuitive and creative social beings who like to celebrate victories and value self-control – but who also need the security and meaning of achieving goals through organisations. From this, Peters and Waterman deduced some general rules for treating workers with dignity and respect, to ensure that people produced quality work in an increasingly uncertain environment.

Peters and Waterman had a significant influence on management thinking: they believed that management had previously relied too much on analytical techniques of the rational goal models, at the expense of more intuitive and human perspectives. They developed the ideas associated with the human relations models and introduced the idea of company culture – discussed in the next chapter.

Current status

The Hawthorne studies showed that the factors influencing performance were certainly more complex than earlier commentators had assumed. Other writers have followed and developed Mayo's emphasis on human factors. McGregor (1960), Maslow (1970) and Alderfer (1972) (see Chapter 13) have suggested ways of integrating human needs with those of the organisation as expressed by management.

An example of a manager who puts this into practice is the chief executive of SAS, a global software company which *Fortune* magazine named in 2010 as the best place to work in America. He says:

> People who are extremely concerned about problems at home tend not to be very productive at work. So our goal is to try to remove as much stress from their lives as we possibly can . . . all these things (medical care, childcare, massage, food, hairdressers and a 35-hour week) tend to make a person's life just a little bit easier. (*Financial Times*, 1 February 2010)

Another example is employee share ownership, as practised by the John Lewis Partnership (**www.johnlewispartnership.co.uk**) (retailing) and Tullis-Russell (**www.tullis-russell.com**) (papermaking). These (still uncommon) methods reflect their managers' theories about how best to encourage staff commitment and motivation.

As the external environments of organisations become less predictable than they were at the time of the Hawthorne experiments, managers and scholars have sought new theories to cope with these conditions, particularly in the idea of open systems models.

2.7 Open systems models

The open systems approach builds on earlier work in general systems theory, and has been widely used to help understand management and organisational issues. The basic idea is to think of the organisation not as a **system**, but as an **open system**.

The open systems approach draws attention to the links between the internal parts of a system, and to the links between the whole system and the outside world. The system is separated from its environment by the **system boundary**. An open system imports resources such as energy and materials, which enter it from the environment across this boundary, undergo some transformation process within the system and leave the system as goods and services. The central theme of the open systems view of management is that organisations depend on the wider environment for inputs if they are to survive and prosper. Figure 2.3 (based on Figure 1.1) is a simple model of the organisation as an open system.

A **system** is a set of interrelated parts designed to achieve a purpose.

An **open system** is one that interacts with its environment.

A **system boundary** separates the system from its environment.

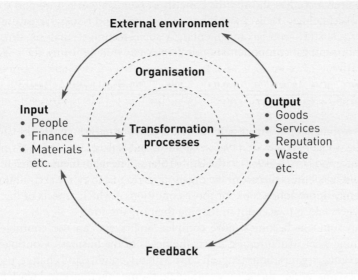

Figure 2.3
The systems model

The figure shows input and output processes, conversion processes and feedback loops. The organisation must satisfy those in the wider environment well enough to ensure that they continue to provide resources. The management task is to sustain those links if the organisation is to thrive. **Feedback** (in systems theory) refers to information about the performance of the system. It may be deliberate, through customer surveys, or unplanned, such as the loss of business to a competitor. Feedback enables those managing the system to take remedial action.

Another idea is that of **subsystems**. A course is a subsystem within a department or faculty, the faculty is a subsystem of a university, the university is a subsystem of the higher education system. This in turn is part of the whole education system. A course itself will consist of several systems – one for quality assurance, one for enrolling students, one for teaching, another for assessment and so on.

These subsystems interact with each other, and how well people manage these links affects the functioning of the whole system: when a university significantly increases the number of students admitted to a popular course, this affects many parts of the system – such as accommodation (*technology*), teaching resources (*people*) and examinations (*business processes*).

A systems approach emphasises the links between systems, and reminds managers that a change in one will have consequences for others. For example, Danny Potter, Managing Director of Inamo (**www.inamo-restaurant.com**) a London restaurant where customers place their order directly to the kitchen from an interactive ordering system on their table explains:

> I think the greatest challenge that we faced is communicating our ideas down through the business about what we're trying to achieve. There is a big overlap between essentially the computer software side and the actual restaurant side, to unite those in a way that people [new staff, suppliers etc.] understand has proven rather tricky.

Socio-technical systems

An important variant of systems theory is the idea of the **socio-technical system**. The approach developed from the work of Eric Trist and Ken Bamforth (1951) at the Tavistock Institute in London. Their most prominent study was of an attempt in the coal industry to mechanise the mining system. Introducing what were in essence assembly line technologies and methods at the coalface had severe consequences for the social system that the older pattern of working had encouraged. The technological system destroyed the social system, and the solution lay in reconciling the needs of both.

Feedback (In systems theory) refers to the provision of information about the effects of an activity.

Subsystems are the separate but related parts that make up the total system.

A **socio-technical system** is one in which outcomes depend on the interaction of both the technical and social subsystems.

This and similar studies showed the benefits of seeing a work system as a combination of a material technology (tools, machinery, techniques) and a social organisation (people, relationships, constitutional arrangements). A socio-technical analysis aims to integrate the social and technical components: optimising one while ignoring the other is likely to be unproductive.

Contingency management

A further development of the open systems view is the contingency approach (Chapter 9). This arose from the work of Woodward (1965) and Burns and Stalker (1961) in the United Kingdom, and of Lawrence and Lorsch (1967) in the United States. The main theme is that to perform well managers must adapt the structure of the organisation to match external conditions.

Contingency approaches look for those conditions – which aspects of the environment should managers take into account in shaping their organisation.

As the environment becomes more complex, managers can use contingency perspectives to examine what structure best meets the needs of the business. Contingency theorists emphasise creating organisations that can cope with uncertainty and change, using the values of the open systems model; they also recognise that some functions need work in a stable and predictable way, using the values of the internal process model.

Managers increasingly have to cope with change and innovation (see Chapter 11). An example would be when senior managers in high-tech firms like Apple (**www.apple.com**) or Microsoft (**www.microsoft.com**) create teams to work with a high degree of autonomy (to encourage creativity) on discrete parts of a larger project. The team members will work creatively within a network of informal contacts and exchanges relevant to their part of the task. These human interactions lead to stable or unstable behaviour, and the skill is to balance these extremes. If an organisation is too stable it will stifle innovation, but if it is too unstable it will disintegrate:

> Successful organisations work between these two conditions. [In changing environments], rather than seeking to control their organisations to maintain equilibrium . . . [managers] need to embrace more flexible and adaptive models of change and innovation. (McMillan and Carlisle, 2007, p. 577)

This way of thinking about organisations sometimes uses the terms 'linear' and 'non-linear' systems. 'Linear' describes a system in which an action leads to a predictable reaction. If you light a fire in a room, the thermostat will turn the central heating down. Non-linear systems are those in which outcomes are less predictable. If managers reduce prices they will be surprised if sales match the forecast – they cannot predict the reactions of competitors, changes in taste or new products. Circumstances in the outside world change in ways that management cannot anticipate, so while short-term consequences of an act are clear, long-run ones are not.

Current status

Although theories of management develop at particular times in response to current problems, this does not mean that newer is better. While new concerns bring out new theories, old concerns usually remain. While recently developed ideas seek to encourage flexibility and change, some businesses, and some parts of highly flexible businesses still require control. Rather than thinking of theoretical development as a linear process, see it as circular or iterative, in which familiar themes recur as new concerns arise. The competing values approach captures the main theoretical developments in one framework and shows the relationships between them – see Table 2.3.

The emerging management challenges come from many sources. One is the widely accepted need to develop a more sustainable economic system. Another is the need to balance innovation and creativity with closer governance and control, especially in financial services. Deregulation of many areas of activity is allowing new competitors to enter previously protected markets

---

Contingency approaches to organisational structure propose that the performance of an organisation depends on having a structure that is appropriate to its environment.

Table 2.3 Summary of the models within the competing values framework

Features/model	Rational goal	Internal process	Human relations	Open systems
Main exponents	Taylor	Fayol	Mayo	Trist and Bamforth
	Frank and Lillian Gilbreth	Weber	Follett	Woodward
			Barnard	Burns and Stalker
			Peters and Waterman	Lawrence and Lorsch
Criteria of effectiveness	Productivity, profit	Stability, continuity	Commitment, morale, cohesion	Adaptability, external support
Means/ends theory	Clear direction leads to productive outcomes	Routinisation leads to stability	Involvement leads to commitment	Continual innovation secures external support
Emphasis	Rational analysis, measurement	Defining responsibility, documentation	Participation, consensus building	Creative problem solving, innovation
Role of manager	Director and planner	Monitor and co-ordinator	Mentor and facilitator	Innovator and broker

(airlines, financial services). Still another is the closer integration between many previously separate areas of business (telecommunications, consumer electronics and entertainment). There is also the growing internationalisation of business. Managers today look for radical solutions – just as Robert Owen did in the early days of the Industrial Revolution.

Activity 2.2   What are 'theories of management'?

Recall the organisation you used in Activity 2.1.

Having read the chapter, make brief notes summarising how 'theory' (even if implicitly) has shaped management decisions:

- Which of the quadrants in Figure 2.1 most closely reflects the way the organisation works?
- What examples of rational goal practices have you found? (Refer to Section 2.4.)
- What examples of internal process practices have you found? (Refer to Section 2.5.)
- What examples of human relations practices have you found? (Refer to Section 2.6.)
- What examples of open systems practices have you found? (Refer to Section 2.7.)

Compare what you have found with other students on your course.

Summary

1 **Explain the value of models of management, and compare unitary, pluralist and critical perspectives**

- Models represent more complex realities, help to understand complexity and offer a range of perspectives on the topic. Their predictive effect is limited by the fact that people interpret information subjectively in deciding how to act.

- A unitary perspective emphasises the common purpose of organisational members, while the pluralist draws attention to competing interest groups. Those who take a critical perspective believe that organisations reflect deep divisions in society, and that attempts to integrate different interests through negotiation ignore persistent differences in the distribution of power.

2 **State the structure of the competing values framework and evaluate its contribution to our understanding of management**

- A way of integrating the otherwise confusing range of theories of management. Organisations experience tensions between control and flexibility and between an external and an internal focus. Placing these on two axes allows theories to be allocated to one of four types – rational goal, internal process, human relations and open systems.

3 **Summarise the rational goal, internal process, human relations and open systems models and evaluate what each can contribute to a manager's understanding of their role**

- Rational goal (Taylor, the Gilbreths and operational research):
  - clear direction leads to productive outcomes, with an emphasis on rational analysis and measurement.
- Internal process (Weber, Fayol):
  - routinisation leads to stability, so an emphasis on defining responsibility and on comprehensive documentation and administrative processes.
- Human relations (Follett, Mayo):
  - people are motivated by social needs, and managers who recognise these will secure commitment. Practices include considerate supervision, participation and seeking consensus.
- Open systems (socio-technical and contingency):
  - Continual innovation secures external support, achieved by creative problem solving.

These theories have contributed to the management agendas in these ways:

- Rational goal – through techniques like time and motion study, work measurement and a variety of techniques for planning operations; also the narrow specification of duties, and the separation of management and non-management work.
- Internal process – clear targets and measurement systems, and the creation of clear management and reporting structures. Making decisions objectively on the basis of rules and procedures, rather than on favouritism or family connections.
- Human relations – considerate supervision, consultation and participation in decisions affecting people.
- Open systems – understanding external factors and being able and willing to respond to them through individual and organisational flexibility especially in uncertain, complex conditions characterised by the idea of non-linear systems. While a linear system is one in which a relatively stable environment makes some planning feasible, a non-linear system is strongly influenced by other systems. This means that actions lead to unexpected consequences.

Review questions

1 Name three ways in which theoretical models help the study of management.
2 What are the different assumptions of the unitary, pluralist and critical perspectives on organisations?
3 Draw the two axes of the competing values framework, and then place the theories outlined in this chapter in the most appropriate sector.

4 List Taylor's five principles of scientific management and evaluate their use in examples of your choice.

5 What was the particular contribution that Lillian Gilbreth made concerning how workers' mental capacities should be treated?

6 What did Follett consider to be the value of groups in community as well as business?

7 Compare Taylor's assumptions about people with those of Mayo. Evaluate the accuracy of these views by reference to an organisation of your choice.

8 Compare the conclusions reached by the Hawthorne experimenters in the relay assembly test room with those in the bank wiring room.

9 Why is an open system likely to be harder to manage than a closed system?

Further reading

Birkinshaw, J. (2010), *Reinventing Management: Smarter choices for getting work done*, Jossey-Bass, San Fancisco, CA.

A small book by a leading management academic gives a short account of the work of general management.

Taylor, F. W. (1917), *The Principles of Scientific Management*, Harper, New York.

Fayol, H. (1949), *General and Industrial Management*, Pitman, London.

The original works of these writers are short and lucid. Taylor (1917) contains illuminating detail that brings the ideas to life, and Fayol's (1949) surviving ideas came from only two short chapters, which are worth reading in the original.

Weblinks

These websites have appeared in, or are relevant to, the chapter:

www.pret.com
www.johnlewispartnership.co.uk
www.tullis-russell.com
www.inamo-restaurant.com
www.apple.com
www.microsoft.com
www.newlanark.org.uk

Visit two of the business sites in the list above, or those of other organisations in which you are interested, and navigate to the pages dealing with recent news, press or investor relations.

● What are the main issues which the organisation appears to be facing?

● Compare and contrast the issues you identify on the two sites.

● What challenges may they imply for those working in, and managing, these organisations?

Annotated weblinks, multiple choice questions and other useful resources can be found on **www.pearsoned.co.uk/boddy**

Case study   Robert Owen – an early management innovator   www.newlanark.org.uk

Robert Owen (1771–1856) was a successful manufacturer of textiles, who ran mills in England and at New Lanark, about 24 miles from Glasgow, in Scotland. David Dale built the cotton-spinning mills at New Lanark in 1785 – which were then the largest in Scotland. Since they depended on water power, Dale had built them below the Falls of Clyde – a well-known tourist attraction throughout the 18th century. Many people continued to visit both the Falls and New Lanark, which combined both manufacturing and social innovations.

Creating such a large industrial enterprise in the countryside meant that Dale (and Owen after him) had to attract and retain labour – which involved building not just the mill but also houses, shops, schools and churches for the workers. By 1793, the mill employed about 1200 people, of whom almost 800 were children, aged from 6 to 17: 200 were under 10 (McLaren, 1990). Dale provided the children with food, education and clothing in return for working 12 hours each day: visitors were impressed by these facilities.

One visitor was Robert Owen, who shared Dale's views on the benefits to both labour and owner of good working conditions. By 1801 Dale wanted to sell New Lanark to someone who shared his principles and concluded that Owen (who had married his daughter) was such a man. Owen had built a reputation for management skills while running mills in England, and did not approve of employing children in them.

Having bought the very large business of New Lanark, Owen quickly introduced new management and production control techniques. These included daily and weekly measurements of stocks, output and productivity; a system of labour costing; and measures of work-in-progress. He used a novel control technique: a small, four-sided piece of wood, with a different colour on each side, hung beside every worker. The colour set to the front indicated the previous day's standard of work – black indicating bad. Everyone could see this measure of the worker's performance, which overseers recorded to identify any trends in a person's work:

> Every process in the factory was closely watched, checked and recorded to increase labour productivity and to keep costs down. (Royle, 1998, p. 13)

Reproduced with kind permission of New Lanark Trust
www.newlanark.org.

At this stage of the Industrial Revolution, most adult employees had no experience of factory work, or of living in a large community such as New Lanark. Owen found that many 'were idle, intemperate, dishonest [and] devoid of truth' (quoted in Butt, 1971). Evening patrols were introduced to stop drunkenness, and there were rules about keeping the residential areas clean and free of rubbish. He also had 'to deal with slack managers who had tolerated widespread theft and embezzlement, immorality and drunkenness' (Butt, 1971).

During Owen's time at the mill it usually employed about 1500 people, and soon after taking over he stopped employing children under 10. He introduced other social innovations: a store at which employees could buy goods more cheaply than elsewhere (a model for the Co-operative Movement), and a school which looked after children from the age of 1 – enabling their mothers to work in the mills. Owen actively managed the links between his business and the wider world. On buying the mills he quickly became part of the Glasgow business establishment, and was closely involved in the activities of the Chamber of Commerce. He took a prominent role in the social and political life of the city. He used these links in particular to argue the case for reforms in the educational and economic systems, and was critical of the effect that industrialisation was having upon working-class life.

Owen believed that education in useful skills would help to release working-class children from poverty and promoted the case for wider educational provision. He also developed several experiments in co-operation and community building, believing that the basis of his successful capitalist enterprise at New Lanark (education, good working conditions and a harmonious community) could be applied to society as a whole.

Sources: Butt (1971); McLaren (1990); Royle (1998); Donachie (2000).

Questions

1 Refer to Section 2.2, and make notes on which theory may have (implicitly) guided Owen's approach to business.

2 What 'rational goal' practices did he use at New Lanark? (Refer to Section 2.4.)

3 What 'human relations' practices did he use? (Refer to Section 2.6.)

4 Draw a systems diagram showing the main inputs, transformation and outputs of Robert Owen's mill. (Refer to Section 2.7, especially Figure 2.3.)

PART 2
THE ENVIRONMENT OF MANAGEMENT

Introduction

Management takes place within a context, and this part examines the external context of organisations. Managers need to be familiar with that external environment, though they do not accept it passively. They try to influence it by lobbying powerful players, by reaching agreement with competitors or by shaping public opinion. Nevertheless, since the organisation draws its resources from the external world, it needs to deliver goods or services well enough to persuade people in that environment to continue their support. This is most obvious in commercial organisations. It is equally relevant in the public service: if a department set up to deliver care is managed badly, it will not deliver. Taxpayers or clients will press their elected representatives to improve performance, and they in turn will demand improved performance from management and staff. If they do not, the enterprise will fail.

Chapter 3 examines the most immediate aspect of the manager's context – the culture of their organisation – and then offers tools for analysing systematically the competitive and general environments and stakeholder expectations. Chapter 4 reflects the international nature of much business today, by examining international features of the general environment – political developments such as the European Union, international economic factors and differences in national cultures.

Pressure from interest groups and some consumers has encouraged many companies to take a positive approach to issues of corporate responsibility. There are conflicting interests here and Chapter 5 presents some concepts and tools that help to consider these issues in a coherent way.

CHAPTER 3
ORGANISATION CULTURES AND CONTEXTS

Learning outcomes

When you have read this chapter you should be able to:

1 Compare systematically the cultures of two organisational units
2 Use the five forces model to analyse an organisation's competitive environment
3 Use the PESTEL framework to analyse the wider environment of an organisation
4 Explain the meaning and purposes of corporate governance
5 Use ideas from the chapter to comment on the management issues in the Nokia case study

Activity 3.1   What are 'organisational cultures and contexts'?

Before reading this chapter, write some notes on what you understand by the term 'organisational cultures and contexts'.

Choose the organisation or people you hope may be able to help you learn about the topic. You may find it helpful to discuss the topic with a manager you know, or reflect on an activity you have managed.

- Make brief notes on the main features of the organisation's culture and how people describe it.
- What are likely to be the main factors outside the organisation which affect it?
- How (if at all) have changes in those external factors altered what managers do?

Keep these notes as you will be able to use them later.

3.1   Introduction

Nokia's performance depends on the ability of its managers to understand what consumers expect from a mobile phone and to meet those requirements more effectively than competitors. It also depends on staff identifying scientific research that may lead to new features in its handsets – and assessing whether customers would value them in the next generation of products. The early success of the company was helped by recognising that many users see a mobile as a fashion accessory, and by using its design skills to meet that need. It also gained when the European Union established common standards for mobile telephony, which the Finnish government supported. In recent years, the company has found it hard to compete with devices such as the iPhone from Apple, and with lower cost producers of basic handsets. It has recently formed an alliance with Microsoft to try to recover its position in the industry.

All managers work within a context which both constrains and supports them. How well they understand, interpret and interact with that context affects their performance. Finkelstein (2003) (especially pp. 63–68) shows how Motorola, an early market leader in mobile communications, failed to take account of changes in consumer preferences (for digital rather than the older, analogue mobile phones). By the time managers understood this change, Nokia had a commanding lead in the market. Each business is unique, so the forces with which they interact differ: those who are able to identify and shape them (Nokia) will perform better than those who are not (Motorola). In 2009, Nokia in turn may have underestimated the effect which smartphones would have on the market, allowing Apple to take market share.

Figure 3.1 shows four environmental forces. The inner circle represents the organisation's **internal environment (or context)** – introduced in Chapter 1. That includes its culture, often a major influence on performance. Beyond that is the immediate **competitive environment (or context)**, sometimes known as the micro-environment. This is the industry-specific environment of customers, suppliers, competitors and potential substitute. The outer circle shows the **general environment (or context)**, sometimes known as the macro-environment – political, economic, social, technological, (natural) environmental and legal factors that affect all organisations. Forces in the internal and competitive environments usually have more impact on, and are more open to influence by, the organisation than those in the general environment.

The competitive and general environments make up an organisation's **external environment (or context)** – a constantly changing source of threats and opportunities: how well people cope with these affects performance.

Forces in the external environment become part of the 'management agenda' in an organisation only when internal or external stakeholders draw attention to them in some way. In

The **internal environment (or context)** consists of elements which make up the organisation – such as its structure, culture, people and technologies.

A **competitive environment (or context)** is the industry-specific environment comprising the organisation's customers, suppliers and competitors.

The **general environment (or context)** (sometimes known as the macro-environment) includes political, economic, social technological, (natural) environmental and legal factors that affect all organisations.

The **external environment (or context)** consists of elements beyond the organisation – it combines the competitive and general environments.

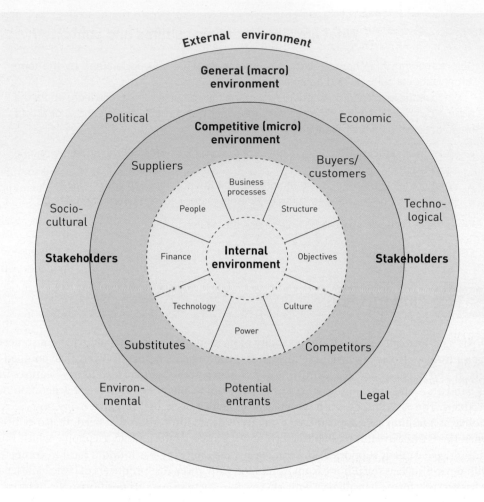

Figure 3.1
Environmental
influences on the
organisation

terms of Figure 3.1, they are a fourth force. Managers (who are themselves stakeholders) balance conflicting interpretations of their context. They work within an internal context, and look outside for actual and potential changes that may affect the centre of Figure 3.1. The figure implies a constant interaction between an organisation and its external environment.

Managers do not passively accept their environment, but try to shape it by actively persuading governments and other agencies to act in their favour (known as 'lobbying'). Car manufacturers and airlines regularly seek subsidies, cheap loans or favourable regulations, while most industry bodies (such as the European Automobile Manufacturers Association – **www.acea.be**) lobby international bodies such as the European Commission – often through professional lobbying companies.

The next section presents ideas on organisational culture. Beyond that, managers need to interact intelligently with their external environments, so the chapter also outlines stakeholder expectations and introduces ideas on governance and control.

Culture is a pattern of shared basic assumptions that was learned by a group as it solved its problems of external adaptation and internal integration, that has worked well enough to be considered valid and transmitted to new members (Schein, 2004, p. 17).

| 3.2 | Cultures and their components |

Developing cultures

Interest in organisation **culture** has grown as academics and managers have come to believe that it influences behaviour. Several claim that a strong and distinct culture helps to integrate individuals into the team or organisation (Deal and Kennedy, 1982; Peters and Waterman,

1982). Deal and Kennedy (1982) refer to culture as 'the way we do things around here' and Hofstede (1991) sees it as the 'collective programming of the mind', distinguishing one group from another. They claim that having the right culture explains the success of high-performing organisations.

Someone entering a department or organisation for the first time can usually sense and observe the surface elements of the culture. Some buzz with life and activity, others seem asleep; some welcome and look after visitors, others seem inward looking; some work by the rules, while others are entrepreneurial and risk taking; some have regular social occasions while in others staff rarely meet except at work.

Distinctive cultures develop as people develop and share common values. They use these to establish beliefs and norms which guide their behaviour towards each other and to outsiders. Positive outcomes reinforce their belief in the values underlying their behaviour, which then become a stronger influence on how people should work and relate to each other: Should people have job titles? How should they dress? Should meetings be confrontational or supportive?

A shared culture provides members with guidelines about how they can best contribute. The more they work on these issues to develop a common understanding, the better they will perform.

Components of cultures

Schein (2004) identifies a culture's three levels, 'level' referring to the degree to which the observer can see its components.

- **Artifacts** represent the visible level – elements such as the language or etiquette which someone coming into contact with a culture can observe:
  - Architecture (open plan offices without doors or private space)
  - Technology and equipment
  - Style (clothing, manner of address, emotional displays)
  - Rituals and ceremonies (leaving events, awards ceremonies and away-days)
  - Courses (to induct employees in the culture as well as the content)

While it is easy to observe artifacts, it is difficult for outsiders to decipher what they mean to the group, or what underlying assumptions they reflect. That requires an analysis of beliefs and values.

- **Espoused beliefs and values** are the accumulated beliefs that members hold about their work. As a group develops, members refine their ideas about what works in this business: how people make decisions, how teams work together, how they solve problems. Practices that work become the accepted way to behave:
  - 'Quality pays'
  - 'We should stick to our core business'
  - 'Cultivate a sense of personal responsibility'
  - 'We depend on close team work'
  - 'Everyone is expected to challenge a proposal – whoever made it'

Some companies codify and publish their beliefs and values, to help induct new members and to reinforce them among existing staff. Such beliefs and values shape the visible artifacts, though companies vary in the degree to which employees internalise them. The extent to which they do so depends on how clearly they derive from shared basic underlying assumptions.

- **Basic underlying assumptions** are deeply held by members of the group as being the way to work together. As they act in accordance with their values and beliefs, those that work become embedded as basic underlying assumptions. When the group holds these strongly, members will act in accordance with them, and reject actions based on others:

- 'We need to satisfy customers to survive as a business'
- 'Our business is to help people with X problem live better with X problem'
- 'People can make mistakes, as long as they learn from them'
- 'We employ highly motivated and competent adults'
- 'Financial markets worry about the short-term: we are here for the long-term'

Difficulties arise when people with assumptions developed in one group work with people from another. Staff in companies that merge with another business sometimes find it difficult to work with their new colleagues because of historic cultural differences.

Management in practice   **A strong culture at Bosch**   **www.bosch.com**   FT

Franz Fehrenbach is chief executive of Bosch, Germany's largest privately owned engineering group, and the world's largest supplier of car parts. In 2009 he said:

> The company culture, especially our high credibility, is one of our greatest assets. Our competitors cannot match us on that because it takes decades to build up.

The cultural traditions include a rigid control on costs, an emphasis on team thinking, employees being responsible for their errors, cautious financial policies and long-term thinking. For example, to cope with the recession in 2009 Mr Fehrenbach explained that:

> We have to cut costs in all areas. We will reduce spending in the ongoing business, but we will not cut back on research and development for important future projects.

Source: Adapted from Space to breathe amid the crisis (Daniel Schaefer), *Financial Times*, 2 March 2009, p. 16.

3.3   Types of culture

This section outlines three ways of describing and comparing cultures.

Competing values framework

The competing values model developed by Quinn *et al.* (2003) reflects inherent tensions between flexibility or control and between an internal or an external focus: Figure 2.1 (p. 30) shows four cultural types.

Rational goal

Members see the organisation as a rational, efficiency-seeking unit. They define effectiveness in terms of production or economic goals that satisfy external requirements. Managers create structures to deal with the outside world. Leadership tends to be directive, goal-oriented and functional. Key motivating factors include competition and the achievement of goals. Examples are large, established businesses – mechanistic.

Internal process

Here members focus on internal matters. Their goal is to make the unit efficient, stable and controlled. Tasks are repetitive and methods stress specialisation, rules and procedures. Leaders tend to be cautious and spend time on technical issues. Motivating factors include security, stability and order. Examples include utilities and public authorities – suspicious of change.

Human relations

People emphasise the value of informal interpersonal relations rather than formal structures. They try to maintain the organisation and nurture its members, defining effectiveness in terms of their well-being and commitment. Leaders tend to be participative, considerate and supportive. Motivating factors include attachment, cohesiveness and membership. Examples include voluntary groups, professional service firms and some internal support functions.

Open systems

This represents an open systems view, in which people recognise that the external environment plays a significant role, and is a vital source of ideas, energy and resources. It also sees the environment as complex and turbulent, requiring entrepreneurial, visionary leadership and flexible, responsive behaviour. Key motivating factors are growth, stimulation, creativity and variety. Examples are start-up firms and new business units – organic, flexible operations.

Charles Handy's cultural types

Charles Handy (1993) distinguished four cultures – **power**, **role**, **task** and **person**.

Power

A dominant central figure holds power: others follow the centre's policy and interpret new situations in the way the leader would. Many entrepreneurial firms operate in this way, with few rules but with well-understood, implicit codes on how to behave and work. The firm relies on the individual rather than on seeking consensus through discussion.

Role

Typical characteristics of this culture are the job description or the procedure. Managers define what they expect in clear, detailed job descriptions. They select those who meet the specifications. Procedures guide how people and departments interact. If all follow the rules, co-ordination is straightforward. Someone's position in the hierarchy determines their formal power.

Task

People focus on completing the task or project rather than their formal role. They value each other for what they can contribute and expect everyone to help as needed. The emphasis is on getting the resources and people for the job and then relying on their commitment and enthusiasm. People often work in teams, combining diverse skills to meet a common purpose.

Person

The individual is at the centre and any structure or system is there to serve them. The form is unusual – small professional and artistic organisations are probably closest to it, and perhaps experiments in communal living. They exist to meet the needs of the professionals or the members, rather than some larger organisational goal.

Multiple cultures

Martin (2002) proposed that organisations have not one, but several cultures: observers take one of three perspectives towards a culture:

- **Integration** – a focus on identifying consistencies in the data, and using those common patterns to explain events.
- **Differentiation** – a focus on conflict, identifying different and possibly conflicting views of members towards events.
- **Fragmentation** – a focus on the fluid nature of organisations, and on the interplay and change of views about events.

A **power culture** is one in which people's activities are strongly influenced by a dominant central figure.

A **role culture** is one in which people's activities are strongly influenced by clear and detailed job descriptions and other formal signals as to what is expected of them.

A **task culture** is one in which the focus of activity is towards completing a task or project using whatever means are appropriate.

A **person culture** is one in which activity is strongly influenced by the wishes of the individuals who are part of the organisation.

Table 3.1 Hierarchical position and cultural perspectives

Position in hierarchy	Cultural perspective	Description	Example
Head office managers	Integration	Cultural values should be shared across the organisation. Unified culture both desirable and attainable	'If we can get every . . . part of the company doing what they should be doing, we'll beat everybody.'
Store managers	Differentiation	Reconciling conflicting views of head office and shop floor. See cultural pluralism as inevitable	'People up at head office are all pushing us in different directions. Jill in Marketing wants customer focus, June in Finance wants lower costs.'
Store employees	Fragmented	Confused by contradictory nature of the espoused values. See organisation as complex and unpredictable	'One minute it's this, the next it's that. You can't keep up with the flavour of the month.'

Source: Based on Ogbonna and Harris (1998).

Ogbonna and Harris (1998) provided empirical support for this view, based on interviews with staff in a retail company. They found that someone's position in the hierarchy determined their perspective on the culture (see Table 3.1). As consensus on culture was unlikely, they advised managers to recognise the range of sub-cultures within their oganisation, and only seek to reconcile those differences that were essential to policy. They also observed that culture remains a highly subjective idea, largely in the eye of the beholder:

and is radically different according to an individual's position in the hierarchy. (p. 45)

Culture and performance

Peters and Waterman (1982) believed that an organisation's culture affected performance, and implied that managers should try to change their culture towards a more productive one. Others are more sceptical about the effects on performance and question whether, even if a suitable culture has a positive effect, managers can consciously change it. Thompson and McHugh (2002), while also critical of much writing on the topic, observe the potential benefits that a suitable culture can bring to not-for-profit organisations:

Creating a culture resonant with the overall goals is relevant to any organisation, whether it be a trade union, voluntary group or producer co-operative. Indeed, it is more important in such consensual groupings. Co-operatives, for example, can degenerate organisationally because they fail to develop adequate mechanisms for transmitting the original ideals from founders to new members and sustaining them through shared experiences. (pp. 208–09)

As managers work within an organisational culture, they also work within an external context – whose participants have expectations of the organisation. They need tools with which to analyse that external world.

3.4   The competitive environment – Porter's five forces

Managers are most directly affected by forces in their immediate competitive environment. According to Porter (1980a, 1985) the ability of a firm to earn an acceptable return depends on five forces – the ability of new competitors to enter the industry, the threat of substitute products, the bargaining power of buyers, the bargaining power of suppliers and the rivalry among existing competitors. Figure 3.2 shows Porter's **five forces analysis**.

Porter believes that the *collective* strength of the five forces determines industry profitability, through their effects on prices, costs and investment requirements. Buyer power influences the prices a firm can charge, as does the threat of substitutes. The bargaining power of suppliers determines the cost of raw materials and other inputs. The greater the collective strength of the forces, the less profitable the industry: the weaker they are, the more profitable. Managers can use their knowledge of these forces to shape strategy.

Five forces analysis is a technique for identifying and listing those aspects of the five forces most relevant to the profitability of an organisation at that time.

Threat of new entrants

The extent of this threat depends on how easily new entrants can overcome barriers such as:

- the need for economies of scale (to compete on cost), which are difficult to achieve quickly;
- high capital investment is required;
- lack of distribution channels;
- subsidies which benefit existing firms at the expense of potential new entrants;
- cost advantages of existing firms, such as access to raw materials or know-how; and
- strong customer loyalty to incumbent companies.

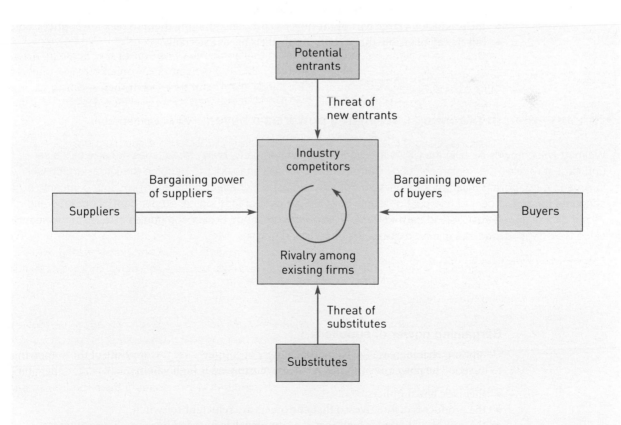

Figure 3.2 The five forces of industry competition
Source: Porter (1980a), p. 5.

Nokia faces competition from new entrants to the mobile phone industry, especially Apple and Research in Motion (BlackBerry), at the top end of the market. The Chinese ZTE Corporation is supplying cheap mobiles to consumers in emerging markets.

Intensity of rivalry amongst competitors

Strong competitive rivalry lowers profitability, and occurs when:

- there are many firms in an industry;
- there is slow market growth, so companies fight for market share;
- fixed costs are high, so firms use capacity fully and overproduce;
- exit costs are high; specialised assets (hard to sell) or management loyalty (in old family firms) deter firms from leaving the industry, which prolong excess capacity and low profitability; and
- products are similar, so customers can easily switch to other suppliers.

A highly competitive market will also be one in which the threat of new entrants is high. While Nokia was still the largest player in the mobile phone industry in 2011, it faced pressure from established competitors Motorola, Siemens and Ericsson, and from new entrants in Asia.

Power of buyers (customers)

Buyers (customers) seek lower prices or higher quality at constant prices, thus forcing down prices and profitability. Buyer power is high when:

- the buyer purchases a large part of a supplier's output;
- there are many substitute products, allowing easy switching;
- the product is a large part of the buyer's costs, encouraging them to seek lower prices; and
- buyers can plausibly threaten to supply their needs internally.

Management in practice　Walmart's power as a buyer　www.walmart.com

Walmart (which owns Asda in the UK) is the world's largest company, being three times the size of the second largest retailer, the French company Carrefour. Growth has enabled it to become the largest purchaser in America, controlling much of the business done by almost every major consumer-products company. It accounts for 30 per cent of hair-care products sold, 26 per cent of toothpaste, 20 per cent of pet food and 20 per cent of all sales of CDs, videos and DVDs. This gives it great power over companies in these industries, since their dependence on Walmart reduces their bargaining power.

Source: *Business Week*, 6 October 2003, pp. 48–53, and other sources.

Bargaining power of suppliers

Conditions that increase the bargaining power of suppliers are the opposite of those applying to buyers. The power of suppliers relative to customers is high when:

- there are few suppliers;
- the product is distinctive, so that customers are reluctant to switch;
- the cost of switching is high (e.g. if a company has invested in a supplier's software);
- the supplier can plausibly threaten to extend their business to compete with the customer; and
- the customer is a small or irregular purchaser.

Threat of substitutes

In Porter's model, substitutes refer to products in other industries that can perform the same function – using cans instead of bottles. Close substitutes constrain the ability of firms to raise prices, and the threat is high when buyers are able and willing to change their habits. Technological change and the risk of obsolescence pose a further threat: online news services (such as that freely available from the BBC) and recruitment sites threaten print newspapers.

Analysing the forces in the competitive environment enables managers to seize opportunities, counter threats and generally improve their position relative to competitors. They can consider how to alter the strength of the forces to improve their position by, for example, building barriers to entry or increasing their power over suppliers or buyers. Chapter 8 (Managing strategy) examines how managers can position their organisation within the competitive environment.

3.5   The general environment – PESTEL

Forces in the wider world also shape management policies, and a **PESTEL analysis** (short for political, economic, socio-cultural, technological, environmental and legal) helps to identify these – see Figure 3.3. GlaxoSmithKline (**www.gsk.com**), like other pharmaceutical companies, works in an environment which includes:

PESTEL analysis is a technique for identifying and listing the political, economic, social, technological, environmental and legal factors in the general environment most relevant to an organisation.

- governments trying to reduce the cost of drugs supplied to citizens;
- companies making cheap generic alternatives to patented drugs;

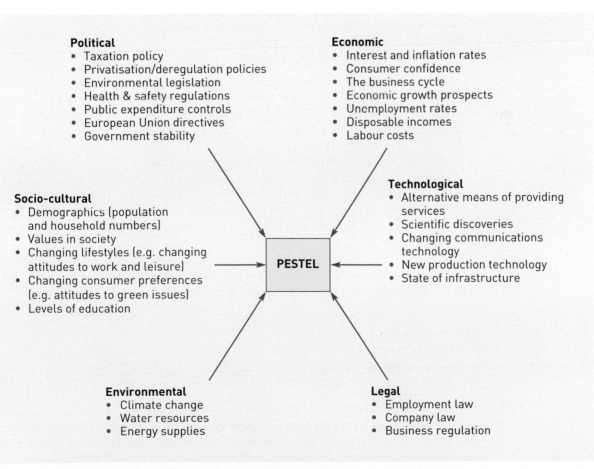

Political
- Taxation policy
- Privatisation/deregulation policies
- Environmental legislation
- Health & safety regulations
- Public expenditure controls
- European Union directives
- Government stability

Economic
- Interest and inflation rates
- Consumer confidence
- The business cycle
- Economic growth prospects
- Unemployment rates
- Disposable incomes
- Labour costs

Socio-cultural
- Demographics (population and household numbers)
- Values in society
- Changing lifestyles (e.g. changing attitudes to work and leisure)
- Changing consumer preferences (e.g. attitudes to green issues)
- Levels of education

Technological
- Alternative means of providing services
- Scientific discoveries
- Changing communications technology
- New production technology
- State of infrastructure

PESTEL

Environmental
- Climate change
- Water resources
- Energy supplies

Legal
- Employment law
- Company law
- Business regulation

Figure 3.3 Identifying environmental influences – PESTEL analysis

- slow transfer of scientific knowledge into commercial products; and
- regulators requiring longer and more costly trials of new drugs.

Political factors

Political systems vary between countries and often shape what managers can and cannot do. Governments often regulate industries such as power supply, telecommunications, postal services and transport by specifying, among other things, who can offer services, the conditions they must meet and what they can charge. Regulations differ between countries and are a major factor in managers' decisions.

When the UK and most European governments altered the law on financial services, non-financial companies like Virgin and Sainsbury's quickly began to offer banking services. Deregulating air transport stimulated the growth of low-cost airlines, especially in the US (e.g. Southwest Airlines), Europe (easyJet), Australia (Virgin Blue) and parts of Asia (Air Asia), though as the Ryanair case in Chapter 1 showed, these companies still work in a political environment. The European Union is developing regulations to try to manage the environmentally friendly disposal of the millions of personal computers and mobile phones that consumers scrap each year.

Managers aim to influence these political decisions by employing professional lobbyists, especially at international institutions. The European Commission relies on contributions from interested parties to inform its decisions and lobbying firms provide this. They focus on those people who have decision-making power, often members of the European parliament.

Economic factors

Economic factors such as wage levels, inflation and interest rates affect an organisation's costs. During the recession, Unilever (**www.unilever.com**) detected significant changes in shopping habits, with many customers doing without expensive bubble baths, body moisturisers and upmarket cleaning products in favour of less expensive purchases. The consumer goods company said that sales of stock cubes were growing very rapidly as more people 'cooked from scratch' instead of buying prepared meals.

Increasing competition and the search for cost advantages drive globalisation. Ford (**www.ford.com**) has invested in a plant to make small cars in India, where demand is growing rapidly as people become more prosperous. The same economic trend encouraged Tata (**www.tata.com**), the Indian conglomerate, to launch a low cost car, the Nano: Renault/Nissan (**www.renault.com**) expect to sell more cars in emerging markets than in developed ones by 2015.

The state of the economy is a major influence on consumer spending, which affects firms meeting those needs. Managers planning capital investments follow economic forecasts: if these suggest slower growth, they may postpone the project.

Socio-cultural factors

Demographic change affects most organisations, apart from those most clearly affected by the ageing population – healthcare and pharmaceuticals businesses. A growing number of single people affects the design of housing, holidays and life assurance. Demographic change affects an organisation's publicity to ensure, for example, that advertising acknowledges racial diversity. Leading banks develop investment and saving schemes that comply with *sharia* law, to attract devout Muslim investors. Rising expenditure on live music encouraged HMV Group (**www.hmv.com**) to buy companies already working in this market (Chapter 8 case study).

> ### Management in practice   Changing tastes challenge pubs
>
> Across Europe people are drinking more alcohol at home and less in pubs. The trend is particularly marked in Britain, where about 40 pubs close each week. They are gradually being usurped as the biggest sellers of beer in the UK, with supermarkets supplying most ale and lager. Many pub managers have adapted to this change by selling more food, some pubs have become gastro-pubs – offering high quality food in the simple 'public house' environment. A manager at a company with several gastro-pubs said:
>
> > **Our pubs are doing really well and we want to raise our exposure to this market. The new pubs are in good areas such as west London where people are going to eat out two or three times a week, and want a relaxed place where they can meet their friends without [having to spend too much].**
>
> Source: *Financial Times*, 26 August 2008, and other sources.

Consumer tastes and preferences change. Commenting on a decision to increase the number of healthier products, the chief executive of Nestlé said:

> I think this shows you where the future direction of the company is. This emphasis on [healthier products] is a strategic decision, reflecting changing economic and demographic conditions.

Technological factors

Companies pay close attention to the physical infrastructure – such as the adequacy of power supplies and transport systems. Even more, they monitor advances in information technology, which are dramatically changing the business environment of many companies. Advances in technology do not only affect data systems. Computers traditionally handled data, while other systems handled voice (telephones) and pictures (film and video). These components of the information revolution are familiar as separate devices, but their use of common digital technology greatly increases their ability to exchange information. Digitisation – presenting images and sounds in digital form – has profound implications for many industries as Table 3.2 illustrates.

Table 3.2 Examples of digital technologies affecting established businesses

Technology	Application	Businesses affected
Digital Versatile Discs (DVDs)	Store sound and visual images	Sales of stereophonic sound systems decline sharply
IPOD, MP3 and smartphones	Digital downloads of talking books	New markets created for talking books, with titles to suit new audience
Broadband services delivering online content	Enables advertisers to use online media rather than print or television	Media companies respond by building an online presence (NewsCorp acquired MySpace)
Voice over Internet Protocol (VoIP)	Enables telephone calls over the internet at very low cost	Threat to revenues of traditional phone companies
Digital photography	Enables people to store pictures electronically and order prints online	Photographic retailers such as Jessops lose significant part of business

Nokia is facing major challenges as the mobile phone and computing industries come together, allowing a company like Apple (originally a computer business) to offer the iPhone range of smartphones. Bernoff and Li (2008) show how social networking (Facebook) and user-generated content sites (YouTube) change the technological context – to which established media companies need to work out a profitable response.

Political pressure is also mounting on Europe's leading telecoms companies to increase their spending on high-speed broadband networks. The European commissioner responsible for the EU's digital agenda has told them that their inadequate investment plans meant that targets to increase broadband speeds across Europe are unlikely to be met (*Financial Times*, 27 April 2011).

Environmental factors

The natural resources available in an economy – including minerals, agricultural land and the prevailing climate – affect the kind of businesses that managers create: the mills at New Lanark (Chapter 2 case study) were built beside a source of water power.

Many senior managers know that climate change will have major implications for their organisations, and are working out how best to respond. It will put most businesses at risk, with the probability of more droughts, floods, storms and heat waves – less rainfall in some places, more in others. For some it represents a threat – insurance companies, house builders and water companies are only the most visible examples of companies that are being affected. For others sustainability brings opportunities – alternative energy suppliers, emission control businesses and waste management companies are all seeing more interest in their products and services.

Legal factors

Governments create the legal framework within which companies operate, most obviously in areas like health and safety, employment, consumer protection and pollution control. They also create the legal basis for business – such as when the UK parliament passed the Joint Stock Companies Act in 1862. People had been reluctant to invest in new companies as they were personally liable for the whole of a company's debts if it failed. The Act of 1862 limited their liability to the value of their shares – they could lose their investment, but not the rest of their wealth. This stimulated company formation and other countries soon passed similar legislation, paving the way for the countless 'limited liability' companies that exist today.

The PESTEL analysis is just as relevant to public and voluntary sector organisations. Many public service organisations are in business to do things that the market does not, so a PESTEL analysis can identify emerging issues that need attention. An example is the age structure of the population: a country with growing numbers of elderly people has to finance changes in community care services, social services and hospitals. Public sector organisations are often unable to expand their operations where new problems or needs are identified, but the results can be used to lobby for increased funding or to target their existing budgets.

The PESTEL framework is a useful starting point for analysis if managers use it to identify factors that are relevant to their business, and how these are changing.

3.6   Stakeholders

All managers need to deal with stakeholders – individuals, groups or other organisations with an interest in, or who are affected by, what the enterprise does. Organisations depend on their micro and macro environments (Figure 3.1) for the resources they need. Stakeholders in these environments make resources available or withhold them, depending on their view of the organisation. Managers in any sector need to pay attention to stakeholder expectations, and meet these to an acceptable degree to ensure a positive view.

Stakeholders may be internal (employees, managers, different departments or professional groups, owners, shareholders) or external (customers, competitors, bankers, local communities, members of the public, pressure groups and government). The challenge is that:

> Different stakeholders do not generally share the same definition of an organization's 'problems', and hence, they do not in general share the same 'solutions'. As a result, the typical approaches to organizational problem solving, which generally presuppose prior consensus or agreement among parties, cannot be used; they break down. Instead a method is needed that builds off a starting point of disagreement . . . (Mitroff, 1983, p. 5)

Stakeholders have expectations of organisations and managers choose whether or not to take account of these. Nutt (2002) shows the dangers of ignoring them: he studied 400 strategic decisions, and found that half of them 'failed' – in the sense that they were not implemented or produced poor results – largely because managers failed to attend to stakeholders.

Faced with evidence of excessive risk-taking in banks, shareholders have begun to become more active in criticising directors over the pay and bonus systems through which they reward senior managers in their companies. This has led to changes in corporate governance arrangements.

3.7   Corporate governance

Why have governance systems?

Scandals and failures in prominent public and private organisations lead people to question the adequacy of their systems of **corporate governance**. They show that senior managers cannot always be trusted to act in the best interests of the citizens or shareholders. To reduce this risk, people develop 'governance systems' – rules and processes to control those managing public and private organisations. They aim to make them accountable to others for what they do, in the hope that this will achieve a closer balance between the interests involved.

Corporate governance refers to the rules and processes intended to control those responsible for managing an organisation.

In capitalist economies, ownership typically becomes separated from control. The founder provides the initial capital but growth requires further finance – which investors provide in exchange for an income. They cannot supervise management decisions, but need to be confident that the business is secure before they provide further funds.

Berle and Means (1932) highlighted the dilemma facing owners who become separated from the managers they appoint to run the business:

> The corporation is a means by which the wealth of innumerable individuals has been concentrated into huge aggregates and whereby control over this wealth has been surrendered to a unified direction . . . The direction of industry other than by persons who have ventured their wealth has raised the question . . . of the distribution of the returns from business enterprise. (p. 4)

Their observations led others to develop what is now termed 'agency theory', which seeks to explain what happens when one party (the principal) delegates work to another party (the agent). In this case, the shareholders (principals) have financed, and own, the business, but delegate the work of running it to managers (agents). The principal faces the risk that managers may not act in their (the principal's) best interests: they may take excessive investment risks, or withhold information so that the state of the business appears better than it is. The agent can use this to personal advantage. Failures at major financial institutions, caused in part by staff lending money to risky borrowers in the hope of high bonuses, show that the separation of ownership from management, of principal from agent, is as relevant as ever.

Similar issues arise in the public sector, where elected members are nominally in charge of local authorities, health boards and other agencies – and who appoint professional managers to run the organisation on behalf of the citizens. Elected members face the risk that the people they have appointed act in their narrow professional or personal interests, rather than of those of the electorate. Hartley (2008) writes:

> a new awareness of the social, economic and cultural contribution of government, public organizations and public services has resulted in a significant period of reform and experimentation. At the heart of these initiatives is the idea that improvements to the way public services can be governed, managed and delivered will produce improved outcomes for citizens. (p. 3)

Stakeholder theory is also relevant, as it tries to explain the evolving relationship between an organisation and its stakeholders. Many believe that governance systems should take account of the interests of this wider group, as well as those of shareholders with only a financial interest.

The substance of corporate governance

Mallin (2007) suggests that governance systems should have:

- an adequate system of internal controls which safeguards assets;
- mechanisms to prevent any one person having too much influence;
- processes to manage relationships between managers, directors, shareholders and other stakeholders (such as the practice of separating the jobs of chairman and chief executive, to avoid a concentration of power in any one person);
- the aim of managing the company in the interests of shareholders and other stakeholders; and
- the aim of encouraging transparency and accountability, which investors and many external stakeholders expect.

Proposals to deal with these issues affect the context in which managers work, and the book will examine the topic as an integrating theme at the end of each chapter.

Activity 3.2   What are 'organisational cultures and contexts'?

Recall the organisation you used in Activity 3.1.

Having read the chapter, make brief notes summarising the main cultural and external factors affecting the company.

- What type of culture do you think is dominant within the company, and how does this affect the way it works? (Refer to Section 3.2 and 3.3.)
- What are the main competitive factors affecting it? (Refer to Section 3.4.)
- What are the main factors in the general environment affecting it? (Refer to Section 3.5.)
- What, if any, governance issues has it had to deal with? (Refer to Section 3.7.)

Compare what you have found with other students on your course.

Summary

1 **Identify the main elements of the environments in which organisations work**
   - They include the immediate competitive environment, the wider general (or macro) environment and the organisation's stakeholders.

2 **Compare the cultures of two organisational units, using Quinn's or Handy's typologies**
   - Quinn *et al*. (2003) – rational goal, internal process, human relations and open systems.
   - Handy (1993) – power, role, task and person.

3 **Use Porter's five forces model to analyse the competitive environment of an organisation**
   - This identifies the degree of competitive rivalry, customers, competitors, suppliers and potential substitute goods and services.

4 **Use the PESTEL framework to analyse the wider environment of an organisation**
   - The PESTEL model of the wider external environment identifies political, economic, social, technological, environmental and legal forces.

5 **Explain the meaning and purpose of corporate governance**
   - Corporate governance frameworks are intended to monitor and control the performance of managers to ensure they act in the interests of organisational stakeholders, and not just of the managers themselves.

Review questions

1 Describe an educational or commercial organisation that you know in terms of the competing values model of cultures.

2 What is the significance of the idea of 'fragmented cultures' for those who wish to change a culture to support performance?

3 Identify the relative influence of Porter's five forces on an organisation of your choice and compare your results with a colleague's. What can you learn from that comparison?

4 How should managers decide which of the many factors easily identified in a PESTEL analysis they should attend to? If they have to be selective, what is the value of the PESTEL method?

5 Since people interpret the nature of environmental forces from unique perspectives, what meaning can people attach to statements about external pressures?

6 Illustrate the stakeholder idea with an example of your own, showing their expectations of an organisation.

7 Explain at least two of the mechanisms which Mallin (2007) recommends should be part of a corporate governance system.

Further reading

Tapscott, E. and Williams, A. D. (2006), *Wikinomics: How mass collaboration changes every-thing*, Viking Penguin, New York.

   Best-selling account of the radical changes which convergent technologies bring to society, especially the relationship between producers and consumers.

Hawken, P., Lovins, A. B. and Lovins. L. H. (1999), *Natural Capitalism: The next industrial revolution*, Earthscan, London.

Generally positive account of the environmental challenges facing us all, and what organisations are doing about it.

Weblinks

These websites have appeared in, or are relevant to, the chapter:

    www.acea.be.
    www.bosch.com
    www.walmart.com
    www.gsk.com
    www.unilever.com
    www.ford.com
    www.tata.com
    www.Renault.com
    www.hmv.com
    www.nokia.com

Visit some of these, or any other companies which interest you, and navigate to the pages dealing with recent news, press or investor relations.

- What can you find about their culture?
- What are the main forces in the external environment which the organisation appears to be facing?
- Compare and contrast the issues you identify on the two sites.
- What challenges may they imply for those working in, and managing, these organisations?

 Annotated weblinks, multiple choice questions and other useful resources can be found on **www.pearsoned.co.uk/boddy**

Case study   Nokia   www.nokia.com

Nokia is struggling to survive in the very competitive mobile phone business. In 2008 it had 40 per cent of the world handset market, but at the end of March 2011 that had fallen to 29 per cent. This was still well ahead of Motorola, and many times the number sold by rivals such as Samsung and Ericsson: but its position was being challenged by competitors. Managers were making big changes in the company to meet the expectations of customers and shareholders. In April 2011, it announced that 4000 jobs would be lost by the end of 2012, most of them in Denmark, Finland and the UK: In June it warned that profits for the year would be well below expectations. The value of shares in the company fell to their lowest level since 1998.

The Finnish company was founded in 1895 as a paper manufacturer, and then grew into a conglomerate with wide interests including electronics, cable manufacture, rubber, chemicals, electricity generation and, by the 1960s, telephone equipment. In the early 1990s senior managers decided to focus on the new mobile phone industry.

Two factors favoured this move. First, the Finnish government had taken a lead in telecoms deregulation and Nokia was already competing vigorously with other manufacturers supplying equipment to the national phone company. Second, the European Union (EU) adopted a single standard – the Global System for Mobile Telephony (GSM) – for Europe's second generation (digital) phones. Two-thirds of the world's mobile phone subscribers use this standard. Finland's links with its Nordic neighbours also helped, as people in these sparsely populated countries adopted mobile phones enthusiastically.

Nokia had strong design skills, but above all, managers were quick to recognise that mobile phones were now a fashion accessory. By offering smart designs, different ring tones and coloured covers, Nokia became the 'cool' mobile brand for fashion-conscious people. Nokia had also mastered the logistics of getting millions of phones to customers around the world.

While many competitors subcontract the manufacture of handsets, Nokia assembles most of its own, with factories in many countries across the world. Managers believe this gives them a better understanding of the market and the manufacturing process. Nokia buys about 80 billion components a

Courtesy of Nokia.

year, and has close relationships with its most important suppliers.

In March 2011 it reported sales of 108.5 million units in the previous quarter. It is continuing to add value to its devices by integrating them with innovative services providing music, maps, apps and email. It also believes that its wide range of handsets means it will be able to meet demand if customers begin to prefer cheaper handsets.

One factor in the company's sustained success was believed to have been a culture which encourages co-operation within teams, and across internal and external boundaries. Jorma Ollila, CEO until 2006, believed that Nokia's innovative capacity springs from multi-functional teams working together to bring new insights to products and services. Staff in the four divisions work in teams which may remain constant for many years – but sometimes combine with other teams to work on a common task.

Informal mentoring begins as soon as someone steps into a new job. Within a few days, the employee's manager lists the people in the organisation whom it would be useful for the employee to meet. They also review what topics the newcomer should discuss with the suggested contact, and why establishing a relationship with them is important. The gift of time – in the form of hours spent on coaching and building networks – is a crucial part of the collaborative culture.

Nokia also encourages a culture of communication by creating small groups to work on a strategic issue for four months. This helps them to build ties

▶

with many parts of the company – some of which continue during later work. The induction process for new employees also encourages team-building and co-operation: the newcomer's manager must introduce them to at least 15 people within and outside the team.

It is struggling to compete at the top end of the market, where smartphones offer a range of multimedia services: these probably represent about 20 per cent of handset sales, and sell for much higher prices than basic models. The convergence of the technologies underlying the mobile and computing industries has enabled companies like Apple (originally a computer business) to launch the iPhone, which has gained a strong position in the smartphone market. Other companies have adopted Google's Android software to develop a further range of devices to compete with Nokia.

As profits declined, shareholders began to demand that Nokia's board act to improve its performance – especially when the company's market share declined from 36.4 per cent at the end of 2009 to 28.6 per cent in the last quarter of 2010. One consequence was to dismiss the then Chief Executive, and replace him with Steve Elop, who had worked for Microsoft.

In early 2011 the company announced it would collaborate with Microsoft to develop a new range of devices and software – which included using the Microsoft Windows Phone 7 operating system for next generation of smartphones. Microsoft has been keen to build presence in smartphones, but its own brands have not established a strong presence. It hoped that an alliance with Nokia would help it improve its position.

Sources: Grattan and Erickson (2007); Doz and Kosonen (2008); *Financial Times*, 17 July 2009, 22 January 2010, 8 April 2011, 28 April 2011, 1 June 2011; company website.

Questions

1 Which of the cultural types identified by Quinn *et al.* (2003) would you expect to find within Nokia's handset business? (Refer to Section 3.3.)

2 Use Porter's five forces model to outline Nokia's competitive (micro) environment. (Refer to Section 3.4.)

3 Which PESTEL factors are most affecting the macro environment of the industry? Are they likely to be positive or negative for Nokia? (Refer to Section 3.5.)

4 Who are the main stakeholders in Nokia, and what are their interests in the success of the company? (Refer to Section 3.6.)

5 Visit Nokia's website, and read their most recent trading statement (under investor relations). What have been the main developments in the last year?

CHAPTER 4
MANAGING INTERNATIONALLY

Learning outcomes

When you have read this chapter you should be able to:

1 List the ways in which organisations conduct international business

2 Show how PESTEL factors affect the decisions of those managing internationally

3 Give an example of an EU policy affecting an organisation

4 Explain and illustrate the evidence on differences in national cultures

5 Describe some differences in national management systems

6 Summarise the forces stimulating the growth of international business

7 Use ideas from the chapter to comment on the management issues in the Starbucks case study

Activity 4.1   What does 'managing internationally' mean?

Before reading the chapter, write some notes on what you think people who are 'managing internationally' are likely to be dealing with in their work.

Choose the organisation or people you hope may be able to help you learn about the topic. You may find it helpful to discuss the topic with a manager you know, or reflect on an activity you have managed.

- Make brief notes on the international aspects of the organisation.
- How do they conduct their international trade?
- What external factors are having most effect on the way they work?

Keep these notes as you will be able to use them later.

4.1   Introduction

Managers at Starbucks decided that as well as expanding in the home (North American) market, they would also expand overseas, as they believed this offered the best route to profitable growth. Some of their overseas ventures have done well and so added value for shareholders, while others have failed, and so destroyed value. 'Going international' brings new and unfamiliar problems – how to create a strategy for a global business, and how to implement it.

Others face the same issues. Retailers like Tesco and IKEA (Chapter 7 case study) are extending their international operations, despite the problems of understanding different customer tastes, and of obtaining government permission to open stores in some countries. Managers in companies like Marlborough and H&M with large overseas sales balance the consistency of the global brand with what local customers expect.

Manufacturers like BMW and service providers like Lloyds TSB have transferred some activities to low-wage countries. That raises new management problems when managing operations in unfamiliar countries: When Kraft, the US food group, bought Cadbury's in 2010 it acquired a brand with strong historical associations: these are part of the context as it re-structures the operation to reduce costs. Managers investing overseas consider not only the economic or market aspects, but also whether the legal system will protect their investments and whether the country is politically stable.

There has been international trade since the earliest times: what is new is the high proportion of production that crosses national boundaries, much of it through businesses operating on a regional or global scale. One-third of all trade takes place within transnational companies, quite apart from external sales of foreign subsidiaries. Rapid economic development in China, India and other Asian countries has transformed them into major players in world trade. High-value/low-weight products are traded across the world, increasing growth – and providing opportunities for the shipping business – see Management in Practice.

Management in practice   Maersk and global trade   www.maersk.com

Maersk is the world's largest container shipping line, and it's growth has reflected that of world trade. Doug Bannister, Managing Director of Maersk Line (UK and Ireland) explained:

> We're involved in the transportation sector, about 90 per cent of world trade is done by sea-borne transportation, it is an incredible industry to be associated with: our primary mission is to create opportunities in global commerce.

The scale of containerised shipping is enormous. Container shipping has been around for 40 years, and it has had incredible growth, 8 to 10 per cent a year. The types of stuff we bring in are anything from lamps to furniture to bananas, about 90 per cent of anything that you'd see in any room was transported in by one of our ships.

Several external factors have really played into Maersk Line's growth, globalisation probably being the primary one, and the explosion of world trade has been incredible. This is down to efficient transport solutions, as well as offshoring of production to low cost areas such as China.

Source: Interview with Doug Bannister.

International management is the practice of managing business operations in more than one country.

From a career point of view, **international management** (managing business operations in more than one country) can mean:

- working as an *expatriate manager* in another country
- joining or managing an *international team* with members from several countries
- managing in a *global organisation* whose employees, systems and structures are truly international in that they no longer reflect its original, national base.

This chapter begins by showing how companies conduct business internationally, and then introduces ideas on the context of international business, with separate sections on trade agreements and culture. It shows the differences between national management systems and examines why international trade develops. Figure 4.1 shows a plan of the chapter.

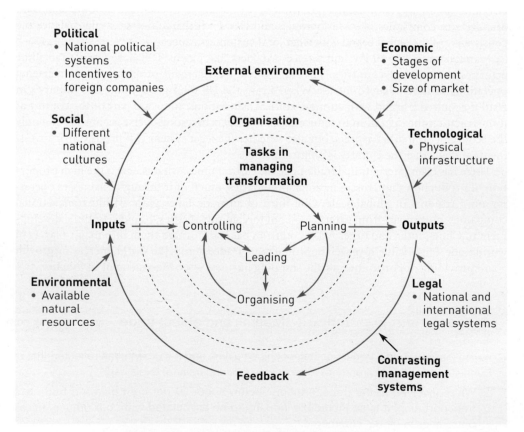

Figure 4.1
Themes in managing internationally

4.2   Ways to conduct business internationally

Companies use one or more of these methods to conduct international business.

Offshoring

Offshoring (sometimes called 'outsourcing') happens when managers decide to transfer some activities to countries which will do them more cost-efficiently. This began when companies in developed Western economies transferred routine manufacturing activities to low-wage developing countries. The practice is now more diverse, with the internet enabling companies to transfer routine administrative activities (such as payroll and accounting) to overseas centres. Companies in India now outsource some work to emerging economies where staff are cheaper or more plentiful.

Exporting and importing

The longest established way of dealing with overseas customers and suppliers is by transporting physical products (raw materials or finished goods) or delivering services (insurance, consultancy or legal advice) across national boundaries. If the final distribution of exports is arranged through a dealer or agent in the receiving country, the implications for people in the exporting company are limited, apart from those directly involved in managing the transactions.

Licensing

Licensing occurs when a business grants the right to (licenses) a firm in another country (the licensee) to produce and sell its products for a specified period – such as the deal between Imperial Tobacco and a Chinese group to produce and distribute Imperial brands in the world's largest cigarette market. The licensing firm receives a payment for each unit sold (usually called a royalty payment), while the licensee takes the risk of investing in manufacturing and distribution facilities. **Franchising** is similar, commonly used by service businesses (like Starbucks) that wish to expand rapidly beyond their home market. The expanding firm sells the right (the franchise) to a company allowing it (the franchisee) to use the brand name and product design to build a business in the target market. The seller usually imposes tight conditions on matters such as quality and working procedures: many fast-food outlets are run by franchisees. Mothercare (**www.mothercareplc.com**) – the mother-and-baby products retailer – used this method to expand overseas (*Financial Times*, 3 July 2008).

> **Licensing** is when one firm gives another firm the right to use assets such as patents or technology in exchange for a fee.
>
> **Franchising** is the practice of extending a business by giving other organisations, in return for a fee, the right to use your brand name, technology or product specifications.

Joint ventures

Joint ventures enable firms in two or more countries to share the risks and resources required to do business internationally. Most joint ventures involve a foreign firm linking with one in the host country to take advantage of its distribution arrangements and knowledge of local customs, politics and ways of working. Both firms agree their respective investment in the venture and how they will share the profits. Starbucks typically uses joint ventures in overseas markets: in Germany this is with KarstadtQuelle, a department store group. Royal Dutch Shell has a joint venture with Shenhua Group, China's largest coal company, to study the possibility of creating a coal-to-liquids facility in western China. The hazards of joint ventures include cultural differences between the partners and misunderstandings about what each expects.

> A **joint venture** is an alliance in which the partners agree to form a separate, independent organisation for a specific business purpose.

Wholly owned subsidiary (or foreign direct investment)

Managers who want to retain close control over their company's international activities can create a subsidiary in another country. Motor companies do this – Nissan manufactures at several sites in the UK, while General Motors built a plant in India to make the Chevrolet

Foreign direct investment (FDI) is the practice of investing shareholder funds directly in another country, by building or buying physical facilities, or by buying a company.

Spark. Such **foreign direct investment (FDI)** to build or acquire facilities in a foreign country, and manage them directly, is costly. The advantages are that all profits stay within the company, which also retains control over its expertise, technology and marketing: it secures local knowledge by employing local staff. The company may establish the subsidiary as a new entity or, if time is scarce, it can acquire an existing company, as when the Indian company Tata bought Jaguar and Land Rover in 2010.

Which route to take (if any) is a significant management decision, as many international ventures fail: their managers have destroyed value – such as Gregg's (the bakery chain) decision to withdraw from the Belgian market after five years of trying to build a significant business there. Johnson and Tellis (2008) studied the success or failure of firms entering India and China. They concluded that firms which retained a high degree of control (by using wholly owned subsidiaries) were more successful than those who did not. Early entrants were more successful than latecomers, and smaller companies were more successful than large.

Companies also develop different forms of organisation for their international business – multinational, transnational and global.

Multinational companies are managed from one country, but have significant production and marketing operations in many others.

Multinational companies are based in one country, but have significant production and marketing operations in many others – perhaps accounting for more than one-third of sales. Managers in the home country make the major decisions.

Transnational companies operate in many countries and delegate many decisions to local managers.

Transnational companies also operate in many countries, but decentralise many decisions to local managers. They use local knowledge to build the business, while still projecting a consistent company image. IBM (the US-based software supplier) no longer performs all functions at HQ – finance is based in Brazil, purchasing in China and service delivery in India.

Global companies work in many countries, securing resources and finding markets in whichever country is most suitable.

Global companies work in many countries, securing resources and finding markets in whichever are most suitable. Production or service processes are performed, and integrated, across many global locations – as are ownership, control and top management. Trend Micro, an anti-virus software company, needed to organise so that staff could respond rapidly to new viruses that appear anywhere and spread very quickly. Trend's financial headquarters is in Tokyo; product development is in Taiwan (a good source of staff with a PhD); and the sales department is in California – inside the huge US market. Nestlé is another example: although headquarters are in Switzerland, 98 per cent of sales and 96 per cent of employees are not. Such businesses are often organised by product, with those in charge of each unit securing resources from whichever country gives best value.

Management in practice   An Indian supplier to Walmart   www.walmart.com

Deep in the Punjab heartland, in the town of Barnala, Rajinder Gupta is a star supplier to the world's biggest company – Walmart. Gupta's Abhishek Industries exports textiles, and has twice been judged the Walmart International Supplier of the year. He says:

> We've grown with Walmart since we first began supplying to them five years ago. Now we've created a dedicated capacity for them, with systems geared to their needs.

From tanneries in Kanpur and rug weavers in Mumbai to shirt manufacturers in Tirupur, Walmart has zeroed in on 142 low-cost quality manufacturing units across India, which will supply to its stores in the US and twelve other countries … It recently set up Walmart Global Procurement Company in Bangalore where a staff of 54 are working towards further expanding business with India. A company official said:

> Indian suppliers are capable, qualified and quality-focused and we intend to grow India as a source of supply, especially in categories like textiles, shoes, jewellery and gift items.

Source: Based on 'Walmart Effect', *Times of India Corporate Dossier*, 28 May 2004.

| 4.3 | **The contexts of international business – PESTEL** |

People managing international operations pay close attention to the international aspects of the general business environment outlined in Chapter 3: the PESTEL framework becomes international. Section 4.3 outlines four of these (beginning, for clarity, with the economic context), and Sections 4.4 and 4.5 present the legal and cultural contexts.

Economic context

One area of economic theory is that which aims to understand why nations trade with each other, rather than being self-sufficient. It uses the idea of the specialisation of effort, from which comes the **theory of absolute advantage**. This states that by specialising in the production of those goods which they can produce more cheaply than other countries, and trading them with others, nations will increase their economic well-being. If countries use the resources in which they have an advantage (such as fertile land, rich raw materials or efficient methods) to produce goods and services, and then exchange them with countries for things in which *they* are most efficient, they will collectively add more value than if everyone was self-sufficient. While being self-sufficient sounds attractive, it is more costly than buying things which someone else can produce more cheaply. The theory is, of course, a great deal more complex than that, but even this simple account begins to explain why nations trade with each other, even though each *could* make the traded goods themselves.

> The **theory of absolute advantage** is a trade theory which proposes that by specialising in the production of goods and services which they can produce more efficiently than others, nations will increase their economic well-being.

Evidence supporting theory comes from the rapid internationalisation of production since the 1960s. At that time, many firms in the developed world realised that labour intensive manufacturing and service operations in their home country was a costly way of working. This was especially the case in electrical and electronic goods, clothing, footwear and toys, which faced growing competition from cheaper imports. Managers looked for new sources of supply, and received a positive response from a small group of Asian countries – Taiwan, Hong Kong, South Korea and especially Singapore. These took the opportunity over the next 30 years to become major 'outsourcing' centres, supplying goods and components to companies around the world. They also developed their education systems so that they now do work of higher value, widening their product range – including a growing trade in services such as software development and the back-office functions of airlines and banks. Table 4.1 gives examples.

Companies sometimes find that operations in remote locations require more management time than they expected, so reducing the cost advantage. Some also find that customers object

Table 4.1 Examples of the internationalisation of production

Company	Work transferred	Reasons given
BT www.bt.com	Opened call centres in India, replacing the jobs of 2000 staff in the UK	'To meet cost-saving targets and remain competitive'
Gillette www.gillette.com	Closed three factories (two UK and one German) and transferred work to new factory in eastern Europe	'Significantly reduce costs and improve operating efficiency'
Dyson www.dyson.co.uk	Moved production of vacuum cleaners and washing machines from UK to Malaysia	'Reduce manufacturing costs help protect UK jobs in design and development'

to talking to a call centre operator in a distant country who may lack the local knowledge to conduct a transaction smoothly. They are then likely to 'repatriate' the outsourced activities.

The internationalisation of markets happens when companies from the wealthier countries see market opportunities in less developed ones. The most common measure of economic development is income per head of population – a measure of a country's total production, adjusted for size of population. As incomes in relatively poor countries rise, foreign companies see them as attractive markets – many see parts of Africa as offering valuable new markets (*Financial Times*, 30 November 2010). Car companies expect emerging economies to buy more than half their output by 2015, as people in these countries become richer and seek greater personal mobility. Consumer products companies (such as British American Tobacco or Phillip Morris) see good prospects in developing countries such as Malaysia and South Africa, whose high birth rates ensure more young consumers. Hong Kong Disneyland reflects the company's belief that Asia's media and entertainment market will grow rapidly. The Chinese government agreed, taking a 57 per cent stake in the project. Disney hopes this will help it win good terms for other ventures there – TV, films, advertising and consumer products.

Political context

Whatever economic theory may predict about the patterns of trade, political factors also influence managers' decisions. These include the nature of a country's political institutions, government involvement in the economy and laws on corruption. Such factors shape the **political risk** a company faces in a country – the risk of losing assets, earning power or managerial control due to political events or the actions of host governments. During the 1990s east European countries offered large incentives to attract Western companies to build power plants in their territories: now they are members of the EU these incentives may be judged as illegal state aid, so the investing companies risk losing money. BP has built a major presence in Russia through it joint venture TNK-BP, giving the company strategically valuable access to huge oil and gas reserves. It also becomes exposed to political risks, as powerful Russian politicians are involved in the oil industry: in 2011 many believed these internal political conflicts were affecting attitudes to the joint venture. Companies planning investments overseas, especially in emerging economies, spend time and money assessing factors like the stability of the regime, the rule of law, the extent of corruption and the risk of terrorism.

The political system in a country influences business, and managers adapt to the prevailing **ideology**. Political ideologies are closely linked to economic philosophies and attitudes towards business. In the United States the political ideology is grounded in a constitution which guarantees the rights of people to own property and to have wide freedom of choice. This laid the foundations of a capitalist economy favourable to business. While countries such as Australia or the UK are equally capitalist in outlook, others such as Brazil or France have political ideologies which give more emphasis to social considerations.

There are close links between political and economic systems – especially in how they allocate resources and deal with property ownership. Governments of all forms set the rules that establish what commercial activity takes place within their jurisdiction, and how it can be conducted – whether in a fundamentally capitalist way, in a centrally controlled way, or a mix of the two. Differences in political systems affect business life through:

- the balance between state-owned and privately owned enterprises;
- the amount of state intervention in business through subsidies, taxes and regulation;
- policies towards foreign companies trading in the country, with or without local partners (India is reluctant to allow foreign retailers like IKEA to enter the country);
- policies towards foreign companies acquiring local firms;
- policies on employment practices, working conditions and job protection (in 2010 the French government ordered Renault to make the new Clio in France, rather than move production to Turkey).

Political risk is the risk of losing assets, earning power or managerial control due to political events or the actions of host governments.

An **ideology** is a set of integrated beliefs, theories and doctrines that helps to direct the actions of a society.

All states are affected to some degree by corruption – when politicians or officials abuse public power for private benefit. Coping with this is part of the job of managers operating internationally.

Technological context

Infrastructure includes the physical facilities that support economic activities – ports, airports, surface transport and, increasingly, telecommunications facilities. Companies operating abroad, especially in less-developed countries, are closely interested in the quality of this aspect of a country as it has a huge effect on the cost and convenience of conducting business in the area. A poor infrastructure is an opportunity for suppliers. European water companies have contracts to apply their expertise to providing water and sanitation services to many developing countries.

Developments in information technology stimulate international trade in two ways. The electronics industry requires billions of high-value, low-weight components, which they produce in globally dispersed factories and transport them to assembly plants – and in turn send finished products to consumers around the world. These movements have been a major driver of the growth of world trade. In addition, companies of all kinds use the internet to help them control international operations. The efficiency this brings encourages them to continue extending these.

Environmental context

The natural environment is a further aspect of the business context, especially the natural resources available in an economy – oil, coal and other minerals, agricultural land and the prevailing climate. A distinction in considering natural resources is between those that are renewable and those that are not: land can be used for several purposes in succession, timber is renewable – but oil is not. Water supplies are increasingly scarce, and a major concern to international food production companies.

These considerations affect the kind of businesses people create in a country, and the pattern of world trade. Technological developments enable the discovery of resources (new oil reserves in central Asia) and fuller use of some that were previously uneconomic. This benefits the countries concerned, and the companies who agree to exploit the resources.

The process is also controversial, as when foreign mining or oil companies come into conflict with local populations whose land they occupy, or over the commercial terms of the concessions.

Management in practice   Insurgency that may threaten business growth   FT

Just as India is emerging as an economic powerhouse on the world stage, landless revolutionaries committed to the class struggle and the destruction of the state are gaining control of large areas of the country. Maoist groups are estimated by the government to be running parallel administrations, including legal systems, in one-quarter of India's 600 districts, and are imposing high costs on the country's ability to attract investment in mineral-rich states such as Orissa and Jharkand. Manmohan Singh, India's Prime Minister, identifies the Maoists, motivated by resentment at generations of social injustice and the inequitable distribution of the country's new wealth, as the single greatest threat to India's security.

Source: After Insurgency in India – how the Maoist threat reaches beyond Nepal (Jo Johnson), *Financial Times*, 26 April 2006, p. 13.

Some object to the environmental degradation associated with timber or mineral exploitation, whose effects spread widely (such as when rivers are polluted in one country before flowing to another). Economic development itself causes pollution – a problem for people in the area, and an opportunity for foreign businesses that specialise in environmental remediation.

4.4   Legal context – trade agreements and trading blocs

Managers planning to enter an overseas market need to ensure they are familiar with local laws and regulations affecting business practice: they also seek to satisfy themselves that the legal system there will protect them in the event of disputes with customers or suppliers. Beyond conditions in an individual country, international managers are closely interested in trade agreements and regional economic alliances.

GATT and the World Trade Organization

The General Agreement on Tariffs and Trade (GATT) reduces the propensity of national governments to put tariffs on physical goods to protect domestic companies. Its main tool is tariff concessions, whereby member countries agree to limit the level of tariffs they impose on imports. GATT has also sponsored a series of international trade negotiations aimed at reducing restrictions on trade – one of which established the World Trade Organization (WTO). This is a permanent global institution which monitors international trade, and arbitrates in disputes between countries over the interpretation of tariffs and other barriers to trade. It is also seeking a world agreement on rules governing foreign investment – both to encourage it and, where thought necessary, to control it.

European Union

Since the leaders of the original member states signed the Treaty of Rome in 1959 the aim of the EU has been to eliminate tariffs and other restrictions that national governments use to protect domestic industries. This was broadly achieved by 1968, and led to further work to integrate the economies of the member states. This culminated in the Single European Act of 1986 that aimed to create a single internal market within the EU. Introducing the euro as a common currency for many of the members encouraged further changes in the European economy by unifying capital markets and making price comparisons more transparent. In 2010 the EU was the world's biggest economy, and the world's largest trading bloc.

The European Commission (responsible for proposing and implementing policy) is encouraging this liberalisation by proposing changes in national laws to make cross-border trade easier. One project will make it easier for investment businesses to sell investment products across Europe – most at present operate only in their home country. This and similar deals have encouraged a rapid growth in trade within the region. Car companies such as BMW and DaimlerChrysler have plants in several countries, specialising in particular components or models. They simultaneously import and export these between the countries as part of a region-wide production system.

Enlargement has long been a feature of the EU agenda, alongside efforts to deepen the integration of member states, enabling free movement of goods and services. The intention is to benefit consumers by increasing competition and efficiency within the EU. Areas covered include:

- harmonising technical regulations between member states;
- common industrial policy (such as subsidies for local businesses and/or foreign investment);
- liberalising services (such as postal services) across the Union;
- harmonising rules on employment and environmental protection;
- facilitating cross-border mergers; and
- recognising professional qualifications (e.g. in medicine and dentistry) between member states to enable freer movement of labour.

The EU is also developing common policies on monetary and political matters, in the hope that it will be able to speak with a single voice on matters as diverse as interest rates, foreign affairs and security. The Lisbon Treaty (2009) aims to enable the enlarged EU to work more effectively. It creates a full-time President of the European Council, appointed by national governments for a period of two and a half years, replacing the system of six-monthly presidencies. It also creates a 'High Representative of the Union for Foreign Affairs and Security Policy' who will conduct the EU's Common Foreign and Security Policy. It also extends Qualified Majority Voting (QMV) to new policy areas, which supporters hope will streamline decision-making in a number of technical areas (e.g. appointments to the European Central Bank's executive board).

4.5 Hofstede's comparison of national cultures

Geert Hofstede is a Dutch academic who has conducted widely quoted studies of national cultural differences. Hofstede (2001) refines the conclusions of his research, which was based on a survey of the attitudes of 116,000 IBM employees, one of the earliest transnational companies. The research inspired other studies with non-IBM employees in both the countries where IBM operated and in those where they did not. Kirkman *et al.* (2006) reviewed many of these, concluding that 'most of the country differences predicted by Hofstede were supported' (p. 308).

Hofstede (2001) defined culture as a collective programming of people's minds, which influences how they react to events in the workplace. He identified five dimensions of culture and sought to measure how people in different countries vary in their attitudes to them.

Power distance

Power distance (PD) is 'the extent to which the less powerful members of ... organisations within a country expect and accept that power is distributed unevenly' (Hofstede and Hofstede, 2005, p. 46). One of the ways in which countries differ is in how power and authority are distributed and in how people view any inequality in this. In some, people see inequality in boss/subordinate relationships as undesirable while in others they see it as part of the natural order. The questionnaire allowed the researchers to calculate scores for PD, countries with a high PD being those where people accepted inequality. Those with high scores included Malaysia, Mexico, Venezuela, Arab countries, China, France and Brazil. Those with low PD scores included Australia, Germany, Great Britain, Sweden and Norway.

Power distance is the extent to which the less powerful members of organisations within a country expect and accept that power is distributed unevenly.

Uncertainty avoidance

Uncertainty avoidance is 'the extent to which the members of a culture feel threatened by ambiguous or unknown situations' (Hofstede and Hofstede, 2005, p. 167). People in some cultures tolerate ambiguity and uncertainty quite readily – if things are not clear they will improvise or use their initiative. Others are reluctant to move without clear rules or instructions. High scores, indicating low tolerance of uncertainty, were obtained in the Latin American, Latin European and Mediterranean countries, and for Japan and Korea. Low scores were recorded in the Asian countries (except Japan and Korea), and in most of the Anglo and Nordic countries – United States, Great Britain, Sweden and Denmark.

Uncertainty avoidance is the extent to which members of a culture feel threatened by uncertain or unknown situations.

Individualism/collectivism

Hofstede and Hofstede (2005) distinguish between **individualism** and **collectivism**:

> Individualism pertains to societies in which the ties between individuals are loose: everyone is expected to look after himself or herself and his or her immediate family. Collectivism as its opposite pertains to societies in which people, from birth onwards, are integrated into strong, cohesive in-groups which throughout people's lifetime continue to protect them in exchange for unquestioning loyalty. (p. 76)

Individualism pertains to societies in which the ties between individuals are loose.

Collectivism 'describes societies in which people, from birth onwards, are integrated into strong, cohesive in-groups which ... protect them in exchange for unquestioning loyalty.' (Hofstede, 1991, p. 51)

Some people live in societies in which the power of the group prevails: there is an emphasis on collective action and mutual responsibility, and on helping each other through difficulties. Other societies emphasise the individual, and their responsibility for their position in life. High scores on the individualism dimension occurred in wealthy countries such as the United States, Australia, Great Britain and Canada. Low scores occurred in poor countries such as the less-developed South American and Asian countries.

Masculinity/femininity

Masculinity pertains to societies in which social gender roles are clearly distinct.

Femininity pertains to societies in which social gender roles overlap.

A society is called **masculine** when emotional gender roles are clearly distinct: men are supposed to be assertive, tough and focused on material success, whereas women are supposed to be more modest, tender and concerned with the quality of life. A society is called **feminine** when emotional gender roles overlap (i.e. both men and women are supposed to be modest, tender and concerned with the quality of life). (Hofstede and Hofstede, 2005, p. 120)

The research showed that societies differ in the desirability of assertive behaviour (which they label masculinity) and of modest behaviour (femininity). Many societies expect men to seek achievements outside the home while women care for things within the home. Masculinity scores were not related to economic wealth: 'we find both rich and poor masculine countries, and rich and poor feminine countries' (p. 120). The most feminine countries were Sweden, Norway, the Netherlands and Denmark. Masculine countries included Japan, Austria, Germany, China and the United States.

Integrating the dimensions

These four dimensions describe the overall culture of a society, and each culture is unique. They also have similarities – for example the UK, Canada and the US all have high individualism, moderately high masculinity, low power distance and low uncertainty avoidance. In these nations managers expect workers to take the initiative and assume responsibility (high individualism), rely on the use of individual (not group) rewards to motivate staff (moderate masculinity), treat their employees as valued people whom they do not treat officiously (low power distance) and keep bureaucracy to a minimum (low uncertainty avoidance). A systematic analysis of Hofstede's data for all the countries in his survey revealed that most of them (the exceptions being Brazil, Japan, India and Israel) fall into a particular cultural cluster. Figure 4.2 illustrates this.

Long-term and short-term orientation

In their 2005 work, Hofstede and Hofstede added this fifth dimension to their account:

Long-term orientation (LTO) stands for the fostering of virtues oriented towards future rewards – in particular perseverance and thrift. Its opposite pole, short-term orientation, stands for the fostering of virtues related to the past and present – in particular respect for tradition, preservation of 'face', and fulfilling social obligations. (Hofstede and Hofstede, 2005, p. 210)

Countries with high LTO scores include China, Hong Kong, Taiwan and Japan. Great Britain, Australia, New Zealand, the United States and Canada have a short-term orientation, in which many people see spending, not thrift, as a virtue.

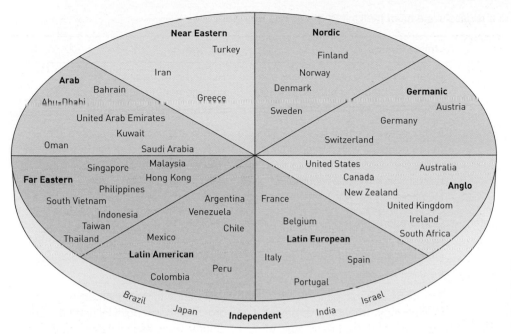

Figure 4.2
A synthesis of
country clusters
Source: Ronen and
Shenkar (1985).

Limitations of Hofstede's work

Other scholars have drawn attention to some limitations of Hofstede's work, including:

- the small (and so possibly unrepresentative) number of respondents in some countries;
- reducing a phenomenon as complex as a nation's culture to five dimensions;
- basing the original sample on the employees of a single multinational;
- the possibility that cultures change over time;
- the variety of cultures within a country (e.g. between religious or ethnic groups); and
- the likelihood of differences of culture within IBM.

Even if the precision of the results is questionable, they are a useful starting point for those working internationally – helping them to reflect on their cultural biases and to deal with different cultural contexts.

4.6 **Contrasting management systems**

Despite the growth of international trade and the growing interdependence of business across the world, countries vary substantially in the way they organise economic activities. There are major differences in the way businesses are organised in different countries – even though all are capitalist economies. As Whitley (1999) explains:

> Different patterns of industrialization developed in contrasting institutional contexts and led to contrasting institutional arrangements governing economic processes becoming established in different market economies... Partly as a result, the structure and practices of state agencies, financial organizations and labour-market actors (in different) countries continue to diverge and to reproduce distinctive forms of economic organization. (p. 5)

Table 4.2 illustrates his ideas in relation to the United States and Europe. There are significant differences between countries within Europe, and in some respects the UK is closer to the United States model than to the rest of Europe.

Table 4.2 Contrasting business systems of the United States and Europe

	United States	Europe
Power of state	Relatively limited, with more scope for discretion by companies to provide employee and social benefits	Relatively strong, with more engagement in economic activity through business regulations
Financial system	Stock market central source of finance for companies, with shareholdings dispersed. Corporations expected to be transparent and accountable to investors	Corporations in network of relations with small number of larger investors. Non-shareholders often play equal role to shareholders
Education and labour system	Corporations have developed policies; relatively local and decentralised labour relations and collective bargaining	Publicly led training and labour market policies, in which corporations participated; national collective bargaining
Cultural systems	Traditions of participation, philanthropy, wary of government, moral value of capitalism; ethic of giving back to society	Preference for representative organisations – political parties, trade unions, trade associations, state

Source: Based on Whitley (1999 and 2009).

He also examines the Japanese model with networks of interdependent relations, and a tradition of mutual ownership between different, but friendly, business units. Companies have close financial and obligational links with each other and the Ministry of Industry actively supports and guides the strategic direction of major areas of business. Firms create a network of mutually dependent organisations and decide strategy by negotiation with their stakeholders – other companies and financial institutions.

At the other extreme, firms in the United States and United Kingdom are more isolated, raising most of their funds from the capital markets. Some observers believe that investors in US and UK companies expect steadily increasing returns from the companies they invest in, which in turn leads those managing the companies to focus on short-term profits at the expense of the long-term health of the business. The collapse of some financial institutions in 2008–09 was in part blamed on executives taking excessive risks to meet capital market expectations.

4.7   Forces driving globalisation

The globalisation of markets?

If you travel to another country, you immediately see many familiar consumer products or services – things that illustrate the idea that global brands are steadily displacing local products. In several industries identical products (Canon cameras, Sony Walkman, Famous Grouse whisky) are sold across the globe without modification – evidence of **globalisation**.

Globalisation refers to the increasing integration of internationally dispersed economic activities.

What has led to this increasingly global business world? Yip (2003) developed a model (Figure 4.3) of the factors that drive globalisation in particular industries – managers (like those at Starbucks) can use such a model to analyse the global potential of a business. Market factors were probably the most significant in Starbuck's case – such as the transferability of brands and advertising, and the ability to develop international distribution channels. In other industries cost factors are more prominent drivers – in motor manufacture or electronics this

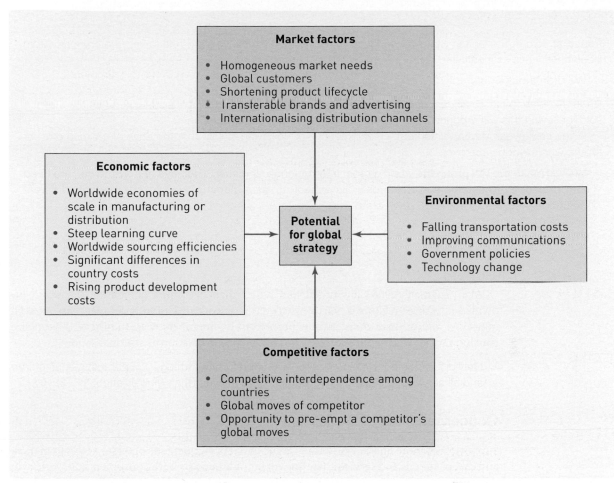

Figure 4.3 Factors driving globalisation in an industry

Source: Based on Yip (2003).

is especially true, with the economies of scale in manufacturing and the ability to buy components around the world. In other cases, government incentives for companies to relocate manufacturing facilities away from their home base have added to globalisation. Developments in information and communication technologies drive globalisation in many industries, by enabling the efficient flow of data on which international operations depend.

There is also evidence of resistance to the forces in Yip's model. Local companies develop new products, and customers may find they offer better value – so global brands offering standard products regardless of local tastes, lose market share. Rather than 'going global' companies began to 'go local' – Coca-Cola, for instance, owns not one brand but 200, many of them in only one or two markets; Starbucks and McDonald's vary what they offer to suit local tastes; Nestlé has about 200 varieties of instant coffee. Two examples from the motor industry show contrasting approaches – see Management in Practice.

Management in practice   Contrast Ford   (www.Ford.com)   FT
with VW (www.VW.com)

In 2008 Ford announced that it was trying to break down the 'regional fiefdoms' which managers of the company's businesses around the world had developed. Designers, engineers and marketing staff focused primarily on their parts of the world producing, for example, a Ford Focus in Europe that was quite different from that sold in the United States. Alan Mulally, Ford's chief executive (who had joined the company from Boeing) saw this as inefficient:

We didn't make different 737s for France and China.

Under his plan, by 2015 all cars of each model will share a common platform, irrespective of where they are sold, believing this will produce great economies of scale for it and its suppliers.

In the same year Martin Winterkorn, chief executive of Volkswagen said that the days of building one car for the whole world were over:

We will make the VW group the world's most international car maker. The days of a 'world car' are dead and buried. Our customers in China or India expect us, as a global player, to offer entirely different solutions than we do in the US or western Europe.

Source: *Financial Times*, 14 March 2008, and 25 July 2008.

Alan Rugman (2005) has noted that rather than becoming globalised, the world has divided into three regions – North America, the European Union and Japan/East Asia. He notes that almost three-quarters of exports from EU members went to other EU countries, concluding that what we are seeing is not so much globalisation as regionalisation:

Only in a few sectors is globalization a successful firm strategy . . . For most manufacturers and all services, regionalization is much more relevant than globalization. (p. 18)

Concerns about globalisation

Supporters of more liberal world trade argue that it brings benefits of wider access to markets and cheaper goods and services. The growth in trade benefits both consumers and workers by encouraging innovation and investment. It has given many consumers a much wider choice of goods, by being able to attract supplies from around the world, often much more cheaply than those produced locally. Others take a more critical view, pointing out that moves towards liberalisation through bodies such as the WTO are driven by the rich countries. They believe the agreements reached serve the interests of multinational businesses and richer economies rather than indigenous producers in local economies.

Activity 4.2   What does 'managing internationally' mean?

Recall the organisation you used in Activity 4.1.

Having read the chapter, make brief notes summarising the main international factors affecting the company.

- How does the company conduct the international aspects of the business? (See Section 4.2.)
- Which of the PESTEL factors have had most effect on the business in the last year? (See Section 4.3.)
- To what extent (if at all) do management practices take account of differences in national cultures? (See Section 4.5.)
- To what extent (if at all) do management practices take account of differences in national management systems? (See Section 4.6.)

Compare what you have found with other students on your course.

Summary

1 Contrast the ways in which organisations conduct international business

 • Offshoring, exporting, licensing, joint ventures, wholly owned subsidiaries.
 • Multinational (independent operations in many countries, run from centre); transnational (independent operations in many countries, decentralised); global (linked and interdependent operations in many countries, closely coordinated).

2 Explain, with examples, how PESTEL factors affect the decisions of those managing internationally

 • This would involve gathering data and information about political, economic, socio-cultural, technological, environmental and legal.

3 Explain and illustrate the evidence on national cultures, and evaluate the significance of Hofstede's research for managers working internationally

 • This would involve gathering evidence (as in the Activities) on differences in national culture (using Hofstede or a similar model), and on whether the cultural differences had a noticeable effect on the task of managing.
 • Hofstede distinguished between cultures in terms of power distance (acceptance of variations in power); uncertainty avoidance (willingness to tolerate ambiguity); individualism/collectivism (emphasis on individual or collective action); masculinity/femininity (preferences for assertive or modest behaviour); and long/short-term orientation.

4 Compare and contrast the features of national management systems

 • These shape the way people interpret generic activities of management:
   • US – individualistic, rational approach, contingent design of organisations
   • Europe – collective, rational approach, pragmatic
   • Japan – collective responsibility, trust of subordinates, consensus building.

5 Summarise the forces stimulating the growth of international business

 • Yip proposes that these factors are market, economic, environmental and competitive.

Review questions

1 Identify a new example of each of the methods of conducting international business.

2 Compare internationalisation and globalisation. Give a specific example of a company of each type about which you have obtained some information.

3 Explain accurately to another person Hofstede's five dimensions of national cultures. Evaluate his conclusions on the basis of discussions with your colleagues from any of the countries in his study. Evaluate the limitations and criticisms of his study.

4 What are the distinctive features of Japanese, European and US management systems?

5 What factors are stimulating the growth in world trade?

6 Compare the implications of globalisation for (a) national governments, (b) their citizens, (c) the management of global companies, (d) the environment.

Further reading

Guthrie, D. (2006), *China and Globalization: The social, economic and political transformation of Chinese society*, Routledge, London.

> An excellent review of China's transition towards a market economy, showing how the visible economic changes depend on supportive social, cultural and political changes.

Friedman, T. (2005), *The World is Flat: A brief history of the globalized world in the 21st century*, Penguin/Allen Lane, London.

> Best-selling account of the forces that are driving globalisation, and enabling greater collaboration between companies wherever they are. The same forces that assist company networks also assist terrorist networks.

Schultz, H. with Gordon, J. (2011), *Onward: How Starbucks fought for its life without losing its soul,* Wiley, Chichester.

> 'A story of leadership and change.' Howard Schultz's account of his role when he returned to Starbucks as CEO in 2008 to rescue the company from crisis.

Weblinks

These websites have appeared in, or are relevant to, the chapter:

> www.maersk.com
> www.mothercareplc.com
> www.walmart.com
> www.bt.com
> www.gillette.com
> www.dyson.co.uk
> www.Ford.com
> www.VW.com
> www.starbucks.com
> www.irisnation.com

Visit two of the sites in the list, or others which interest you, and navigate to the pages dealing with recent news, press or investor relations.

● What signs are there of the international nature of the business, and what are the main issues in this area that the business appears to be facing?

● Compare and contrast the issues you identify on the two sites.

● What challenges may they imply for those working in, and managing, these organisations?

 Annotated weblinks, multiple choice questions and other useful resources can be found on **www.pearsoned.co.uk/boddy**

Case study   Starbucks   www.starbucks.com

Starbucks sells coffee, pastries, confectionery and coffee-related accessories through over 17000 retail stores – about 12000 in the United States and 5000 in more than 50 countries (early 2011). In the financial year to the end of September 2010 its total revenue amounted to $10.7 billion, and profits to almost $900 million.

Three entrepreneurs created the company in 1971 to sell coffee in Seattle, and by 1981 they had five stores. The owners decided to sell the business in 1987 and Howard Schultz (a former employee) bought it: he expanded it rapidly, so that by 1991 there were 114 Starbucks stores. The company was also innovative with new products to attract customers – such as introducing low-fat iced coffee for the diet conscious. It grew by about 20 per cent a year during the 1990s, but some believed that the market in the US would become saturated.

To maintain rapid growth, the company began to expand overseas, through Starbucks Coffee International, a wholly owned subsidiary. It entered the Asia Pacific rim first, as the eagerness of young people there to imitate Western lifestyles made them attractive markets for Starbucks. In 2011 it owned about 9000 of the stores, and licensed, or had joint ventures in, about 8000.

Initially it opened a few stores in trendy parts of a country, with the company's managers from Seattle handling the operation. Local *baristas* (brew masters) were trained in Seattle for 13 weeks, to ensure consistent standards across the world. Similar products were stocked, and all stores were 'No Smoking'.

The company's managers adapted the business to local tastes – such as offering curry puffs and meat buns in Asia, where people prefer to eat something while having coffee. In the Middle East the coffee shops had segregated sections for ladies. In 1998 the company opened in Europe, with stores in the UK, Switzerland, Germany and Greece. The company believed that it was successful not because it was selling coffee, but because it was selling an experience. In many markets it faces local competition and is subject to the same economic conditions as other businesses of its type.

The company has also received criticism from activists in several countries. Some criticise it for an apparently relentless expansion, offering a similar global brand that tends to push out local

Purestock/Alamy.

companies, reducing the variety of local shopping areas.

Others have cast doubt on its claims to treat coffee growers fairly. It has taken these criticisms seriously, and has for ten years been working with Conservation International to help farmers grow coffee in ways that are better for people and for the planet. The goal is that 100 per cent of coffee will be responsibly grown and ethically traded – at present about 75 per cent meets that standard. It also has targets that by 2015 all of the cups will be reusable or recyclable, and that it will contribute more that 1 million community service hours each year.

It expects all suppliers to comply with the conditions set out in a detailed statement of social responsibility standards, covering matters like transparency, worker health and safety, worker treatment and rights, hours and pay and environmental protection.

By January 2008 the company was in severe trouble, which many blamed on too rapid an expansion. Founder Howard Schultz returned as Chief Executive (he had remained as Chairman after giving up as CEO in 2000) and acted quickly to turn the business round. He closed 600 under-performing stores, improved internal processes to cut costs, improved customer service, and improved the coffee and food. Speaking to a conference of store managers he warned against complacency:

> We can't allow mediocrity to creep back into the business. The worst thing we could do is not understand what happened three years ago.

By 2011 the company was recovering strongly, reporting record sales in the 2010 financial year of $10.7 billion.

Sources: *Fortune*, 13 November 2006; company website; *Financial Times*, 19 January 2007, 22 March 2010; Starbucks Corporation *Annual Report 2010* (on website).

Questions

1 Which of the modes of conducting international business has Starbucks used? (Refer to Section 4.2.)

2 Which of the PESTEL factors have had most effect on the business in the last year? (Refer to Section 4.3.)

3 In what ways does the company reflect the diversity of national cultures? (Refer to Section 4.5.)

4 Which of Yip's list of factors driving globalisation has affected the company? What other factors may have encouraged this move? (Refer to Section 4.7.)

CHAPTER 5
CORPORATE RESPONSIBILITY

Learning outcomes

When you have read this chapter you should be able to:

1 Give examples of controversial, and of philanthropic, business practices
2 Distinguish criteria that people use to evaluate individual and corporate actions
3 Use a model of ethical decision-making to explain behaviour
4 Show how stakeholders, strategies and responsible behaviour interact
5 Evaluate an organisation's methods for managing corporate responsibility
6 Use ideas from the chapter to comment on the management issues in the Pinto case study

Activity 5.1 What does 'corporate responsibility' mean?

Before reading the chapter, write some notes on what you think 'corporate responsibility' means. Choose the organisation or people you hope may be able to help you learn about the topic. You may find it helpful to discuss the topic with a manager you know, or reflect on an activity you have managed.

- Make brief notes on what, if any, issues of 'ethics' or 'corporate responsibility' those running the business have had to deal with.
- What factors appeared to have affected the decisions they made?
- Did the outcomes relate to wider organisational strategies?

Keep these notes as you will be able to use them later.

5.1 Introduction

Ford managers dealing with the Pinto chose to put profit before safety. Yet they did not act illegally, and customers then were not as interested in safety features as they are today. A manager who tried to delay the model launch would have damaged their career, their family economy – and the livelihood of other Ford workers. But the managers' decisions led to death and injury.

Most people are only aware of corporate responsibility (or the lack of it) when there is a controversy about (say) food safety or the use of child labour. They also take note of events like the collapse of Enron (Swartz and Watkins, 2002) and Arthur Andersen (Toffler and Reingold, 2003). The high salary and pension paid to Fred Goodwin, whose leadership almost destroyed The Royal Bank of Scotland in 2008, increase distrust of corporate bodies. While these situations seem clear-cut, many controversies about corporate behaviour are ambiguous:

> there is no consensus on what constitutes virtuous corporate behavior. Is sourcing overseas to take advantage of lower labor costs responsible? Are companies morally obligated to insist that their contractors pay a 'living wage' rather than market wages? Are investments in natural resources in poor countries with corrupt governments always, sometimes or never irresponsible? (Vogel, 2005, pp. 4–5)

Should BP gain credit for acknowledging climate change before many of its competitors, or criticised for its poor safety record? Is Shell acting responsibly by extracting oil in Nigeria which supports the nation's development, but which may damage local communities?

These issues arise at each stage of the value-adding chain. They arise over

- inputs (e.g. whether to use existing staff or to outsource work);
- transformation (e.g. treatment of employees, use of energy, transport and other resources); and
- outputs (e.g. pollution, treatment of customers, effects on reputation).

The chapter begins with examples of contrasting business practice, and shows the practical topics which managers face in the area of corporate responsibility. It outlines models for evaluating actions by individuals and organisations, and follows this with three 'contextual' perspectives – ethical decision-making models, stakeholders and strategy. A further section illustrates practices which organisations use to support their policies on corporate responsibility.

| Management in practice | Bernard Madoff – the biggest fraud ever? | FT |

In 2009 Bernard Madoff (71) was sentenced to 150 years in prison for running a fraudulent investment scheme in the United States that took £39bn from thousands of investors around the world. He attracted investors by offering unusually large returns and by cultivating an image of competence and trustworthiness – clients were eager for him to accept their money. Instead of investing it, he used it to pay dividends to earlier investors – so the scheme depended on continually attracting new ones. When the world economic decline began in 2008 many asked for their money back – revealing that it was no longer there. Individuals and charitable foundations lost large amounts of money.

A remarkable feature of the story was that regulatory bodies set up after previous financial frauds failed to see what Madoff was doing: the agency responsible for regulating that part of the financial services industry was understaffed, and never inspected his accounts.

Source: *Financial Times*, 24 June 2009, 30 June 2009.

5.2 Contrasts in business practice

The Pinto case is a prominent example of questionable corporate actions, and Table 5.1 notes some recent cases – some of which were illegal while others, though dubious, were not. There is an equally long tradition of ethical behaviour in business: Robert Owen (Chapter 2 case study) campaigned against the employment of children in the mines and mills of nineteenth-century Britain. From the start of the Industrial Revolution some entrepreneurs acted philanthropically:

1803–76	Titus Salt	Textiles	Employee welfare; Saltaire Village
1830–98	Jeremiah Coleman	Mustard	Charities; Salvation Army; YMCA
1839–1922	George Cadbury	Chocolate	Employee welfare; Bournville Village
1836–1925	Joseph Rowntree	Chocolate	Employee welfare; New Earswick Village
1851–1925	William Lever	Soap	Employee welfare; Port Sunlight Village

Table 5.1 Recent financial scandals at major companies

Company	Incident	Outcome
Bernard Madoff, 2009, US investment company	Fraudulent investment company, paying early investors dividends with money raised from new ones	Thousands of investors, including charities, lost money. Madoff sentenced to 150 years in jail
The Royal Bank of Scotland, 2008, UK Bank	Used short-term borrowing to fund high-risk investments. The investments failed, and the company almost collapsed	UK government buys majority stake. Fred Goodwin, chief executive, retires with £800,000 annual pension
Volkswagen, 2007, German car manufacturer	Former head of personnel admits illegal payments to trade union leaders, managers and prostitutes	Initially denies involvement, then resigns and pleads guilty; receives short jail sentence. Trade union leaders charged
Ahold, 2006, Dutch retailer	Conceals documents about joint ventures from auditors, so that revenues appeared higher than they should have been	Chief Executive and Chief Financial officer convicted for fraud. Shareholder groups criticised lenient sentences

They recognised the social impact of industry and tried to use its potential to improve social conditions. By fostering an ethos of care, these industrialists offered an unconventional business model and showed society what was possible. Their **philanthropy** helped to position **enlightened self-interest** as a viable approach to business. Some of today's business leaders give substantial donations to charities. Bill Gates (founder of Microsoft) gives very large sums to health and educational causes, and Jeff Skoll (ex-president of eBay) gave £5m to the Said Business School at Oxford University. Lord Sainsbury, former head of the UK supermarket chain, is the UK's most generous charitable donor: he has put £400m into his Gatsby Charitable Foundation and plans to give another £600m before he dies. Sir Tom Hunter (founder of JJB Sports) has given generously to projects helping young people, and has pledged a further £1bn.

Between these extremes of (often illegal) behaviour and unstinting philanthropy there are many ambiguous issues of **corporate responsibility**. This is a broad term, which refers here to the awareness, acceptance and management of the wider responsibilities of organisations – in the public as well as the private sectors. These topics arise throughout an organisation, at any stage of the value chain – Table 5.2 lists examples.

Public interest has encouraged more companies to manage issues of corporate responsibility, and to report publicly on how they do so. Business in the Community (**www.bitc.org.uk**) encourages organisations of all kinds to respond to this interest, and publicises their achievements.

Philanthropy is the practice of contributing personal wealth to charitable or similar causes.

Enlightened self-interest is the practice of acting in a way that is costly or inconvenient at present, but which is believed to be in one's best interest in the long-term.

Corporate responsibility refers to the awareness, acceptance and management of the wider implications of corporate decisions.

Table 5.2 Common topics of corporate responsibility: content and process

Content (or substance) of corporate responsibility

Topics	Examples
Inputs and resource supplies	Dealing fairly with producers and suppliers, sustainable sourcing of raw materials and supplies, avoiding exploitation of labour by suppliers in poor countries
Workforce activities	Promoting diversity, equality, health and safety, work-life balance, and other elements of the employment relationship; reward and risk – fair pay, bonus and pension schemes
Operations	Help the environment by reducing energy in production and transport, using resources efficiently to reduce waste (e.g. less packaging)
Product and service impacts	Responsible customer relations, including advertising and promotion ('Drink responsibly'), protecting children, limit harmful ingredients, clear and accurate labels, product accessibility
Community activities	Education, employability and regeneration in communities – donations, employee volunteering, gifts in kind, being a good neighbour

Processes of corporate responsibility

Leadership	Defining commitment to responsible action, resourcing it, identifying roles and reporting relationships, monitoring compliance with policies and codes
Stakeholder engagement	Mapping stakeholders and their main concerns, consulting them

5.3   Perspectives on individual actions

Three domains of human action

'Ethics' refers to a code of moral principles that guide human action by setting standards of what is acceptable. We can understand this more clearly if we compare ethics with actions that are governed by law and by free choice – Figure 5.1. Some actions are the subject of legislation which can be enforced in the courts: it is illegal to steal. At the other extreme are actions in the domain of free choice – anyone can apply for another job.

In between are acts which have an ethical dimension. Laws do not prohibit them, but nor are people free to act as they wish: they are constrained by shared principles and values about acceptable behaviour in the circumstances. An ethically acceptable action is one that is legal *and* meets a society's ethical standards – which raises the question of how people form and express those standards: a standard that you think should be respected may be ignored by others.

Ethical dilemmas arise when an action which benefits one person or group will harm others, such as when someone:

- believes that a parent has given inaccurate information to secure a place for their child at a popular school – should they tell?
- sees a golfer surreptitiously move their ball to improve their chance of winning a prize – should they tell?
- sees a thief steal a valuable item from a small shop while the owner is attending to an elderly customer – should they tell?

People may disagree on which answer is right, which probably means they are using different criteria: what might they be?

Four criteria for evaluating an action

Philosophers have identified four principles that people use to evaluate whether an action is ethical – moral principle, utilitarianism, human rights and individualism. Understanding these may help to understand what people expect of others.

- **Moral principle** People use this criterion when they evaluate an action against a moral principle – the rules that societies develop, and which members generally accept as valid guides to behaviour (e.g. people do not steal, cheat or deliberately injure each other). If someone acts in a way that conforms to these principles, it is right: if not, it is wrong.
- **Utilitarianism** People use this criterion when they evaluate an action against its effect not on individual pleasure and pain, but on the total balance of pleasure and pain in society. An act is right if it brings pleasure to more people than it hurts. An act is wrong if the amount of pain is greater than the amount of pleasure.

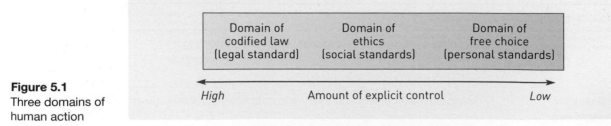

Figure 5.1
Three domains of
human action

- **Human rights** People use this criterion when they evaluate an action against its effect on human rights which a society recognises (such as privacy, free speech or fair treatment). An act is right if it supports the human rights of those whom it affects, and wrong if it damages them.
- **Individualism** People use this criterion when they evaluate an action against its effect on their interests. An act is right (provided that it is also legal) if they can show that it serves those interests. This may seem strange, but philosophers use it to justify a free enterprise economy, on the grounds that apparently selfish behaviour helps society as a whole: entrepreneurs acting selfishly only benefit in the long-term if their actions benefit others – by producing things that people want to buy, for example.

These tools from moral philosophy may show the reasoning behind someone's decision on an ethical issue – though Table 5.3 shows that others could challenge these criteria.

Figure 5.2 shows why people often find it difficult to agree on whether or not a decision is ethical. It shows that the people (B,C,D . . .) who observe an action by A, and the criteria that A uses to justify it, will themselves be evaluating the action *and* the criteria. Their diverse personalities, backgrounds and experiences makes it likely that they will attach different meanings to what they see, and so make different judgements.

Table 5.3 Questions within each philosophy

Philosophy	Questions
Moral principle	Who determines that a moral principle is 'generally accepted'? What if others claim that a principle leading to a different decision is equally 'accepted'?
Utilitarianism	Who determines the majority, and the population of which it is the greatest number? Is the benefit assessed over the short-term or the long-term?
Human rights	Actions usually involve several people – what if the decision would protect the rights of some, but breach the rights of others? How to balance them?
Individualism	Whose self-interest comes first? What if the action of one damages the self-interest of another?

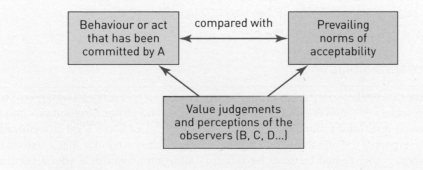

Figure 5.2
Making ethical judgements
Source: Based on Carroll (1989), p. 84.

5.4   Perspectives on corporate actions

Managers can take account of four responsibilities as they develop their decisions.

Legal responsibilities

Society expects managers to obey the law – by not misleading investors, exploiting staff or selling faulty goods. These are among countless issues upon which nations create laws regulating company behaviour. Some companies take these responsibilities seriously – but go no further. Their only criterion is that what they do is legal: as long as a decision meets that test they will take it, even if it has damaging consequences for others. Managers involved with the Pinto scandal took this view, as did, more recently, many of those involved in trading complex financial instruments which contributed to the financial crisis of 2008.

Economic responsibilities – Milton Friedman

Here managers focus on serving the economic interests of the company and its shareholders. Milton Friedman was clear that:

> [In a free economy] there is one and only one social responsibility of business – to use its resources and engage in activities designed to increase its profits so long as it stays within the rules of the game, which is to say, engages in open and free competition, without deception or fraud. (Friedman, 1962, p. 113)

He believed that operating business 'without deception or fraud' provided sufficient social benefit by creating wealth and employment, implying that managers should consider only their legal and economic responsibilities. To give money to charitable purposes was equivalent to self-imposed taxation. He argued that the directors in charge of a business should concentrate on generating wealth for shareholders, and distributing it to them. They could then decide if they wished to give that income to charity.

Many agree, claiming that stringent environmental or other regulations increase costs for a business, and make it less competitive (Stavins, 1994). Spending money on socially responsible but unprofitable ventures will damage the firm, and be unsustainable. An example of this was when Burberry's, the luxury goods retailer, decided to close one of its few remaining UK factories. A journalist questioned the finance director, and she commented:

> Ultimately if a factory isn't commercially viable you have to take the decision to close . . . that's what your obligations to your shareholders dictate. When you know you've made the right decision commercially, you have to stay true to that. These are the facts – commercial realities reign. (*Financial Times,* 15 February 2007, p. 3)

Ethical responsibilities

Some believe that while society depends on business for goods and services, business in turn depends on society. It requires inputs – employees, capital and physical resources – and the socially created institutions that enable business to operate – such as a legal and education system. This is part of the moral case for corporate responsibility – namely that it reflects this interdependency: society and business have mutual obligations within a **social contract**. Actions in this area are not specified by law, and may not serve a company's narrow economic interests. Managers may act as part of their perceptions of the social contract – such as acting to

The **social contract** consists of the mutual obligations that society and business recognise they have to each other.

meet a wider social interest, by discouraging tobacco consumption, protecting the natural environment or supporting a socially disadvantaged group. They may also do so in the belief that it will help meet their economic responsibilities by enhancing their reputation with customers.

Discretionary responsibilities

This covers actions which are entirely voluntary, not being shaped by economic, legal or ethical considerations. They include anonymous donations with no expectation or possibility of a pay-back, sponsorship of local events and contributions to charities – the actions are entirely philanthropic. Innocent Drinks donates 10 per cent of profits to charities such as the Rainforest Alliance (**www.innocentdrinks.com**).

Friedman believed that managers' responsibilities are to do what is best for the business and the shareholders. Those advocating a more inclusive view of corporate responsibility believe that recognising wider interests is enlightened self-interest, in the sense that it can satisfy both economic *and* moral expectations. Managers may add more value (and serve their shareholders better) if they meet ethical and discretionary responsibilities, in ways that benefit the business. Both consider stakeholders, but in different ways.

What factors influence managers' decisions? The next section introduces an ethical decision-making model.

5.5	An ethical decision-making model

Trevino and Weaver (2003) note that attempts to develop universal guidelines for responsible behaviour in business have a long history: Aristotle commented on the ethical propriety of commercial practices. They also find much of the commentary on modern scandals – suppliers bribing government officials to secure contracts or banks paying their staff high salaries – is essentially normative, in that it prescribes what people should and should not do. They go on:

> important as it is to engage in the normative study of what is, and is not, ethically proper in business, it is just as important to understand the organizational and institutional context within which ethical issues, awareness and behavior are situated. (p. xv)

Figure 5.3 may help that understanding, by showing a simple **ethical decision-making model** (there is a complex one with more variables in Trevino, 1986). The figure predicts that an individual's choice of behaviour when facing an ethical dilemma depends on factors unique to the individual and on factors within their context.

The individual factors are:

Ethical decision-making models examine the influence of individual characteristics and organisational policies on ethical decisions.

- *Stage of moral development* – the extent to which the person can distinguish between right and wrong; the higher this is, the more likely the person is to act ethically.
- *Ego strength* – the extent to which they are able to resist impulses and follow their convictions; the greater this is, the more likely the person will do what they think is right.
- *Locus of control* – the extent to which the person believes they have control over their life, rather than this being determined by others; the more a person sees themselves as having control, the more likely they are to act ethically.

The contextual factors are:

- *Work group norms* – the beliefs within the work group about how to behave in a situation.
- *Incentives* – such as management policies on rewards and disciplines.
- *Rules and regulations* – management policies about relevant ethical dilemmas.

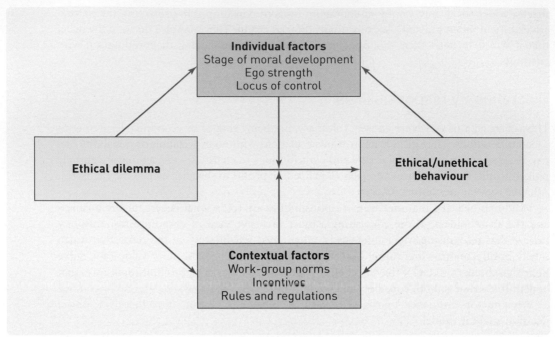

Figure 5.3 A simple model of ethical decision-making

The figure also shows that behaviour has consequences which feed back to, and possibly change, the individual and their context – which shape the way the person responds to future dilemmas. Many other factors could be added, but in this context the purpose of the figure is to indicate the type of factors which influence ethical choices.

Pierce and Snyder (2008) illustrate this by showing that the willingness of staff to commit fraud varied with their employer's policies. They analysed vehicle testing records in a state over two years, during which time some testers moved between employers (typically small workshops). They found that testers' leniency varied with their employer – norms of behaviour and incentives at their current workshop encouraged them to behave ethically (making decisions in line with regulations) or unethically (passing vehicles that should fail).

Many believe that the 2008 financial crises was caused by senior managers in some banks encouraging a culture of risk. This rewarded staff for taking risks which benefited them, but brought financial ruin to others. Governments sometimes use the ideas behind Figure 5.3 to influence corporate behaviour – the US Government announced in 2009 that it would make billions of dollars available in cheap loans to car companies, to encourage them to invest in new plants to build electric and other fuel-efficient vehicles (*Financial Times*, 24 June 2009).

Figure 5.3 also illustrates the dilemma some people face when working in countries with different views on giving and taking bribes to influence management decisions. On the universal perspective, people should act in an ethically consistent way irrespective of where they are. **Ethical relativism** suggests taking account of the local context, and incorporating prevailing norms and values when deciding issues with an ethical dimension: if local and home country norms conflict, people should follow the local norms. Ethical relativism is a convenient philosophy for international companies, but causes difficulties for individual managers if their personal views are more universal than relative.

Ethical relativism is the principle that ethical judgements cannot be made independently of the culture in which the issue arises.

5.6   Stakeholders and corporate responsibility

Stakeholder priorities – balancing trade-offs

Chapter 3 explained that organisations have internal and external stakeholders with an interest in what the organisation does. Table 5.4 lists the main groups, and illustrates the issues to which they are likely to give priority.

Each stakeholder category will express conflicting views. Multinationals deal with the governments (national and local) in many countries, which inevitably expect different things. Communities within one country will show similar diversity – managers can satisfy one only at the expense of another. Scottish and Southern Energy wants to increase the amount of power it generates from wind farms, which will help to meet the UK government's renewable energy target. Some stakeholders object that building wind farms, and the associated distribution lines, will damage landscapes, endanger migrating birds and require large subsidies which could be used for other public services. In 2011 several UK companies were keen to build plants to turn household waste into 'green' energy – but some residents near the proposed sites objected to their plans, leading to long delays in obtaining planning permission.

Almost any major decision involves trade-offs, in the sense that a benefit in one area is likely to bring a disadvantage somewhere else: this applies to decisions aimed at promoting responsibility as much as in any other areas of management action. As much as an organisation does to satisfy one set of stakeholders, others are likely to object.

Table 5.4 Stakeholders and interests in relation to corporate responsibility (CR)

Stakeholders	Expectations
Employees	Employment, security, safe working conditions, rewarding work, fairness in promotion, security and pay
Shareholders	Financially centred investors: high return on investment
	Ethical investors: strong CR policies and reputation
Suppliers	Fair terms, prompt payment, long-term relationships
Customers	Majority – price, quality, durability and safety
	Minority (ethical consumers) – Fair Trade sources, fair treatment of staff, care for environment
Communities	Employment; income; limits on pollution and noise
Competitors	Fair competition, follow the norms of behaviour in the industry
Governments	Pay taxes, obey laws, provide economic opportunities
Environmental campaigners	Minimise pollution, emissions and waste and assist recycling
Charities and causes	Donations and gifts in kind

Ethical investors are people who only invest in businesses that meet specified criteria of ethical behaviour.

Stakeholders influence managers

Stakeholders vary in their influence over managers. If the most powerful expect a company to follow a Friedmanite position, managers will deliver that, perhaps with some public commitment to socially acceptable practice. Other companies have powerful shareholders who, while expecting a financial return, are willing to take a longer view: they believe their managers can best deliver long-term returns by meeting, to some degree, the expectations of other stakeholders.

> Firms with this perspective will invest in social initiatives because they believe that such investments will result in increased profitability. (Peloza, 2006, p. 54)

Many companies differentiate themselves less by their products than by the ideas, emotions and images that their brand conveys – they value their reputation. Managers who allow their brand to become associated with hostility to people, communities or the natural environment risk their reputation and profits. Adopting responsible practices enables a firm to imbue the brand with positive themes that coincide with the beliefs of many customers. This valuable asset can be damaged if activists target the company. Companies like Nike, Shell, McDonald's and Starbucks have all faced well organised campaigns.

Managers influence stakeholders – the lobbying business

Consistently with the interaction model, managers also influence their context by, for example, lobbying powerful interest groups to make decisions in their favour. Companies and industry associations invest substantial resources protecting their interests against legislation which they believe is against their interests – see Management in Practice feature.

Management in practice   **Lobbying for the motor industry**   **www.acea.ch**   **FT**

Ivan Hodac is chief executive of the European Automobile Manufacturers Association, and many regard him as one of the most successful of the 15,000 lobbyists who influence European Union decisions.

Automakers are fighting for survival, and Mr Hodac's talents are often called for. In December 2008, his organisation was credited with delaying environmental legislation which would have forced automakers to cut vehicle carbon dioxide emissions 18 per cent by 2012. Now they have until 2015 and the penalties for failure will be less severe. Environmental groups were furious, but Mr Hodac argued that it was a reasonable compromise for an industry on its knees and with little cash for research and development.

Source: Adapted from Lobbyist driving a hard bargain (Joshua Chaffin), *Financial Times*, 16 June 2009.

5.7   Corporate responsibility and strategy

Will responsible behaviour pay? If it does not, how will the responsible organisation survive? Vogel (2005) believes that responsible corporate action is only sustainable if it yields a financial return – otherwise less responsible players gain a competitive advantage over the more responsible. There are three ways in which responsible action may support wider strategy and bring a financial return – as their mission; to meet customer needs; and by being integral to strategy.

Responsible action as the corporate mission

Some companies position corporate responsibility at the heart of their business, reflecting the beliefs and values of founders and senior managers. An early example was The Body Shop which became a major retailing group by, among many other things, taking a strong ethical position on issues such as testing cosmetics on live animals. Its unique position was gradually eroded – partly by its own success. Animal testing of cosmetics (one of the firm's early campaigns) was stopped, and more people are aware of environmental issues. So a strategically valuable position became less distinctive, and L'Oréal now owns the company. Unilever (**www.unilever.com**) has a history of community involvement, and tries to continue that tradition – while stressing that 'sustainability' has to be consistent with financial requirements.

> ### Management in practice   The co-operative   www.co-operative.coop
>
> Established in the early nineteenth century, the Co-op is now Britain's fifth largest retail chain, with a strong financial services business. It is run democratically by its members, who twice a year receive a share of the profits, based on how much they have spent in the business, and how much profit the business made in the year.
>
> Working in line with ethical principles has always been part of the Co-op's mission and way of working – so it has been quick to take into account current concerns of corporate responsibility, such as climate change and world poverty. The company produces an annual sustainability report, outlining what the group has done throughout the business to manage it in a more sustainable way. The fund managers in its investment businesses, for example, take a distinctive approach to investing, in that they consider environmental, social and governance issues alongside financial measures.
>
> The company website gives more information about all the group's activities supporting responsible corporate behaviour.
>
> Source: Company website.

Responsible action to meet customer needs

Other companies, while not focused on responsibility as a mission, focus on meeting the needs of **ethical consumers** – those who take ethical issues into account when making a purchase, and try to avoid buying products from companies that damage the environment, deal with oppressive regimes, have a poor record on animal rights or pay low wages. Such consumers have supported the growth of the Fair Trade scheme, under which companies guarantee that suppliers in poor countries receive higher prices for their products than they would from market forces alone. Café Direct, Green and Black Chocolate are examples of such products.

Ethical consumers are those who take ethical issues into account in deciding what to purchase.

Not all customers share these concerns, but there are enough of them to encourage some companies to meet their requirements, without necessarily adding to their costs. Hawken *et al.* (1999) provide many examples of companies finding that environmentally friendly practices are cost-neutral: by looking carefully at supply, manufacture and distribution, they work out how to make responsible practices pay. Walmart encourages suppliers to use less packaging, and in 2010 Marks & Spencer (**www.marksandspencer.com**) announced that it aims to become the world's most sustainable retailer by 2015. Many banks are re-designing offices and branches to use less energy.

Management in practice   Red – Bono and Aids in Africa   www.joinred.com

In 2006 Bono announced the creation of his new brand – Red – which will dedicate some of its revenue to fight Aids in Africa. The effort will include a series of joint ventures with companies like American Express, Georgio Armani and Gap to sell products under the brand (for example, go to **www.gap.com** and you will see the RED brands featured). They will be marketed first in the UK to an estimated 1.5m 'conscience consumers' who are seen as more likely to buy products associated with a social benefit. Other products available will include Converse sports shoes made with African mud-cloth, a new line of Gap vintage T-shirts and wrap-around Armani sunglasses:

> I think doing the Red thing, doing good, will turn out to be good business for them, said Bono, who has long been associated with campaigns on African debt relief, Aids, and unfair trading rules that hurt the continent's poor. This and similar efforts are being supported by big companies worried that television advertising is losing its punch. The idea is that using good works or services will gain consumer attention – what some call 'corporate social opportunity'.

Sources: *Financial Times*, 26 January 2006, *Independent*, 13 May 2006; U2 and RED websites.

Responsible action as part of strategy

Others follow responsible practices towards, for example, their use of resources, because it fits their business strategy. Using energy efficiently, avoiding waste and treating staff with respect are established daily practices in many companies – some of whom now present such practices as part of a responsible image. In 2009 Mars, the world's biggest confectioner, announced that its entire cocoa supply will be produced sustainably by 2020. It will achieve this by working with the Rainforest Alliance, which encourages farmers to preserve their environment. Cadbury (**www.cadbury.com**) announced that all the cocoa in Dairy Milk, Britain's biggest-selling chocolate, would be certified by Fair Trade, the organisation which works to ensure a minimum price for farmers. Both companies have substantial business reasons for their actions – they are worried about how much cocoa will be available a decade from now, as world production is falling.

Does responsible action affect performance?

The evidence is not clear. One review found a positive relationship between responsible corporate behaviour and financial performance (Orlitzky *et al.*, 2003). Ambec and Lanoie (2008) found that under pressure from stakeholders, some firms use responsible practices to increase revenue (gaining better access to markets; differentiating products; or selling pollution control technologies) and/or reduce costs (risk management; lower costs of materials, energy, capital and labour). Their examples appear to show that companies can both act responsibly and perform well economically.

Vogel (2005) is more sceptical. He found studies which showed a positive relationship between, for example, the level of emission reduction and financial performance, but the direction of causality was unclear – perhaps profitable firms could afford to invest in equipment to reduce emissions. Another possibility was that factors not included in the research affected both variables. Overall, he found an inconclusive picture of the relationship between responsibility and profitability, perhaps due to limitations in the studies:

- different measures of financial performance (one review of 95 studies found that they had 49 different accounting measures);
- different measures of corporate responsibility (95 studies used 27 different data sources); and
- questionable validity of some measures (some rankings only included the views of executives in the industry).

His overall conclusion is that the relationship between responsible behaviour and performance is unclear:

> just as firms that spend more on marketing are not necessarily more profitable than those that spend less, there is no reason to expect more responsible firms to outperform less responsible ones. (p. 33)

5.8   Managing corporate responsibility

Managers use several methods to promote responsible behaviour, including leading by example, codes of ethics, and ethical structures and reporting systems.

Leading by example

Senior managers set the tone for an organisation by their actions. If others see that they are acting in line with stated ethical principles, their credibility will rise and others are likely to follow. Leaders known to be engaging in malpractice are likely to encourage it to spread throughout the business.

Codes of practice

A code of practice is a formal statement of the company's values, setting out general principles on matters such as quality, employees or the environment. Others set out procedures for situations – such as conflicts of interest or the acceptance of gifts. Their effectiveness depends on the extent to which top management supports them with sanctions and rewards.

Corporate responsibility structures and reporting

These are the formal systems and roles that companies create to support responsible behaviour. This may include staff with direct responsibilities for developing and implementing company policies and practices, together with procedures for regular monitoring and reporting, both within the company and to external stakeholders. Most companies now include a corporate responsibility statement in their Annual Report, and may include in this an **ethical audit** profiling current practice.

Ethical audits are the practice of systematically reviewing the extent to which an organisation's actions are consistent with its stated ethical intentions.

Activity 5.2   What does 'corporate responsibility' mean?

Recall the organisation you used in Activity 5.1.

Having read the chapter, make brief notes summarising the organisation's practices in the area of corporate responsibility.

- What, if any, examples of CR issues did you identify (Refer to Table 5.2.)
- Which criteria appear to have most influence on their decisions (Refer to Section 5.4.)
- Can you identify examples of the company relating responsible actions to the wider strategy? (Refer to Section 5.7.)
- What formal practices has the company introduced to support its CR activities? (Refer to Section 5.8.)

Compare what you have found with other students on your course.

Summary

1 **Give examples of controversial, and of philanthropic, business practices**
   - Negative examples include poor treatment of suppliers or staff, wasteful uses of energy and other resources during transformation, and unfair treatment of customers. Reputations are also damaged by cases of senior management fraud or high compensation to failed managers.
   - In contrast there are many examples of philanthropy, in which people give to charities and other causes without expecting any specific benefit in return.

2 **Distinguish criteria that people use to justify individual and corporate actions**
   - Individual
     - Moral principle – the decision is consistent with generally accepted principles.
     - Utilitarianism – the decision that benefits the greatest number of people is the right one to take.
     - Human rights – decisions that support one of several human rights (such as privacy) are right.
     - Individualism – decisions that serve the individual's self-interest are right – in the long run they will benefit society as well.
   - Corporate
     - Legal responsibilities – obey the law.
     - Economic responsibilities – Friedman's view that the only function of business is to act legally in the interests of shareholders.
     - Ethical responsibilities – that business has wider responsibilities, since it depends on aspects of the society in which it operates.
     - Discretionary – actions that are entirely philanthropic.

3 **Use a model of ethical decision-making to explain behaviour**
   - Figure 5.3 shows a simple model of individual and contextual factors that shape ethical or unethical behaviour.

4 **Show how stakeholders, strategies and responsible behaviour interact**
   - Stakeholders' expectations and relative power will influence how managers interpret responsible behaviour, bearing in mind Vogel's point that this is only sustainable if it supports strategy. The chapter showed how this happens – when corporate responsibility is part of the mission, meets customer needs, or otherwise supports strategy.

5 **Evaluate an organisation's methods for managing corporate responsibility**
   - These include leading by example, codes of practice, CR structures and reporting mechanisms.

Review questions

1 Identify two recent examples of dubious corporate behaviour (including one from the public sector) and two of philanthropic behaviour. What were their effects?

2 Describe in your own terms each of four schools of ethical theory mentioned in the chapter, and illustrate each with an example of how it has been used to justify a decision.

3 Summarise the four responsibilities which corporations may choose to meet (or not), illustrating each with an example.

4 Sketch the ethical decision-making model and use it to analyse the Pinto case – that is, to explain why managers acted as they did.

5 How can managers take account of the diverse interests of stakeholders?

6 Why is it important, in Vogel's view, to link corporate responsibility to strategy?

7 Illustrate each of the ways in which organisations do this with a current example.

Further reading

Vogel, D. (2005), *The Market for Virtue: The potential and limits of corporate social responsibility*, Brookings Institution Press, Washington, DC.

Places issues of corporate responsibility within a wider consideration of company strategy. Many current examples support the discussion.

Blowfield, M. and Murray, A. (2008), *Corporate Responsibility: A critical introduction*, Oxford University Press, Oxford.

Comprehensive account of the topic with many examples from practice, and activities to illustrate the themes.

Weblinks

These websites have appeared in, or are relevant to, the chapter:

www.bitc.org
www.innocentdrinks.co.uk
www.acea.ch
www.unilever.com
www.co-operative.coop
www.marksandspencer.com
www.joinred.com
www.gap.com
www.cadbury.com

Visit two of the sites in the list, and navigate to the pages dealing with corporate responsibility, sustainability or corporate governance.

- What are the main concerns that they seem to be addressing?
- What information can you find about their policies?
- Compare the concerns and policies expressed on the sites.

 **www** Annotated weblinks, multiple choice questions and other useful resources can be found on **www.pearsoned.co.uk/boddy**

Case study   The Ford Pinto

In the late 1960s, Lee Iacocca, then president of Ford, sought to improve the company's market position by having a new car, the Ford Pinto, on the market by the 1971 model year. This would be a basic vehicle selling for $2000, which meant that it had to be produced very cheaply, with a small margin between production costs and selling price.

The designers placed the petrol tank at the back of the car, six inches from a flimsy rear bumper. Bolts were placed just three inches from the tank. Other sharp metal edges surrounded the tank, and the filler pipe tended to break loose from the tank in low-speed crashes. These features could have been re-designed, but the extra expense would go against Iacocca's aim of 'a 2000 pound car for $2000'.

In testing its new design Ford found that when it was struck from behind at 20 mph the bumper would push the bolts into the tank, causing it to rupture. This posed a significant risk to those inside and contravened proposed legislation which required cars to withstand an impact at 30 mph without fuel loss. No one informed Iacocca of these findings, for fear of being fired. He was fond of saying 'safety doesn't sell'.

The car went on sale and in 1976 a magazine exposed the dangers of the Pinto petrol tank. This prompted the National Highway Traffic Safety Administration (NHTSA) to launch an investigation, which in 1977 identified 28 rear-end crashes in which petrol had leaked and caused a fire. Twenty-seven occupants had died and 24 suffered burns.

Feeling some pressure to fix the tank, Ford officials devised a polythene shield to prevent it from being punctured by the bolts, and a jacket to cushion it against impact. The engineers calculated that these improvements would cost $11 per car, and had to decide whether to recall the cars to make these repairs. They conducted a cost–benefit analysis. Using NHTSA figures for the cost to society of death or serious injury, and an estimate of the likely number of future deaths and serious injuries, Ford's calculations were:

Benefits of altering design

Savings:	180 deaths; 180 serious injuries; 2100 vehicles
Unit cost:	$200,000 per death; $67,000 per serious injury; $700 per vehicle
Total benefit:	$49.5 million

Costs of altering the design

Sales:	11 million cars; 1.5 million light trucks
Unit cost:	$11 per car; $11 per truck
Total cost:	$137.5 million

Since the costs of recalling and altering the cars outweighed the benefits they decided not to do so, continuing to produce the Pinto in its original form. They reasoned that the current design met federal safety standards at the time. While it did not meet proposed legislation, it was as safe as current competing models.

In 1977 the proposed fuel tank legislation was adopted and Ford decided to recall all 1971–76 Pintos to modify their fuel tanks. A month before the recall began three people in a Pinto were struck from behind in a low-speed crash and burned to death. A $120 million lawsuit followed, but Ford escaped on a technicality. Ford won the lawsuit, but its reputation suffered badly.

Court records showed that Ford's top managers knew that the Pinto was unsafe, but concluded that it was cheaper to incur the losses from lawsuits than to fix the cars. Production staff also knew of the risks, but were never given the opportunity to tell top management about it. Fords 'profit drives principle' philosophy of the time discouraged staff from drawing attention to risks. Actions were guided by the original aim for the Pinto – '2000 pounds for $2000' – and a 'safety doesn't sell' mindset. Insiders believed they were acting in line with company values. Richard Pascale (1990) noted that during the 1970s:

© Bettmann/CORBIS.

The company was financially focussed. Cost accounting drove suboptimal design decisions at the front edge of the product development process. In the factories, a system tied a large percentage of plant managers' compensation to volume, driving plants to build cars as rapidly as possible and worry about the defects later. (Pascale, 1990, pp. 116–117)

These practices were rooted in the distant past, and did not address the issues the company was facing in the late 1970s, when consumers were more concerned about safety and less concerned about price.

When a new chief executive took over, he went to great lengths to consult with top managers about major decisions. He wanted to break away from the previously autocratic 'do as I say' style of management, and to encourage debate and discussion: which may enable people to raise ethical issues early in the decision-making process.

Sources: Pascale (1990); Shaw (1991); Nutt (2002).

Questions

1 Imagine you worked for Ford as an engineer and were aware of this potential design fault. What would you do? What, if any, are your responsibilities to the customer and/or your employer? (Refer to Sections 5.2, 5.3.)

2 Evaluate the actions of Ford's managers in this case. (Refer to Section 5.4.)

3 Does the ethical decision-making model help explain the decisions made by Ford at that time? How did the style of the new chief executive alter the likelihood of a similar scandal arising? (Refer to Section 5.5.)

4 Consider how Ford's actions at the time may have related to their strategy at the time, and then consider how the company would be likely to manage a similar situation if it arose today. (Refer to Section 5.6.)

PART 3
PLANNING

Introduction

This part examines the generic management activities of planning and decision-making, and then looks at their application to the task of managing strategy. This depends on understanding the environment of the business and on building an internal capability to deliver whatever strategy management decides upon.

Chapter 6 provides an overview of planning in organisations, setting out the purposes of planning, the types of plan and the tasks of planning. While all these tasks are likely to be part of the process, their shape will always depend on the circumstances for which a plan is being made.

Decision-making is closely linked to planning, made necessary by finite resources and infinite demands. People in organisations continually decide on inputs, transformation processes and outputs – and the quality of those decisions affects organisational performance. Chapter 7 therefore introduces the main decision-making processes, and contrasts several theories of decision-making in organisations.

Chapter 8 outlines the strategy process, and introduces techniques that managers use to analyse the options facing businesses of all kinds. This analysis can then lead to clearer choices about future direction.

CHAPTER 6
PLANNING

Learning outcomes

When you have read this chapter you should be able to:

1 Explain the purposes of planning and the content of different types of plan
2 Compare planning processes, and say when each may be most suitable
3 Outline the seven iterative steps in planning, and some techniques used in each
4 Explain how the goals in a plan affect motivation to achieve them
5 Assess the completeness of a plan
6 Use ideas from the chapter to comment on the management issues in the Crossrail case study

Activity 6.1   What is 'planning'?

Before reading this chapter, write some notes on what you understand by the term 'planning'.

Choose the organisation or people who may be able help you to learn about the topic. You may find it helpful to discuss it with a manager you know, or use an activity you have managed.

- Identify a planning issue you can use for this activity, and make a brief note about it.
- What types of plan do managers in the company make?
- How do they typically develop their plans – can they describe their planning process?
- Can they explain some of the planning techniques they use?

Keep these notes as you will be able to use them later.

6.1   Introduction

Crossrail is an example of a major project which managers can only achieve by doing a great deal of planning. From the early political processes to secure support from many interested parties – some in favour of the project, some against – through raising capital and securing public consent, managers have been planning what to do. That continues, as completing the project depends on the ever more detailed planning required to drive a new railway through a crowded capital city. The case will illustrate how Crossrail's managers deal with these challenges, some of which are unforeseen.

Perhaps paradoxically, as business conditions become more unstable, companies plan more, not less. Change creates uncertainty, and planning helps people adapt to this by clarifying objectives, specifying how to achieve them and monitoring progress. Plans include both ends (what to do) and means (how to do it).

Informal plans (not written down, nor widely shared) work perfectly well in many situations – but as the number of people involved in an activity increases they need something more to guide them. That is the focus here – on more formal plans, which record the goals of a business or unit, and who will do what to achieve them. When senior managers at Hiscox, a small but rapidly growing insurance company, decided to add an online service to its traditional way of doing business through insurance brokers, it needed a plan for the website AND a plan to reassure the brokers they still had a role. When two entrepreneurs decided to create the City Inn hotel chain they planned in detail the kind of hotels they would be – contemporary, city centre, newly built, 'active and open' atmosphere and a consistent room design across the group.

Figure 6.1 provides an overview of the themes. At the centre are seven generic tasks in planning – but people vary the order and how much attention they give to each. The chapter outlines the benefits of planning and their content. Later sections describe the process of planning and outlines some of the techniques that people use to create a plan which will help them achieve their objectives.

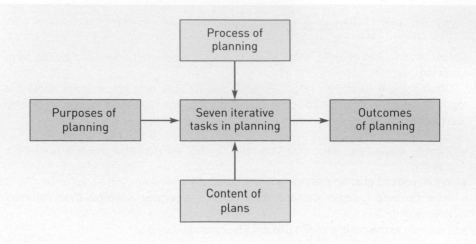

Figure 6.1
An overview
of the chapter

6.2   Purposes of planning

Planning is the iterative
task of setting goals,
specifying how to
achieve them, imple-
menting the plan and
evaluating the results.

A **goal** (or **objective**)
is a desired future state
for an activity or
organisational unit.

A planner is an individual contemplating future actions: the activity of **planning** involves establishing the **goals (or objectives)** for the task, specifying how to achieve them, implementing the plan and evaluating the results. Goals are the desired future state of an activity or organisational unit, and planning to meet them typically includes allocating resources and specifying what people need to do to meet the goals.

If people plan well it helps them to:

- clarify direction;
- motivate people;
- use resources efficiently; and
- increase control, as they can measure progress against goals.

The act of planning may in itself add value, by ensuring that people base decisions on a wider range of evidence than if there was no planning system. Giraudeau (2008) shows how the planning process in one of Renault's divisions enhanced debate among managers, and stimulated their strategic imagination. By observing the company's planners as they developed their plan to build a plant in Brazil, the author shows how providing detailed draft plans to other managers (many of whom were unfamiliar with that country) led them to see opportunities they had not considered. If done badly, planning has the opposite effect, leading to confusion and waste.

Good plans give direction to the people whose work contributes to their achievement. If everyone knows the purpose of an activity and how their task contributes, they work more effectively. They adjust their work to the plan (or vice versa), and co-operate and co-ordinate with others. It helps them cope with uncertainty: if they know the end result they can respond to unexpected changes, without waiting to be told. People like to know how their task fits the bigger picture, as it adds interest and enables them to take more responsibility.

Management in practice   **Maersk – planning key to strategy**   www.maersk.com

Maersk is the world's largest container operator, and depends on planning. Mark Cornwall, Operations Manager, explains:

Maersk operates 470 container ships with 1.9 million individual containers that are all travelling around the world, and our job is to build efficiencies into the system – moving the cargo to the customer on time.

Part of our strategy is to deliver unmatched reliability, and operations is key to that. From the top of the company right down to the clerks on the desk, everybody's focused on meeting deadlines and the requirements of the customer every step of the way. So whether it's a ship arriving in a port on time, or a container loading on a ship on time, or a truck delivery to a warehouse, everybody's focused all the way through the chain on making sure that everything happens against the deadline as planned.

Efficiency's all about making the best use of your assets, so whether it's putting as many containers as possible on a ship, or maximising your utilisation of a particular train, or getting as many miles out of a truck as you can during a shift, it's all about planning your assets to get the biggest use out of them during that period.

Source: Interview with Mark Cornwall.

Planning reduces overlap and at the same time ensures that someone is responsible for each activity. A plan helps people co-ordinate their separate tasks, so saving time and resources; without a plan they may work at cross-purposes. If people are clear on the goal they can spot inefficiencies or unnecessary delays and act to fix them.

Setting final and interim goals lets people know how well they are progressing and when they have finished. Comparing actual progress against the intended progress enables people to adjust the goal or change the way they are using resources.

The content of a plan is the subject – *what* aspect of business it deals with: strategic, business unit, operational, tactical or special purpose. The next section deals with those topics, while Section 6.4 deals with *how* – the planning process.

6.3 The content of plans

People starting a new business or expanding an existing one prepare a **business plan** – a document that sets out the markets the business intends to serve, how it will do so and what finance they require. It does so in considerable detail, as it needs to convince potential investors to lend money. Managers seeking capital investment or other corporate resources need to convince senior managers to allocate them – which they do by presenting a convincing plan. People in the public sector do the same – a director of roads (for example) needs to present a plan to convince the chief executive or elected members that planned expenditure on roads will be a better use of resources than competing proposals from (say) the director of social work. Service managers inevitably compete with each other for limited resources and develop business plans to support their case.

> A **business plan** is a document which sets out the markets the business intends to serve, how it will do so and what finance they require.

Strategic plans apply to the whole organisation. They set out the overall direction and cover major activities – markets and revenues, together with plans for marketing, human resources and production. Strategy is concerned with deciding what business an organisation should be in, where it wants to be and how it is going to get there. These decisions involve major resource commitments and usually require several consequential operational decisions.

> A **strategic plan** sets out the overall direction for the business, is broad in scope and covers all the major activities.

In a large business there are divisional plans for each major unit. If subsidiaries operate as autonomous **strategic business units** (SBUs) they develop their plans with limited inputs from the rest of the company, as they manage distinct products or markets.

> A **strategic business unit** consists of a number of closely related products for which it is meaningful to formulate a separate strategy.

Management in practice   British Airways plans survival   www.ba.com

In 2009 British Airways reported that it expected to lose money for the second successive year, and said it was planning more cost reductions to help it survive an expected two-year recession. It was shrinking operations at Gatwick Airport reducing the aircraft fleet based there from 32 to 24.

Other plans included:

- cutting thousands of jobs across the business;
- negotiating a merger with Spain's Iberia to create Europe's third-largest aviation group;

- reducing absenteeism among staff;
- negotiating more efficient working practices for cabin staff;
- reducing capacity at London City Airport by a further 17 per cent from an earlier plan.

Source: Adapted from BA cuts costs as it anticipates two years of recession (Kevin Done), *Financial Times,* 6 March 2009.

Strategic plans usually set out a direction for several years, though in businesses with long lead times (energy production or aircraft manufacture) they look perhaps 15 years ahead. Ryanair plans to grow capacity to meet demand, and makes a plan showing the financial and other implications of enlarging the fleet, recruiting staff and opening new routes. Such plans are not fixed: managers regularly update them to take account of new conditions, so they are sometimes called 'rolling plans'.

Operational plans detail how the overall objectives are to be achieved, by specifying what senior management expects from specific departments or functions.

Operational plans detail how managers expect to achieve the strategic objectives. They are narrower in scope, indicating what departments or functions should do to support the strategy. So there may be a family of related plans forming a hierarchy – a strategic plan for the organisation and main divisions, and several operational plans for departments or teams. Sainsbury announced an aggressive expansion plan in 2009, with the aim of opening 50 new supermarkets and extending another 50, over the next two years. Justin King, chief executive, said that it would concentrate the expansion in areas where it was weak, such as the west of England, Wales and Scotland. Such plans will contain linked objectives and will become more specific as they move down the organisation – eventually dealing with small activities that need to be dealt with for each new store – but aiming to be consistent with the wider expansion strategy. Table 6.1 shows this hierarchical arrangement, and how the character of plans changes at each level.

Most organisations prepare annual plans which focus on finance and set budgets for the coming year – these necessarily include sales, marketing, production or technology plans as well. Activity plans are short-term plans which deal with immediate production or service delivery – a sheet scheduling which orders to deliver next week, or who is on duty tomorrow. Standing plans specify how to deal with routine, recurring issues like recruitment or customer complaints. Some use a method called **enterprise resource planning** to integrate the day-to-day work of complex production systems – Chapter 10 describes this technique in Section 10.5.

Enterprise resource planning (ERP) is a computer-based planning system which links separate databases to plan the use of all resources within the enterprise.

Managers also prepare special purpose plans. Disasters like the explosion in 2010 at BP's oil rig in the Gulf of Mexico severely damage a company's reputation, but a well-prepared and regularly rehearsed disaster recovery plan can limit the damage. They also prepare plans to organise and implement specific changes, such as introducing a new computer system or launching a new product. When The Royal Bank of Scotland took over NatWest Bank,

Table 6.1 A planning hierarchy

Type of plan	Strategic	Operational	Activity
Level	Organisation or business unit	Division, department, function or market	Work unit or team
Focus	Direction and strategy for whole organisation	Functional changes or market activities to support strategic plans	Actions needed to deliver current products or services
Nature	Broad, general direction	Detail on required changes	Specific detail on immediate goals and tasks
Timescale	Long-term (2–3 years?)	Medium (up to 18 months?)	Very short-term (hours to weeks?)

managers quickly developed over 160 interlocking plans to incorporate NatWest operations into those of RBS (Kennedy *et al.*, 2006). People starting a new business have to prepare business plans to persuade potential investors – even though the majority change their plans significantly in the first few years of trading.

6.4   The process of planning

The process of planning refers to how people plan – do they develop them at the top of the organisation, or do staff contribute ideas? How frequently do they revise them? Who monitors them? A **planning system** organises and co-ordinates these activities, thus shaping the quality and value of a plan. Designing and maintaining a suitable planning system is part of the planning task.

One issue is participation – who should take part in making the plan? One approach is to appoint a group of staff specialists to be responsible for producing plans, with or without consultation with the line managers or staff concerned. Others believe the quality and acceptability of the plan will be higher if staff who are familiar with local conditions help to create it.

A **planning system** refers to the processes by which the members of an organisation produce plans, including their frequency and who takes part in the process.

Management in practice   A new planning process at Merck   www.merck.com   FT

In the early 1990s Merck was the world's leading pharmaceutical company, but by 2006 it was ranked only eighth. Dick Clark, the new Chief Executive, was charged with reviving a company: one of his first actions was to make radical changes in the company's planning process. Teams of employees were asked to present the business cases to senior managers to test possible directions for the company – such as whether to build a generic drugs business. This process was vital, said Mr Clark, as it showed the 200 senior executives that Merck would now operate in an atmosphere where assumptions would be openly questioned by anyone. He has also changed the way the company sets its earnings projections. Formerly set by top managers, projections are now set by lower-level teams. 'It wasn't like Dick Clark said "We're going to have double-digit growth, go out and find it!" We tested it and tweaked it . . . but it was legitimate and we believe in it, so let's go public with it. And that's the first time we'd done that as a company.'

Source: Adapted from The man who has to shake up Merck (by Christopher Bowe), *Financial Times*, 27 March 2006, p. 10.

Another issue is how fixed or flexible the planning should be. Some advocate a rational approach to planning, taking care to assemble all relevant data and information, and setting clear, fixed objectives and how they will be met. Others favour 'learning' or 'emergent' approaches. They believe that, in rapidly changing conditions, plans are essentially temporary and provisional, so that managers can adapt them to suit changing circumstances.

Planning and doing may seem like separate activities, and in stable conditions they may be. In volatile conditions, with markets or technologies changing quickly, people conduct them simultaneously. In their study of strategic planning, Whittington *et al.* (2006) conclude that strategising and organising:

> become very similar, or even common: in the heat of the moment practitioners may be unable to distinguish the two. (p. 618)

Jennings (2000) shows how companies change their approach to planning as conditions change. A study of the UK electricity generating company PowerGen (now owned by the German company E.on) traced the evolution of the company's corporate planning process since it was privatised in 1991. It had retained a formal process with a five-year planning horizon, but it is more devolved. A small central team focuses on overall strategy while business units develop local plans, quickly completing the planning cycle. These changes created a more adaptive style of planning which suited the (new) uncertainty of the business.

Figure 6.2
Seven iterative tasks in making a plan

Figure 6.2 shows the seven generic tasks which people can perform when they make a plan. They use them iteratively, often going back to an earlier stage when they find new information that implies, say, that they need to reshape the original goals. And they may miss a stage, or spend too little or too much time on them: the figure only indicates a way of analysing the stages of planning.

6.5   Gathering information

Any plan depends on information – including informal, soft information gained from casual encounters with colleagues, as well as formal analyses of economic and market trends.

Chapter 3 outlined the competitive and general environments, and planners usually begin by drawing on information about these. External sources include government economic and demographic statistics, industry surveys and business intelligence services. Managers also commission market research on, for example, individual shopping patterns, attitudes towards particular firms or brand names and satisfaction with existing products or services.

Management in practice   Inamo – planning the start-up   www.inamo-restaurant.com

Danny Potter, Managing Director, explained the information they needed before they started:

Well, in terms of market research, we looked into what other interactive ordering restaurants and concepts there might be, a lot of research on the world wide web and just going round London to various restaurants. We also looked at good guides which give you a quick summary. Also meeting people in the industry, going to shows and exhibitions are quick ways of learning a great deal. Also a few brainstorming sessions to get feedback on what people thought of the concept – one piece of feedback from that was that this would not fit a formal French dining environment, for example. We came to the conclusion that Oriental fusion was the appropriate cuisine type.

We spent a great deal of time finding the right location. We went through the government statistics database and built a database of our own, analysing demographics of the whole of London. What we found was that a very small area around central London is really where all the buzz happens, where all of the restaurants want to be. And then focused on finding the right location in this area.

Source: Interview with Danny Potter.

SWOT analysis

At a strategic level, planning will usually combine an analysis of external environmental factors with an internal analysis of the organisation's strengths and weaknesses. A **SWOT analysis** does this, bringing together the internal strengths and weaknesses and the external opportunities and threats. Internally, managers would analyse the strengths and weaknesses of the resources within, or available to, the organisation (Grant, 1991) – such as a firm's distinctive research capability or its skill in integrating acquired companies. The external analysis would probably be based on PESTEL and Porter's (1980a) five forces model (see Chapter 3). These tools help to identify the opportunities and threats that people believe could affect the business.

A **SWOT analysis** is a way of summarising the organisation's strengths and weaknesses relative to external opportunities and threats.

While the method appears to be a rational way of gathering information, its usefulness depends on recognising that it is a human representation of reality: participants will differ about the significance of factors – a debate which may itself add value to the process.

Critical success factors analysis

In considering whether to enter a new market, a widely used planning technique is to assess the **critical success factors** in that market. These are the things which customers most value about a product or service: some value price, others quality, others some unusual feature of the product – but in all cases they are things that a company must be able to do well to succeed in that market.

Critical success factors are those aspects of a strategy that *must* be achieved to secure competitive advantage.

Forecasting

Forecasts or predictions are usually based on an analysis of past trends in factors such as input prices (wages, components etc.), sales patterns or demographic trends. In relatively stable environments, people can reasonably assume that past trends will continue, but in uncertain conditions they need alternative assumptions. A new market might support rapid sales growth, whereas in a saturated market (basic foods, paid-for newspapers) it might be more realistic to assume a low or zero growth rate.

Forecasting is big business, with companies selling analyses to business and government, using formal techniques such as time-series analysis, econometric modelling and simulation. These become less useful as uncertainty increases. Grant (2003) reports that oil companies have reduced the resources they spend on forecasting oil demand and prices, preferring to rely on broader assumptions about possible trends.

Sensitivity analysis

One way to test assumptions is to make a **sensitivity analysis** of key variables in a plan. This may assume that the company will attain a 10 per cent share of a market within a year: what will be the effect on the calculations if they secure 5 per cent, or 15 per cent? What if interest rates rise, increasing the cost of financing the projects? Planners can then compare the robustness of the options and assess the relative risks.

A **sensitivity analysis** tests the effect on a plan of several alternative values of the key variables.

Scenario planning

An alternative to forecasting is to consider possible scenarios. **Scenario planning** typically begins by considering how external forces such as the internet, an ageing population or climate change might affect a company's business over the next 5–10 years. Doing so can bring managers new ideas about their environment enabling them to consider previously unthinkable possibilities. Advocates (Van der Heijden, 1996) claim that it encourages managers to develop their awareness of the business environment and of the most critical uncertainties they are likely to face. Few companies use the technique systematically, as it

Scenario planning is an attempt to create coherent and credible alternative stories about the future.

is time consuming and costly. A notable exception is Shell, which began developing the technique in 1971:

> Scenario thinking now underpins the established way of thinking at Shell. It has become a part of the culture, such that people throughout the company, dealing with significant decisions, normally will think in terms of multiple, but equally plausible futures to provide a context for decision making. (Van der Heijden, 1996, p. 21)

The company has a team of 14 staff based in the Netherlands developing scenarios, alongside the company's strategy analysts (*Financial Times*, 30 November 2010).

A combination of PESTEL and five forces analysis should ensure that managers recognise major external factors. Forecasting and scenario planning can help them to consider possible implications for the business.

6.6   Setting goals (or objectives)

A useful plan depends on being clear about the ultimate purpose of a task – whether this concerns the organisation or a unit. This seems obvious, but managers favour action above planning and often spend too little time on this (difficult) step.

Goals (or objectives)

Goals give focus to a task – what will we achieve, by when? Setting goals is difficult, as we need to look beyond a (relatively) known present to an unknown future. Goals provide the reference point for other decisions, and the criteria against which to measure performance. At the business level they include quantified financial objectives – earnings per share, return on shareholders' funds and cash flow. At the project level, the targets will be expressed in other ways – such as the energy performance of a building.

A hierarchy of goals

A way of relating goals to each other is to build them into a hierarchy, in which the overall goals are transformed into more specific goals for different parts of the organisation – such as marketing, finance, operations and human resources. Managers in those areas develop plans setting out the actions they must undertake to meet the overall goal. Figure 6.3 illustrates this by using IKEA's plan to expand in Japan. To meet its planned sales growth, managers decided to open many stores across Asia, of which the first were to be in Japan. That evolved into a plan for their probable location, and then into a precise plan for two near Tokyo. That in turn led managers to develop progressively more detailed plans for the thousands of details that will need to be in good order if the venture is to succeed.

Plans like this need to be flexible, as they will need to change between design and completion. Managers often stress their firm commitment to the highest level goals – but leave staff with more discretion about how to achieve lower level plans.

However convincingly set out, statements of goals only have value if they guide action. Effective goal setting involves balancing multiple goals, considering whether they meet the SMART criteria, and evaluating their likely motivational effects.

Single or multiple goals?

Company statements of goals – whether short- or long-term – are usually expressed in the plural, since a single measure cannot indicate success or failure. Emphasis on one goal, such as growth, ignores another, such as dividends. Managers balance multiple, possibly conflicting goals: Gerry Murphy, who became chief executive of Kingfisher (a UK DIY retailer), recalled:

> Alan Sheppard, my boss at Grand Metropolitan and one of my mentors, used to say that senior management shouldn't have the luxury of single point objectives. Delivering growth

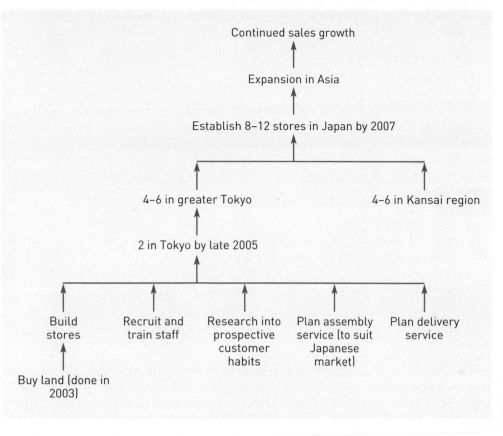

Figure 6.3
Developing a plan for IKEA (Japan)

without returns or returns without growth is not something I find attractive or acceptable. Over time we are going to do both. (*Financial Times*, 28 April 2004, p. 23)

As senior managers try to take account of a range of stakeholders, they balance their diverse interests. This can lead to conflict between **stated goals**, as reflected in public announcements, and the **real goals** – those to which people pay most attention. The latter reflect senior managers' priorities, expressed through what they say and how they reward and discipline managers.

Criteria for assessing goals

The SMART acronym summarises some criteria for assessing a set of goals. What form of each is effective depends on circumstances (specific goals are not necessarily better than directional ones). The list simply offers some measures against which to evaluate a statement of goals.

- **Specific** Does the goal set specific targets? People who are planning a meeting can set specific goals for what they hope to achieve, such as:

   By the end of the meeting we will have convinced them to withdraw their current proposal, and to have set a date (within the next two weeks) at which we will start to develop an alternative plan.

   Having a clear statement of what the meeting (or any other activity in a plan) is intended to achieve helps people to focus effort.

- **Measurable** Some goals may be quantified ('increase sales of product X by 5 per cent a year over the next three years') but others, equally important, are more qualitative ('to offer a congenial working environment'). Quantitative goals are not more useful than qualitative ones – what can be measured is not necessarily important. What matters is that goals are defined precisely enough to measure progress towards them.

Stated goals are those which are prominent in company publications and websites.

Real goals are those to which people pay most attention.

- **Attainable** Goals should be challenging, but not unreasonably difficult. If people perceive a goal as unrealistic, they will not be committed. Equally, goals should not be too easy, as this too undermines motivation. Goal-setting theory (see Chapter 13, Section 13.5) predicts the motivational consequences of goal setting.
- **Rewarded** People need to see that attaining a goal will bring a reward – this gives meaning and helps ensure commitment.
- **Timed** Does the goal specify the time by which it will be achieved, and is that also a reasonable and acceptable standard?

6.7 Identifying actions and communicating the plan

This part of the planning process involves deciding what needs to be done, who will do it and communicating that. In a small activity like planning a project in a club, this would just mean listing the tasks and dividing them clearly among a few able and willing members. At the other extreme, Ford's plan to build a new car plant in China probably runs to several volumes.

Identifying what needs to be done – and by whom

Figure 1.3 (reproduced as Figure 6.4) provides a model to help envisage the implications of a goal, by enabling managers to ask what, if any, changes do they need to make to each element? If the goal is to launch a new product, the plan could identify which parts of the organisation will be affected (structure), what investment is needed (finance), how production will fit with existing lines (business processes) and so on. Computer projects often fail because planners pay too much attention to the technological aspects and too little to contextual elements such as structure, culture and people (Boddy *et al.*, 2009a). Each main heading will require further actions that people can identify and assign.

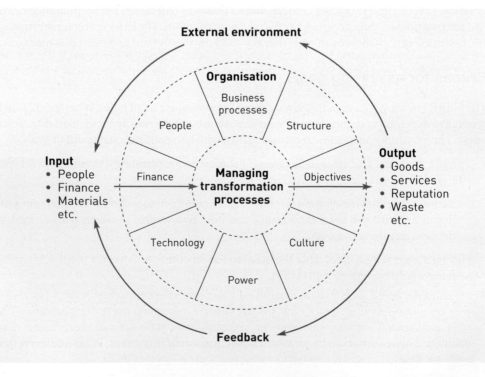

Figure 6.4
Possible action
areas in a plan

Communicating the plan

In a small organisation or where the plan deals with only one area, communication in any formal way is probably unnecessary. Equally, those who have been involved in developing the objectives and plans will be well aware of it. However, in larger enterprises managers will probably invest time and effort in communicating both the objectives and the actions required throughout the areas affected. They do this to:

- Ensure that everyone understands the plan;
- Allow them to resolve any confusion and ambiguity;
- Communicate the judgements and assumptions that underlie the plan; and
- Ensure that activities around the organisation are co-ordinated in practice as well as on paper.

6.8   Implementing plans and monitoring results

However good the plan, nothing worthwhile happens until people implement it by making visible, physical changes to the organisation and the way people work within it. Many managers find this the most challenging part of the process – when plans, however well developed, are brought into contact with current ways of working. The plan then meets organisational and environmental obstacles – possibly showing that some of the assumptions in the plan are wrong.

Organisations are slower to change than plans are to prepare – so events may overtake the plan. Miller *et al.* (2004) tracked the long term outcomes of 150 strategic plans to establish how managers put them into action and how that affected performance. They defined implementation as

> all the processes and outcomes which accrue to a strategic decision once authorisation has been given to . . . put the decision into practice. (Miller *et al.*, 2004, p. 203)

Their intention was to identify the conditions in which implementation occurs, the managerial activities involved in putting plans into practice, and the extent to which they achieved the objectives. They concluded that success was heavily influenced by:

- managers' experience of the issue, and
- **organisational readiness** for a change.

> Having relevant experience of what has to be done . . . enables managers to assess the objectives [and to] specify the tasks and resource implications appropriately, leading [those affected to accept the process]. (p. 206)

Organisational readiness refers to the extent to which staff are able to specify objectives, tasks and resource requirements of a plan appropriately, leading to acceptance.

Readiness means a receptive organisational climate that enables managers to implement the change within a positive environment.

The statistical results were illustrated by cases which showed, for example, how managers in a successful company were able to implement a plan to upgrade their computer systems because they had *experience* of many similar changes. They were

> able to set targets, detail what needed doing and allocate the resources . . . That is, they could plan and control the implementation effectively. (p. 209)

In another illustration, a regional brewer extending into the London area had no directly relevant experience, and so was not able to set a specific plan. But people in the organisation were very *receptive* to new challenges, and could implement the move with little formal planning.

The authors concluded that the activities of planning do not in themselves lead to success, but are a means for gaining acceptance of what has to be done. Planning helps by inducing confidence in the process, leading to high levels of acceptability:

> Planning is a necessary part of this approach to success, but it is not sufficient in itself. (p. 210)

The final stage in planning is to set up a system that allows people to monitor progress towards the goals. This happens at all levels of planning – from a project manager monitoring and controlling the progress of a discrete project to a board committee monitoring the progress of a broad strategic change that affects many parts of the business – such as integrating an acquisition or entering a new line of business. This is sometimes called a programme, and monitoring then focuses on the interdependencies between many smaller specific projects.

Project plans define and display every task and activity, but someone managing a programme of linked projects would soon become swamped with such detail. The programme manager needs to maintain a quick-to-understand snapshot of the programme. This should show progress to date, the main events being planned, interdependencies, issues and expected completion dates. This also helps the programme manager to communicate with senior executives and project managers.

Activity 6.2   What is 'planning'?

Having read the chapter, make brief notes summarising the main planning issues affecting the organisation.

- What types of plan do managers in the company make? (See Sections 6.2 and 6.3.)
- Can you describe their planning processes? (Refer to Section 6.4.)
- Which planning techniques did they use to gather information? (Refer to Section 6.5.)

Compare what you have found with other students on your course.

Summary

1 **Explain the purposes of planning and the content of different types of plan**
   - Effective plans can clarify direction, motivate people, use resources efficiently and allow people to measure progress towards objectives.
   - Plans can be at strategic, tactical and operational levels and, in new businesses, people prepare business plans to secure capital. Strategic business units also prepare plans relatively independently of the parent. There are also special-purpose or project plans, and standing plans. All can be either specific or directional in nature.

2 **Compare alternative planning processes and say when each may be most suitable**
   - Plans can be formal/rational/top-down in nature, or they can be adaptable and flexible (logical incrementalism). Firms in volatile conditions are likely to use several methods.

3 **Outline the seven iterative steps in planning and describe techniques used in each**
   - Recycling through the tasks of gathering information, developing a mission, setting goals, identifying actions and allocating resources, implementing plans, monitoring progress and evaluating results.
   - Planners draw information from the general and competitive environments using tools such as Porter's five forces analysis. They can do this within the framework of a SWOT analysis, and also use forecasting, sensitivity analysis, critical success factors and scenario planning techniques.

4 **Use theory to evaluate the quality of the goals stated in a plan**
   - Goals can also be evaluated in terms of whether they are specific, measurable, attainable, rewarded and timed.

5   Use a framework to evaluate whether a plan is sufficiently comprehensive
   ● The 'wheel' provides a model for recalling the likely areas in an organisation which a plan should cover, indicating the likely ripple effects of change in one area on others.

Review questions

1   What types of planning do you do in your personal life? Describe them in terms of whether they are (a) strategic or operational, (b) short- or long-term, (c) specific or directional.

2   What are four benefits that people in organisations may gain from planning?

3   What are the main sources of information that managers can use in planning? What models can they use to structure this information?

4   What are SMART goals?

5   In what ways can a goal be motivational? What practical things can people do in forming plans that take account of goal-setting theory?

6   What is meant by the term 'hierarchy of goals', and how can the idea help people to build a consistent plan?

7   Explain the term 'organisational readiness', and how people can use the idea in developing a plan that is likely to work.

8   What are the main ways to monitor progress on a plan, and why is this a vital task in planning?

Further reading

Sahlman, W. A. (1997), 'How to write a great business plan', *Harvard Business Review*, vol. 75, no. 4, pp. 98–108.

   Valuable guidance by an experienced investor, relevant to start-ups and established businesses.

Weblinks

These websites have appeared in the chapter:

   www.maersk.com
   www.ba.com
   www.merck.com
   www.inamo-restaurant.com
   www.crossrail.co.uk

Visit two of the sites in the list, and navigate to the pages dealing with corporate news, or investor relations.

● What planning issues are managers in the company likely to be dealing with?

● What kind of environment are they working in, and how may that affect their planning processes?

 Annotated weblinks, multiple choice questions and other useful resources can be found on **www.pearsoned.co.uk/boddy**

Case study   Crossrail   www.crossrail.co.uk

Crossrail is a new railway for London and the south east of England which will connect the City, Canary Wharf, the West End and Heathrow Airport to commuter areas east and west of the capital. It aims to be a world-class, affordable railway, with high frequency, convenient and accessible services across the capital. The plans are intended to:

- relieve congestion on many Underground and rail lines;
- provide new connections and new services;
- bring modern trains; and
- provide six new stations in central London.

It will add 10 per cent to London's overall transport capacity and provide 40 per cent of the extra rail capacity London needs. Main construction of the railway began in 2010, with services commencing in 2018. Crossrail will make travelling in the area easier and quicker and reduce crowding on London's transport network. It will operate with main line size trains, each carrying more than 1500 passengers.

It is the largest civil engineering project in the UK and the largest single addition to the London transport network for over 50 years. It will run 118 km from Maidenhead and Heathrow in the west, through new twin-bore, 21 km tunnels under Central London out to Shenfield and Abbey Wood in the east, joining the Great Western and Great Eastern railway networks.

The project has a long history – it was first proposed in 1990, but amidst considerable opposition from other players it was cancelled in 1996. Support for building the line continued to grow, as many saw it a major contribution to solving London's transport problems: the company had wide support from businesses and from business organisations such as the CBI, London First and London Chamber of Commerce and Industry.

Political conditions changed again, and Royal Assent was given to the Crossrail Act in July 2008, giving the company authority to build the railway, and in December 2008 the Government and the Mayor of London signed the key funding agreements for Crossrail. The cost (estimated at £14.8 billion) will be met by UK Government, Transport for London and London businesses. Passengers will contribute towards the debt raised during construction by Transport for London and Network Rail will pay for using the line to run train services. Other beneficiaries will also contribute to the cost, including The City of

By kind permission, Crossrail.

London Corporation, British Airports Authority and property developers such as Canary Wharf Group.

By March 2010, the plan began to turn into reality as many of the smaller elements were implemented. For example, the company announced the award of contracts for what it calls enabling work such as various pieces of complex demolition work at several stations and their surrounding area. The company also announced that the Learning & Skills Council had agreed to provide £5 million towards the cost of a new tunnelling and underground construction academy. A senior manager said:

> This is great news for the programme and great news for the tunnelling and underground construction industry. This decision means we can now progress our plans to build this fantastic training facility, which the industry so urgently needs. (private communication)

In 2009, the company published its outline plans for the station building and tunnelling work to be done – making it clear that as detailed design and development of the scheme progressed there would be increasing certainty over the exact times that works will start and finish at each location.

The two 21 km tunnels will present a particular challenge as they run at depths of up to 36m below the busy streets of London. In doing so, they will weave between existing underground railway tunnels, sewers and building foundations. In early 2011, the company indicated that the choice of tunnelling boring machines to use would depend on local circumstances. They estimated that the tunnelling work and the excavation of new stations would create 6 million tonnes of material: they plan to remove most of this by moving it along the tunnels to disposal sites, so avoiding as far as possible the need for lorry movements through central London.

At some locations, enabling works (such as the diversion of utilities like gas mains and demolition of existing buildings) will need to take place before main works. The sites may also be required after main works, for example to support fitting out of stations and tunnels. Enabling works for the station at Tottenham Court Road were planned to start in January 2009, construction in early 2010, and the works would be completed in 2016.

Work on stations and tracks on the existing surface railway to be served by Crossrail will be carried out by Network Rail.

Meanwhile, work was progressing on the timetable for the services to be offered. The unusual complexity of this task arises because the new services will, for much of their routes, run on the existing railway lines, so they will need to fit into the existing timetables. Crossrail is therefore working closely with Network Rail and freight and passenger companies to create a timetable for the new services. They have carried out extensive simulation of future services on the railway, showing that a high level of punctuality can be achieved with at least 24 trains an hour running in each direction at peak times

Source: Company website and other published sources.

Questions

Visit the Crossrail website (see above).

1 What are the main items of recent news about the progress of the project?

2 What types of plan is the company likely to have made? (See Section 6.3.)

3 What planning processes will it probably have used? (Refer to Section 6.4.)

4 Which of the planning tools mentioned in Sections 6.5, 6.6 and 6.7 are they likely to have used?

CHAPTER 7
DECISION-MAKING

Learning outcomes

When you have read this chapter you should be able to:

1. Outline the (iterative) stages of the decision-making process and the tasks required in each
2. Explain, and give examples of, programmed and non-programmed decisions
3. Distinguish decision-making conditions of certainty, risk, uncertainty and ambiguity
4. Contrast rational, administrative, political and garbage can decision models
5. Give examples of common sources of bias in decisions
6. Explain the contribution of Vroom and Yetton, and of Irving Janis, to our understanding of decision-making
7. Use ideas from the chapter to comment on the management issues in the IKEA case study

Activity 7.1   **What does 'decision-making' mean?**

Before reading the chapter, write some notes on what you think 'decision-making' means. Choose the organisation or people who may be able to help you to learn about the topic. You may find it helpful to discuss it with a manager you know, or use an activity you have managed.

- Identify a decision to use for this activity, and describe it briefly.
- Was it an easy decision to make, or complex and messy? Why was that?
- Can you identify the conditions in which people made the decision?
- Do they believe they made it through a logical, rational process, or by some other route?

Keep your notes as you will be able to use them later.

7.1   Introduction

The chapter case study outlines the recent history of one of Europe's biggest and most successful companies, which is now a global player in the home furnishing market. To develop the business from a Swedish general retailer to its present position, senior managers at IKEA had to decide where to allocate time, effort and other resources. Over the years, their decisions paid off and they now face new issues, such as how to attract customers and well-qualified staff against competition from other companies. They also face critical comments from environmental campaigners about their sources of timber, and need to decide how to respond. How they do so will shape IKEA's future. A constant dilemma for managers is how much to base decisions on quantitative, structured data – 'evidence' – and how much to rely on qualitative, unstructured ideas and hunches – 'judgement'. Both approaches have their place – the skill is to recognise the conditions when each is suitable.

The performance of every organisation reflects (as well as luck and good fortune) the decisions which people at all levels of an organisation make as they see problems that need attention, or ideas they can use. Resources are limited, there are many demands and people have different goals. Choices relate to all aspects of the management task – inputs (how to raise capital, who to employ), outputs (what products to make, how to distribute them) and transformations (how to deliver a new service, how to manage the finances). In 2011, Nokia decided to form an alliance with Microsoft to develop a new mobile phone operating system, rather than with Google – which would have allowed it to use the successful Android system. This was a critical decision, with significant risks for the company, which will affect whether it adds sufficient value to ensure survival. Choice brings tension as we worry about 'what if' we had selected the other option. Speed is sometimes more important than certainty – the chief executive of Eli Lilly (pharmaceuticals) recalled that when he took over, he realised the company needed to make decisions more quickly:

> We've had the luxury of moving at our own pace. Sometimes you can think for so long that your competitors pass you by. We need to act with 80 per cent, not 99.5 per cent, of the information.

He gives the example of a biotech company for which a rival company made a take-over offer, triggering a rapid and ultimately successful counter-bid from Lilly.

> We had them on our radar, and we had no premonition the other company would bid. But we were well-prepared and, within a couple of days, we convinced ourselves that we should get into the process. (From an article by John Lechleiter, *Financial Times*, 6 April 2009)

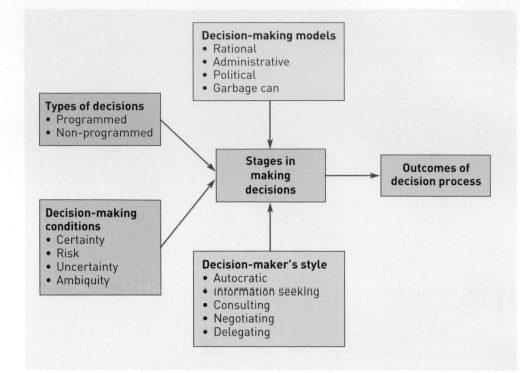

Figure 7.1
Overview of
decision-making
in organisations

Figure 7.1 illustrates the themes of the chapter, showing that decision-making involves:

- identifying the type of decision;
- identifying the conditions surrounding the decision;
- using one or more models to guide the approach;
- selecting a decision-making style; and
- working through the stages in making a decision.

The chapter outlines the iterative steps in any decision process, and explains the difference between 'programmed' and 'non-programmed' decisions. It identifies four 'conditions' surrounding a decision, compares four models of the process, shows how bias affects decisions and finally examines how managers can shape the context of decision-making.

7.2 Stages in making decisions

A **decision** is a specific commitment to action (usually a commitment of resources).

A **decision** is a specific commitment to action (usually a commitment of resources). People make such choices at all levels – some affecting the business significantly (Barclays Bank deciding during the 2008 banking crisis to raise capital privately, rather than accept support from the UK Government – The Royal Bank of Scotland and HBOS made the opposite decision). Others affect local operations – whether to recruit staff, how much to spend on advertising next week.

Management in practice   Deciding which treatment to provide   www.nice.org.uk

Expenditure on health care is limited by competing demands for public funds, while scientific advances bring new treatments to prolong life – and so increase the demand for services from an aging population.

This means that managers at all levels in the health service decide how to ration care; which patients or conditions should receive treatment, and which not. People at the centre do most of this implicitly, when they set budgets for the units delivering care: their managers must then ration care to stay within budget. Others are made explicitly, by specifying criteria about which patients, or which conditions, are eligible for treatment. In the UK the National Institute for Clinical Excellence (NICE) decides which drugs or technologies are cost effective. It then gives explicit guidance to hospitals on whether, and in what circumstances, they should use them to treat patients.

The committees making these decisions include representatives of medical and patient interests, as well as those of the pharmaceutical industries. They make their (sometimes controversial) decisions public.

Source: Published information, and NICE website.

Such choices follow from a wider process of **decision-making** – which includes identifying problems, opportunities and possible solutions, and involves effort before and after the actual choice. In deciding whether to select Jean, Bob or Rasul for a job the manager would, among other things, have to:

> **Decision-making** is the process of identifying problems and opportunities and then resolving them.

- identify the need for a new member of staff;
- persuade their boss to authorise the budget;
- decide where to advertise the post;
- interview candidates;
- select the preferred candidate;
- decide whether or not to agree to their request for a better deal; and
- arrange their induction into the job so that they work effectively.

At each of these stages, the manager may go back in the process to think again, or to deal with another set of decisions – such as whom to include on the selection committee. In Nokia's case the choice of model would follow decisions about the target market and basic design concept, and lead to decisions about production volumes and price. A manager makes small but potentially significant decisions all the time – which of several urgent jobs to deal with next, whose advice to seek, which report to read, which customer to call. These shape the way people use their time, and the issues they decide are sufficiently important to earn a place on the agenda.

As we make decisions we attend to the tasks shown in Figure 7.2 – the arrows showing the iterative nature of the process, as we move back and forwards between the tasks. As we move through an activity we find new information, reconsider what we are doing, go back

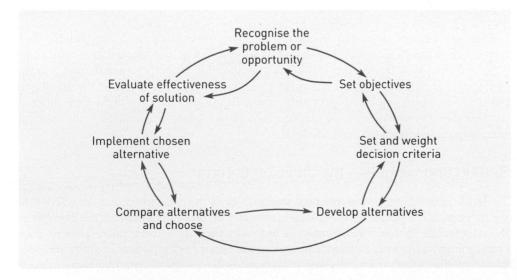

Figure 7.2
Stages in making decisions

a stage or two and perhaps decide on a different route. People may miss a stage, or pay too much attention to one topic and too little to others. Giving just enough time to each task is a decision-making skill.

Recognising a problem or opportunity

A **problem** is a gap between an existing and a desired state of affairs.

An **opportunity** is the chance to do something not previously expected.

People make decisions when they become aware of a **problem** – a gap between an existing and a desired state of affairs, or an **opportunity** – the chance to do something new.

An example to illustrate the steps is that of a manager who needs to decide whether to buy new laptops for the sales team. They say their present machines are too slow and waste time – and are presenting the manager with a clear problem.

Most situations are more ambiguous, and people will have different views about the significance of an event or a piece of information: labelling a problem as significant is a subjective, possibly contentious matter. Before a problem (or opportunity) gets onto the agenda, enough people have to be aware of it and feel sufficient pressure to act. Managers at Microsoft were slow to realise that Linux software was a serious threat to their growth, and this delay lost valuable time.

Management in practice   The opportunity for Iris   www.irisnation.com

Ian Millner explains the decision to start Iris:

We started about ten years ago, and we were essentially a group of friends all working within a really large advertising agency group, and we just decided that we could do it better. And then I guess one thing led to another and before we knew it we were having conversations with one of the clients that we had at the time which was Eriksson. Once we had that conversation Iris was quite quickly born, and then over a period of months myself and those friends, we sort of left the building and set Iris up.

I think without doubt the biggest success that we've had is around momentum and being able to keep the momentum high and continue to change as we've gone from being a small company which is just defined by a group of friends, to a large company that is global, expanding really quickly and driving the strategic agenda of a lot of clients all over the world. We've always had a strong kind of entrepreneurial streak, we've always been willing to try things and learn quickly.

Source: Interview with Ian Millner.

Managers become aware of a problem as they compare existing conditions with the state they desire. If things are not as they should be – in the laptop example, the sales team complain that their slow laptops prevent them doing their job properly – then there is a problem. People are only likely to act if they feel pressure – such as a sales person threatening to leave, or a customer complaining. Pressure comes from many sources – and people differ in whether they pay attention: some react quickly, others ignore uncomfortable information and postpone a difficult (to them) decision.

Setting and weighting the decision criteria

Decision criteria define the factors that are relevant in making a decision.

To decide between options people need **decision criteria** – the factors that are relevant to the decision. Until people set these, they cannot choose between options: in the example of the sales team's laptops, criteria could include usefulness of features, price, delivery, warranty, compatibility with other systems, ease of use and many more. Some criteria are more important than others and the decision process needs to represent this in some way – perhaps by assigning 100 points between the factors depending on their relative importance. We can measure some of these criteria (price or delivery) quite objectively, while others (features, ease of use) are subjective.

Like problem recognition, setting criteria is subjective: people vary in the factors they wish to include, and the weights they give them. They may also have private and unexpressed criteria – such as 'will cause least trouble', 'will do what the boss wants', 'will help my career'. Changing the criteria or their relative weights will change the decision – so the manager in the laptop case has to decide whether to set and weight the criteria themselves, or to invite the views of the reps.

Developing alternatives

Another task is to identify solutions: in the laptop case this would be a list of available brands. In more complex problems the alternatives need to be developed – but how many and at what cost? Too few will limit choice, too many will be costly. If we have too many options we experience stress, frustration and become anxious that we might make the wrong choice.

Comparing alternatives and making a choice

As in daily life, management decisions need a system for comparing and choosing. Since criteria and weights are subjective, several people making a choice can easily end in argument.

Figure 7.3 illustrates the tasks in making a decision through a simple personal example. Although superficially simple, people find it difficult to set criteria, which are often subjective and thus open to different interpretations – especially if several people take part.

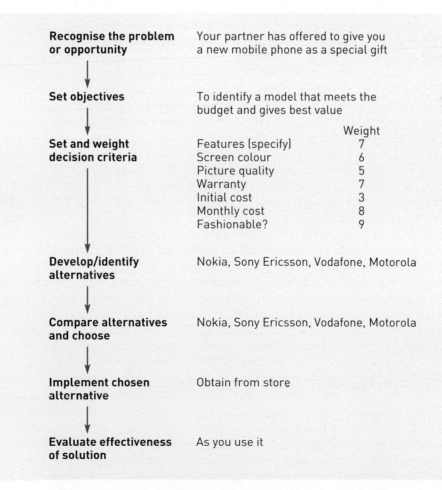

Recognise the problem or opportunity	Your partner has offered to give you a new mobile phone as a special gift	
Set objectives	To identify a model that meets the budget and gives best value	
Set and weight decision criteria		Weight
	Features (specify)	7
	Screen colour	6
	Picture quality	5
	Warranty	7
	Initial cost	3
	Monthly cost	8
	Fashionable?	9
Develop/identify alternatives	Nokia, Sony Ericsson, Vodafone, Motorola	
Compare alternatives and choose	Nokia, Sony Ericsson, Vodafone, Motorola	
Implement chosen alternative	Obtain from store	
Evaluate effectiveness of solution	As you use it	

Figure 7.3
Illustrating the decision-making tasks – a new mobile phone

A **decision tree** helps someone to make a choice by progressively eliminating options as additional criteria or events are added to the tree.

Another way to structure a situation in which there are several alternative actions is to draw a **decision tree**. This helps to assess the relative suitability of the options by assessing them against identified criteria – successively eliminating the options as each relevant factor is introduced. The main challenge in using the technique is to identify the logical sequence of intermediate decisions and how they relate to each other.

Implementing the choice

In the laptop case this is a simple matter if the manager has conducted the process well. In bigger decisions this will be a much more problematic stage as it is here that the decision commits scarce resources – and perhaps meets new objections. Thus implementing often takes longer than expected, and depends on people making other supportive decisions to release resources or change methods. It also shows the effects of the decision-making process: if the promoter involved others in the decision, they may be more willing to co-operate with the consequential changes.

Evaluating the decision

The final stage is evaluation – looking back to see if the decision has resolved the problem, and what can be learned. It is a form of control, which people are often reluctant to do formally, preferring to turn their attention to the next urgent job, rather than reflect on the past. That choice inhibits their ability to learn from experience.

Having given this simplified overview of the process, the following sections outline different types of decisions, and some models that seek to explain how people make them.

7.3   Programmed and non-programmed decisions

Many decisions which managers face are straightforward and need not involve intense discussion; others can be deferred until there is more information to make the decision clear.

Programmed decisions

A **programmed (or structured) decision** is a repetitive decision that can be handled by a routine approach.

A **procedure** is a series of related steps to deal with a structured problem.

A **rule** sets out what someone can or cannot do in a given situation.

A **policy** is a guideline that establishes some general principles for making a decision.

Programmed (or structured) decisions (Simon, 1960) deal with problems that are familiar, and where the information required is easy to define and obtain – the situation is well structured. If a store manager notices that a product is selling more than expected there will be a simple, routine procedure for deciding how much extra to order from the supplier. Decisions are structured to the extent that they arise frequently and can be dealt with routinely by following an established **procedure** – a series of related steps, often set out in a manual, to deal with a structured problem. They may also reach a decision by using an established **rule**, which sets out what someone can or cannot do in a given situation. They may also refer to a **policy** – a guideline that establishes some general principles for making a decision.

People make programmed decisions to resolve recurring problems – to reorder supplies when stocks drop below a defined level, to set the qualifications required for a job, to decide whether to lend money to a bank customer. Once managers formulate procedures, rules or policies, others can usually make the decisions. Computers handle many decisions of this type – the checkout systems in supermarkets calculate the items sold and order new stock.

Non-programmed decisions

A **non-programmed (unstructured) decision** is a unique decision that requires a custom-made solution when information is lacking or unclear.

Simon (1960) also observed that people make **non-programmed (unstructured) decisions** to deal with situations that are novel or unusual, and so require a unique solution. The issue has not arisen in quite that form, and the information required is unclear, vague or open to several interpretations. Major management decisions are of this type – such as the choice which managers at Marks and Spencer faced in deciding whether to launch their (2010) programme to become the world's most sustainable retailer by 2015. This will bring many benefits to the environment and the company, but will be challenging and time-consuming to introduce as it involves changing the way suppliers work. While the company will have done a lot of research before making the decision, no one has made this commitment before, and it cannot be sure how customers and competitors will respond. Most issues of strategy are of this type, because they involve great uncertainty and many interests.

Management in practice   Inamo – choosing a designer www.inamo-restaurant.com

Inamo is a London restaurant where customers place their order directly to the kitchen from an interactive ordering system on their table. Selecting the designer for such a novel idea was a big step. Noel Hunwick, Chief Operating Officer:

> An early and crucial decision we had to make was to select our interior design company. The way we've always worked is to make sure that we always [have] options from which to choose, so based on recommendations and on web research, and going to various shows and events, I put together a large portfolio of work . . . to get a rough price per square foot that these companies generally charged.
>
> We then selected eight companies to give us a full design brief, and then cut that down to three – who came out with three entirely different concepts, so I think that then allowed us to narrow it down to two and have a final showdown. [Given that our ordering system was so novel] I think that was a crucial decision – we had to make sure it wasn't an overload on the customer, so I think that was a very delicate and difficult business decision. We always want options. Every single decision, whether it's the cleaning company that we use, everything, we want three options at least. I think that's very important.

Source: Interview with Noel Hunwick.

People need to deal with programmed and non-programmed decisions in different ways. The former are amenable to procedures, routines, rules and quantitative analytical techniques such as those associated with operational research (see Chapter 2). They are also suitable for resolution by modern information systems. Non-programmed decisions depend on judgement and intuition.

The type of decision people make reflects their level in the organisation. Those lower in the hierarchy typically deal with routine, structured problems by using set rules. As people move up the hierarchy they face more unstructured decisions – junior staff pass decisions that do not fit the rules to someone above them, while the latter pass routine matters to subordinates.

Many decisions have elements of each type – non-programmed decisions will usually contain some issues that can be handled in a programmed way.

Dependent or independent

Another way to categorise decisions is in terms of their links to other decisions. People make decisions in a historical and social context and so are influenced by past and possible future decisions and the influence of other parts of the organisation. Legacy computer systems (the result of earlier decisions) frequently constrain how quickly a company can adopt new systems. Some decisions have few implications beyond their immediate area, but others have significant ripples around the organisation. Changes in technology, for example, usually require consistent, supportive changes in structures and processes if they are to be effective – but decisions on these areas are harder to make than those affecting the technology. People managing a local unit may find that wider company policy limits the scope of the decisions they can make.

Decisions arise within a wider context, and the conditions in this context, as measured by the degree of **certainty**, **risk**, **uncertainty** and **ambiguity** materially affect the decision process.

Certainty describes the situation when all the information the decision-maker needs is available.

Risk refers to situations in which the decision-maker is able to estimate the likelihood of the alternative outcomes.

Uncertainty is when people are clear about their goals, but have little information about which course of action is most likely to succeed.

Ambiguity is when people are uncertain about their goals and how best to achieve them.

Certainty

Certainty is when the decision-maker has all the information they need and are fully informed about the costs and benefits of each alternative. A company treasurer wanting to invest reserve funds can readily compare comparative rates of interest from several banks and calculate exactly the return from each. Few decisions are that certain, and most contain risk and/or uncertainty.

Risk

Risk refers to situations in which the decision-maker can estimate the likelihood of the alternative outcomes, possibly using statistical methods. Banks have developed tools to assess credit risk, and so reduce the risk of borrower not repaying the loan. The questions on an application form for a loan (home ownership, time at this address, employer's name etc.) enable the bank to assess the risk of lending money to that person. This allows them to decide on requests more efficiently and cheaply, and to increase the amount of money they lend – but as the financial crisis showed, this does not avoid the risk that some borrowers cannot repay the loan.

Uncertainty

Uncertainty means that people know what they wish to achieve, but do not have enough information about alternatives and future events to estimate the risk confidently. Factors that may affect the outcomes of deciding to launch a new product (future growth in the market, changes in customer interests, competitors' actions) are difficult to predict.

Managers at GSK (**www.gsk.com**), the pharmaceutical group, experience great uncertainty in deciding how to allocate research funds. Scientists who wish to develop a new range of drugs have to persuade the board to divert resources to their project. Uncertainties include the fact that the science is evolving rapidly, other companies are making competing discoveries, and it will be many years before the company receives income from the research results (if any).

Ambiguity

Ambiguity describes a situation in which the intended goals are unclear, and so the alternative ways of reaching them are equally fluid. Ambiguity is by far the most difficult decision situation. Students experience ambiguity if their teacher creates student groups, asks each to work on a project – but gives them unclear guidance on the topic, direction or completion date. Ambiguous problems are often associated with rapidly changing circumstances, and unclear links between the elements in the decision. An example is the conflicts which sometimes arise in EADS (**www.eads.com**), the parent company of Airbus, where there is tension between French and German shareholders. A decision to launch a project to build a new fleet of aircraft to compete with Boeing's Dreamliner was delayed while managers tried to decide how to divide the work between operations in France, Germany, Spain and the UK: national political conflicts at the highest level delayed the managers' choice.

7.5 Decision-making models

James Thompson (1967) distinguished decisions on two dimensions – agreement or disagreement over goals, and the beliefs that decision-makers hold about the relationship between cause and effect. A decision can be mapped on these two dimensions – whether or not there is agreement on goals, and how certain people are about the consequences of their decisions. Figure 7.4 shows these, and an approach to making decisions that seems best suited to each cell.

Computational strategy – rational model

The **rational model of decision-making** is based on economic assumptions. Traditional economic models suggested that the role of a manager was to maximise the economic return to the firm, and that they did this by making decisions on economically rational criteria. The assumptions underlying this model are that the decision-maker:

*The **rational model of decision-making** assumes that people make consistent choices to maximise economic value within specified constraints.*

- aims for goals that are known and agreed, and that the problem is structured;
- strives for conditions of certainty, gathering complete information and calculating the likely results of each alternative;
- selects the alternative that will maximise economic returns;
- is rational and logical in assigning values, setting preferences and evaluating alternatives.

The rational model is normative, in that it defines how a decision-maker should act – it does not describe how managers make decisions. It aims to help decision-makers to act more rationally, rather than rely solely on intuition and personal preferences and is most valuable for programmed decisions where there is little conflict. Where the information required is available and people can agree the criteria for choice, the approach works well.

Developments in technology enable computers to take some decisions traditionally made by people, using what are known as decision support systems. These work best when decisions require rapid analysis of large quantities of data, with complex relationships – such as in power supply, transport management and banking. Automated decision systems:

sense online data or conditions, apply codified knowledge or logic and make decisions – all with minimal amounts of human intervention. (Davenport and Harris, 2005, p. 84)

Table 7.1 gives examples.

	Agreement on goals?	
	High	*Low*
Certainty	I Computational strategy Rational model	III Compromise strategy Political model
Uncertainty	II Judgemental strategy Administrative, incremental and intuitional models	IV Inspirational strategy Garbage-can model

Beliefs about cause-and-effect relationships

Figure 7.4 Conditions favouring different decision processes

Source: Huczynski and Buchanan (2007, p. 754).

Table 7.1 Examples of automated decision systems

Type of decision	Examples of automated decision system
Solution configuration	Mobile phone operators who offer a range of features and service options: an automated programme can weigh all the options, including information about the customer, and present the most suitable option to the customer.
Yield optimisation	Widely used in the airline industry to increase revenue by enabling companies to vary prices depending on demand. Spreading to other transport companies, hotels, retailing and entertainment.
Fraud detection	Credit card companies, online gaming companies and tax authorities use automated screening techniques to detect and deter possible fraud.
Operational control	Power companies use automated systems to sense changes in the physical environment (power supply, temperature or rainfall), and respond rapidly to changes in demand, by redirecting supplies across the network.

Source: Based on Davenport and Harris (2005).

Such applications support managers who face decisions that require rational methods. When decisions are more controversial, the rational approach itself will not be sufficient.

Judgemental strategies – administrative, incremental and intuitional

Administrative models

The **administrative model of decision-making** describes how people make decisions in uncertain, ambiguous situations.

Bounded rationality is behaviour that is rational within a decision process which is limited (bounded) by an individual's ability to process information.

Satisficing is the acceptance by decision-makers of the first solution that is 'good enough'.

Simon's (1960) **administrative model of decision-making** aims to describe how managers make decisions in situations which are uncertain and ambiguous. Many management problems are unstructured and not suitable for the precise quantitative analysis implied by the rational model. People rely heavily on their judgement to resolve such issues.

Simon based the model on two concepts – bounded rationality and satisficing. **Bounded rationality** expresses the fact that people have mental limits, or boundaries, on how rational they can be. While organisations and their environments are complex and uncertain, people can process only a limited amount of information. This constrains our ability to operate in the way envisaged by the rational model, which we deal with by **satisficing** – we choose the first solution that is 'good enough'. While searching for other options may eventually produce a better return, identifying and evaluating them costs more than the benefits. Suppose we are in a strange city and need coffee before a meeting. We look for the first acceptable coffee shop that will do the job – we satisfice. In a similar fashion, managers may seek alternatives only until they find one they believe will work. Richard Cyert, James March and Herbert Simon (Simon, 1960; Cyert and March, 1963; March, 1988) developed an influential model of decision-making. It is sometimes referred to as the behavioural theory of decision-making since it treats decision-making as an aspect of human behaviour. Also referred to as the administrative model, it recognises that in the real world people are restricted in their decision processes and therefore have to accept less than perfect solutions. It introduced the concepts of 'bounded rationality' and 'satisficing'.

The administrative model focuses on the human and organisational factors that influence decisions. It is more realistic than the rational model for non-programmed, ambiguous decisions. According to the administrative model, managers:

- have goals that are vague and conflicting, and are unable to reach a consensus on what to do;
- have different levels of interest in the choices to be made, and interpret information subjectively;
- rarely use rational procedures in a sufficiently comprehensive way;
- limit their search for alternatives; and
- usually settle for a satisficing rather than a maximising solution – one that is 'good enough'.

The administrative model is descriptive, aiming to show how managers make decisions in complex situations rather than stating how they *should* make them.

Management in practice   Satisficing in e-health projects

Boddy *et al.* (2009b) studied the implementation of several 'e-health' projects, in which modern information and communication technologies assist clinicians in delivering care. Such methods offer significant savings in patient travel time, and in the better use of scarce consultants' time, especially in remote parts of the country. Despite this, uptake of e-health systems has been slow.

To secure the fullest benefits, managers and staff also need to make significant changes throughout the organisation. The processes for interacting with patients change, as does the work of consultants, nurses and other medical staff. Many small pilot projects are producing modest benefits, but nothing like those which could flow from a national programme. A reasonable conclusion is that managers have unconsciously decided to satisfice – they can show they are trying the new methods and producing benefits: to secure the full potential would require more effort than they are willing to give.

Source: Boddy *et al.* (2009b).

Incremental models

Charles Lindblom (1959) developed what he termed an **incremental model**, which he observed people using when they were uncertain about the consequences of their choice. In the rational model these are known, but people face many decisions where they cannot know the effects. Lindblom built on Simon's idea of bounded rationality to show that if people made only a limited search for options their chosen solution would differ only slightly from what already existed. Current choices would be heavily influenced by past choices – and would not move far from them.

> People use an **incremental model** of decision-making when they are uncertain about the consequences. They search for a limited range of options, and policy unfolds from a series of cumulative small decisions.

On this view, policy unfolds not from a single event, but from many cumulative small decisions. Small decisions help people to minimise the risk of mistakes, and to reverse the decision if necessary. He called this incrementalism, or the 'science of muddling through'. Lindblom contrasted what he called the 'root' method of decision-making with the 'branch' method. The root method required a comprehensive evaluation of options in the light of defined objectives. The branch method involved building out, step-by-step and by small degrees, from the current situation. He claimed that the root method is not suitable for complex policy questions, so the practical person must follow the branch approach – the science of muddling through. The incremental model (like the administrative one) recognises human limitations.

Intuitional models

George Klein (1997) studied how effective decision-makers work, including those working under extreme time pressure like surgeons, fire fighters and nurses. He found they rarely used classical decision theory to weigh the options: instead they used pattern recognition to relate the situation to their experience. They acted on intuition – a subconscious process of using experience and judgement – sometimes called 'tacit knowledge'. Klein concluded that experienced managers act quickly on what seems like very little information, using their intuition as much as formal processes – perhaps using both as the situation demands. Hodgkinson *et al.* (2009) quote the co-founder of Sony, Akio Mariata, who was the driving force behind one of the great entertainment innovations of the twentieth century:

> Creativity requires something more than the processing of information. It requires human thought, spontaneous intuition and a lot of courage. (p. 278)

Compromise strategy – political model

The **political model** is a model of decision-making that reflects the view that an organisation consists of groups with different interests, goals and values.

The **political model** examines how people make decisions when managers disagree over goals and how to pursue them. It recognises that an organisation is not only a working system, but also a political system, which establishes the relative power of people and functions. A decision will enhance the power of some people and limit that of others. People pursue personal and sub-unit goals, as well as those of the organisation as a whole. They will evaluate a decision in terms of its likely effects on those possibly conflicting objectives.

They will often try to support their position by building a coalition with those who share their interest. This gives others the opportunity to contribute their ideas and enhances their commitment if the decision is adopted.

The political model assumes that:

- organisations contain groups with diverse interests, goals and values. Managers disagree about problem priorities and may not understand or share the goals and interests of others;
- information is ambiguous and incomplete. Rationality is limited by the complexity of many problems as well as personal interests; and
- managers engage in the push and pull of debate to decide goals and discuss alternatives – decisions arise from bargaining and discussion.

Inspirational strategy – garbage can model

This approach is likely when those concerned are unclear about cause-and-effect relationships, AND uncertain about the outcome they seek. James March (1988) observed that in this situation the processes of reaching a decision become separated from the decisions reached. Most models assume that decision-makers work through a process which results in a decision. In situations of extreme uncertainty this is not the case, as the elements that constitute the decision problem are independent of each other, coming together in random ways.

March proposed that decisions arise when four independent streams of activities meet – and when this happens will depend largely on accident or chance. The four streams are:

- **Choice opportunities** Organisations have occasions at which there is an expectation that a decision will be made – budgets must be set, there are scheduled, regular management meetings, and unscheduled ones when people meet by chance.
- **Participants** A stream of people who have the opportunity to shape decisions.
- **Problems** A stream of problems which represent matters of concern to people – a lost sale, a new opportunity, a vacancy.
- **Solutions** A stream of potential solutions seeking problems – ideas, proposals, information – that people continually generate.

In this view, the choice opportunities (scheduled or unscheduled meetings) act as the container (garbage can) for the mixture of participants, problems and solutions. One combination of the three may be such that enough participants are interested in a solution, which they can match to a problem – and take a decision accordingly. Another group of participants may not have made those connections, or made them in a different way, thus creating a different outcome.

Table 7.2 Four models of decision-making

Features	Rational	Administrative/ incremental	Political	Garbage can
Clarity of problem and goal	Clear problem and goals	Vague problems and goals	Conflict over goals	Goals and solutions independent
Degree of certainty	High degree of certainty	High degree of uncertainty	Uncertainty and/or conflict	Ambiguity
Available information on costs and benefits	Full information about costs and benefits of alternatives	Little information about costs and benefits of alternatives	Conflicting views about costs and benefits of alternatives	Costs and benefits unconnected at start
Method of choice	Rational choice to maximise benefit	Satisficing choice – good enough	Choice by bargaining among players	Choice by accidental merging of streams

This may at first sight seem an unlikely way to run a business, yet in highly uncertain, volatile environments this approach may work. Creative businesses depend on a rapid interchange of ideas, not only about specified problems but on information about new discoveries, research at other companies, what someone heard at a conference. They depend on people bringing these solutions and problems together – and deliberately foster structures that maximise opportunities for face-to-face contact and rapid decisions. The practical implication is that encouraging frequent informal contact between creative people will improve decisions and performance.

Table 7.2 summarises these four models – which are complementary in that a skilful manager or a well-managed organisation will use all of them, depending on the decision and the immediate context. A new product idea may emerge from a process resembling the garbage can model – but will then need a rational business investment case to persuade the board to develop it.

7.6 Biases in making decisions

Since people are subject to bounded rationality (limited capacity to process information) they tend to use **heuristics** – simple rules, or short cuts, that help us to overcome our limited capacity to deal with information and complexity (Kahneman and Tversky, 1974). While these short cuts help us to make decisions, they expose us to the danger of biases.

Heuristics Simple rules or mental short cuts that simplify making decisions.

Prior hypothesis bias

People who have strong prior beliefs about the relationship between two alternatives base their decisions on those beliefs, even when they receive evidence that the beliefs are wrong. In doing so they fall victim to the **prior hypothesis bias**, which is strengthened by a tendency to use information consistent with their beliefs, and ignore that which is inconsistent. People recall vivid events more readily than others – and these bias their decisions, even if circumstances have changed.

Prior hypothesis bias results from a tendency to base decisions on strong prior beliefs, even if the evidence shows that they are wrong.

Representativeness bias

This is the tendency to generalise from a small sample or single episode, and to ignore other relevant information. Examples of this **representativeness bias** are:

- predicting the success of a new product on the basis of an earlier success;
- appointing someone with a certain type of experience because a previous successful appointment had a similar background.

Optimism bias

Lovallo and Kahneman (2003) believe that a major reason for poor decisions is the 'planning fallacy', which is the tendency for people to systematically underestimate the costs and overestimate the benefits of a proposal. One source of this fallacy is what they call **optimism bias** – a human tendency to judge future events in a more positive light than is warranted by experience. People often exaggerate their talents and their role in success, leading them to make optimistic assessments. Large construction and computer projects often appear to suffer from this, as actual costs regularly exceed budgeted costs.

Illusion of control

Other errors in making decisions result from the **illusion of control**, which is the human tendency to overestimate our ability to control activities and events. Those in senior positions, especially if they have a record of successes, are prone to this bias which causes them to over-estimate the odds of a favourable outcome.

Escalating commitment

Managers may also be influenced by the phenomenon known as the **escalation of commitment**, which is an increased commitment to a previous decision despite evidence that it may have been wrong. People are reluctant to admit mistakes, and rather than search for a new solution, they increase their commitment to the original decision. This happens in the venture capital industry – whose firms lend money to entrepreneurs starting and building a business – when investors continue to put money into ventures they have supported, even though they are clearly failing.

Emotional attachment

A final source of bias is emotional attachments to people, ideas or places. Finkelstein *et al.* (2009a, b) note that people are frequently influenced by emotional attachments to:

- family and friends;
- communities and colleagues; and
- objects – things and places which have meaning for us.

Finkelstein and his colleagues suggest that these attachments (negative or positive), which bring us meaning and happiness, are bound to influence our decisions. Most of the effects are insignificant, but sometimes a manager's emotional attachments can lead them to make bad business decisions. They give examples such as Samsung's disastrous investment in car manufacturing which was widely opposed in the company as a poor use of resources, but initiated and supported by a chairman who liked cars.

 7.7   Group decision-making

While people often make decisions as individuals, they also do so within the context of a group. This section looks at two ideas – Vroom and Yetton's decision model and Irving Janis' identification of groupthink.

Vroom and Yetton's decision model

The idea behind Vroom and Yetton's (1973) contingency model of decision-making is to influence the quality and acceptability of decisions. This depends on the manager choosing how best to involve subordinates in making a decision – and being willing to change their style to match the situation. The model defines five leadership styles:

- **Autocratic** – you solve the problem or make the decision yourself using information available to you at that time.
- **Information-seeking** – you obtain the necessary information from your subordinate(s), then decide on the solution to the problem yourself. You may or may not tell your subordinates what the problem is in getting the information from them. The role played by your subordinates in making the decision is clearly one of providing the necessary information to you rather than generating or evaluating alternative solutions.
- **Consulting** – you share the problem with relevant subordinates individually, getting their ideas and suggestions without bringing them together as a group. Then *you* make the decision that may or may not reflect your subordinates' influence.
- **Negotiating** – you share the problem with your subordinates as a group, obtaining their collective ideas and suggestions. Then you make the decision that may or may not reflect your subordinates' influence.
- **Group** – you share the problem with your subordinates as a group. Together you generate and evaluate alternatives and attempt to reach agreement (consensus) on a solution. Your role is much like that of a chairperson. You do not try to influence the group to adopt 'your' solution, and you are willing to accept any solution that has the support of the entire group.

The idea behind the model is that no style is in itself better than another. Some believe that consultative or delegating styles are inherently preferable to autocratic approaches, as being more in keeping with democratic principles. Vroom and Yetton argue otherwise. In some situations (such as when time is short or the manager has all the information needed for a minor decision), going through the process of consultation will waste time and add little value. In other situations, such as where the subordinates have the relevant information, it is essential to consult them. The point of the model is to make managers more aware of the range of factors to take into account in using a particular decision-making style, such as whether the manager or the subordinate has the most relevant information, and the amount of time available to make a choice.

The theory implies that managers need to be flexible in the style they adopt. The style should be appropriate to the situation rather than consistent among all situations. The model is used in training to alert managers to the style they prefer to use, and to the range of options available. It also prompts them to consider whether that preferred style is always appropriate. They may then handle situations more deliberately than if they relied only on their preferred style.

Irving Janis and groupthink

Groupthink is a pattern of biased decision-making that occurs in groups that become too cohesive – members strive for agreement among themselves at the expense of accurately and dispassionately assessing relevant, and especially disturbing, information. An influential analysis of how it occurs was put forward by the social psychologist Irving Janis. His research (Janis, 1972) began by studying major and highly public failures of decision-making, looking for some common theme that might explain why apparently able and intelligent people were able to make such bad decisions – such as President Kennedy's decision to have US forces invade Cuba in 1961. One common thread he observed was the inability of the groups involved to consider a range of alternatives rationally, or to see the likely consequences of the choice they made. Members were also keen to be seen as team players, and not to say things

Groupthink is 'a mode of thinking that people engage in when they are deeply involved in a cohesive in-group, when the members' striving for unanimity overrides their motivation to realistically appraise alternative courses of action' (Janis, 1972).

that might end their membership of the group. Janis termed this phenomenon 'groupthink', and defined it as:

> . . . a mode of thinking that people engage in when they are deeply involved in a cohesive in-group, when the members' striving for unanimity overrides their motivation to realistically appraise alternative courses of action. (Janis, 1972, p. 9)

He identified eight symptoms of groupthink.

- **Illusion of invulnerability** – a belief that any decision they make will be successful.
- **Belief in the morality of the group** – justifying a decision by reference to a higher value.
- **Rationalisation** – playing down the negative consequences or risks of a decision.
- **Stereotyping out-groups** – referring to opponents in unfavourable or dismissive terms.
- **Self-censorship** – suppressing legitimate doubts in the interest of group loyalty.
- **Direct pressure** – members (or the leader) make it very clear that dissent is unwelcome.
- **Mindguards** – keeping uncomfortable facts or opinions out of the discussion.
- **Illusion of unanimity** – minimising doubts or questions to support appearance of unity.

When groupthink occurs, pressures for agreement and harmony within the group have the unintended effects of discouraging individuals from raising issues that run counter to the majority opinion. An often-quoted example is the *Challenger* disaster in 1986, when the space shuttle exploded shortly after take-off. Investigations showed that NASA and the main contractors, Morton Thiokol, were so anxious to keep the Shuttle programme on schedule that they ignored or discounted evidence that would slow the programme down. On a lighter note, Professor Jerry Harvey tells the story of how members of his extended family drove 40 miles into Abilene on a hot day, to no obvious purpose – and everyone was miserable. Discussing the episode with the family later, each person admitted that they had not wanted to go, but went along to please the others. Harvey (1988) coined the term 'Abilene paradox' to describe this tendency to go along with others to avoid conflict.

Activity 7.2　　What does 'decision-making' mean?

Having read the chapter, make brief notes summarising the decision-making issues evident in the organisation you chose for this activity.

- Was the decision you used 'programmed' or 'non-programmed'? (See Section 7.3.)
- To what extent did the conditions of certainty, risk, uncertainty and ambiguity affect those making the decision? (See Section 7.4.)
- Which of the models described in Section 7.5 most accurately describes the way people reached their decision?
- Comments on the processes by which they made their decision. (See Section 7.7.)

Compare what you have found with other students on your course.

Summary

1 **Outline the (iterative) stages of the decision-making process and the tasks required in each**

- Decisions are choices about how to act in relation to organisational inputs, outputs and transformation processes. The chapter identifies seven *iterative* steps in the process:
- Recognise the problem – which depends on seeing and attending to ambiguous signals.

- Set objectives – what the decision may lead to.
- Set and weight criteria – the features of the result most likely to meet problem requirements and that can guide the choice between alternatives.
- Develop alternatives – identify existing or develop custom-built ways of dealing with the problem.
- Compare and choose – using the criteria to select the preferred alternative.
- Implement – the task that turns a decision into an action.
- Evaluate – check whether the decision resolved the problem.

2   **Explain, and give examples of, programmed and non-programmed decisions**
- Programmed decisions deal with familiar issues within existing policy – recruitment, minor capital expenditure, small price changes.
- Non-programmed decisions move the business in a new direction – new markets, mergers, a major investment decision.

3   **Distinguish decision-making conditions of certainty, risk, uncertainty and ambiguity**
- Certainty – decision-makers have all the information they need, especially the costs and benefits of each alternative action.
- Risk – where the decision-maker can estimate the likelihood of the alternative outcomes. These are still subject to chance, but decision-makers have enough information to estimate probabilities.
- Uncertainty – when people know what they wish to achieve, but information about alternatives and future events is incomplete. They cannot be clear about alternatives or estimate their risk.
- Ambiguity – when people are unsure about their objectives and about the relation between cause and effect.

4   **Contrast rational, administrative, political and garbage can decision models**
- Rational models are based on economic assumptions which suggest that the role of a manager is to maximise the economic return to the firm, and that they do this by making decisions on economically rational criteria.
- The administrative model aims to describe how managers actually make decisions in situations of uncertainty and ambiguity. Many management problems are unstructured and not suitable for the precise quantitative analysis implied by the rational model.
- The political model examines how people make decisions when conditions are uncertain, information is limited, and there is disagreement among managers over goals and how to pursue them. It recognises that an organisation is not only a working system, but also a political system, which establishes the relative power of people and functions.
- The garbage can model identifies four independent streams of activities which enable a decision when they meet. When participants, problems and solutions come together in a relevant forum (a 'garbage can'), then a decision will be made.

5   **Give examples of common sources of bias in decisions**
- Sources of bias stem from the use of heuristics – mental short cuts which allow us to cope with excessive information. Six biases are:
- Prior hypothesis bias – basing decisions on prior beliefs, despite evidence they are wrong
- Representativeness bias – basing decisions on unrepresentative samples or single incidents
- Optimism bias – human tendency to anticipate more positive outcomes than is plausible
- Illusion of control – excessive belief in one's ability to control people and events
- Escalating commitment – committing more resources to a project despite evidence of failure
- Emotional attachment – to family, colleagues or objects.

6 Explain the contribution of Vroom and Yetton, and of Irving Janis, to our understanding of decision-making in groups

- Vroom and Yetton introduced the idea that decision-making styles in groups should reflect the situation – which of the five ways of involving subordinates in a decision (Autocratic, Information-seeking, Consulting, Negotiating and Delegating) to use depended on identifiable circumstances – such as whether the manager has the information required
- Irving Janis observed the phenomenon of groupthink, and set out the symptoms which indicate that it is affecting a group's decision-making processes.

Review questions

1 Explain the difference between risk and ambiguity. How may people make decisions in different ways for each situation?

2 List three decisions you have recently observed or taken part in. Which of them were programmed, and which non-programmed?

3 What are the major differences between the rational and administrative models of decision-making?

4 What is meant by satisficing in decision-making? Can you illustrate the concept with an example from your experience? Why did those involved not try to achieve an economically superior decision?

5 List and explain three common biases in making decisions.

6 The Vroom and Yetton model describes five styles. How should the manager decide which to use?

7 Recall four of the symptoms of groupthink, and give an example to illustrate each of them.

Further reading

Harrison, E. F. (1999), *The Managerial Decision-Making Process* (5th edn), Houghton Mifflin, Boston, MA.

Comprehensive interdisciplinary approach to the generic process of decision-making, with a focus on the strategic level. The author draws on a wide range of scholarly perspectives and presents them in a lucid and well-organised way.

Buchanan, L. and O'Connell, A. (2006), 'A brief history of decision-making', *Harvard Business Review*, vol. 84, no. 1, pp. 32–41.

Informative overview, placing many of the ideas mentioned in the chapter within a historical context. Part of a special issue of the *Harvard Business Review* devoted to decision-making.

Weblinks

These websites have appeared in the chapter:

www.nice.org.uk
www.irisnation.com
www.inamo-restaurant.com
www.gsk.com

www.eads.com
www.FT.com
www.ikea.com

Visit two of the business sites in the list, or any other company that interests you, and navigate to the pages dealing with recent news or investor relations.

- What examples of decisions which the company has recently had to take can you find?
- How would you classify those decisions in terms of the models in this chapter?
- Gather information from the media websites (such as **www.FT.com**) which relate to the companies you have chosen. What stories can you find that indicate something about the decisions the companies have faced, and what the outcomes have been?

 **WWW**   Annotated weblinks, multiple choice questions and other useful resources can be found on **www.pearsoned.co.uk/boddy**

Case study   IKEA   www.IKEA.com

At the end of 2010 there were 316 IKEA home furnishing stores in 38 countries (up from 301 a year earlier). The company recorded total sales in 2010 of 23.8 billion euros, up from 22.7 billion in 2009. In that year, management had decided to slow the rate at which they would open new stores, and to reduce the 130,000 staff by about 5,000.

The IKEA Concept is founded on a low-price offer in home furnishings. It aims to offer a wide range of well-designed home furnishing products at prices so low that as many people as possible can afford them. The way IKEA products are designed, manufactured, transported, sold and assembled all contribute to transforming the Concept into reality.

The Concept began when Ingvar Kamprad, a Swedish entrepreneur had the idea of offering well-designed furniture at low prices. He decided to achieve this not by cutting quality, but by applying simple cost-cutting solutions to manufacture and distribution. IKEA's first showroom opened in 1953 and until 1963 all the stores were in Sweden. In that year, the international expansion began with a store in Norway – it has entered one new country in almost every year since then.

The objective of the parent company, Inter IKEA Systems BV, is to increase availability of IKEA products by the world-wide franchising of the IKEA Concept through very large stores near to major cities. IKEA employs its own designers, though other companies manufacture most of the products. It is renowned for modern innovative design and for supplying large products in a form that customers must assemble themselves. An example of its innovative approach is 'Children's IKEA', introduced in 1997. The company worked with child psychologists to develop products that would help children develop their motor skills, social development and creativity. Children helped to make the final selection of the range.

The company employs about 130,000 staff – whom it calls co-workers. In 1999, Ingvar Kamprad initiated the Big Thank You Event as a millennium reward for the co-workers. The total value of all sales on that day was divided equally among everyone in the company – for most it was more than a month's pay.

The company vision is to create a better everyday life for many people, and acknowledges that it is the co-workers who make that possible. They aim to give people the possibility to grow both as individuals

IKEA Ltd

and in their professional roles 'we are strongly committed to creating a better life for ourselves and our customers'. The company tries to recruit staff who share its values – including togetherness, cost-consciousness, respect and simplicity. The website explains that, as well as being able to do the job, it seeks people with many other personal qualities such as a strong desire to learn, the motivation to continually do things better, simplicity and common sense, the ability to lead by example, efficiency and cost-consciousness:

> **These values are important to us because our way of working is less structured than at many other organisations.**

In mid 2009, the founder of IKEA warned that the Swedish retailer must lose more jobs after the recession squeezed sales of flat-pack furniture. Ingvar Kamprad believed that the 5,000 jobs that the company had already shed would not be enough to deal with the tougher economic climate.

> **We need to decrease the number of staff further, particularly within manufacturing and logistics. It's about adjusting to sales being a lot less and becoming more efficient.**

The Swedish billionaire revealed that sales were running at about 7 per cent below its target, adding that the company could no longer match its recent rate of expansion when up to 20 stores had opened every year. Kamprad said:

> **The forecast is that our margins and profits are decreasing substantially this year. This is proof that we have been too negligent in how we take care of our existing stores. Actually, I have long**

tried to warn about our excessive focus on expansion, and now the board has decided to hit the brakes,

A spokeswoman confirmed that there may be further job cuts, but insisted that the company was also hiring at its new stores, and was committed to opening between 10 and 15 stores a year. It had, however, suspended its investment in Russia, a major target, blaming the 'unpredictability of administrative processes'.

In June 2009, the company announced it was abandoning efforts to set up stores in India, after failing to persuade the Indian government to ease restrictions on foreign investment. It has tried to do this for over two years, and had believed the change was imminent – but it did not happen. IKEA's Asia-Pacific retail manager said:

> We still face a very high level of uncertainty. It is a very sensitive political issue in India and it may take a new government more time to negotiate with the different parties and agree the changes that are required to open up and develop the retail sector.

More generally, managers in IKEA have placed great emphasis on developing a strong culture within the company, transmitting this to new employees and reinforcing it with events for existing ones. The belief is that if co-workers develop a strong sense of shared meaning of the IKEA concept, they deliver good service wherever in the group they are. As Edvardsson and Enquist (2002) observe:

> The strong culture in IKEA can give IKEA an image as a religion. In this aspect the *Testament of a Furniture Dealer* [written by Kamprad and given to all co-workers] is the holy script. The preface reads: 'Once and for all we have decided to side

with the many. What is good for our customers is also good for us in the long run.' After the preface the testament is divided into nine points: (1) The Product Range – our identity, (2) The IKEA Spirit. A Strong and Living Reality, (3) Profit Gives us Resources, (4) To Reach Good Results with Small Means, (5) Simplicity is a Virtue, (6) The Different Way, (7) Concentration of Energy – Important to Our Success, (8) To Assume Responsibility – A Privilege, (9) Most Things Still Remain to be Done. A Glorious Future! (p. 166)

Sources: Edvardsson and Enquist (2002); *Guardian*, 7 July 2009; company website.

Questions

1 Visit the company's website, and note examples of recent decisions that have shaped the company.

2 Which of the decisions in the case study, or which you have identified on the website, seem to be 'programmed', and which 'non-programmed'? (See Section 7.3.)

3 Reflect on IKEA's decision to invest in Russia, and its attempts to enter India. What risks, uncertainties or ambiguities were probably associated with these situations? (See Section 7.4.)

4 In which decisions mentioned in the case study might managers have been guided by one or more of the models described in Section 7.5? Try to match at least two of the models with a decision.

5 What insights does the case give into decision-making processes at IKEA? (See Section 7.7.)

CHAPTER 8
MANAGING STRATEGY

Learning outcomes

When you have read this chapter you should be able to:

1 Explain the significance of managing the process, content and context of strategy

2 Compare views on the strategy process, and explain the steps in the strategy loop

3 Describe tools for external and internal analysis

4 Use the product/market matrix to compare corporate-level strategies

5 Use the generic strategies matrix to compare business-level strategies

6 Illustrate the alternative ways in which managers deliver a strategy

7 Use ideas from the chapter to comment on the management issues in the HMV case study

Activity 8.1   Describing strategy

Before reading the chapter, write some notes on what you think 'strategy' means. Choose the organisation or people who may be able to help you to learn about the topic. You may find it helpful to discuss it with a manager you know, or use an activity you have managed.

- Identify a strategic issue someone has faced and summarise it briefly.
- How did they seem to create their strategy?
- How do they assemble information to guide their choices?
- Have there been any major changes in their strategy or in how they deliver it?

Record your ideas as you may be able to use them later.

8.1   Introduction

Senior managers at HMV (see chapter case study) are facing strategic challenges as technology and consumer preferences change. If you visit one of their stores, or go to their website, you will see tangible evidence in the design of the stores, the products they stock, and the services they provide: these are all the results of conscious decisions by managers to try to create more value from their resources. In 2011, the company reported heavy losses – in part because customers can download music instead of buying it from music stores. Simon Fox, the chief executive, needs to reassure investors that he has a strategic plan to rebuild the company's profits: in 2011 he announced many store closures, and sold Waterstone's. He was also considering whether to increase the amount of floor space for other products such as tablet computers, MP3 players and headphones.

All organisations face issues of this kind. In 1998, Tesco opened its first store in Thailand, as part of a wider plan to expand overseas – and in 2010 had over 700 stores there: it was that country's leading grocery retailer, with over 12 per cent of the market. It was now considering whether to expand equally vigorously in China and South Korea. Established businesses such as National Express (the bus, coach and rail operator) concluded in 2010 that prospects for expansion in the UK were limited, and decided to bid for contracts to run rail services in, among others, the US and Portugal. Charities such as the National Trust or Cancer Research UK fear their income will decline in difficult economic times and must make strategic decisions: should they continue their current strategy, or will they serve their cause better by making radical changes – perhaps closing some properties or research activities, and/or seeking new sources of income? Procter & Gamble (the world's largest consumer goods company) has been losing market share for several years, and is working to change this – including re-designing some brands to make them more acceptable to consumers with less money than the traditional P&G customer.

Strategic management enables companies to be clear about how they will add value to resources, even though much is changing in their world. Strategy links the organisation to the outside world, where changes in the competitive (micro) and wider (macro) environment bring opportunities and threats. Table 8.1 gives some examples of organisations managing their strategies.

The common theme in these examples is that they present managers with big decisions: they are expensive, visible and hard to reverse. They also link the organisation and the world outside: each example arises when managers become aware of external trends and events – but to respond effectively they need to make possibly significant internal changes. Most managers and commentators refer to such issues as 'strategic', in the sense that they are big, visible and hard to reverse. Successful organisations often link their success to the way they

Table 8.1 Examples of organisations making strategic changes

Organisation and strategic issue	Strategic decisions or moves
MySpace – in 2011 facing competition from Facebook, and a slow growth in advertising revenues. Owner (News Corporation) seeking better financial return (www.MySpace.com)	New management abandons international expansion strategy, and closes several overseas offices, making about 30 per cent of staff redundant. Also scraps plans for a new corporate campus in Los Angeles
Procter & Gamble (world's largest supplier of consumer goods (like soap and toothpaste) – how to ensure long-term growth (www.p&g.com)	Changed from focus on people in rich economies to those in poor countries – affects R & D, market research and manufacturing to identify and make suitable products
Nestlé (global food and beverage company) – how to stimulate sales and profits in a mature business (www.nestle.com)	Increased emphasis on healthy foods, by adapting current products and taking over companies with established reputations for healthy products

have managed their strategies. The organisations you work for will, in varying degrees, face 'strategic' challenges. This chapter will help you to learn the vocabulary, and to be better able to understand, and contribute to, discussions about it.

The first sections of the chapter give you some ideas about the strategy process, how managers develop their strategy, and the tools they use to analyse their business environments. Two sections then present models with which to analyse corporate and business unit strategies, followed by one showing how managers can deliver their chosen strategy.

8.2   Strategy – process, content and context

What is strategy?

> **Strategy** is about how people decide to organise major resources to enhance performance of an enterprise.

Strategy is about organising major resources to enhance the performance of an enterprise. It is about resource decisions that are large, relatively long-term, expensive and visible – with correspondingly large implications for performance: decisions that are not strategic are operational or tactical. Elaborating on the definition:

- **People** – strategy is typically the responsibility of senior management, but some believe that in conditions of rapid change enabling more people to contribute will improve the result.
- **Decide** – in formal planning processes and/or informal conversations among managers.
- **Organise** – how to divide and co-ordinate activities to add most value.
- **Major** – significant, expensive, visible – decisions with long-term implications.
- **Resources** – inputs the enterprise needs – including those in other organisations.
- **To enhance performance** – the intended outcome of strategic decisions.
- **Enterprise** – all kinds of organisation can benefit from managing their strategy.

As people work on their strategy (through formal and informal processes) they end up with a distinctive strategy (things they will try to do – the content of their strategy), which they hope is suitable for their circumstances (the context within which the business operates).

Process

People, usually senior managers, talk and email and argue about their present and future strategy – this is their strategy process. This perspective suggests asking who develops a strategy (a few senior managers or a larger group?), what information they gather (much formal analysis, or mostly impressions and hunches?) and how they use it. Do they set a strategy for several years ahead, or does it emerge informally from discussions among managers, and then change again as conditions change? Sections 8.3 and 8.4 deal with these topics.

Content

The existing strategy is the starting point of, and the new one is the result of, the strategy process. Something stimulates managers to question current strategy, such as a takeover bid or a new product from R&D which customers may value. Most managers develop strategy to perform well against competitors. They try to identify what gives their enterprise an edge, so that they can define their **competitive strategy**. This includes deciding what to offer, to which markets, using what resources. Sections 8.5 and 8.6 deal with these topics.

Competitive strategy explains how an organisation (or unit within it) intends to achieve competitive advantage in its market.

Context

Context here refers to the setting in which the organisation works, which affects the issues managers face. Not-for-profit (NFP) or public sector organisations share some characteristics with commercial businesses (they need to attract and retain enthusiastic and capable staff) and differ in others (their performance criteria and sources of funding). Managers in multi-national businesses have to decide the overall direction of the business and how to organise their dispersed units to deliver it. Rapidly expanding new firms in innovative sectors (such as Facebook in social networking) need to decide how to continually create innovative products that customers will pay for. Public sector organisations need to decide how to reorganise their services so that they can meet rising demand with fewer resources. All hope their work on strategy will enhance performance by clarifying and unifying purpose, reducing uncertainty and ensuring that what people do supports the strategic direction.

8.3 Planning, learning and political processes

Table 8.2 shows three perspectives on the strategy process, comparing their approach, content, nature and outcomes – and the context in which they may be suitable.

Planning

The 'planning view' is prescriptive and based on a belief that the complexity of strategic decisions requires an explicit and formalised approach to guide management through the process. In the 1960s and 1970s many writers, notably Ansoff (1968), took this approach, presenting strategy development as a systematic process, following a prescribed sequence of steps and making extensive use of analytical tools and techniques. Those favouring this perspective assume that events and facts can be expressed objectively and that people respond rationally to information.

Those who challenge these assumptions of objectivity and rationality advocate two alternative views – the learning and the political.

Learning

This sees strategy as an *emergent* or adaptive process. Mintzberg (1994a, b) regards formal strategic planning as a system developed during a period of stability, and designed mainly for the centralised bureaucracies typical of Western manufacturing industry in the mid twentieth century. This style of planning is appropriate for those conditions, but not for businesses in rapidly changing sectors: they require a more flexible approach.

He therefore distinguishes between intended and **emergent strategy**. He acknowledges the validity of strategy as a plan, setting out intended courses of action, and recognises that some deliberate intentions may be realised. But it is also likely that some plans are not

Emergent strategies are those that result from actions taken one by one that converge in time in some sort of consistent pattern.

Table 8.2 Alternative perspectives on the strategy process

	Planning	Learning	Political
Approach	Prescriptive; assumes rationality	Descriptive; based on bounded rationality	Descriptive; based on bounded rationality
Content	Analytical tools and techniques; forecasting; search for alternatives, each evaluated in detail	Limited use of tools and techniques, limited search for options: time and resources don't permit	As learning view, but some objectives and options disregarded as politically unacceptable
Nature of process	Formalised, systematic, analytical; top-down – centralised planning teams	Adaptive, learning by doing; top-down and bottom-up	Bargaining; use of power to shape strategies; top-down and bottom-up
Outcomes	Extensive plans made before work begins; plans assumed to be achieved with small changes	Plans are made but not all are 'realised'; some strategies are not planned but emerge in course of 'doing'	Plans may be left ambiguous to secure agreement; need interpretation during implementation; compromises
Context/ environment	Stable environment; assumption that future can be predicted; if complex, use of more sophisticated tools	Complex, dynamic, future unpredictable	Stable or dynamic, but complex; stakeholders have diverging values, objectives and solutions

implemented (unrealised strategies) and that others which he describes as 'emergent strategies' were not expressly intended. They resulted from:

> actions taken one by one, which converged in time in some sort of consistency or pattern. (Mintzberg, 1994a, p. 25)

Management in practice   **Emergent strategy at IKEA**   www.ikea.com

Barthélemy (2006) offers an insight into the strategy process at IKEA (Chapter 7 case study). Their strategy has clearly been highly successful, but how did it come about? A close examination of the company's history shows that many of the specifics of the strategy were not brought about through a process of deliberate formulation followed by implementation.

Instead, the founder, Ingvar Kamprad, started with a very general vision. IKEA's specific strategy then emerged as he both proactively developed a viable course of action and reacted to unfolding circumstances. (p. 81)

Examples include:

- The decision to sell furniture was an adaptation to the market, not a deliberate strategy – furniture was initially a small part of the retail business, but was so successful that he soon dropped all other products.
- The flat pack method which symbolises the group was introduced to reduce insurance claims on the mail order business – its true potential only became clear when the company started opening stores, and realised that customers valued this type of product.
- The company only began to design its own furniture because other retailers put pressure on established furniture companies not to sell to IKEA.

Source: Barthélemy (2006).

A flexible approach to strategy recognises that:

> the real world inevitably involves some thinking ahead of time as well as some adaptation *en route*. (Mintzberg, 1994a, p. 26)

The essence of the learning view is adaptation, reacting to unexpected events, experimenting with new ideas 'on the ground'. Mintzberg gives the example of a salesperson coming up with the idea of selling an existing product to some new customers. Soon all the other salespeople begin to do the same, and

> one day, months later, management discovers that the company has entered a new market. (Mintzberg, 1994a, p. 26)

This was not planned but learned, collectively, during implementation.

Political

Strategy as an emergent process has much in common with political perspectives, since both draw on the concepts of bounded rationality and satisficing behaviour (Chapter 7). While the learning view reflects the logic that planning can never give complete foresight, the political view adds dimensions of power, conflict and ambiguity.

Drawing on his experience in the public sector, Lindblom (1959) was an early advocate of the political view (Chapter 7). He showed how personal values influence policy (or strategy) and how conflicts of interest between stakeholders can frustrate attempts to agree a direction. He concluded that policy-making is not a scientific, comprehensive or rational process, but an iterative, incremental one, as players bargain with each other about the direction of the enterprise. Lindblom called this the method of 'successive limited comparisons' whereby 'new' strategy is made by marginal adjustments to existing strategy:

> Policy is not made once and for all; it is made and remade endlessly . . . [through] . . . a process of successive approximation to some desired objectives. (p. 86)

It is not a comprehensive, objective process but a limited comparison of options, restricted to those that are politically acceptable and possible to implement.

While advocating a learning view, Mintzberg also recognises the value of planning:

> Too much planning may lead us to chaos, but so too would too little, more directly. (Mintzberg, 1994a, p. 416)

The planning style suited the relative stability of the 1960s. Uncertain business conditions probably require a different approach, of which the next section provides some evidence.

The strategy loop

Empirical research shows that managers use each of these approaches, depending on circumstances, and will often draw on all three – especially when planning in highly uncertain conditions. Grant's (2003) study of strategic planning in eight major oil companies, showed how, in the relatively stable conditions of the 1970s, they had developed formal planning systems which were conducted by staff at corporate HQ. By the late 1990s, when they faced volatile oil prices, economic uncertainty and greater competition, they were using a new strategy process: they now spent less time making detailed forecasts, more time in face-to-face discussion between corporate and business unit staff; and had moved responsibility from planning staff to line management.

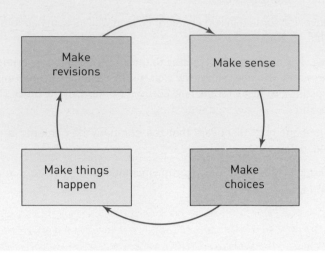

Sull (2007) believes that since volatile markets throw out a steady stream of opportunities and threats, managers cannot predict the form, magnitude or timing of events. He therefore sees the strategy process as inherently iterative – a loop instead of a line:

> According to this view, every strategy is a work in progress that is subject to revision in light of ongoing interactions between the organization and its shifting environment. To accommodate those interactions, the strategy loop consists of four major steps: making sense of a situation, making choices on what to do (and what not to do), making those things happen and making revisions based on new information. (p. 31)

Figure 8.1 shows the strategy loop, the most important feature of which is that it implies that managers incorporate and use new information as it becomes available, closely linking strategy formation and implementation.

The following sections provide ideas and examples about:

- making sense – using information about external and internal environments;
- making choices – deciding strategy at corporate and business unit levels;
- making things happen – ways to deliver strategy; and
- making revisions – reflecting on results and taking in new information.

8.4 Making sense – external and internal analysis

External analysis

Chapter 3 outlined Porter's view of the five forces which affect the profitability of an industry. Each of the forces points to the action points which managers need to consider in their strategy.

- **Threat of entry** What are the barriers that new entrants need to overcome if they are to compete successfully? High barriers are good for incumbents: they fear barriers that are becoming lower, as this exposes them to more competition. Government legislation in the 1980s reduced the barriers protecting banks from competition, and allowed other companies like Citibank and HSBC to enter the industry.

- **Threat of substitutes** What alternative products and services may customers choose? Many people choose to receive their news online rather than in print, seriously threatening print newspapers, who are searching for survival strategies – *The Times* and the *Sunday Times* now charge for access to their online editions.
- **Power of buyers** If they have strong bargaining power they force down prices and reduce profitably. The major supermarket groups dominate the retail food market, and are able to use that position to demand favourable prices and terms from suppliers.
- **Power of suppliers** If suppliers have few competitors they can raise prices at the expense of customers. The UK domestic energy market is dominated by a small number of companies, who have considerable power over their customers.
- **Competitive rivalry** The four forces combine to affect the intensity of rivalry between an organisation and its rivals. Factors such as industry growth or the ease with which companies can leave it also affect this.

The model remains popular, and Porter published a revised version in 2008 (Porter, 2008) with more current examples: the five forces remain the same. They help strategists to understand the fundamental conditions of their industry, and to work out how to make their company less vulnerable and more profitable.

At the macro-level of the general environment, the PESTEL framework (Chapter 3) helps to identify major drivers of change affecting strategy. The Management in Practice feature below shows what happened when Motorola misread some of these signals about changes in the outside world.

Management in practice   Motorola misreads the market   www.motorola.com   FT

In 2009, Greg Brown, Motorola's joint chief executive, explained the dramatic decline in the company's mobile phone business. He said that the company did not spot quickly enough how mobiles were evolving from simple devices for making phone calls into sophisticated handsets for surfing the internet and sending email. Smartphones have thrived with the arrival of third-generation mobile technology, and Motorola has been weak in that area.

> Motorola didn't see the trends coming in smartphone and 3G with the kind of foresight and customer attention it should have.

He went on to describe Motorola's failure to anticipate the growing importance of mobile software rather than handset design – accepting that most of the challenges the company faces were their own doing.

The company was the world's largest mobile maker in the 1990s until Nokia stole that mantle in 1998. It then followed a strategy of selling cheap handsets in developing countries – but abandoned that as it was unprofitable. In the fourth quarter of 2006 the company's market share of mobile sales was 23.3 per cent – in the same quarter of 2008 it was 6.6 per cent.

Source: Adapted from 3G wrong number forces change of strategy (Andrew Parker and Paul Taylor), *Financial Times*, 2 March 2009.

Strategy tries to match an organisation's external world with its internal capabilities – so before establishing a direction, managers need an internal analysis to show how well they can cope with external conditions.

Internal analysis: resources and competencies

Managers analyse the internal environment to identify the organisation's strengths and weaknesses. This means identifying what the organisation does well, where it might do better and whether it has the resources and competencies to deliver a preferred strategy. Those that are considered essential to outperforming the competition are sometimes called critical success factors.

Chapter 1 introduced the idea that the performance of an organisation depends on the resources available to it *and* its competence in using them. Tangible resources are the physical assets such as buildings, equipment, people or finance, while intangible resources include reputation, knowledge or information. **Unique resources** are those that others cannot obtain – a powerful brand, access to raw material or a distinctive culture – and which can be a source of competitive advantage. The chief executive of Virgin Media believes the company's high-speed cable network is a durable source of competitive advantage.

A company also needs to develop competencies – activities and processes which enable it to deploy resources effectively. Joe Morris, operations director at TJ Morris, a Liverpool-based chain of discount stores (in 2010, the second largest independent grocer in the UK) claims that their information system (which his brother Ed designed) gives them a competitive advantage:

> It is our own bespoke product. It is extremely reliable and simple. We can do what we want to do very quickly.

While the amount and quality of resources matter, how people use them matters more. If managers encourage staff to develop higher skills, co-operate with each other, be innovative and creative, the company is likely to perform better than one where managers treat staff indifferently.

Ryanair has prospered not because it has resources (such as a fleet of modern, standard aircraft) – other airlines have similar resources, but are unprofitable. The difference is that Ryanair has developed competencies – such as quick turnrounds – which enable it to use aircraft more efficiently. GlaxoSmithKline has a strategy to acquire half of its new drugs from other organisations: for this to work, it will use a **unique competence** of identifying and working with suitable partners.

Management's task in internal analysis is to identify those resources and competencies that distinguish it in customers' minds. At the *corporate level*, this could be the overall balance of activities that it undertakes – the product or service portfolio. Does it have sufficient strength in growing rather than declining markets? Does it have too many new products (which drain resources) relative to established ones? Are there useful synergies between the different lines of business? At the *divisional or business unit level*, performance depends on having adequate resources (physical, human, financial and so on) and competencies (such as design, production or marketing).

Value chain analysis

The concept of the **value chain**, introduced by Porter (1985), calculates the value added at each stage of a manufacturing or service process. Porter applied this idea to the activities of the whole organisation, as an analysis of each activity could identify sources of competitive advantage.

Figure 8.2 shows primary and support activities. *Primary* activities transform inputs into outputs and deliver them to the customer:

- **inbound logistics:** receiving, storing and distributing the inputs to the product or service; also material handling and stock control etc.;
- **operations:** transforming inputs into the final product or service, by machining, mixing and packing;
- **outbound logistics:** moving the product to the buyer – collecting, storing and distributing; in some services (a sports event) these activities will include bringing the customers to the venue;
- **marketing and sales:** activities to make consumers aware of the product;
- **service:** enhancing or maintaining the product – installation, training, repairs.

Unique resources are those which are vital to competitive advantage and which others cannot obtain.

A **unique competence** is an activity or process through which resources are deployed to give competitive advantage in ways that others cannot imitate or obtain.

A **value chain** 'divides a firm into the discrete activities it performs in designing, producing, marketing and distributing its product. It is the basic tool for diagnosing competitive advantage and finding ways to enhance it.' (Porter, 1985)

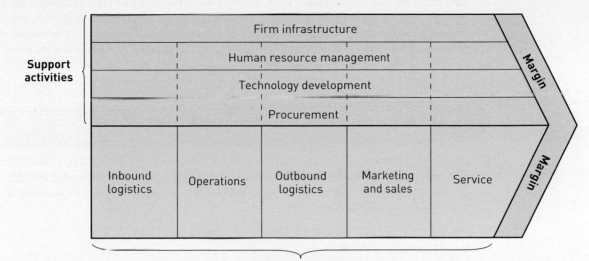

Figure 8.2 The value chain

Source: Porter (1985), copyright © 1985 Michael E. Porter, reprinted with permission of The Free Press, a division of Simon & Schuster.

These depend on four *support* activities:

- **firm infrastructure**: structure, together with planning, financial and quality systems;
- **human resource management**: recruitment, training and rewards;
- **technology development**: supporting inputs, transformation and outputs;
- **procurement**: acquiring materials and other resources.

Value chain analysis enables managers to consider which activities benefit customers, and which are more troublesome – perhaps destroying value rather than creating it. It might, say, be good at marketing, outbound logistics and technology development – but poor at operations and human resource management. That awareness may lead managers to consider which activities the business should do itself, and which it should outsource to other firms. Each activity in the chain

> can contribute to a firm's relative cost position and create a basis for differentiation. (Porter, 1985, p. 33)

– the two main sources of competitive advantage. Analysing the value chain helps management to consider:

- Which activities have most effect on reducing cost or adding value? If customers value quality more than costs, then that implies a focus on ensuring quality of suppliers.
- What linkages do most to reduce cost, enhance value or discourage imitation?
- How do these linkages relate to the cost and value drivers?

SWOT analysis

Strategy follows a 'fit' between internal capabilities and external changes – managers try to identify key issues from each and draw out the strategic implications. A SWOT analysis (see Chapter 6) summarises the internal and external issues facing the business. Managers use the technique in strategy workshops, though, like any technique, the value depends on how thoroughly people engage with it. Done well, the results help them to develop and evaluate strategic alternatives, aiming to select those that make the most of internal strengths and external opportunities. Managers in large enterprises develop strategies at corporate, business unit and functional levels, though in smaller organisations there will be less complexity.

8.5   Making choices (1) – deciding strategy at corporate level

---

Corporate-level strategy reflects the overall direction of the organisation. What is the overall mission and purpose? Should it focus on a small range of activities or diversify? Should it remain a local or national business, or seek to operate internationally? These decisions establish the distinctive direction of an enterprise.

The corporate mission

A **mission statement** is a broad statement of an organisation's scope and purpose, aiming to distinguish it from similar organisations.

Defining the mission is intended to provide a focus for work. A broad **mission statement** can guide those setting more specific goals and the strategies to achieve them, by express-ing the underlying beliefs and values held within the organisation – see the examples in the Management in Practice feature below.

Management in practice   Examples of missions and visions

IKEA (www.ikea.com)
A better everyday life.

Google (www.google.com)
To organise the world's information.

Royal Society for the Protection of Birds (www.rspb.org.uk)
To secure a healthy environment for birds and wildlife, helping to create a better world for us all.

Cancer Research UK (www.cancerresearchuk.org)
Together we will beat cancer.

Mission statements may be idealistic aspirations rather than guides to action. People only believe, and act upon, the mission statement if they see managers doing so. The mission needs to be cascaded through the structure to ensure it guides day-to-day actions.

Setting a strategic direction

Strategies can aim for growth, stability or renewal. Growth strategies try to expand the number of products offered or markets served. Stability is when the organisation offers the same products and services to much the same group of customers. Renewal often follows a period of trouble and involves significant changes to the business to secure the required turnaround.

Managers can decide how to achieve their chosen option by using the product/market matrix, shown in Figure 8.3. They can achieve growth by focusing on one or more of the quadrants; stability by remaining with existing products and services; and renewal by leaving some markets followed by entry into others.

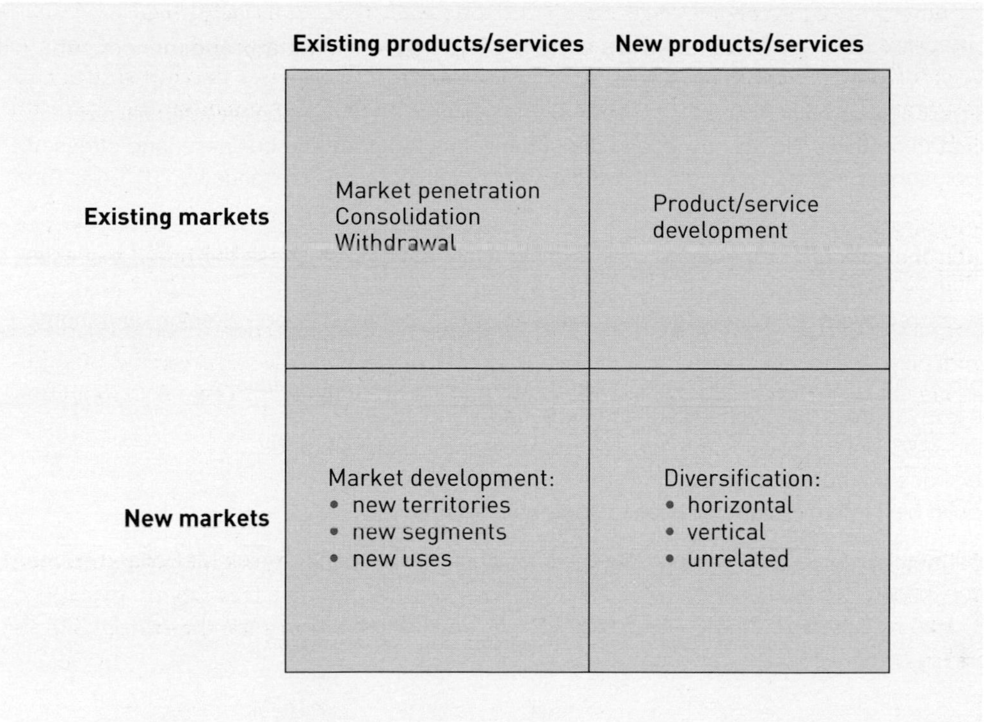

	Existing products/services	**New products/services**
Existing markets	Market penetration Consolidation Withdrawal	Product/service development
New markets	Market development: • new territories • new segments • new uses	Diversification: • horizontal • vertical • unrelated

Figure 8.3
Strategy develop-
ment directions –
the product/market
matrix

Source: As adapted in
Johnson *et al.* (2008)
from Chapter 6 of
H. Ansoff, *Corporate
Strategy*, published by
Penguin 1968.

Existing markets, existing product/service

Choice within this segment depends on whether the market is growing, declining or has reached maturity. Each box shows several possibilities:

- A market penetration strategy aims to increase market share, perhaps by reducing price, increasing advertising or improving distribution.
- Consolidation aims to protect the company's share in existing markets. In growing or mature markets this could mean improving efficiency and/or service to retain custom. In declining markets management might consolidate by acquiring other companies.
- Withdrawal is a wise option when, for instance, competition is intense and the organisation is unable to match its rivals: staying in that line of business would destroy value, not create it. In the public sector, changing priorities lead to the redeployment of resources. Health boards have withdrawn A&E services from some hospitals to make better use of limited resources.

Existing markets, new products/services

A strategy of product or service development allows a company to retain the relative security of its present markets while altering products or developing new ones. Fashion and consumer electronics companies continually change products to meet changes in consumer preferences. Car manufacturers compete by adding features and extending their model range.

New markets, existing products/services

Market development aims to find new outlets by:

- extending geographically (from local to national or international);
- targeting new market segments (groups of customers, by age, income or lifestyle); or
- finding new uses for a product (a lightweight material developed for use in spacecraft is also used in the manufacture of golf clubs).

> ### Management in practice   M&S creates a new strategy   www.marksandspencer.com
>
> When Marc Bolland took over as chief executive of Marks and Spencer in 2010 he soon revealed his strategy for improving profits at the retailer. He acknowledged the underlying strength of the business, and stressed the changes were evolutionary – with the aim of achieving a 10 per cent increase in revenue by 2013–14. The plan included:
>
> - Brand – building on the strength of the brand by launching 'Only at M&S' to stress the brand's special qualities and innovative products
> - Stores – change store layout to encourage customers to move between food, clothing and home departments
> - Clothing – strengthen the core M&S brand, by improving style and fashion credentials
> - Home – focus on growth areas like kitchenware and bedding
> - Food – reduce non-M&S brands to 100, and add 100 exclusive international brands
> - Space – increase space by 3 per cent a year
> - Multi-channel – build new internet platform to encourage online sales.
>
> These changes will require significant (and thus 'strategic') financial investment – which Mr Bolland hopes will bring a satisfactory return to shareholders.
>
> Source: Adapted from M&S brand value (Emiko Terazono), *Financial Times*, 10 November 2010; company website.

New markets, new products/services

Often described as diversification, this can take three forms:

- **Horizontal integration** Developing related or complementary activities, such as when mortgage lenders extend into the insurance business, using their knowledge of, and contact with, existing customers to offer them an additional service. The advantages include the ability to expand by using existing resources and competences – such as Kwik-Fit using the database of depot customers to create a motor insurance business, or GKN expanding from supplying components to the motor industry to supplying them to the aerospace industry as well.
- **Vertical integration** Moving either backwards or forwards into activities related to the organisation's products and services. A manufacturer might decide to make its own components rather than buy them from elsewhere. Equally, it could develop forward, for instance into distribution.
- **Unrelated diversification** Developing into new markets outside the present industry. Virgin has used its strong brand to expand into sectors as diverse as airlines, trains, insurance and soft drinks. The extension by some retailers into financial services is another example. It is a way to spread risk where demand patterns fluctuate at different stages of the economic cycle, and to maintain growth when existing markets become saturated.

Alternative development directions are not mutually exclusive: companies can follow several at the same time. Apple Inc. has a clear strategy to move away from being a computer manufacturer and into areas which would give their products a very wide appeal. One observer predicted, at the time of the iPad launch in 2010:

> Get on any train in five years' time, and people will be reading the newspaper (downloaded at home or automatically when they walk through Waterloo Station on the way home), books, watching TV, playing games (quite possibly with fellow passengers!) on their iPads.

8.6   Making choices (2) – deciding strategy at business unit level

At the business unit level, firms face a choice about how to compete. Porter (1980b, 1985) identified two types of competitive advantage: low cost or differentiation. From this he developed the idea that there are three generic strategies that a firm can use to develop and maintain competitive advantage: cost leadership, differentiation and focus. Figure 8.4 shows these strategies. The horizontal axis shows the two bases of competitive advantage. Competitive scope, on the vertical axis, shows whether company's target market is broad or narrow in scope.

Cost leadership

Cost leadership strategy is when a firm aims to compete on price rather than, say, advanced features or excellent customer service. They will typically sell a standard no-frills product and try to minimise costs. This requires **economies of scale** in production and close attention to efficiency and operating costs, although other factors such as preferential access to raw material, also help. A low cost base will not in itself bring competitive advantage – consumers must see that the product represents value for money. Retailers using this strategy include Wal-Mart (Asda in the UK), Argos and Superdrug; Dell Computers is another example, as is Ryanair.

> A **cost leadership strategy** is one in which a firm uses low price as the main competitive weapon.
>
> **Economies of scale** are achieved when producing something in large quantities reduces the cost of each unit.

Differentiation

A **differentiation strategy** is seen when a company offers a service that is distinct from its competitors, and which customers value. It is 'something unique beyond simply offering a low price' (Porter, 1985) that allows firms to charge a high price or retain customer loyalty. Examples of differentiation:

- Nokia differentiates through the fashionable design of its handsets;
- Sony achieves it by offering superior reliability, service and technology;
- BMW differentiates by stressing a distinctive product/service image;
- Coca-Cola differentiates by building a widely recognised brand.

> A **differentiation strategy** consists of offering a product or service that is perceived as unique or distinctive on a basis other than price.

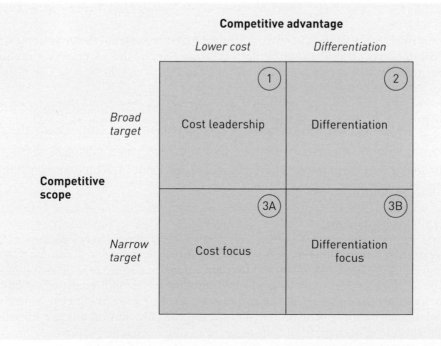

Figure 8.4
Generic competitive strategies

Source: Porter (1985), copyright © 1985 Michael E. Porter, reprinted with permission of The Free Press, a division of Simon & Schuster.

The form of differentiation varies. A maker of construction equipment will stress durability and quick service, while in cosmetics, firms will build an image of sophistication, exclusivity and eternal youth. Cities compete by stressing differentiation in areas such as cultural facilities, available land or good transport links.

Focus

A **focus strategy** is when a company competes by targeting very specific segments of the market.

A **focus strategy** involves targeting a narrow market segment, either by consumer group (teenagers, over-60s, doctors) or geography. The two variants – cost focus and differentiation focus – are simply narrow applications of the broad strategies. Examples include:

- Saga offers travel and insurance for those over 50;
- Rolls-Royce offers luxury transport to the wealthy;
- Female Direct offers insurance for women;
- Hiscox offers insurance to the wealthiest 10 per cent of the population.

Management in practice   Strategic focus at Maersk   www.maersk.com

I think because of the size of our organisation now, our strategy is really targeted to focus on certain segments. One of the things we did this year was start a brand new service from Costa Rica to the UK, specifically bringing in bananas. That was a new service for us and provided a different service for the customer, whereas before they've always been shipped in bulk vessels, and now we've containerised them. So we try and be very specific about the marketing. Once the customer is on board, then we have small teams of customer service people looking after specific customers, both here and elsewhere in the world.

Once we've locked them into the customer experience, what we want to do then is build a long-term relationship with the customer, get to know the business, get to know where we can improve them. Not just on the service but also from a cost point of view, because obviously cost is very important in this market. So we like to go into partnerships. Some of the biggest retailers in the UK, for instance, we have long-term relationships with, one of those being Tesco, where we've been able to take a lot of costs out of their supply chain by giving them a personalised service by actually knowing their business.

Source: Interview with Brian Godsafe, Customer Services Manager.

Some companies try to follow cost leadership and differentiation strategies at the same time. If they control costs better than competitors, they can reinvest the savings in features that differentiate them.

8.7   Making things happen – deciding how to deliver strategy

Organisations deliver their strategies through internal development, acquisition or alliance – or a combination of these.

Internal development

The organisation delivers the strategy by expanding or redeploying relevant resources that it has or can employ. This enables managers to retain control of all aspects of the development of new products or services – especially where the product has technologically advanced features. Marks and Spencer's current strategy includes securing a much bigger revenue from online sales (£1bn by 2014) – and plans to do so by investing heavily in developing its website internally (instead of outsourcing the site to Amazon, which is its current practice).

Public organisations typically favour internal development, traditionally providing services through staff whom they employ directly. Changes in the wider political agenda have meant that these are often required to compete with external providers, while some – such as France Telecom, Deutsche Post or the UK Stationery Office – have been partially or wholly sold to private investors.

Merger and acquisition

One firm merging with, or acquiring, another allows rapid entry into new product or market areas and is a quick way to build market share. It is also used where the acquiring company can use the other company's products to offer new services or enter new markets. Companies like Microsoft and Cisco Systems frequently buy small, entrepreneurial companies and incorporate their products within the acquiring company's range. Like Marks and Spencer, Wm. Morrison is planning to increase online revenue – but (unlike M&S) it has acquired an existing online retailer, and the right to use that company's online system. Other mergers extend the range of activities – Vodafone made several acquisitions to become the world's largest mobile phone company.

Mergers and acquisitions frequently fail, destroying rather than adding value. When Sir Roy Gardner took over as chairman of Compass (a UK catering company) at which profits and the share price had fallen rapidly, he was critical of the previous management:

> [They] concentrated far too much on growing the business through acquisition. They should have stopped and made sure [that] what they had acquired delivered the expected results. Compass was being run by its divisional managers, which resulted in a total lack of consistency. (*Financial Times*, 19 January 2007, p. 19)

Joint developments and alliances

Organisations sometimes turn to partners to co-operate in developing products or services. Arrangements vary from highly formal contractual relationships to looser forms of co-operation but there are usually advantages to be gained by both parties. One attraction of this method is that it limits risk. UK construction firm, John Laing, has a joint venture with the Commonwealth Bank of Australia to invest in UK hospital and European road projects: rather than borrow funds for a project, Laing shares the risk (and the reward) with the bank. HMV acquired a 50 per cent equity stake in 7digital in September 2009, as this will enable it to use that company's technological expertise to enhance its own digital offers in entertainment and e-books.

Alliances and partnership working have also become commonplace in the public sector. In many cities, alliances or partnerships have been created between major public bodies, business and community interests. Their main purpose is to foster a coherent approach to planning and delivering services. Public bodies often act as service commissioners rather than as direct providers, developing partnerships with organisations to deliver services on their behalf.

| 8.8 | Making revisions – implementing and evaluating |

Implementation turns strategy into action, moving from corporate to operational levels. Many strategies fail to be implemented, or fail to achieve as much as management expected. A common mistake is to assume that formulating a strategy will lead to painless implementation. Sometimes there is an 'implementation deficit', when strategies are not implemented at all, or are only partially successful. A common reason for this is that while formulating strategy may appear to be a rational process, it is often a political one. Those who were content with the earlier strategy may oppose the new one if it affects their status, power or career prospects. Chapter 11 shows how implementing change is a complex, often conflicting process.

Evaluate results

Managers, shareholders (current and potential) and financial analysts routinely compare a company's performance with its published plans. Only by tracking results can these and other interested parties decide if performance is in line with expectations or if the company needs to take some corrective action. Many targets focus on financial and other quantitative aspects of performance, such as sales, operating costs and profit.

Although monitoring is shown as the last stage in the strategy model, it is not the end of the process. This is continuous, as organisations adjust to changes in their business environment. Regular monitoring alerts management to the possibility that targets might not be achieved and that operational adjustments are needed. Equally, and in conjunction with continuous scanning of the external environment, performance monitoring can prompt wider changes to the organisation's corporate and competitive strategies.

Donald Sull (2007) advises that in any discussions to revise strategy, people should treat actions as experiments:

> they should analyse what's happened and use the results to revise their assumptions, priorities and promises. As such, the appropriate time to have such conversations is after the team has reached a significant milestone in making things happen . . . Managers must acknowledge that that their mental models are merely simplified maps of complex terrain based on provisional knowledge that is subject to revision in the light of new information. (pp. 36–37)

Activity 8.2 Describing strategy

Having read the chapter, make brief notes summarising the strategy issues evident in the organisation you chose for this activity.

- What examples did you find of the strategic decisions they have made? (Refer to Sections 8.1 and 8.2.)
- What were the main features of the strategy process in the company? (Refer to Section 8.3.)
- Which internal or external factors had most influence on the strategy? (Refer to Section 8.4.)
- Describe the changes at corporate- and/or business unit level in terms of the models in Sections 8.5 and 8.6.
- How did the company plan to deliver the strategy? (Refer to Section 8.7.)

Compare what you have found with other students on your course.

Summary

1 **Explain the significance of managing the process, content and context of strategy**
   - Strategy is about the survival of the enterprise; the strategy process sets an overall direction with information about the external environment and internal capabilities. Defining the purposes of the organisation helps to guide the choice and implementation of strategy.

2 **Compare views of the strategy process, and the steps in the strategy loop**
   - The planning approach is appropriate in stable and predictable environments; while the emergent approach more accurately describes the process in volatile environments,

since strategy rarely unfolds as intended in complex, changing and ambiguous situations. A political perspective may be a more accurate way of representing the process when it involves the interests of powerful stakeholders. It is rarely an objectively rational activity, implying that strategy models are not prescriptive but rather frameworks to guide managers.

3   Describe tools for external and internal analysis

- External analysis can use Porter's five forces model and the PESTEL framework to identify relevant factors.
- Internally managers can use the value chain to analyse their current organisation.
- The two sets of information can be combined in a SWOT diagram.

4   Use the product/market matrix to compare corporate-level strategies

- Strategy can focus on existing or new products, and existing or new markets. This gives four broad directions, with options in each – such as market penetration, product development, market development or diversification.

5   Use the generic strategies matrix to compare business level strategies

- Key strategic choices are those of cost leader, differentiation or a focus on a narrow segment of the market.

6   Illustrate alternative ways of delivering a strategy

- Strategy can be delivered by internal (sometimes called organic) development by rearranging the way resources are deployed. Alternatives include acquiring or merging with another company, or by forming alliances and joint ventures.

Review questions

1   Why do managers develop strategies for their organisation?

2   How does the planning view of strategy differ from the learning and political views respectively?

3   Describe the main features of the ways in which recent research suggests managers develop strategy.

4   Draw Sull's strategy loop and explain each of the elements.

5   What are the main steps to take in analysing the organisation's environment? Why is it necessary to do this?

6   Describe each stage in value chain analysis and illustrate them with an example. Why is the model useful to management?

7   The chapter described three generic strategies that organisations can follow. Give examples of companies following each of these.

8   Give examples of company strategies corresponding to each box in the product/market matrix.

9   What are the main ways of delivering strategy?

Further reading

Mintzberg, H., Ahlstrand, B. and Lampel, J. (1998), *Strategy Safari*, Financial Times/Prentice Hall, Harlow.

Excellent discussion of the process of strategy making from various academic and practical perspectives.

Johnson, G., Scholes, K. and Whittington, R. (2008), *Exploring Corporate Strategy* (8th edn), Financial Times/Prentice Hall, Harlow.

A concise overview of the topic by the authors of the leading UK textbook on strategy.

Weblinks

These websites have appeared in, or are relevant to, the chapter:

www.myspace.com
www.p&g.com
www.nestle.com
www.ikea.com
www.unilever.com
www.motorola.com
www.gsk.com
www.google.com
www.rspb.org.uk
www.cancerresearchuk.org
www.marksandspencer.com
www.maersk.com
www.hmv.com

Visit two of the business sites in the above list, or any other company that interests you, and navigate to the pages dealing with news or investor relations.

- What are the main strategic issues they seem to be facing?
- What information can you find about their policies?

Annotated weblinks, multiple choice questions and other useful resources can be found on **www.pearsoned.co.uk/boddy**

Case study   HMV Group   www.hmv.com

HMV and Waterstone's are two familiar retailing brands, specialising in music, films, games and books. In 2011, the HMV Group had over 400 entertainment stores and websites in the UK and overseas, and Waterstone's. This is the UK's only specialist book chain, and includes most of the 130 Ottakar's stores acquired when it took over that company in 2006.

The music side of the business was part of EMI Group, but separated in 2002 to create a purely retail company, rather than being part of the diversified EMI Group, which also owned Dillon's, another bookselling chain. HMV bought Waterstone's from WH Smith.

The group experienced severe losses in 2005, as illegal music downloading damaged sales of CDs. Management were confident they could recover from this and, led by chief executive Simon Fox, began to develop a new strategy. This had three strands – *revitalising the HMV and Waterstone's stores, growing revenue* from new channels and *becoming more efficient*.

In the HMV *stores,* the company is changing the mix of products to offset the decline in physical music sales. They are stocking more games software and consoles, as well as introducing MP3/4 players and accessories. They expected market growth at Waterstone's to come mainly from non-book sales, so began to extend the range of high-quality gift stationery, and to concentrate on rapidly growing book categories, such as fiction and children's books. The need to reduce debt led the company to sell Waterstone's in early 2011.

To help understand customers' needs and to encourage sales to the most loyal and high spending, the company launched the Pure HMV loyalty card. Customers can exchange the points earned – at Waterstone's for future purchases and at HMV for entertainment-related rewards. They are also developing the HMV store format to become a more inspiring shopping venue, with more interactive features.

The second strand in the new strategy is to *grow revenue* from new channels, instead of relying on physical purchases in the stores. The HMV Group is therefore investing in both stores' online sites. Customers can download music through the **HMV .com** site, giving the choice of a digital download or a physical album. The company plans to extend the site to offer video downloads as soon as this becomes worthwhile to customers and the company. They are also planning to grow revenue from live music events and ticket sales.

HMV

To become *more efficient*, the company is changing major parts of the cost base. For example in Waterstone's they had invested in a centralised book hub, to which all book suppliers deliver their products. These are then sorted and delivered to each store as a single daily delivery, rather than having several deliveries to a store each day by individual suppliers. They are also centralising their purchasing to reduce costs, and consolidating many back office functions of the two store chains.

They are growing revenue from live music and ticket sales. In late 2009, HMV expanded its already small presence in the live music market by buying venue owner MAMA Group for £46m. MAMA Group runs 11 concert venues in the UK including the Hammersmith Apollo, and has other interests including an artist management business. The group chief executive said he was delighted with the deal as the two companies were already partners in the Mean Fiddler joint venture, which run venues in London, Birmingham, Edinburgh and Aberdeen. Mr Fox believed the deal would enable HMV to accelerate the growth into live music, which the company expected would have higher sales than recorded music by 2012. MAMA is also a leading operator of live music festivals and expects to add new events to the range. HMV also believes a significant opportunity exists in the market for tickets, and aims to sell 3 million tickets for MAMA and third-party venues in 2012/13.

In 2011, the company appointed a new finance director, David Wolffe, in the hope that he would help it to offset falling book and music sales by diversifying into new markets.

Sources: Company website.

Questions

1 Refer to Section 8.1, and explain why the issues facing HMV Group were 'strategic'. Support your answer with examples.

2 What clues can you find in the case about the strategy process in HMV. (Refer to Section 8.3.)

3 What external factors have affected the company's strategy? (Refer to Section 8.4.)

4 What choices has it made at corporate and business unit levels? (Refer to Sections 8.5 and 8.6.)

5 How has it delivered the chosen strategy? (Refer to Section 8.7.)

6 Go to the HMV website and look for evidence that helps you to evaluate the strategy the company has been following.

PART 4
ORGANISING

Introduction

Part 4 examines how management creates the structure within which people work. Alongside planning the direction of the business, managers need to consider how they will achieve the direction chosen. A fundamental component of that is the form of the organisation. This is a highly uncertain area of management, as there are conflicting views about the kind of structure to have and how much influence structure has on performance.

Chapter 9 describes the main elements of organisation structure and the contrasting forms they take. Chapter 10 focuses on information technology and e-business, showing how information technologies have deep implications for organisations and their management. Chapter 11 looks at how people seek to manage change and innovation – both of which are essential parts of the management task of adding value.

CHAPTER 9
ORGANISATION STRUCTURES

Learning outcomes

When you have read this chapter you should be able to:

1 Outline the links between strategy, structure and performance

2 Give examples of how managers divide and co-ordinate work

3 Compare the features of mechanistic and organic structures

4 Summarise the ideas about structure developed, respectively, by Woodward, Burns and Stalker, Lawrence and Lorsch, and Child

5 Use ideas from the chapter to comment on the management issues in the GSK case study

Activity 9.1   What does 'organisation structure' mean?

Before reading the chapter, write some notes on what you think 'organisation structure' means. Choose the organisation or people who may be able to help you learn about the topic. You may find it helpful to discuss the topic with a manager you know, or reflect on an activity you have managed.

- Identify a structural issue someone has faced, and describe it briefly.
- How (if at all) did they discuss any links between structure and strategy?
- What methods did they use to divide and coordinate work?
- What reasons, if any, did they give for choosing those methods?

Keep these notes as you will be able to use them later.

9.1   Introduction

Managers at GlaxoSmithKline (GSK) regularly revise the structure of the business to ensure it performs well. Although the market for pharmaceutical products is growing, so is the cost of developing them – and the company faces competition from cheap 'generic' brands of products which are no longer protected by patents. Managers are especially concerned about how best to organise their large research and development (R&D) activity (on which they spend about 14 per cent of revenue). They also face decisions about how to organise its global business – avoiding duplication while also responding to local conditions.

Senior managers of other companies face similar choices. Motorola's mobile devices had been losing market share for several years and, in 2009, the board responded by dividing the company in two – one unit to focus on the handset market, the other on communication networks. Others follow a policy of frequent small changes. The (then) Chairman of L'Oréal, the world's biggest beauty company refers to its

> culture of permanent mini-restructuring. I don't think there has ever been a major restructuring in the whole of L'Oréal's corporate history . . . but there have been hundreds of little ones. What we do is try to live a life of permanent small change to avoid the major disasters. (*Financial Times*, 3 March 2008)

Structural choices also include decisions about whether to acquire another business, and then how to integrate it. **Outsourcing** is also a practice which changes an organisation's structure.

When an owner-manager is running a small business they decide what tasks to do and co-ordinate them. If the enterprise grows, the entrepreneur usually passes some of the work to newly recruited staff, though the division will probably be flexible and informal – direct communication makes co-ordination easy. If the business continues to grow, they find that informal ways of working begin to cause problems – so introduce more formality. They divide and clarify tasks to ensure people know what to do, and devise ways to co-ordinate the separate tasks.

This chapter outlines how people divide and co-ordinate work, and how these choices lead to the contrasting 'mechanistic' and 'organic' forms of structure. These choices reflect personal preferences, views (even if implicit) about theories of structure and knowledge of the organisation's strategy. A central theme of the chapter is that developing the right structure for the situation (context) is likely to benefit an organisation's performance. Figure 9.1 shows these themes.

Outsourcing is the practice of contracting out defined functions or activities to companies who can do the work more cost-effectively.

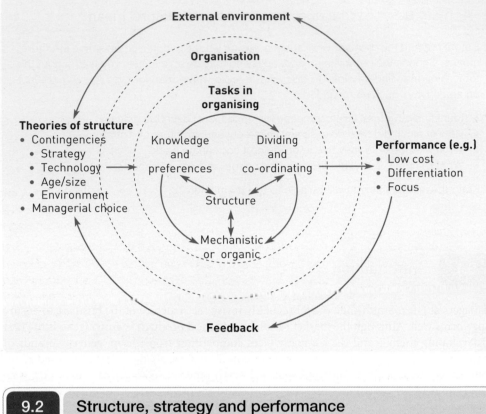

Figure 9.1
Themes of the chapter

9.2 Structure, strategy and performance

Alfred Chandler (1962) traced the evolution of America's largest industrial firms, showing how their strategies of growth and diversification placed too many demands on the centralised structures they had created. As the diversity of products and geographies grew, issues arose which those at the (increasingly remote) centre could not handle, as they lacked the knowledge of local circumstances. Chandler's historical analysis of Du Pont, General Motors, Standard Oil and Sears, Roebuck shows how they responded by creating decentralised, divisional structures – a significant organisational innovation which many companies use today. It allowed managers at corporate headquarters to provide overall guidance and control, leaving the detailed running of each division to local managers ('strategy shaped structure').

Chandler also shows that structure could influence strategy. A new legal requirement to break Standard Oil into small regional companies encouraged one of these – Standard Oil (New Jersey) to expand into foreign markets as a way of increasing profits ('structure shaped strategy').

Chandler's aim was to study the interaction of strategy and structure in a changing business environment. In successive cases he traces how strategies to launch new products or enter new regions strained current structures, and how managers responded by gradually, through trial and error, developing new ways of dividing and co-ordinating work.

That research tradition continues in, for example, Grant's (2003) study of strategy in major oil companies – see Chapter 8. Eli Lilly (**www.lilly.com**), a pharmaceutical company, provides further evidence. The company faced commercial disaster when it unexpectedly lost patent protection of Prozac, at the time its most profitable drug. Colville and Murphy (2006) show how managers had intense debates about a new strategy and a new structure, followed by rapid implementation. This was so successful that the group began launching new drugs at an unprecedented rate, rapidly returning to profit.

Table 9.1 Examples of strategic and organisational decisions

Example	Strategic issue	Structural issue
Royal Dutch Shell, 2009 www.shell.com	Shell's new CEO decided the present structure was too complex and costly. Aim of change was to cut costs and speed up large projects	Combined two largest divisions into one; some common functions (such as IT) moved from divisions to a central service
Co-operative Group, 2010 www.co-op.co.uk	Mutual group (owned by its customers) tries to secure economies of scale to compete more effectively in the retail and banking sectors	Acquires the Somerfield supermarket chain and the Britannia Building Society, and begins to integrate them into the Co-op Group
Multi-show Events (see p. 177)	How to control growing business to ensure continued success	Divided staff into departments to improve focus and skill; created distinct management roles
Sony Ericsson joint venture, 2009 www.sonyericsson.com	Had not yet developed a smartphone, and lacked a plan to sell cheap mobiles in emerging markets. Development groups competing	New CEO cut 30 per cent of staff; centralised decision-making to end internal rivalry; will use other companies' technology in first smartphone

Table 9.1 gives examples of visible structural change. While senior managers discuss these prominent changes, those at other levels work on similar issues within their respective units, such as:

- should we divide a job into three parts and give each to a separate employee, or have them work as a team with joint responsibility for the whole task;
- should Team A do this task, or Team B?
- should that employee report to supervisor A or supervisor B?

Whether the issue is at a multi-national business like Motorola or a small company like Multi-show Events (see p. 177) the fundamental structural task is the same – to clarify what people should do, and to ensure they co-ordinate with others.

The next section introduces the main tools people can use to shape the structure of an organisation, or of a unit within it.

9.3   Designing a structure

Organisation structure describes how managers divide and co-ordinate work. It gives those appointed to a job a reasonably clear idea of what they should do – the marketing assistant deals with marketing, not finance.

The organisation chart

The **organisation chart** shows the main departments and job titles, with lines linking senior executives to the departments or people for whose work they are responsible. It shows who people report to, and clarifies four features of the **formal structure**:

- tasks – the major tasks or activities of the organisation;
- subdivisions – how they are divided;

Organisation structure
'The structure of an organisation [is] the sum total of the ways in which it divides its labour into distinct tasks and then achieves co-ordination among them' (Mintzberg, 1979).

An **organisation chart** shows the main departments and senior positions in an organisation and the reporting relations between them.

Formal structure consists of guidelines, documents or procedures setting out how the organisation's activities are divided and co-ordinated.

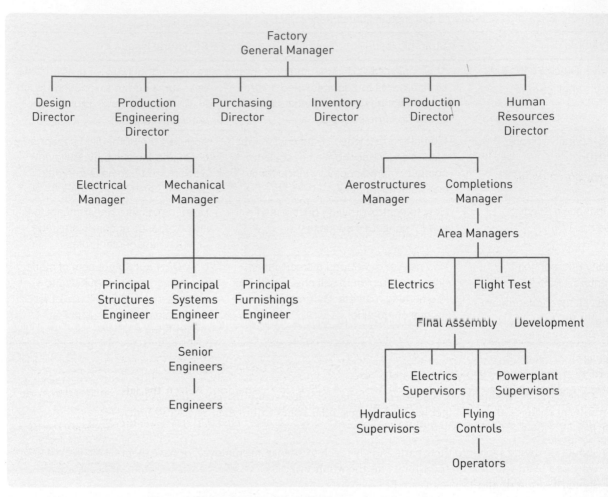

Figure 9.2 The structure within a BAE aircraft factory (**www.baesystems.com**)

- levels – the position of each post within the hierarchy; and
- lines of authority – these link the boxes to show who people report to.

Organisation charts give a convenient (though transient) summary of tasks and who is responsible for them. Figure 9.2 shows that for an aircraft factory which at the time was part of BAE Systems, a UK defence contractor. It shows six departments – design, production engineering, purchasing, inventory, production and human resources. It also shows the chain of command within the plant and the tasks of the respective departments (only some of which are shown). In this case, the chart includes direct staff such as operators and engineers, and shows the lines of authority throughout the factory. It does *not* show the **informal structure** – the many patterns of work and communication that are part of organisational life.

Informal structure is the undocumented relationships between members of the organisation that emerge as people adapt systems to new conditions and satisfy personal and group needs.

Work specialisation

Within the formal structure, managers divide work into smaller tasks, in which people or departments specialise. They become more expert in one task than they could be in several and are more likely to come up with improved ideas or methods. Taken too far it leads to the negative effects on motivation described in Chapter 13.

Management in practice   Multi-show Events

Multi-show Events employs 11 people providing a variety of entertainment and promotional services to large businesses. When Brian Simpson created the business there were two staff – so there was no formal structure. He reflected on the process of growth and structure:

> While the company was small, thinking about a structure never occurred to me. It became a consideration as sales grew and the complexity of what we offered increased. There were also more people around and I believed that I should introduce a structure so that clear divisions of responsibility would be visible. It seemed natural to split sales and marketing from the actual delivery and production of events as these were two distinct areas. I felt that by creating 'specialised' departments we could give a better service to clients as each area of the company could focus more on their own roles.
>
> We had to redesign the office layout and introduce a more formal communication process to ensure all relevant information is being passed on – and on the whole I think this structure will see us through the next stage of business growth and development.

Source: Private communication.

Figure 9.2 shows specialisation in the BAE factory – at the top it is between design, production, purchasing and so on. It shows a **vertical specialisation**, in that people at each level deal with distinct activities, and a **horizontal specialisation**. Within production engineering some specialise in electrical problems and others in mechanical. Within the latter, people focus on structures, systems or furnishings. Though Multi-show Events is still a small company, they too have begun to create a structure showing who is responsible for which tasks.

Vertical specialisation refers to the extent to which responsibilities at different levels are defined.

Horizontal specialisation is the degree to which tasks are divided among separate people or departments.

Chain of command

The lines of authority show the links between people – to whom they report and who reports to them. It shows whom they can ask to do work, whom they can ask for help – and who will be expecting results from them. In Figure 9.2 the production director can give instructions to the aerostructures manager, but not to the electrical manager in production engineering.

In drawing lines of authority, managers decide where to allocate **formal authority** – giving people the right to make decisions, allocate resources or give instructions. It is based on the position, not the person. The production engineering director at BAE has formal authority over defined matters – and anyone else in the job would have the same formal authority.

Formal authority is the right that a person in a specified role has to make decisions, allocate resources or give instructions.

Subordinates comply with instructions when they accept the person has the formal (sometimes called legitimate) authority to issue them. An operator in the hydraulics area of final assembly would accept an instruction from the hydraulics foreman, but probably not from the powerplant foreman (they may help as a personal favour, but that is different from accepting formal authority). If managers give instructions beyond their area of formal authority, they meet resistance.

Responsibility is a person's duty to meet the expectations associated with a task. The production director and the hydraulics foreman are responsible for the tasks that go with those positions. To fulfil those responsibilities they require formal authority to manage relevant resources.

Responsibility refers to a person's duty to meet the expectations others have of them in their role.

Accountability means that people with formal authority over an area are required to report on their work to those above them in the chain of command. The principal systems engineer is accountable to the mechanical manager for the way they have used resources: have they achieved what was expected as measured by the cost, quantity, quality or timeliness of the work?

Delegation is when people transfer part of their work to people below them in the hierarchy. While the production director is responsible and accountable for all the work in that area, they can only do this by delegating. They remain responsible for results, but pass the necessary authority and resources to subordinates – and this continues down the hierarchy. If managers delegate to their subordinates this enables quicker decisions and more rapid responses, though some managers are reluctant to delegate in case it reduces their power (Chapter 12).

Delegation occurs when one person gives another the authority to undertake specific activities or decisions.

The span of control

The **span of control** is the number of subordinates reporting to a supervisor. If managers supervise staff closely there is a narrow span of control: if staff have more autonomy and responsibility that means less supervision, so the span of control becomes wider, and the structure flatter.

A **span of control** is the number of subordinates reporting directly to the person above them in the hierarchy.

Centralisation and decentralisation

As an organisation grows, managers divide work vertically, as they delegate decisions to those below them – and so begin to create a hierarchy such as that shown in Figure 9.2. As the business grows, the hierarchy becomes more complex, but it is usually possible to see three levels – corporate, divisional and operating – such as at The Royal Bank of Scotland (RBS) (**www.rbs.com**).

- **Corporate** The most senior group, such as the board of RBS, has overall responsibility for leading and controlling the company. It approves strategy across the group, monitors performance at major units and maintains links with significant external institutions such as regulators and political bodies.
- **Divisional** Responsible for implementing policy and for allocating budgets and other resources. RBS is organised by customer (UK Retail and UK Corporate and Commercial); by product (RBS Insurance); and by geography (Ulster Bank and Citizens Bank which operates in the USA). Divisional managers are responsible for meeting targets set by the board. They also represent the division's interests to the board and monitor the performance of their operating units.
- **Operating** Responsible for the technical work of the organisation – making products, catching thieves, caring for patients or delivering services. Within UK Personal at RBS, teams are responsible for ensuring that, for example, branches and cash machines work smoothly. In 2011, the company acknowledged that customers were queuing too long at branches, and promised that operating staff would improve operating processes to overcome this.

The vertical hierarchy establishes the decisions which people at each level can make. The theme is especially relevant in large multi-national companies, which experience constant tension between calls for global integration and local responsiveness.

Centralisation is when those at the top make most decisions, with managers at divisional level ensuring those at operating level follow the policy.

Centralisation is when a relatively large number of decisions are taken by management at the top of the organisation.

Decentralisation is when a relatively large number of decisions are taken in the divisions or operating units. Branch managers in ATMays, a chain of retail travel agents (now part of Going Places) had considerable freedom over pricing and promotional activities, but were required to follow very tight financial reporting routines.

Decentralisation is when a relatively large number of decisions are taken lower down the organisation in the operating units.

> ## Management in practice   A decentralised structure at Roche   www.roche.com FT
>
> Roche, based in Switzerland, is one of the world's most successful and profitable pharmaceutical companies. The board appointed a new chief executive in 2010 – Severin Schwan (a graduate in business and law) – who, at the age of 40, has spent his career in the company. The group has a decentralised structure and a hands-off relationship with subsidiaries, which analysts believe has been a major factor in its success. The federal structure fosters focused research with each company concentrating on specific diseases, but supple enough to collaborate on marketing. Mr Schwan says teamwork is essential in this knowledge-based business:
>
> > When I toured our labs, I grasped the potential and the enthusiasm of our people. We have to capitalise on that. If you tell your people all the time what to do, don't be surprised if they don't come up with new ideas. Innovative people need air to breathe. Our culture of working together at Roche is based on mutual trust and teamwork. An informal friendly manner supports this: at the same time this must not lead to negligence or shoddy compromises – goals must be achieved and, at times, tough decisions have to be implemented.
>
> Source: Adapted from A healthy attitude to risk-taking (Andrew Jack and Haig Simonian), *Financial Times*, 4 August 2008.

Many organisations display a mix of both. Network Rail (responsible for the railway track and signals) has highly standardised processes and highly centralised control systems: but local managers have high autonomy in deciding how to organise their resources. They can co-ordinate track improvements and engineering schedules to meet the needs of local train operating companies (*Financial Times*, 23 July 2007). SABMiller is a highly decentralised business, as selling beer is essentially a local business with tastes and preferences varying widely – but it is centralising many support functions such as finance and procurement. It hopes this will bring great economies of scale and allow general managers to concentrate on growing sales revenue.

This tension between centralising and decentralising is common, with the balance at any time reflecting managers' relative power and their views on their respective advantages and disadvantages – see Table 9.2.

Table 9.2 Advantages and disadvantages of centralisation

Factor	Advantages	Disadvantages
Response to change	Thorough debate of issues	Slower response to local conditions
Use of expertise	Concentration of expertise at the centre makes it easier to develop new services and promote best practice methods	Less likely to take account of local knowledge or innovative people
Cost	Economies of scale in purchasing Efficient administration if use common systems	Local suppliers may be better value than corporate suppliers
Policy implications	Less risk of local managers breaching legal requirements	More risk of local managers breaching legal requirements
Staff commitment	Backing of centre ensures wide support	Staff motivated by greater local responsibility
Consistency	Provides consistent image to the public – less variation in service standards	Local staff discouraged from taking responsibility – can blame centre

Formalisation

Formalisation is the practice of using written or electronic documents to direct and control employees.

Formalisation is when managers use written or electronic documents to direct and control employees. These include rules, procedures, instruction manuals, job descriptions – anything that shows what people must do. Operators in most call centres use scripts to guide their conversation with a customer: managers create these to bring consistency and predictability to the work.

There is always tension between formality and informality. If people want to respond to individual needs or local conditions, they favour informal arrangements with few rules, as this seems the best way to meet those needs. Industry regulators or consumer legislation may specify detailed procedures that companies must follow: these are meant to protect customers against unsuitable selling methods, or to protect staff against unfounded complaints. This leads to more formal systems and recording procedures.

9.4	Grouping jobs into functions and divisions

While work specialisation divides tasks into smaller jobs for individuals, an opposite process groups them together in functional, divisional or matrix forms. Two other forms use teams and networks as the basis of structure.

Specialisation by function

A **functional structure** is when tasks are grouped into departments based on similar skills and expertise.

In a **functional structure**, managers group staff according to profession or function – the BAE chart shows design, production engineering, purchasing, inventory, production and human resources functions. This can be efficient, as people with common expertise work together to provide a service, and follow a professional career path. It can lead to conflict if functions have different perceptions of organisational goals. Staff in sales and marketing experience this – the former stressing immediate sales, the latter long-term customer relations. Functional staff face conflicts when product managers compete for access to functional resources such as information technology.

Specialisation by divisions

A **divisional structure** is when tasks are grouped in relation to their outputs, such as products or the needs of different types of customer.

Managers create a **divisional structure** when they group staff around products, services or customers, giving those in charge of each unit the authority to design, produce and deliver the product or service. Functions within the division are likely to co-operate as they depend on satisfying the same set of customers.

Product or customer

Divisional structures enable staff to focus on a distinct group of customers. In 2011, HMV Group had two divisions – the HMV stores and Waterstone's bookshops (though it sold the latter early in the year). Hospitals can use the 'named-nurse' system, in which one nurse is responsible for several identified patients. That nurse is the patient's point of contact with the system, managing the delivery of services from other (functional) departments. Figure 9.3 contrasts 'task' and 'named-nurse' approaches.

Geographic divisions

Here managers in companies with many service outlets – like Tesco or Wetherspoon's – group tasks by geography. This allows front-line staff to identify local needs, and makes it easier for divisional managers to control local performance – see Table 9.3.

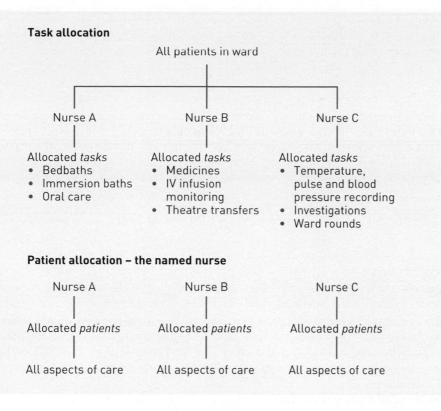

Task allocation

All patients in ward

Nurse A   Nurse B   Nurse C

Allocated *tasks*   Allocated *tasks*   Allocated *tasks*
• Bedbaths   • Medicines   • Temperature,
• Immersion baths   • IV infusion   pulse and blood
• Oral care   monitoring   pressure recording
                    • Theatre transfers • Investigations
                                         • Ward rounds

Patient allocation – the named nurse

Nurse A   Nurse B   Nurse C

Allocated *patients* Allocated *patients* Allocated *patients*

All aspects of care All aspects of care All aspects of care

Figure 9.3
Task and named-nurse structures

Table 9.3 Advantages and disadvantages of functional and divisional structures

Structure	Advantages	Disadvantages
Functional	Clear career paths and professional development Specialisation leads to high standards and efficiency Common professional interests support good internal relations	Isolation from wider interests damages promotion prospects Conflict over priorities Lack of wider awareness damages external relations
Divisional	Functional staff focus on product and customer needs Dedicated facilities meet customer needs quickly Common customer focus enables good internal relations	Isolation from wider professional and technical developments Costs of duplicate resources Potential conflict with other divisions over priorities Focus on local, not corporate, needs

9.5   Grouping jobs in matrices, teams and networks

Matrix structure

A **matrix structure** combines functional and divisional structures: function on one axis of the matrix and products or projects on the other. Functional staff work on one or more projects, moving between them as required. They report to two bosses – a functional head and

A **matrix structure** is when those doing a task report both to a functional and a project or divisional boss.

the head of the current project. The risk with the method is that the complex management structure may mean that staff are unclear about accountability and responsibility, leading to confusion and poor performance.

Teams

In their search for more flexibility, lower costs and faster response, some companies organise work into teams – especially those which depend on a steady flow of new products, such as Nokia or EMI Music. Management delegates significant authority to an identifiable team, which is then accountable for results (Chapter 15).

Management in practice   **Team launches new albums at EMI**   www.emi.com

New music albums often fail when managers are unable to manage the launch effectively. There is often tension between marketing staff who have a short-term outlook, being expected to satisfy current consumers by exploiting existing resources, and creative staff who take a medium-term view. The latter do so as they are expected to find new artists to change the repertoire – and who therefore need longer to become credible.

Ordanini *et al.* (2008) show how EMI Music adopted a team approach to launching new albums. They appointed a single team to be responsible for all aspects of the launch of an album by an unknown and possibly controversial artist. The team included marketing and creative staff, and enabled them to work together in this way for the first time. In this case, the launch was successful on several dimensions and appeared to vindicate the choice of a team approach.

Source: Ordanini *et al.* (2008).

Networks

A **network structure** is when tasks required by one company are performed by other companies with expertise in those areas.

Network structures refer to situations in which organisations remain independent but agree to work together to deliver products or services. Sometimes this happens when managers outsource activities to other companies who can produce them more cost-effectively. The remaining organisation concentrates on setting strategy direction and managing the core units. Electronic companies often do this: Dell employs other companies to make its products. The arrangement is becoming common in public services – Care UK runs schools for disturbed children on behalf of local government. The danger is that while it is easy to outsource the delivery of a product or service in the hope of reducing costs, the *outsourcer* remains responsible to the customer. A supplier may be doing the work, but the company is still responsible and accountable to the customers, and cannot evade that by blaming their suppliers – as BP initially tried to do after the Gulf of Mexico disaster.

Mixed forms

Large organisations typically combine functional, product and geographical structures within the same company.

The counterpart of dividing work is to co-ordinate it, or there will be confusion and poor performance.

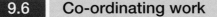

9.6   Co-ordinating work

There are six common ways to co-ordinate work.

Direct supervision

This is where a manager ensures co-ordination by directly supervising their staff to ensure they work as expected. The number of people whom a manager can effectively supervise directly reflects the idea of the span of control – that beyond some (variable) point direct supervision is no longer sufficient.

Hierarchy

If disputes or problems arise between staff or departments, they can put the arguments to their common boss in the hierarchy, making it the boss's responsibility to reach a solution. At BAE (Figure 9.2), if the engineer responsible for structures had a disagreement with the systems engineer, they could ask the mechanical manager to adjudicate. If that failed they could escalate the problem to the production engineering director – but this would take time. In rapidly changing circumstances, the hierarchy cannot cope with the many issues requiring attention, and so delays decisions.

Standardising inputs and outputs

If the buyer of a component specifies exactly what is required, and the supplier meets that specification, co-ordination between users will be easy. If staff meet the specifications, that helps them to co-ordinate with the next stage. If they receive the same training they will need less direct supervision, as their manager is confident they will work together. All new staff at Pret A Manger must complete a very precise training course before they begin work, which is then constantly reinforced as long as they work at the firm.

Rules and procedures

Another method is to prepare rules or procedures, like that in the Management in Practice feature below, which aim to ensure that all operators follow the same safe working methods. Most organisations have strict procedures for managing expensive investments, such as in new equipment or acquisitions. To compare proposals accurately, they specify the questions those seeking approval should answer, how they should prepare the case and to whom they should submit it. Software developers have to co-ordinate the work of the designers working on different parts of a project, so they use strict change control procedures to ensure that the sub-projects fit together.

Management in practice   Safety procedures in a power station

The following instructions govern the steps that staff must follow when they inspect control equipment in a nuclear power station:

1 Before commencing work you must read and understand the relevant Permit-to-Work and/or other safety documents as appropriate.
2 Obtain keys for relevant cubicles.
3 Visually inspect the interior of each bay for dirt, water and evidence of condensation.
4 Visually inspect the cabling, glands, terminal blocks and components for damage.
5 Visually check for loose connections at all terminals.
6 Lock all cubicles and return the keys.
7 Clear the safety document and return it to the Supervisor/Senior Authorised person.

Information systems

Information systems help to ensure that people who need to work in a consistent way have common information, so that they can co-ordinate their activities. Computer systems and internet applications enable different parts of an organisation, as well as suppliers and customers, to work from common information, making co-ordination easier – though managers frequently underestimate the organisational obstacles to implementing such systems (see Chapter 10).

Direct personal contact

The most human form of co-ordination is when people talk to each other in person, which clearly works well in simple situations where people can readily exchange information about customer requirements and so on. It is also often the best means of co-ordination in complex situations. These contain so much uncertainty that information systems cannot cope: only direct contact can do this, by enabling people to make personal commitments to staff in other business units.

Management in practice   Co-ordination in a social service

The organisation cares for the elderly in a large city. Someone who had worked there for several years reflected on co-ordination:

> Within the centre there was a manager, two deputies, an assistant manager, five senior care officers (SCOs) and thirty officers. Each SCO is responsible for six care officers, allowing daily contact between the supervisor and the subordinates. While this defines job roles quite tightly, it allows a good communication structure to exist. Feedback is common, as there are frequent meetings of the separate groups, and individual appraisals of the care officers by the SCOs. Staff value this opportunity for praise and comments on how they are doing.
>
> Contact at all levels is common between supervisor and care officers during meetings to assess the needs of clients – for whom the care officers have direct responsibility. Frequent social gatherings and functions within the department also enhance relations and satisfy social needs. Controls placed on the behaviour of the care officers come from senior management, often derived from legislation such as the Social Work Acts or the Health and Safety Executive.

Source: Private communication.

Managers make a succession of decisions on any or all of these ways to divide and co-ordinate work. As they do so, they build a structure which in varying degrees corresponds to a mechanistic or an organic form.

9.7   Mechanistic and organic structures

A **mechanistic structure** means there is a high degree of task specialisation, people's responsibility and authority are closely defined and decision-making is centralised.

Some structures emphasise the vertical hierarchy by defining responsibilities clearly, taking decisions at the centre, delegating tightly defined tasks and requiring frequent reports. This enables those at the centre to know what is happening and whether staff are working correctly. The organisation presents a uniform image and ensures that customers, patients or service-users receive consistent treatment. Communication is mainly vertical, as those at the centre pass instructions down and staff pass queries up. Burns and Stalker (1961) called this a **mechanistic structure**.

Table 9.4 Characteristics of mechanistic and organic systems

Mechanistic	Organic
Specialised tasks	Contribute experience to common tasks
Hierarchical structure of control	Network structure of contacts
Knowledge located at top of hierarchy	Knowledge widely spread
Vertical communication	Horizontal communication
Loyalty and obedience stressed	Commitment to goals more important

Others develop a structure with broadly defined, flexible tasks, many cross-functional teams and base authority on expertise rather than position. Senior managers realise that they depend on those nearest the action to deal effectively with local problems. Most communication is 'horizontal' – between those lower down the hierarchy who are most familiar with the task and its setting. There may not be an organisation chart, as the division of work is so fluid. Burns and Stalker (1961) called this an **organic structure**. Table 9.4 compares the two forms.

Within a large organisation some units will correspond to a mechanistic form and others to an organic. A company may have a centralised information system and tightly controlled policies on capital expenditure – while also allowing business units autonomy on research or advertising budgets.

Why do managers favour one form of structure rather than another? A widely held (though disputed) view is that it depends on how they interpret **contingencies**:

> the essence of the contingency paradigm is that organizational effectiveness results from fitting characteristics of the organization, such as its structure, to contingencies that reflect the situation of the organization. (Donaldson, 2001, p. 1)

Successful organisations appear to be those in which managers maintain a good fit between contingent factors and the structure within which people work. Figure 9.1 illustrates these – strategy, technology, age/size and environment.

An **organic structure** is one where people are expected to work together and to use their initiative to solve problems; job descriptions and rules are few and imprecise.

Contingencies are factors such as uncertainty, interdependence and size that reflect the situation of the organisation.

Strategy

Chapter 8 outlined the view that firms adopt one of three generic strategies – cost leadership, differentiation or focus. Managers following a cost-leadership strategy concentrate on increasing efficiency to keep costs low, and a mechanistic structure is likely to support this, by defining tasks clearly within a functional structure. A hierarchical chain of command ensures people work to plan and vertical communication keeps senior managers informed. Powergen, an electricity utility, initially had a cost-leadership strategy, which it supported with a functional structure, detailed rules and clear performance measures.

Managers following a differentiation strategy focus on innovation – aiming to develop new products rapidly. An organic structure is most likely to support this, by enabling ideas to flow easily between people able to contribute, regardless of their function. Companies which allow business units a high degree of decision-making authority are likely to be more successful than those which try to exercise tight control over what they do. They often use a team-based structure to encourage people to share ideas quickly – the example of Monsanto in the Management in Practice feature below.

Management in practice   Changing Monsanto   www.monsanto.com   **FT**

Although many see Monsanto as a predatory chemical company pressing genetically modified seeds on the world, its chief executive (Mr Grant) sees it as a vibrant biotechnology company with all the dynamism of a Silicon Valley start-up.

> In some companies the scientists are in the back room, separate from the business people. The culture here is much closer to a software company, where there are developers that invent cool stuff and there is a very intimate link between the scientists and the business people.

This is reflected, Mr Grant says, in the company's day-to-day operations.

> If we're making decisions, there's usually five or six people at the table. That makes for a culture that is extraordinarily team-based – not in the sense of group hugs and the fluff factor, but because most decisions we make are multi-disciplinary and if you want to make a decision once, you had better have those people at the table.
>
> It's an environment where people need to have an equal voice . . . Quite often you will have a business person, a regulatory person, a breeding person, a production person and a couple of others. That has created a culture where people come together, form teams, make decisions, break up and move on to the next thing. It's more amorphous than the hierarchical corporate structure, and that makes it feel more like a modern company than an old world company.

Source: Adapted from Prepared to wait for a bigger yield (Hal Weitzman), *Financial Times*, 15 June 2009.

Figure 9.4 expresses the idea that different strategies require different structures. The more the strategy corresponds to cost leadership, the more likely it is that managers will support it with a functional structure. If the balance is towards differentiation, the more likely there will be a divisional, team or network structure. In 2011, Siemens, the German conglomerate, was reported to be planning a new 'infrastructure' division (by re-combining some units in its industrial division) to supply products and services to the world's 600 largest cities – such as urban trains, road traffic management, smart energy grids and building technology.

Technology

Technology is the knowledge, equipment and activities used to transform inputs into outputs.

Technology refers to the knowledge, tools and techniques used to transform inputs into outputs. It includes buildings, machines, computer systems and the knowledge and procedures associated with them.

Joan Woodward (1965) gathered information from 100 British firms to establish whether structural features such as the span of control or the number of levels in the hierarchy varied between them, and whether this affected performance. The researchers saw no pattern until

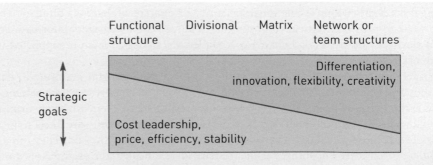

Figure 9.4
Relationship between strategies and structural types

they analysed companies by their manufacturing process, grouping these into three types according to their technical complexity. This showed a relationship between technical complexity and company structure.

- **Unit and small batch production** Firms make unique goods to a customer's order. It is similar to craft work, as people and their skills are deeply involved in the process – custom-built cycles, designer furniture, luxury yachts.
- **Large batch and mass production** Large quantities of standard products move along an assembly line, with people complementing the machinery – mobile phones, Ford cars or Electrolux washing machines.
- **Continuous process** Material flows through complex technology which makes the product as operators monitor it, fixing faults and generally overseeing the process – a Guinness Brewery, a BP refinery or a Mittal steel plant.

Woodward concluded that the different technologies impose different demands on people. Unit production requires close supervision to ensure that staff meet the customer's unique requirements. Supervisors can communicate directly with those working on different parts of the task and so manage the uncertainties involved in producing 'one-off' items. On an assembly line the work is routine and predictable, so a supervisor can monitor more staff: there is a wide span of control. Commercially successful firms were those where managers had created a structure providing the right support to staff using the technology.

Technology also delivers services, and managers create structures to shape the way staff interact with customers. Bank staff traditionally handled many cash transactions, and sat behind secure glass screens which made them remote. Technology such as online banking means that branches now handle very little cash, so banks re-designed them to bring staff and customers closer together.

Environment

Chapter 3 showed how environments vary in terms of their complexity and dynamism: does this mean that firms need a structure which suits the nature of their environment? Burns and Stalker (1961) compared the structure of a long-established rayon plant in Manchester with the structures of several new electronics companies then being created in the east of Scotland. Both types of organisation were successful – but had different structures.

The rayon plant had clearly set out rules, tight job descriptions, clear procedures and co-ordination was primarily through the hierarchy. There was a high degree of specialisation, with tasks divided into small parts. Managers had defined responsibilities clearly and discouraged people from acting outside of their remit. They had centralised decisions, with information flowing up the hierarchy and instructions down.

The small companies in the newly created electronics industry had few job descriptions, while procedures were ambiguous and imprecise. Staff were expected to use their initiative to decide priorities and to work together to solve problems. Communication was horizontal, rather than vertical (see Table 9.4).

Burns and Stalker (1961) concluded that both forms were appropriate for their circumstances. The rayon plant had a stable environment, as its purpose was to supply a steady flow of rayon to the company's spinning factories. Delivery schedules rarely changed and the technology of rayon manufacture was well known. In contrast, the electronics companies were in direct contact with their customers, mainly the Ministry of Defence. The demand for commercial and military products was volatile, with frequent changes in requirements. The technology was new, often applying the results of recent research. Contracts were often taken in which neither the customer nor the company knew what the end product would be: it was likely to change during the course of the work.

A stable business environment is likely to encourage managers to use a mechanistic structure, while in unstable ones they are likely to find that a more organic form works better.

Recognising that environmental conditions place different demands upon organisations was a major step in understanding why companies adopt contrasting structures.

Organisations do not face a single environment. People in each department try to meet the expectations of players in the wider environment, and develop structures which help them to do that. A payroll section has to meet legal requirements on, among other things, salary entitlements, taxation and pensions records. Staff must follow strict rules, with little scope to use their initiative: they work in a mechanistic structure. Staff in product development face different requirements – and will expect to work in a structure which encourages creativity and innovation: they expect to work in an organic structure.

An implication of this is that co-ordination between such departments will be difficult, as they will work in different ways (Lawrence and Lorsch, 1967).

Size and life cycle

Small organisations tend to be informal – people work on several tasks and co-ordinate with each other through face-to-face contact or direct supervision. Weber (1947) noted that larger organisations had formal, bureaucratic structures: research by Blau (1970) and Pugh and Hickson (1976) confirmed that as organisations grow they develop formal structures, hierarchies and specialised units. Like the head of Multi-show Events, as managers divide a growing business into separate units they need more controls such as job descriptions and reporting relationships.

This implies that organisations go through stages in their life cycle, with structures adapting to suit. The entrepreneur creates the business alone, or with a few partners or employees. They operate informally with little division of labour – tasks overlap and there are few rules or systems for co-ordination. The owner makes the decisions, so they have a centralised structure. If the business succeeds it will need to raise more capital to finance growth. The owner no longer has sole control, but shares decisions with members of the growing management team. Tasks become divided by function or product, creating separate departments and more formal controls to ensure co-ordination. Many small companies fail when they expand rapidly without imposing controls to prevent people from taking too many risks. A manager at a failing publishing company recalled:

> We were editors and designers running a large show, and we were completely over-stretched. Our systems were simply not up to speed with our creative ambitions.

This observation is consistent with a study by Sine *et al.* (2006), which shows how successful internet companies balanced the essential creative spirit of their companies with a degree of formalisation, specialisation and administrative intensity. They survived, while those without an adequate structure did not.

If a business continues to grow, it becomes more bureaucratic with more division of responsibilities and more rules to ensure co-ordination. There are more professional and specialist staff in finance or human resources, with systems for budgeting, financial control and rewards. Mature, established firms tend to become mechanistic, with a strong vertical system and well-developed controls. More decisions are made at the centre – bringing the danger of slow response to new conditions, and so becoming less competitive in some industries than new small firms.

Contingencies or managerial choice?

Contingency approaches propose
that the performance of
an organisation depends
on having a structure
that is appropriate to its
environment.

Contingency approaches propose that the most effective structure will depend (be contingent) upon the situation in which the organisation is operating:

> The organization is seen as existing in an environment that shapes its strategy, technology, size and innovation rate. These contingent factors in turn determine the required structure; that is, the structure that the organization needs to adopt if it is to operate effectively. (Donaldson, 1996, p. 2)

Effective management involves formulating an appropriate strategy and developing a structure which supports that strategy by encouraging appropriate behaviour. The emphasis is **determinist** (the form is determined by the environment) and functionalist (the form is intended to serve organisational effectiveness). Management's role is to make suitable adjustments to the structure to improve performance as conditions change – such as by increasing formality as the company grows. Others, like GSK, introduce greater divisional autonomy to encourage creativity or responsiveness to local conditions.

Determinism is the view that the business environment determines an organisation's structure.

John Child (2005) disagrees, suggesting that contingency theorists ignore the degree of **structural choice** which managers have. The process of organisational design is not a solely rational matter but one also shaped by political processes. The values and interests of powerful groups are able to influence the structure that emerges even if this reduces performance to some degree. The standards used to assess performance are in any case not always rigorous, and people may tolerate some under-performance caused by an inappropriate structure.

Structural choice emphasises the scope which management has to decide the form of structure, irrespective of environmental conditions.

Another consideration is that the direction of causality is not necessarily from strategy to structure. It is also possible that an organisation with a given structure finds that that makes it easier to embark on a particular strategy.

Activity 9.2   What does 'organisation structure' mean?

Having read the chapter, make brief notes summarising the structural issues evident in the organisation you chose for this activity.

- How (if at all) did people discuss any links between structure and strategy? (Refer to Section 9.2.)
- What methods did they use to divide work? (Refer to Sections 9.4 and 9.5.)
- What methods did they use to co-ordinate work? (Refer to Section 9.6.)
- What reasons, if any, did they give for choosing one method rather than another? (Refer to Section 9.7.)

Compare what you have found with other students on your course.

Summary

1 **Outline the links between strategy, structure and performance**

- The structure signals what people are expected to do within the organisation, and is intended to support actions that are in line with strategy, and so enhance performance. Equally, a structure may enable a new strategy to emerge which a different structure would have hindered.

2 **Give examples of management choices about dividing and co-ordinating work, with their likely advantages and disadvantages**

- Managers divide work to enable individuals and groups to specialise on a limited aspect of the whole, and then combine the work into related areas of activity. Task division needs to be accompanied by suitable methods of co-ordination.
- Centralisation brings consistency and efficiency, but also the danger of being slow and out of touch with local conditions. People in decentralised units can respond quickly to local conditions but risk acting inconsistently.
- Functional forms allow people to specialise and develop expertise and are efficient; but they may be inward-looking and prone to conflicting demands.

- Divisional forms allow focus on particular markets of customer groups, but can dupli-cate facilities thus adding to cost.
- Matrix forms try to balance the benefits of functional and divisional forms, but can again lead to conflicting priorities over resources.
- Networks of organisations enable companies to draw upon a wide range of expertise, but may involve additional management and co-ordination costs.

3 **Compare the features of mechanistic and organic structures**

- Mechanistic – people perform specialised tasks, hierarchical structure of control, knowledge located at top of hierarchy, vertical communication, loyalty and obedience valued.
- Organic – people contribute experience to common tasks, network structure of con-tacts, knowledge widely spread, horizontal communication, commitment to task goals more important than to superiors.

4 **Summarise the work of Woodward, Burns and Stalker, Lawrence and Lorsch and Child, showing how they contributed to this area of management**

- Woodward: appropriate structure depends on the type of production system ('technol-ogy') – unit, small batch, process.
- Burns and Stalker: appropriate structure depends on uncertainty of the organisation's environment – mechanistic in stable, organic in unstable.
- Lawrence and Lorsch: units within an organisation face different environmental de-mands, which implies that there will be both mechanistic and organic forms within the same organisation, raising new problems of co-ordination.
- John Child: contingency theory implies too great a degree of determinism – managers have greater degree of choice over structure than contingency theories implied.

Review questions

1 What did Chandler conclude about the relationship between strategy, structure and performance?

2 Draw the organisation chart of a company or department that you know. Compare it with the structure shown in Figure 9.2, and note points of similarity and difference.

3 List the advantages and disadvantages of centralising organisational functions?

4 Several forms of co-ordination are described. Select two that you have seen in operation and describe in detail how they work – and how well they work.

5 Explain the difference between a mechanistic and an organic form of organisation.

6 Explain the term 'contingency approach' and give an example of each of the factors that influence the choice between mechanistic and organic structures.

7 If contingency approaches stress the influence of external factors on organisational structures, what is the role of management in designing organisational structures?

Further reading

Woodward, J. (1965), *Industrial Organization: Theory and practice* (2nd edn 1980), Oxford University Press, Oxford. Second edition 1980.

Burns, T. and Stalker, G. M. (1961), *The Management of Innovation*, Tavistock, London.

Lawrence, P. and Lorsch, J. W. (1967), *Organization and Environment*, Harvard Business School Press, Boston, MA.

These influential books give accessible accounts of the research process, and it would add to your understanding to read at least one of them in the original. The second edition of Woodward's book (1980) includes a commentary on her work by two later scholars.

Weblinks

These websites have appeared in, or are relevant to, the chapter:

www.lilly.com
www.shell.com
www.co-op.co.uk
www.sonyericsson.com
www.baesystems.com
www.rbs.com
www.roche.com
www.emi.com
www.monsanto.com
www.gsk.com

Visit two of the business sites in the list, and navigate to the pages dealing with corporate news, investor relations or 'our company'.

- What structural issues can you identify that managers in the company are likely to be dealing with?
- What kind of environment are they likely to be working in, and how may that affect their structure?

 Annotated weblinks, multiple choice questions and other useful resources can be found on **www.pearsoned.co.uk/boddy**

Case study GlaxoSmithKline (GSK) www.gsk.com

GSK is one the world's largest pharmaceutical companies, formed in 2000 by the merger of Glaxo-Wellcome and SmithKlineBeecham. In 2010, it had sales of £28.4 billion, with over 98,000 staff working in 100 countries – including 16,000 in Research & Development.

Like other major pharmaceutical companies, the company's survival depends on developing new drugs which it can sell profitably. New products are discovered, developed and launched – and are protected by patents for about ten years. These prevent other companies from taking the idea and manufacturing and selling an equivalent product. This means that while the drug has patent protection the company has a monopoly over its supply – enabling it to make high profits (if doctors find the drug useful to their patients).

When the patent expires, other companies can copy the drug and produce what are known as 'generic' versions. These sell at very low prices, and radically reduce the original company's income. Their R&D must therefore continually replace older product with new ones, to stop the company's revenue from falling. Without an adequate revenue flow, the company is unable to invest in the R&D required for new drugs.

Companies like GSK are finding it increasingly difficult to maintain an adequate flow of the new drugs they aim to launch each year. Common reasons are that the diseases that are relatively easy to treat have been tackled; tighter regulations have greatly increased the cost of getting approval from the regulatory authorities before it can sell the drug; and the rising costs of every aspects of scientific research. Discovering and developing a new medicine takes about 12 years before it begins to produce revenue – and during that time it is draining resources from the company.

Senior management at GSK also believe that part of the problem is the way in which they organise R&D. Their R&D activity had become very large and bureaucratic, and this had become an impediment to the creative atmosphere in which scientists work best. Increasing the size of the organisation had led to an industrial-type process, which was impeding the personal accountability, transparency and personal enthusiasm essential for drug discovery and development.

Roger Bamber/Alamy

In the 1960s, the company employed fewer than a 1000 scientists, who worked in a functional structure – chemists, pharmacologists, clinical development and so on. There were few management layers, few projects and most scientists worked on a single campus. Communication, co-ordination and the exchange of ideas with colleagues was quite easy. In the following decades, employment grew rapidly and the early functional structure was unable to cope. Scientists were spread over several sites and countries, so communication was difficult. Matrix structures were created, whereby scientists reported to the head of their discipline, and also to the head of the one or more projects on which they were working. Continuing growth meant that these structures became more complex, further slowing communication and decision-making.

The chief executive of GSK concluded that this traditional structure was obsolete, and replaced it with a set of 'Centres of Excellence for Drug Discovery' (CEDD). Each is focused on a family of related diseases (such as Alzheimer's or obesity), has a CEO with the authority to initiate and end projects, and contains several hundred scientists from the relevant disciplines. There are only two or three management layers between the CEO and the bench scientists.

The intention was to increase the speed of decision-making and restore freedom of action to the scientist conducing the research. It had also overhauled the incentive system, to ensure that those who made the discoveries could expect a share in the financial rewards they brought. By 2008 it had 12 CEDDs, and the results appeared promising. When it began changing the structure in 2005, GSK had only two products in the 'late stage development' phase: by 2008 it had 34 – the most in the industry.

A more recent structural innovation is to work much more closely with external partners. To speed up the development process it will no longer depend on its own research: by 2020 half of the new drug discovery projects at the company may be undertaken by external partners as part of a radical overhaul designed to improve the pipeline of new drugs at the group. The research and development will be co-ordinated by the CEDDs. The company's Research Director estimated that between one-quarter to one-third of GSK's existing research pipeline of new drugs already involved work conducted with external partners and a growing role would be played by the CEDD, managing a 'virtual' portfolio of research run by such companies:

In the future we are going to have many more external projects.

In 2010, it announced a further change: a group of 14 scientists would move into a separate, stand-alone company specialising in pain relief. They will take with them the rights to several patents, in exchange for an 18 per cent stake in the company. This will enable GSK to reduce overhead costs, while still benefiting from the revenue from sales. It is expected that the scientists will be more highly motivated in their own small company than as a small group within the pharmaceutical giant.

Sources: *Financial Times*, 31 May 2006; 5 October 2010; Garnier (2008).

Questions

1 What links can you see between strategy, structure and performance in the case? (Refer to Section 9.2.)

2 Note which structural forms mentioned in the chapter have been used at GSK. (Refer to Sections 9.3, 9.4 and 9.5.)

3 How does the company co-ordinate activities? (Refer to Section 9.6.)

4 How would you describe the balance between mechanistic and organic structures in GSK? (Refer to Section 9.7.)

5 Is this change consistent with the ideas of contingency theory? (Refer to Section 9.7.)

CHAPTER 10
INFORMATION SYSTEMS AND E-BUSINESS

Learning outcomes

When you have read this chapter you should be able to:

1 Explain how converging technologies change the ways in which people add value to resources
2 Recognise that benefits depend on managing both technology and organisation
3 Distinguish between operations information systems and management information systems
4 Outline two common systems – customer relations and enterprise resource planning
5 Understand the relationship between IS, organisation and strategy
6 Use ideas from the chapter to comment on the management issues in the Asos case study

Activity 10.1   What does 'information systems and e-business' mean?

Before reading the chapter, write some notes on what you think 'information systems and e-business' means.

Choose the organisation or people who may be able to help you learn about the topic. You may find it helpful to discuss the topic with a manager you know, or reflect on an activity you have managed.

- Identify an information systems or e-business issue you can use in this activity, and make a brief note about it.
- How (if at all) did people expect it to change the way they added value to resources?
- Did they consciously manage the organisational *and* the technical aspects?
- Did they see the potential links between the project and their business strategy?

Keep these notes as you will be able to use them later.

10.1   Introduction

Asos was founded in 2000, and has been an e-business player from the beginning. From its initial focus on fashion, it has shown how an effective management team can build a successful new business on the internet, and continues to widen its range. Asos (like eBay, Facebook or YouTube) is a company created to use the internet – it is a pure 'e-business' company, whose founders and managers built it around computer-based information systems (IS).

In that sense it differs from companies founded long before the internet but which now depend on it. Their managers have built, over many years, and through much trial and error, complex systems affecting all aspects of the business. Firms like British Airways, Ford or Sainsbury depend on information about each stage of the value-adding process:

- inputs – e.g. on cost and availability of materials, staff and equipment;
- transformation – e.g. on delivery schedules, capacity, efficiency, quality and costs;
- outputs – e.g. on prices, market share and customer satisfaction.

They have designed information systems which gather data about inputs, transformations and outputs, process it and (ideally) pass analyses to people at all levels to help them in their work. Figure 10.1 shows how information systems support the task of managing.

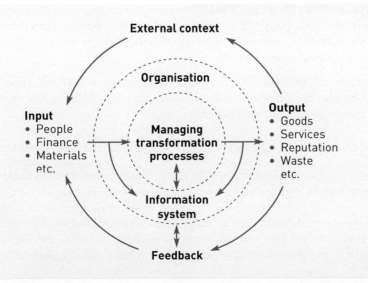

Figure 10.1
The role of information systems in organisations

Source: Boddy et al. (2005).

Computer-based information systems can make operations more efficient, change the way people work together and bring new strategic possibilities and threats. Used well, they help managers to add value to resources. Used badly they destroy wealth – as when managers decide to implement an expensive IS project which does not deliver what they expected, and is abandoned or replaced. The UK National Health Service Programme for Information Technology (NPƒIT) (**www.connectingforhealth.nhs.uk**) contains examples of both – some parts (the Picture Archiving and Communication System) work well; a project to implement an Electronic Patient Record System was a controversial failure, abandoned in 2010.

Many managers face this responsibility, as organisations no longer use information systems only for background activities (accounting and stock control) but for many foreground activities (online banking or sponsored websites) which connect directly with customers. Social networking sites mean that no organisation is immune: if customers post critical comments on Facebook, or on a company's website, managers need to respond to avoid further damage to their reputation.

This chapter explains how IS can transform organisations. It shows how they have steadily widened the role of computer-based systems in managing data about their operations, and how technical developments have led to the convergence of data, voice and vision systems. This led to the new phenomenon of 'co-creation', in which users both view and create content – media sites such as **www.FT.com** or company sites such as **www.ikea.com**. Social networking brings radical change to the way some organisations interact with customers. More broadly, managers face the challenge of using the technologies to add value in new ways: they have to deal with organisational as well as technological issues, which the chapter will illustrate.

10.2　Converging technologies bring new ways to add value

Using IS to add value to data

Since the 1950s, organisations have progressively extended the tasks which computer-based information systems (IS) undertake, beginning with routine accounting and stock control systems, extending to manufacturing and transport, and now covering almost every aspect of the organisation:

- Allied Bakeries use engineering maintenance systems to monitor equipment and plan maintenance to minimise disruption to production;
- The UK Vehicle Licensing Agency encourages drivers to pay their road tax online;
- BP maintains all human resource information on a single database, allowing staff to access their records and company policies online, so all work to common information;
- Tesco links internal processes electronically with suppliers to receive orders, arrange supplies and pay invoices electronically.

Such systems are embedded throughout the organisation and still raise management issues as requirements change or new systems become available: managers then begin costly projects to change or enhance their systems.

Using convergence to add value to data, sound and vision

The information systems just described are all computer-based. The revolutionary changes now taking place – blogging, social networking, downloading music – follow from the convergence of three technologies – computer, telephone and television. Engineers developed these devices independently, so they have always worked in different ways and as isolated systems. As the cost of computing power fell, they used the digital technology at its heart to re-design how telephones transmit voice signals, and then how television transmits images. They were then able to combine the three technologies within a single device – such as your mobile phone. The common language and set of rules specifying how to send data between devices enabled them to communicate electronically, creating the **internet** (Berners-Lee, 1999). Another relevant term is an **intranet**, a private computer network operating within an organisation by using internet standards and protocols. The opposite is an **extranet**, a network that uses the internet to link organisations with specified suppliers, customers or trading partners, who gain access to it through a password system.

Linking mobile phones to the internet led to the explosive growth of the 'Wireless internet', freeing the computer from the desk top, and opening the way for the iPod, iPad, smartphones and the countless other communication devices which allow us to send and/or receive text, voice and images wherever we are. Demand for these devices has grown very rapidly with customers being attracted by the many functions (applications) now available. Smartphone suppliers compete to offer devices with more and better applications than their rivals, most supplied by independent software developers. Apple's App store enables iPhone users to download an application directly to their mobile – with Apple receiving a share of the price (if any) which the developer sets.

Organisations in all sectors of the economy use modern information systems to change traditional enterprises and create new ones. Many now only accept orders online, and use the internet to manage all stages in the transaction. Established media companies offer online as well as paper copies of their publications; national and local governments increasingly expect to interact with their citizens online. The BBC claims that the iPlayer is changing the way people watch television, with over a million programmes being viewed over the online video site each day (**www.bbc.co.uk**). But the most dramatic shift currently observable is that of co-creation.

Co-creating value

One effect of **blogs**, **social networking sites** and **online communities** is to erode the boundaries between producers and consumers. Wikipedia, written by volunteers, soon became the world's largest encyclopaedia. YouTube claims to hold the world's largest collection of videos, including a large collection of professional work. Amazon encourages visitors to provide book reviews, which others visitors can rate. All are examples of **user-generated content (UGC)**.

The **internet** is a web of hundreds of thousands of computer networks linked together by telephone lines and satellite links through which data can be carried.

An **intranet** is a version of the internet that only specified people within an organisation can use.

An **extranet** is a version of the internet that is restricted to specified people in specified companies – usually customers or suppliers.

A **blog** is a web log that allows individuals to post opinions and ideas.

Social networking sites use internet technologies which enable people to interact within an online community to share information and ideas.

Online communities are groups of people loosely joined together by a common interest who exchange information using web tools.

User-generated content (UGC) is text, visual or audio material which users create and place on a website for others to view.

Management in practice	**SelectMinds – social networks for professionals**

www.selectminds.com

The company helps organisations to build connections between groups of employees, former employees and other constituencies to increase knowledge sharing and productivity. It offers secure, online social networking solutions that organisations use to recruit and retain scarce knowledge workers and increase the speed of information and knowledge flow.

It pioneered an early form of corporate social networking in 2000 when it began delivering online networks to connect former employees of organisations with each other and their former employer. Employees of professional services firms often leave to work for customers, so are able to refer business to their former employer. Seeding this population with information about their previous company (new services, client successes) helps them to become better brand ambassadors, speaking knowledgeably about it. The site enables companies to benefit from customer and employee relationships as well as to build new relationships based on continued personal connections among current and ex-employees.

Products now include systems to link organisations with customers, retirees, potential new staff and among current employees.

Source: Company website.

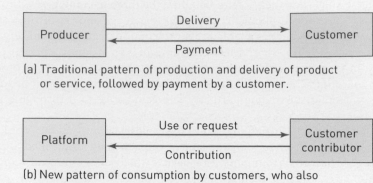

Figure 10.2
Traditional delivery and customer participation

Source: Boddy et al. (2009a).

wikinomics describes a business culture in which customers are no longer only consumers but also co-creators and co-producers of the service.

co-creation is product or service development that makes intensive use of the contributions of customers.

Tapscott and Williams (2006) refer to this as **wikinomics**, a business culture that sees customers not as passive consumers but as active co-producers who engage in **co-creation**. In a traditional economic system, producers create products which consumers order, receive and pay for (Figure 10.2a). The alternative is when companies provide a platform for customers to offer and view information. They add value to the platform as they provide information, enhancing its perceived quality. Consumption does not reduce value, but increases it (Figure 10.2b) – see the Management in Practice feature below.

Management in practice   An online forum in healthcare

A physician dealing with fertility treatment spent a lot of time informing couples on the pros and cons of the treatments, and in providing emotional support. As an experiment he started an online forum in which his clients (exclusively) share information and anxieties. It also provides relevant medical information. From time to time the doctor and other staff join the sessions. The 'electronic fertility platform' saves a lot of the time the doctor used to spend advising and supporting clients. Clients contribute anonymously to the platform, and so help each other.

Source: Boddy *et al.* (2009a), p. 62.

Metcalfe's law states that the value of a network increases with the square of the number of users connected to the network.

Customers create the content, and the more people view it, the more valuable the network becomes. This follows from **Metcalfe's law** '*the value of a network increases with the square of the number of users connected to the network*'. The more people have phones, the more valuable a phone becomes to the next adopter. This 'network effect' encourages people to use an existing website, and creates barriers for new entrants who have few users to attract others.

10.3   Managing the new opportunities to add value

Adding value in traditional delivery systems

The internet, combined with political changes, is creating a wider, often international, market for many goods and services. The challenge for managers is to make profitable use of these possibilities. This includes looking beyond technology – which receives most attention – to the wider organisation. A manager who played a major role in guiding internet-based changes at his company commented:

> The internet is not a technology challenge. It's a people challenge – all about getting structures, attitudes and skills aligned. (private communication)

The significance of the internet for everyone who works in an organisation cannot be overstated. It affects all aspects of their work, enabling new forms of organisation and new ways of doing business. Established organisations typically go through successive stages in the way they use the internet. The simplest applications provide information, enabling customers to view product or other information on a company website; suppliers show customers what they can offer. The next stage is to use the internet for interaction. Customers ask questions about offers and prices, to which the system responds. Conversely a supplier who sees a purchasing requirement from a business can make an online bid to meet the order. A third use is for transactions, when customers buy goods and services through a supplier's website. The whole transaction, from accessing information through ordering, delivery and payment, takes place electronically.

A company achieves integration when it links its internal system to the website, so that when a customer orders a product online, that automatically passes to the internal operating systems, which then begin all the processes (including the links with suppliers' systems) required to manufacture and/or deliver the product. Transformation refers to situations in which customers are actively involved in the design and consumption of the products, and where the company is actively engaging with online customer communities.

Adding value through co-creation

Many managers are working out how to use social networking sites to their advantage, for instance by creating customer platforms or by contributing actively to others. While people use these applications to interact socially with friends or with people who share a common interest, the trend gives managers a potentially useful opportunity. While initially uneasy, many now host customer communities, to move closer to their customers, hoping that this will help them see how best to improve a product or service. If customers are being critical, wise managers want to know this as soon as possible so that they can deal with the problem. A blog discussion among users might identify new uses for a product, or hint at features the company could add.

Whether a business is in a traditional or co-creation mode, technology will only add value if managers look beyond the hardware, however sophisticated, to the management and organisational issues.

Adding value depends on managing technology AND organisation

Whether the company is an internet-based start-up or a century-old business, it requires deliberate management action to create the IS infrastructure to engage with the internet. **Information systems management** is the term used to describe the activities of planning, acquiring, developing and using IS such as this – the Management in Practice feature below gives the views of one IS manager.

Information systems management is the planning, acquisition, development and use of these systems.

Management in practice	Jean-Pierre Corniou – Renault's CIO www.renault.com

Frankly, my job (as Chief Information Officer) consists of being a bilingual guy: I speak both the language of business and the language of technology. Renault, like other companies, started investing in information technology (IT) in the middle 1960s. It was pioneering work – there were just a few people in IT, working on large systems of great complexity. People inside still have that pioneering attitude, of an era when IT was seen as secret, and complex . . . but we need to open up, to build transparency, to build the confidence and trust of all stakeholders in the company.

We have invested a lot of money in [advanced applications] and websites, and when we analysed the level of utilization of these products and tools, we were very surprised to see how much money had been spent on products that people were not using.

I spend a lot of time in plants, in discussions with foremen in the field, trying to understand how they use technology to increase their efficiency. I spend lots of time in commercial departments too, to understand the key business processes. Bringing IT to the business community means the CIO has to be embedded in the day-to-day life of the organization, and of course to have a seat on the board. I consider myself more a business guy than an IT guy.

Source: Bringing business technology out into the open (Fiona Harvey), *Financial Times*, 17 September 2003.

As M. Corniou's comments clearly show, any information system (internet-based or otherwise) includes people and processes as well as hardware and software – as shown in Figure 10.3.

A computer-based student record system illustrates this. The hardware consists of computers and peripherals such as printers, monitors and keyboards. This runs the record system, using software to manipulate the data and to either print the results for each student or send them electronically – which they see as information. The system also requires people (course administrators) to enter data (name and other information about students and their results) following certain processes – such as that one person reads from a list of grades while another keys the data into the right field on the student's record. Managers of a department might use the output to compare the pass rate of each course – so the record system is now part of the university's management information. Staff will use their knowledge (based on learning and experience) to interpret trends and evaluate their significance.

Figure 10.3 also shows that the hardware and software is part of a context, which includes people, working processes, structures and cultures. Any IS includes identifiable elements of this context: they affect the outcomes of an IS project just as much as the design of the technological elements of hardware and software.

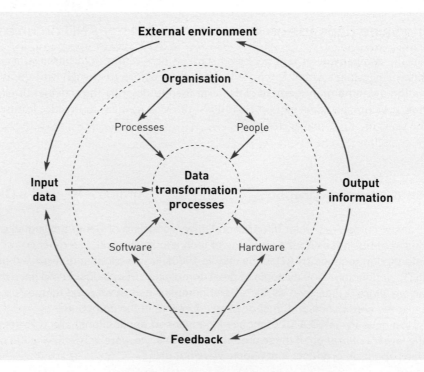

Figure 10.3
The elements of a computer-based IS

Source: Boddy et al. (2009a).

10.4 | Types of information system

Operational information systems support the needs of the day-to-day business operations, and how front-line staff and their supervisors work. Management information systems typically guide the decisions of middle and senior managers.

Both types of system turn 'data' into 'information'. **Data** refers to recorded descriptions of things, events, activities and transactions – their size, colour, cost, weight, date and so on. It may be a number, a piece of text, a drawing or photograph or a sound. In itself it may or may not convey information to a person. **Information** is a subset of data that means something to the person receiving it, which they judge to be useful, significant or urgent. It comes from data that have been processed (by people or with the aid of technology) so that it has meaning and value – by linking it to other pieces of data to show a comparison, a sequence of events or a trend. The output is subjective, since what one person sees as valuable information, another may see as insignificant data – their interpretation reflects diverse backgrounds and interests.

Data are raw, unanalysed facts, figures and events.

Information comes from data that have been processed so that it has meaning for the person receiving it.

Operational information systems

Operational systems support the information processing needed to keep current work moving efficiently. They include technologies that help people perform standalone tasks more efficiently, such as word processors and spreadsheets. Most professional people use these technologies routinely – for instance, R&D engineers can use a computer-aided design (CAD) program to improve the way they work, as the system includes software that performs routine tasks automatically, so that the engineer can focus on design issues.

Transaction processing systems (TPS) record and process data from customer and supplier transactions as well as those with banks and tax authorities. A TPS collects data as transactions occur and stores them in a database, which is then the source of other reports such as customer statements or supplier payments. Such systems help managers to monitor transactions, especially their financial implications.

A **transaction processing system (TPS)** records and processes data from routine transactions such as payroll, sales or purchases.

They also need systems to monitor and control physical processes. So breweries, bakeries, refineries and similar operations use **process control systems** to monitor variables such as temperature, pressure or flow, compare them with the required state and adjust as necessary. Staff monitor the systems to check if they need to take further action.

A **process control system** monitors and controls variables describing the state of a physical process.

Office automation systems bring together email, word processing, spreadsheet and many other systems to create, process, store and distribute information. They can also link to TPS or process control systems to make structured decisions. Banks analyse the pattern of a customer's transactions to decide whether to grant a request for credit. Office automation systems streamline the administrative processes of a business, and pass data and information to other systems.

An **office automation system** uses several systems to create, process, store and distribute information.

Management information systems (MIS)

A **management information system (MIS)** is a computer-based system that provides managers with the information they need to make decisions. The MIS is supported by the operations information systems, as well as other sources of internal and external information. They typically include systems for information reporting, decision support and executive information, each of which is described below. A significant management choice is how many people throughout the organisation can access and use information from these systems.

A **management information system** provides information and support for managerial decision-making.

Managers in charge of production or service facilities constantly face choices about (for example) whether to engage more or fewer staff, arrange schedules or accept a reservation. To increase the chances that their decisions add value, they need information about capacity, orders or materials. Good information increases their confidence: IS help to achieve this by providing accurate and up-to-date information on the current operation.

Decision support systems help people to calculate the consequences of alternatives before they decide which to choose.

Decision support systems (DSS), sometimes called expert or knowledge systems, help managers to calculate the likely consequences of alternative actions. A DSS incorporates a model of the process or situation and will often draw data from operational systems. Some examples:

- businesses use DSS to calculate the financial consequences of investments;
- banks use knowledge systems to analyse proposed loans. These incorporate years of lending experience and enable less experienced staff to make decisions;
- NHS Direct in the UK uses an expert system to enable nurses in a call centre to deal with calls from patients who would otherwise visit their doctor. The system suggests what to ask, interprets the answers and advises the nurse on what to say to the caller.

An **executive information system** provides those at the top of the organisation with easy access to timely and relevant information.

Executive information systems are management information systems aimed at the most senior people in the business. Rather than great detail, they aim to provide easy access to data that have been derived from many sources, and processed in a way that meets top management requirements – often presenting this visually in the form of a 'dashboard'. These systems collect data from operating systems and processes, and process it to show critical information in the form of bar chart and dials like the dashboard of a car. Users can then 'drill down' to the data on which the screen presentation is based, to query assumptions and gain a fuller knowledge of what lies behind the big picture. Avis Europe (a car rental company) uses a system which helps all parts of the business to keep track of their financial performance in a timely way:

> We try to measure everything, and we have precise key performance indicators to measure the results of processes. It is a real quality jump to have a system that provides online access to relevant data. Reporting is one of the critical parts of our business, and we can report our numbers confidently. (*Financial Times*, 8 December 2010)

10.5 The internet and e-business

The internet is clearly transforming the way many organisations work, and creating new relationships between them and their customers, suppliers and business partners. Two commonly used terms are **e-commerce** and **e-business**.

E-commerce and e-business

e-commerce refers to the activity of selling goods or service over the internet.

e-business refers to the integration, through the internet, of all an organisation's processes from its suppliers through to its customers.

Many businesses use the internet to support their distribution, by offering goods and services through a website – which is defined here as e-commerce. A more radical way to use the internet is for what is here called e-business, when companies use a website to manage information about sales, capacity, inventory, payment and so on – and to exchange that information with their suppliers or business customers. They use the internet to connect all the links in their supply chain, thereby creating an integrated process to meet customer needs – see the Management in Practice feature below.

Management in practice   **Using the internet at Siemens** www.siemens.com

Siemens (a large engineering company) plans to do much of their business over the internet including:

1 Knowledge management – using a company-wide system to capture and share knowledge about scientific and technical developments throughout the business.
2 Online purchasing (or e-procurement). Large savings are expected from pooling the demands of buying departments through a company-wide system called click2procure.

3 Online sales. Most of Siemens' customers are other companies who can click on 'buy from Siemens' on the website and place orders for most Siemens products.

4 Internal administrative processes – such as by handling 30,000 job applications a year online, or expecting employees to book their business travel arrangements over the internet.

The chief executive at the time said:

> If you want to transform a company to an e-business company, the problem is not so much e-procurement and the face to the customer. All this can be done rather fast. What is truly difficult is to reorganise all the internal processes. That is what we see as our main task and where the main positive results will come from.

Source: Boddy *et al.* (2009a) and company website.

The internet changes the relationship between a company, its suppliers and its customers, as electronic networks can bypass intermediaries – as more airlines require passengers to book tickets online, fewer people use independent travel agents. Cutting out intermediaries reduces a company's costs and brings them into closer contact with their customers. The internet allows entrepreneurs to create new intermediaries like Yahoo, Google and Amazon which offer search and comparison services. Apple's App store allows mobile users to download new applications directly to their handset.

Two widely used internet applications are known as customer relationship management, and enterprise resource planning systems.

Customer relationship management (CRM)

Customer relationship management (CRM) is a process by which companies aim to build long-term, profitable relationships with customers. This involves many changes in the way the organisation works, and information systems play a major role in supporting this. CRM software tries to align business processes with customer strategies to recruit, satisfy and retain profitable customers by:

Customer relationship management (CRM) is a process of creating and maintaining long-term relationships with customers.

- gathering customer data swiftly;
- identifying valuable customers while discouraging less valuable ones;
- increasing customer loyalty and retention by providing customised products; and
- reducing the costs of serving customers.

Some CRM systems consolidate customer data from many sources to answer questions such as:

- Who are our most loyal customers?
- Who are our most profitable customers?
- What do these profitable customers want to buy?

The Tesco Clubcard is a good example, as it appears to have had a major role in the success of the company – see the Management in Practice feature below. The system processes information about what each customer purchases, and uses this to identify promotional vouchers that are most likely to be useful to that customer, given what the company knows about them from their application form. Suitable vouchers encourage them to return to the store to make further purchases.

Management in practice   Tesco www.tesco.com

The Tesco Clubcard scheme has over 11 million active holders, and is believed to be a factor in the company's success. Shoppers join the scheme by completing a simple form with some personal information about their age and where they live. Their purchases earn vouchers based on the amount they spend. Every purchase they make at Tesco is electronically recorded, and the data analysed to identify their shopping preferences. This is then used to design a package of special offers which are most likely to appeal to that customer, based on an analysis of what they have bought. These offers are mailed to customers with their quarterly vouchers, and each mailing brings a large increase in business.

More broadly, the data is analysed to identify the kind of person the Clubcard holder is – whether they have a new baby, young children, whether they like cooking and so on. Each product is also ascribed a set of attributes – expensive or cheap? An ethnic recipe or a traditional dish? Tesco own-label or an upmarket brand? The information on customers, shopping habits and product attributes is used to support all aspects of the business.

The database is believed to be the largest holding of personal information about named individuals within the United Kingdom. This information has also informed a series of strategic decisions, such as the move into smaller store formats, and the launch of the internet shopping site. It also shaped the development and sale of Tesco mobile phones, pet insurance and the Finest food range.

Sources: Published information and company website.

Banks value current accounts, even though they earn little direct revenue. Their real benefit is that they provide the bank with detailed information about each account holder's financial and personal circumstances, and at what point they might require other services such as a mortgage or a loan (from which the banks earn large revenues): 'current accounts are a key relationship builder' (*Financial Times*, 2 March 2011).

Implementing a successful CRM system depends more on strategy than on technology, and on ensuring that other dimensions like business processes, systems, structure and people change to support it. If a company wants to develop better relationships with its customers, it needs to rethink all the working processes that relate to customers. If they can use several channels to contact the company (ordering by phone, using the web page to check the status of the order, sending a complaint by email) managers must ensure these are integrated to provide one comprehensive and up-to-date view of each customer.

For companies focused on products or services, this means realigning around the customer – which can be a radical change in a company's culture. All employees, but especially those in marketing, sales, service and any other customer contact functions, have to think in a customer oriented way. Much time and financial resource of CRM projects has to be spent on organisational issues. Successful CRM depends on co-ordinated actions by all departments within a company rather than being driven by a single department.

Enterprise resource planning (ERP) systems

Fulfilling a customer order requires that people in sales, accounting, production, purchasing and so on co-operate with each other to exchange information. However their IS were often designed independently to meet the needs of a single function and cannot automatically exchange information. A common solution is to use an enterprise resource planning (ERP) system, which aims to co-ordinate activities and decisions across many functions by creating an integrated platform.

At the heart of an enterprise system is a central database that draws data from, and feeds data to, applications throughout the company. Using a single database streamlines the flow of information. Table 10.1 shows examples of business processes and functions which enterprise systems support. These 'modules' can be implemented separately, but promise much

Table 10.1 Examples of business processes supported by enterprise systems

Application	Description
Financial	Accounts receivable and payable, cash management and forecasting, management information, cost accounting, profitability analysis, profit-centre accounting, financial reporting
Human resources	Payroll, personnel planning, travel expenses, benefits accounting, applicant tracking
Operations and logistics	Inventory management, maintenance, production planning, purchasing, quality management, vendor evaluation, shipping
Sales and marketing	Order management, pricing, sales management, sales planning, billing

greater benefits when they are linked to exchange information continuously through the central database.

ERP systems give management direct access to current operating information and so enable companies to, among other things:

- integrate customer and financial information;
- standardise manufacturing processes and reduce inventory;
- improve information for management decisions across sites;
- enable online connections with suppliers' and customers' systems.

One snag with ERP systems is that they promote centralised co-ordination and decision-making, which may not suit a particular firm, and some companies do not need the level of integration they provide:

> Enterprise systems are basically generic solutions. The design reflects a series of assumptions about the way companies operate in general. Vendors of ES [enterprise systems] try to structure the systems to reflect best practices, but it is the vendor that is defining what 'best' means. Of course, some degree of ES customisation is possible, but major modifications are very expensive and impracticable. As a result, most companies installing ES will have to adapt or rework their processes to reach a fit with the system. (Davenport, 1998, p. 125)

Some believe that ERP systems lock companies into rigid processes which make it difficult to adapt to market changes, and there is little evidence of significant differences in performance between adopters and non-adopters of ERP systems.

10.6 IS, strategy and organisation – the big picture

Computer-based IS can contribute to an organisation's strategy, in the same way as any other capability – human resources, finance or marketing. They are all resources which managers can incorporate into their strategic planning, ensuring that they complement each other, rather than pull in opposite directions. The following sections show how managers can take a strategic perspective on IS, and on the organisational changes this requires.

IS and strategy

Chapter 8 showed that strategy sets the overall direction of the business, and showed how the 'product/market matrix' distinguishes the broad options – see Figure 8.3 (p. 159). They can use IS to support any of these strategies:

Existing markets, existing product/service

- Using CRM systems to improve customer service by understanding their needs more fully.
- Using ERP systems to deliver goods and services more efficiently.

Existing markets, new products/services

- Offering an online service to customers – M&S Online, RBS Digital Banking, Sainsbury's Bank.
- Using CRM systems to identify new products to current customers (see Tesco Clubcard).

New markets, existing products/services

- Using a website to widen the customer base – Asos rapidly expanding overseas sales by customising the website by country.
- Advertising products or services on mobile phones to attract new types of customer.

New markets, new products/services

- Apple – developing from a computer manufacturer to one offering mobile phones, iPads, the App store.
- Kwik-Fit's use of a database of depot customers to create a motor insurance business.

Managers also use IS to support their chosen strategy – such as a *differentiation* or *cost leadership*. They can use IS to achieve a cost-leadership strategy by using:

- computer-aided manufacturing to replace manual labour;
- stock control systems to cut expensive inventory; or
- online order entry to cut order processing costs.

They can support a differentiation strategy by using:

- computer-aided manufacturing to offer flexible delivery;
- stock control systems to extend the range of goods on offer at any time; or
- using online systems to remember customer preferences, and suggest purchases.

They can support a focus by using:

- computer-aided manufacturing to meet unique, non-standard requirements;
- online ordering to allow customers to create a unique product by selecting its features.

IS, strategy and organisation

Managers who wish to use IS to support their strategy also need to ensure that their organisation structure supports the strategy, as there is abundant evidence that having a structure and culture that complements, or is aligned with, the strategy will produce better results than one that is not. Kanter (2001) found that the move to e-business for established companies involves a deep change in their organisation, with successful companies being those who, as well as using technology also:

- created experiments and acted quickly to convert the sceptics;
- created dedicated teams to lead the project, with adequate resources and autonomy;
- recognised that e-business requires systemic changes in many ways of working.

A study by Boddy *et al.* (2009b) showed how attempts to implement e-health systems (such as electronic booking systems or video links allowing doctors to conduct surgeries far away from the patients) depended on managers relating the change to the strategy of the unit, and on making supportive organisational changes. After studying many e-health systems they concluded that those responsible for them would be more successful if they focus on:

- **Embedding e-health applications in normal care activities**, so that e-health clearly contributes to the wider health care strategy. They should aim to build the system into the normal patient workflow, and to adapt performance measurement systems to show how e-health applications support strategic targets.
- **Implementing national systems in a way that respects local conditions.** To do this, senior managers need to allow nurses or other health professionals to adapt the national system to local circumstances, and to meet the costs of training, maintenance and upgrades.
- **Designing systems that match the culture** of a profession or unit. To do this, promoters need to identify the cultural values in a unit or professional group, and work with people there to design a system that supports that culture, or allow the time and resources needed to adapt the culture to the system.
- **Redesigning working processes** in conjunction with e-health systems to support care. This involves taking time to understand how doctors and nurses currently deliver the service, and seeking users' advice on how technologies and working practices can be jointly re designed to improve performance.
- **Ensuring that people see systems as useful,** by working with users to identify the information that is most useful to them in their tasks, and designing the e-health systems to provide that.

Above all, the interviews show that the scale of the e-health implementation task goes far beyond procuring the technology, since it involves redesigning the wider systems for delivering care. The central theme was of the benefits of ensuring that managers are conscious of aligning strategy, organisation and information systems.

Activity 10.2	What does 'information systems and e-business' mean in management?

Having read the chapter, make brief notes summarising the IS and e-business issues evident in the organisation you chose for this activity.

- How (if at all) did people expect IS to change the way they added value to resources? (Refer to Section 10.2.)
- To what extent did they consciously manage both the organisational and the technical aspects? (Refer to Sections 10.3 and 10.6.)
- To which of the types of IS described in Sections 10.4 and 10.5 did the system correspond most closely?
- How (if at all) did people discuss any links between structure and strategy? (Refer to Sections 10.5 and 10.6.)

Compare what you have found with other students on your course.

Summary

1 **Explain how converging technologies change the way people add value to resources**

- Continuing advances in information systems for processing data have been enhanced by the convergence of systems so that they now integrate data, sound and visual systems.
- The radical result is that this enables producers and customers to co-create value.

2 Recognise that, to use these opportunities, managers change both technology and organisation

- Established organisations use IS to make radical changes in the services they offer and how they work.
- They also, as do new internet-based organisations, find ways to benefit from the possibilities of co-creation with customers.
- Both depend on managing both technical and organisational issues.

3 Distinguish between operations information systems and management information systems

- Operations information systems – such as transaction processing and office automation systems – support processes that keep current work running smoothly.
- Management information systems – for information reporting, decision support and executive systems provide managers with information to support decision-making.

4 Illustrate how organisations use the internet to add value by using customer relations, management and enterprise resource planning systems

- Internet-based (e-business) are systems which operate across organisational boundaries, enabling new relations with business partners and customers.
- Customer relations systems aim to capture and process information about each customer, so that products and services can be tailored more closely to individual needs.
- Enterprise systems use a central database to integrate data about many aspects of the business as an aid to planning.

5 Understand the relation between IS, strategy and organisation

- Computer-based IS can support strategy: each of Porter's five forces are potentially affected by IS, leading to either threats or opportunities.
- Similarly managers can use IS to support a low cost, differentiation or niche strategy.
- Whatever strategy they follow, it will be more successful if they ensure that complementary organisational changes – such as ensuring the alignment of strategy and structure, and the appropriate governance structures for the IS function – are in place.

Review questions

1 Explain the significance of information systems to the management of organisations. How do they relate to the core task of managing?

2 Give some original examples of companies using information systems to add value.

3 Identify examples of co-creation or 'wikinomics', and explain the benefits to company and customer.

4 For what purposes are commercial companies using social networking sites?

5 Draw a sketch to illustrate why computer-based information systems require more than the management of technology.

6 Give examples of how an information system can affect at least two of the forces in Porter's model, and so affect the competitiveness of a business.

7 Outline the stages though which organisations go in using the internet, giving an original example of each.

8 Describe how the five forces model can show the likely effects of information systems on strategy.

Further reading

Laudon, K. C. and Laudon, J. P. (2010), *Essentials of Management Information Systems,* (9th edn), Pearson Education, Harlow.

> This text, written from a management perspective, focuses on the opportunities and pitfalls of information systems.

Tapscott, E. and Williams, A. D. (2006), *Wikinomics: How mass collaboration changes everything*, Viking Penguin, New York.

> Best-selling account of the rise of co-creation.

Weblinks

These websites have appeared in, or are relevant to, the chapter:

> www.connectingforhealth.nhs.uk
> www.FT.com
> www.ikea.com
> www.bbc.co.uk
> www.selectminds.com
> www.renault.com
> www.siemens.com
> www.tesco.com
> www.asos.com

Visit two of the business sites in the list, or any others that interest you, and answer these questions:

- If you were a potential employee, how well does it present information about the company and the career opportunities available? Could you apply for a job online?
- Evaluate the sites on these criteria, which are based on those used in an annual survey of corporate websites:
  - Does it give the current share price on the front page?
  - How many languages is it available in?
  - Is it possible to email key people or functions from the site?
  - Does it give a diagram of the main structural units in the business?
  - Does it set out the main mission or business idea of the company?
  - Are there any other positive or negative features?

Annotated weblinks, multiple choice questions and other useful resources can be found on **www.pearsoned.co.uk/boddy**

Case study   Asos www.asos.com

Asos is an online fashion retailer founded by Nick Robertson in 2000 to sell replicas of dresses worn by actresses. He has transformed the business since then, and it is now an international fashion business which claims to be the largest online-only fashion business in the UK.

About 700,000 people a day visit the website – most of them 16- to 34-year-olds who are the company's target group of customers. In 2007, non-UK sales amounted to 10 per cent of annual sales – now it is 44 per cent and Mr Robertson expects it will be over 50 per cent by the end of 2011. The company's HQ is in Camden, North London, and the fulfilment centre – which receives orders from customers and then packs and delivers the goods to them – is in Hemel Hempstead (about 30 miles north).

The Camden office is where most of the images that appear on the website are produced – including photo shoots (the company photographs 2000 items a week) and catwalk videos. Spread over four floors, the open-plan floors are full of rails of clothes ready to be modelled, and with accessories. Mr Robertson joked:

It's like a teenager's bedroom times 100.

Keeping the fashion and technology parts of the company under one roof (the company employs 16 designers whose products for Asos's own label account for half of all sales) and 120 people in information systems – enables both sides of the business to learn from each other:

We are a fashion and a technology business.

While many companies discourage blogging or tweeting in the office, Mr Robertson encourages it, as an ideal way to keep in touch with customers and fashion trends:

They're doing what they would be doing anyway, but they're doing it for Asos.

This is no coincidence. Most of Asos staff fit the demographic of the company's customers – young, trendy, mainly female. Understanding exactly who its customers are is a great strength of the company.

Since launch, everything Asos does has been aimed at 'the imagined 22-year-old', the median age of its shoppers. They fall into three groups:

Fashion Forward – those who set the trend;
Fashion Passengers – those who follow them; and
Functional Fashion – the less fashion-conscious.

M4OS Photos/Alamy

Mr Robertson believes that employing the same types of people as Asos sells to means the company knows how to meet them – as shown by a marketing strategy built upon social networking sites. Teenagers think they have 'discovered' Asos through blogs and tweets, instead of feeling as if they have responded to a sales pitch.

The company has also created its own sites that build on existing platforms. In 2009, it launched Asos Life an online community that is a blend of staff and shoppers who blog, chat and post on fashion forums. Asos Marketplace allows designers to set up boutique stores on the Asos site selling their own creations and one-off vintage items. Like a concession in a department store, the designers rent web space from the company, which also receives 10–15 per cent of the sales revenue.

Much of Asos success is believed to come from their guarantee of free returns – essential to build customer confidence in online shopping. It also offers free delivery, and is discussing with other leading retailers the possibility of enabling customers to collect their goods at locations other than their home or office.

A management incentive plan aims to ensure that the senior management team's objectives are directly aligned with those of the shareholders. The plan has a three-year performance period, and managers' performance is measured over that period, based on earnings per share and measures of total shareholder value. Managers have an incentive to deliver high performance, from which shareholders will benefit.

Mr Robertson aims to achieve sales of £1billion in five years, across five markets. Four of the five target countries are the US, France, Germany and the UK – with the fifth not yet known to the public. In 2010, he reported that international sales were expanding rapidly, reaching £63 million that year (44 per cent of the total). All sales come from the website, and the company ships to 167 countries from the distribution hub in Hemel Hempstead. In 2011, the dedicated US website will go live, followed by country-specific sites for France and Germany by the end of the year.

The company's Head of People outlined her five goals:

- ensure that inspirational leadership runs throughout **Asos.com**;
- we have amazing talent at **Asos.com**, we need to ensure we unleash that talent by giving everyone a chance to shine;
- innovation is what makes **Asos.com** stand out from the crowd, and is a key part of our culture. Driving initiatives across the business that build on innovation is key to keeping our culture alive, as well as delivering innovations to excite our customers;
- engaging communication – involving our people and collaborating to achieve results;
- celebrating success – creating a rewarding and high performance culture.

Sources: *Financial Times*, 22 February 2011; company website.

Questions

1 What examples are there in the story of Asos managing organisational as well as technical issues? (See Sections 10.3 and 10.6.)

2 How does it add value to the resources it uses? (See Section 10.3.)

3 Which of the types of IS mentioned in Sections 10.4 and 10.5 do you think the company will be using?

4 What kind of strategy is Asos following? (Refer to Section 10.6 and Section 8.5.)

5 Go to the Asos website and note recent developments at the company.

CHAPTER 11
MANAGING INNOVATION AND CHANGE

Learning outcomes

When you have read this chapter you should be able to:

1 Outline the links between creativity, innovation, change and strategy
2 Describe types of innovation, with examples
3 Explain the links between innovation and its context
4 Compare life-cycle, emergent, participative and political theories of change
5 Explain the forms and sources of innovation
6 Illustrate the organisational factors believed to support or hinder innovation and change
7 Use ideas from the chapter to comment on the management issues in the Google case study

11.1   Introduction

Google is an organisation founded on innovation and continual change (see chapter case study). The founders developed a search engine that works at astonishing speed to supply internet users with the information they need – and they continue to adjust the algorithm to improve the relevance of the search results to users. They regularly add new features, and are using the accumulating revenues from the search business to invest in new areas such as blogging, online payments, mobile phone operating systems (Android) and an online bookstore. Google managers are also innovative in the way they manage the business: as well as extending their services, they are refining the management processes and skills they need to deliver them. Consumer products companies like Unilever and Procter & Gamble also depend on a constant flow of innovation.

Others work in organisations which change very slowly, even when the evidence is clear that something is wrong. Senior managers at BP face the challenge of continuing to transform the company from a relatively small (for that industry), diversified business into the world's second-largest oil company, and to embed a strong safety culture. The scandal at Mid Staffordshire NHS Trust (Chapter 17 case study) clearly showed the need for radical change in control systems and ways of working – but these will be hard to introduce into such an established organisation. Anecdotal evidence suggests that while most managers accept the need for innovation and change, many are critical of their organisation's ability to introduce it. They experience great difficulty in implementing major changes – often underestimating how long it takes people to accept the need for change, how uncomfortable it can be for those on the receiving end, and the organisational complexity of making apparently small changes.

This chapter presents theories about the nature of innovation and change in organisations. It shows how the external environment is the main source of pressure for change, and how this may prompt people to change one or more elements of the (internal) organisation: there is a continuing interaction between internal and external contexts. It presents four complementary perspectives on how people manage that interaction, and suggests the sources of innovation. It concludes with ideas on the organisational factors that can help or hinder innovation and change. Figure 11.1 shows the themes of the chapter.

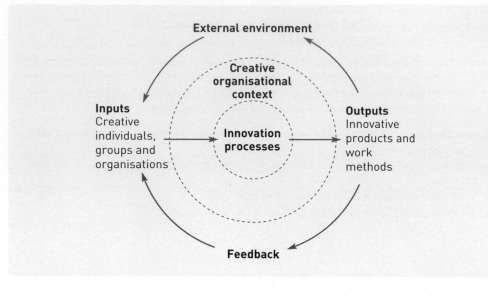

Figure 11.1
A systems view
of innovation
and change

11.2   Initiating innovation and change

Chapter 1 introduced the idea that managers interact with their contexts (external and internal environments) in the sense that the contexts shape what they do, and managers in turn shape their contexts. People begin to innovate and change when they see an actual or potential gap between current outputs and those they desire – products do not perform well enough, new ideas show they can re-design what they do and how they do it, or present working methods are too costly to sustain in a competitive market. They see a gap between desired and actual performance – usually because the internal context of the organisation is unable to meet external opportunities and threats. They try to generate innovative ideas from individuals, groups or other organisations, and implement them – in the hope that this will close (or prevent) the performance gap. Practical issues of design and implementation affect the outcomes – which in turn shape external and internal contexts – the starting point for future innovation and change.

The external context

Chapter 3 described the external environment (or context) of business and successive chapters have illustrated the changes taking place, such as internationalisation and the radical effects of the internet. Together with deregulation and the privatisation of former state businesses, these transformed the competitive landscape of established businesses. Managers at British Airways and KLM had to respond to competition from low-cost airlines. Established banks faced competition from new entrants such as retailers (Sainsbury's) or conglomerates (Virgin) offering financial services. The internet enables online news organisations to compete with print newspapers – some of which now offer online editions. Apple and Facebook were created as innovative businesses, but continually strive to increase the pace and quality of successive innovations.

These forces have collectively meant a shift of economic power from producers to consumers, many of whom now enjoy greater quality, choice and value. Managers wishing to retain customers continually seek new ways to add value and retain their market position. Unless they do so they will experience a widening performance gap.

A **perceived perform-
ance gap** arises when
people believe that the
actual performance of a
unit or business is out of
line with the level they
desire.

Perceived performance gap

A **perceived performance gap** arises when people believe that the performance of a unit or business is out of line with the level they desire. If staff do not meet a customer's expectations, there is an immediate performance gap. Cumulatively this will lead to other performance gaps – such as revenue from sales being below the level needed to secure further resources. If uncorrected, this will, sooner or later, cause the business to fail.

In the current business climate, two aspects of performance dominate discussion – what Prastacos *et al.* (2002) call '**performance imperatives**': the need for flexibility and the need for innovation. In a very uncertain business world, the scope for long-term planning is limited. Successful businesses are those which are both flexible and efficient. This paradox reflects the fact that while companies need to respond rapidly they also need to respond efficiently. This usually depends on having developed a degree of stability in the way they transform resources into outputs. Apple is very flexible in the way it brings out new products, but has very stable and robust systems to produce and deliver them.

> **Performance imperatives** are aspects of performance that are especially important for an organisation to do well, such as flexibility and innovation.

The other imperative identified by Prastacos *et al.* (2002) is innovation:

> to generate a variety of successful new products or services (embedding technological innovation), and to continuously innovate in all aspects of the business. (p. 58)

In many areas of business, customers expect a constant flow of new products, embodying the latest scientific and technological developments: companies that fail to meet these expectations will experience a performance gap. Nokia selling an advanced mobile phone profitably depends not only on the quality of the applied research which goes into producing a better screen display, but also on turning that research into a desirable product *and* delivering it at a price which customers will pay. This depends on organisation – the internal context.

The internal context

Chapter 1 introduced the internal context (Figure 1.3) as the elements within an organisation that shape behaviour. Change begins to happen when sufficient influential people believe, say, that outdated technology or a confusing structure is causing a performance gap, by inhibiting flexibility or innovation. They notice external or internal events and interpret them as threatening the performance that influential stakeholders expect. This interpretation, and their (implicit) theory of change, encourages them to propose changing one or more aspects of the internal context organisation (see Table 11.1).

Table 11.1 Examples of change in each element of the organisation

Element	Example of change to this element
Objectives	Developing a new product or service Changing the overall mission or direction
Technology	Creating an online community Building Terminal 5 at Heathrow
Business processes	Improving the way maintenance and repair services are delivered Redesigning systems to handle the flow of cash and funds
Financial resources	A set of changes, such as closing a facility, to reduce costs New financial reporting requirements to ensure consistency
Structure	Reallocating functions and responsibilities between departments Redesigning work to give staff more responsibility
People	Designing a training programme to enhance skills Changing the tasks of staff to offer a new service
Culture	Unifying the culture between two or more merged businesses Encouraging greater emphasis on quality and reliability
Power	An empowerment programme giving greater authority to junior staff Centralising decisions to increase the control of HQ over subsidiaries

They then have to persuade enough other people that the matter is sufficiently serious to place on the management agenda. People in some organisations are open to proposals for change, others tend to ignore them – BP faced new competitive pressures throughout the 1980s, but it was only around 1990 that sufficient senior people took the threats seriously enough to initiate rapid change.

People initiate change for reasons other than a conscious awareness of a performance gap – fashion, empire building or personal whim can all play a part. Employees or trade unions can propose changes in the way things are done to improve working conditions. The need for innovation and change is subjective – what some see as urgent others will leave till later. People affect that process by managing external information – magnifying customer complaints to support change, minimising them to avoid it.

11.3 Forms of innovation and change

Creativity and innovation

Creativity refers to the ability to combine ideas in a new way, or to make unusual associations between ideas. This helps people and organisations to generate imaginative ideas or ways of working: but that in itself does not bring value. Figure 11.1 shows that achieving more valuable outputs (more innovative products or work methods) depends on both the inputs AND the transformation of those inputs.

Inputs include having creative people and groups who are able to generate novel ideas and methods, but they only flourish in a favourable context. Managers need to create a context which encourages both creative people *and* the application of their ideas into goods and services that people buy. In the business context, it is useful to see **innovation** as the process through which new ideas, objects, behaviours and practices are created, developed and implemented into a product or service.

> **Innovation** is the process through which new ideas, objects, behaviours and practices are created, developed and implemented into a product or service that can be sold for profit.

The 4 Ps of innovation

Innovations become manifest in one or more of four areas – the product itself, the process of delivery or manufacture, its position in the market and the overall paradigm of the business.

Product innovations

This refers to a new function or feature of a product such as incorporating a music player into a mobile phone or offering an online banking facility. They are intended to enhance the utility of the product to increase sales – such as the Nike+ (developed with Apple), which contains a sensor that transmits data from one of the shoes to the runner's iPod or iPhone.

Process innovations

An example is adding a self-service checkout at a supermarket so that customers can scan and pay for their purchases using a barcode reader. An example in manufacturing would be using robots to assemble higher quality products more efficiently, while another (very radical) would be when managers try to change their underlying philosophy and approach to managing the business.

Position innovations

These are changes in the target market for a product or service. Lucozade is a familiar example – once aimed at people recovering from illness, it is now for healthy people engaged in sport. Another example is the four-wheel drive vehicle: originally intended for off-road work, now sold as fashionable family cars.

Paradigm innovations

These are changes in how companies frame what they do; for example reframing a supermarket such as Tesco from a food retailer to one which provides many more of a family's needs such as petrol, clothing and financial products. This also brings further synergies, since shoppers can buy food, petrol and clothes – and pay for it all with their Tesco credit card.

Degrees of innovation – radical and incremental

Some innovations – such as the aerofoil that allows heavier than air flight and the transistor that is the basis of all modern electronics – have fundamentally changed society. Others such as Velcro or the ball-point pen are useful, but have more modest effects on our lives.

The effects of an innovation depend on what people use them for, what they replace and who is evaluating them. Using hydrogen-fuelled engines instead of fossil-fuelled ones will have little effect on how people drive cars, so from the driver's perspective it is an **incremental** innovation. It will have a large environmental benefit – so from the point of view of those who care about the environment it will be a **radical** innovation.

> **Incremental** innovations are small changes in a current product or process which brings a minor improvement.

> **Radical** innovations are large game-changing developments that alter the competitive landscape.

Organisational change

Turning innovative ideas or products into something that adds value depends on **organisational change** – an attempt to change one or more of the elements shown in Figure 1.3. Table 11.1 illustrates this with examples of changes that people initiate under each element. Most change combines several of these – when Paul Polman (chief executive of Unilever, the food and consumer products company) began to make substantial changes to the way it worked, he acknowledging it would be a long process, because:

> **Organisational change** is a deliberate attempt to improve organisational performance by changing one or more aspects of the organisation, such as its technology, structure or business processes.

> we need to change the strategy and structure as well as the culture. (*Financial Times*, 5 April 2010)

Change in any of these areas will have implications for others – and these interconnections make change difficult. When Tesco introduced its online shopping service, managers evidently needed to create a website (technology). They also needed to decide issues of structure and people (would it be part of the existing stores, or a separate unit with its own premises and staff?) and about business processes (how would an order on the website be transformed into a box of groceries delivered to the customer's door?). They had to manage these ripples initiated by the main decision. Managers who ignore, or are unable to manage, these consequential changes achieve less than they expect.

11.4   The interaction of context and change

> The **interaction model** is a theory of change that stresses the continuing interaction between the internal and external contexts of an organisation, making the outcomes of change hard to predict.

How managers implement change depends on their theory about its nature. This section presents an **interaction model**, a theory of how change and context interact, and the next section outlines four complementary perspectives on managing that interaction.

People introduce change to alter the context

Management attempts to change elements of its context to encourage behaviours that close the performance gap. If Google's online bookstore is to be a success, the company will need (at least) to change technology, structure, people and business processes to enable staff to deliver the new service. When people plan and implement a change they are creating a new context, which they hope will guide the behaviour of people involved in the activity.

People do not necessarily accept the new arrangements, or without adapting them in some way: in doing so they make further changes to the context. As people begin to work in new circumstances – with a new IS or a new job description – they make small adjustments to the original plan, deciding which aspects to ignore, use or adapt. In time, some of these changes in behaviour become routine and taken for granted – and so become part of the context that staff have created informally. These add to, or replace, the context that those formally responsible for planning the change created, and may or may not support the original intentions of the project. People and context continue to interact.

The context affects the ability to change

While people managing a project aim to change the context, the context within which they work will itself help or hinder them. All of the elements of Table 11.1 will be present as the project begins, and some of these will influence how people react. Managers who occupy influential positions will review a proposal from their personal career perspective, as well as that of the organisation. At Tesco the existing technology (stores, distribution systems, information systems) and business processes would influence managers' decisions about how to implement the internet shopping strategy.

The prevailing culture (Chapter 3) – shared values, ideals and beliefs – influences how people view change. Some will welcome a project they believe fits their culture, and resist one that threatens it. Culture is a powerful influence on the success or failure of innovation. Some cultures, like those at Asos or Facebook, encourage people to welcome and support change – they provide a **receptive context**. A manager in a leading electronics company commented on his fast-moving business:

Receptive contexts are those where features of the organisation (such as culture or technology) appear likely to help change.

> A very dynamic organisation, it's incredibly fast and the change thing is just a constant that you live with. They really promote flexibility and adaptability in their employees. Change is just a constant, there's change happening all of the time and people have become very acclimatised to that, it's part of the job. The attitude to change, certainly within the organisation, is very positive at the moment.

In others, the culture discourages change and encourages caution – especially if the change proposed would challenge ways of thinking that have worked well for many years. Music publishers like EMI found it hard to respond to competition from digital downloading, in part because they have a **non-receptive context**. Book publishers think of their business from the perspective of printed books, and some find it hard to see how they can work with digital methods of delivering content, such as Kindle. Cultural beliefs shape how people respond, and are hard to change, yet:

Non-receptive contexts are those where the combined effects of features of the organisation (such as culture or technology) appear likely to hinder change.

> Managers learn to be guided by these beliefs because they have worked successfully in the past. (Lorsch, 1986, p. 97)

The distribution of power also affects receptiveness to change. Change threatens established practice, and those who benefit from present arrangements will resist it. Innovation depends on those promoting it being able to use, or develop, sufficient power and expertise to overcome entrenched interests – who will, of course, resist changes in the distribution of power.

The context has a history and several levels

The present context is the result of past decisions and events, so managers implement change against that background. The promoter of a project in a multinational firm noted his colleagues' attitudes:

> They were a little sceptical and wary of whether it was actually going to enhance our processes. Major pan-European redesign work had been attempted in the past and had failed miserably. The solutions had not been appropriate and had not been accepted by the divisions. Europe-wide programmes therefore had a bad name. (Boddy, 2002, p. 38)

Beliefs about the future also affect how people react. Optimists are more open to change than those who feel threatened and vulnerable.

The context represented by Table 11.1 occurs at corporate, divisional and operating levels. People at any of these will be acting to change their context – which may help or hinder those managing change elsewhere. A project at one level may depend on decisions at another about resources, as this manager leading an oil refinery project discovered:

> One of the main drawbacks was that commissioning staff could have been supplemented by skilled professionals from within the company, but this was denied to me as project manager. This threw a heavy strain and responsibility on myself and my assistant. It put me in a position of high stress, as I knew that the future of the company rested upon the successful outcome of this project. One disappointment (and, I believe, a significant factor in the project) was that just before commissioning, the manager of the pilot plant development team was transferred to another job. He had been promised to me at the project inception, and I had designed him into the working operation. (Boddy, 2002, pp. 38–39)

The manager's job is to create a coherent context that encourages creativity and innovation, by using their preferred model of change.

11.5   Four models of change

There are four complementary models of change, each with different implications for managers – life-cycle, emergent, participative and political.

Life-cycle

Much advice given to those responsible for managing projects uses the idea of the project **life-cycle**. Projects go through successive stages, and results depend on managing each one in an orderly and controlled way. The labels vary, but common themes are:

* define objectives;
* allocate responsibilities;
* fix deadlines and milestones;
* set budgets; and
* monitor and control.

Life-cycle models of change are those that view change as an activity which follows a logical, orderly sequence of activities that can be planned in advance.

This approach (sometimes called a 'rational – linear' approach) reflects the idea that people can identify smaller tasks within a change and plan the (overlapping) order in which to do them. It predicts that people can make reasonably accurate estimates of the time required to complete each task and when it will be feasible to start work on later ones. People can use tools such as bar charts (sometimes called Gantt charts after the American industrial engineer Henry Gantt, who worked with Frederick Taylor), to show all the tasks required for a project and their likely duration. These help to visualise the work required and to plan the likely sequence of events – illustrated in Figure 11.2.

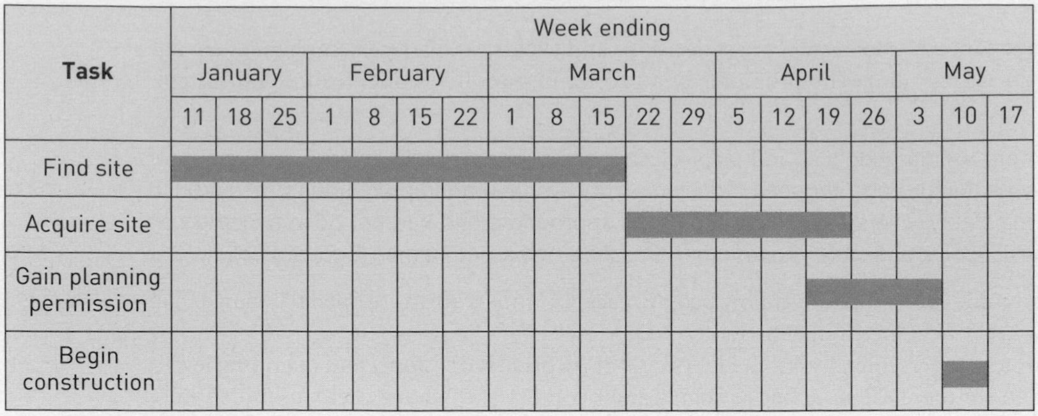

Task	Week ending																	
	January			February				March					April				May		
	11	18	25	1	8	15	22	1	8	15	22	29	5	12	19	26	3	10	17
Find site	███	███	███	███	███	███	███	███	███	███									
Acquire site											███	███	███	███					
Gain planning permission															███	███			
Begin construction																		███	

Figure 11.2 A simple bar chart

The life-cycle model implies that managing change depends on specifying these elements at the start and monitoring them to ensure the project stays on target. Large industrial research laboratories tend to work in this way.

Many books on project management, such as Lock (2007), present advice on tools for each stage of the life cycle. Those advising on IS changes may recommend 'system development life cycle' approaches (Chaffey, 2003). These give valuable guidance, but may not be sufficient, since people may be unable at the start to specify the end point – or the tasks which will lead to it. In uncertain conditions, it makes little sense to plan the outcomes in detail. It may be wiser to set the general direction, and adapt the target to suit new conditions that develop during the change. Those managing such change need an additional theory to cope with emergent change.

Emergent

Chapter 8 (Section 8.3) mentions the strategy process at IKEA, showing how many of its major business ideas emerged from chance events or external conditions. Evidence of similar processes in other firms led scholars to see companies' strategies as an *emergent* or adaptive process. These ideas apply to innovation and change projects as much as they do to broad strategy. People with different interests and priorities influence the direction of a project and how they want to achieve it. The planning techniques associated with the life-cycle approach can help, but their value will be limited if the change is closer to the **emergent model**.

Emergent models of change emphasise that in uncertain conditions a project will be affected by unknown factors, and that planning has little effect on the outcome.

Boddy *et al.* (2000) show how this emergent process occurred when Sun Microsystems began working with a new supplier of the bulky plastic enclosures that contain their products, while the supplier wished to widen their customer base. There were few discussions about a long-term plan. As Sun became more confident in the supplier's ability it gave them more complex work. Both gained from this emerging relationship. A sales co-ordinator:

> It's something we've learnt by being with Sun – we didn't imagine that at the time. Also at the time we wouldn't have imagined we would be dealing with America the way we do now – it was far beyond our thoughts. (Boddy *et al.*, 2000, p. 1010)

Mintzberg believes that managers should not expect rigid adherence to a plan. Chance and 'eureka moments' (see Section 11.6) are valuable sources of innovation. Some departure from plan is inevitable as circumstances change, so a wise approach to change recognises that

> the real world inevitably involves some thinking ahead of time as well as some adaptation en route. (Mintzberg, 1994a, p. 24)

Participative

Those advocating **participative models** stress the benefits of personal involvement in, and contribution to, events and outcomes. The underlying belief is that if people can say 'I helped to build this', they will be more willing to live and work with it, whatever it is. It is also *possible* that since participation allows more people to express their views, the outcome will be better. Employees who participate fully in planning a change are more likely to view the issues from the perspective of the organisation, rather than their own position or function. Participation can be good for the organisation, as well as the individual. Many innovative firms invite customers to participate in product and service design.

The **participative model** is the belief that if people are able to take part in planning a change they will be more willing to accept and implement the change.

While participation is consistent with democratic values, it takes time and effort and may raise unrealistic expectations. It may be inappropriate when:

- the scope for change is limited, because of decisions made elsewhere;
- participants know little about the topic;
- decisions must be made quickly;
- management has decided what to do and will do so whatever views people express;
- there are fundamental disagreements and/or inflexible opposition to the proposed change.

Participative approaches assume that a sensitive approach by reasonable people will result in the willing acceptance and implementation of change. Some situations contain conflicts that participation alone cannot solve.

Political models

Change often involves people from several levels and functions pulling in different directions:

> Strategic processes of change are . . . widely accepted as multi-level activities and not just as the province of a . . . single general manager. Outcomes of decisions are no longer assumed to be a product of rational . . . debates but are also shaped by the interests and commitments of individuals and groups, forces of bureaucratic momentum, and the manipulation of the structural context around decisions and changes. (Whipp *et al.*, 1988, p. 51)

Several analysts propose using a **political model of change**. Pettigrew (1985) was an early advocate of the view that change requires political as well as rational (life-cycle) skills. Successful change managers encourage others to accept the change as necessary – often by manipulating apparently rational information to build support for their ideas and enhance their power.

Political models of change reflect the view that organisations are made up of groups with separate interests, goals and values, and that these affect how they respond to change.

Power is essential to get things done, since decisions in themselves change nothing – people only see a difference when someone implements a visible change. Change frequently threatens the *status quo*: people who have done well are likely to resist it. Innovators need to ensure the project is put onto the senior management agenda, and that influential people support and resource it. Innovators need to develop a political will, and to build and use their power. Buchanan and Badham (1999) conclude that the roots of political behaviour

> lie in personal ambition, in organisation structures that create roles and departments which compete with each other, and in major decisions that cannot be resolved by reason and logic alone but which rely on the values and preferences of the key actors. Power politics and change are inextricably linked. Change creates uncertainty and ambiguity. People wonder how their jobs will change, how their work will be affected, how their relationships with colleagues will be damaged or enhanced. (p. 11)

Reasonable people may disagree about means and ends, and fight for the action they prefer. This implies that successful project managers understand that their job requires more than technical competence, and are able and willing to engage in political actions.

The political perspective recognises the messy realities of organisational life. Major product and service innovations will be technically complex and challenge established interests. These will pull in different directions and pursue personal as well as organisational goals. To manage these tensions, managers need political skills as well as those implied by life-cycle, emergent and participative perspectives.

Management in practice   **Political action in hospital re-engineering**

Managers in a hospital responded to a persistent performance gap (especially unacceptably long waiting times) by 're-engineering' the way patients moved through and between clinical areas. This included creating multi-functional teams responsible for all aspects of the flow of the patient through a clinic, rather than dealing with narrow functional tasks. The programme was successful, but was also controversial. One of those leading the change recalled:

> I don't like to use the word manipulate, but ... you do need to manipulate people. It's about playing the game. I remember being accosted by a very cross consultant who had heard something about one of the changes and he really wasn't very happy with it. And it was about how am I going to deal with this now? And it is about being able to think quickly. So I put it over to him in a way that he then accepted, and he was quite happy with. And it wasn't a lie and it wasn't totally the truth. But he was happy with it and it has gone on.

Source: Buchanan (2001), p. 13.

These perspectives (life-cycle, emergent, participative, political) are complementary in that successful large change is likely to require elements of each. Table 11.2 illustrates how each perspective links to management practice.

Table 11.2 Perspectives on change and examples of management practice

Perspective	Themes	Example of management practices
Life cycle	Rational, linear, single agreed aim, technical focus	Measurable objectives; planning and control devices such as Gantt charts and critical path analysis
Emergent	Objectives change as learning occurs during the project, and new possibilities appear	Open to new ideas about scope and direction, and willing to add new resources if needed
Participative	Ownership, commitment, shared goals, people focus	Inviting ideas and comments on proposals, ensuring agreement before action, seeking consensus
Political	Oppositional, influence, conflicting goals, power focus	Building allies and coalitions, securing support from powerful players, managing information

11.6 Sources of innovation

Innovative ideas can come from any or all of the elements shown in Figure 11.1, if managers create a suitable context.

Eureka moments – capturing the unexpected

The word 'eureka' is associated with the experience of having an idea. A common example is when Art Fry used a recently invented 'sticky but not too sticky' adhesive to keep his bookmark in place. This gave him the idea for the Post-It note which, after more design and development, became the familiar product range. The Management in Practice feature describes a recent example.

Management in practice   Plugging a 'mole' in the market   www.magnamole.co.uk

Sharon Wright had her eureka moment while having a phone-line installed in her home. Under pressure for time she offered to help the engineer thread the cable through the wall of her house. To Sharon's surprise the engineer produced a makeshift tool made out of a wire coat-hanger. As well as being difficult to use Sharon's experience in health and safety management told her this device was unsuitable and hazardous. Market research showed there were no alternatives tools available for cable threading.

Within hours she had sketched the design of the Magnamole tool, a plastic rod with a magnet at one end and an accompanying metallic cap for attaching to the wire to be threaded through the wall. She soon had a prototype, and orders followed from large customers around the world.

What is remarkable about Sharon is that she had little knowledge or experience of this area of business, but that did not stop her from taking advantage of an obvious gap in the market.

Source: Company website.

Knowledge push

Most innovation now comes from the research and development laboratories of large companies. GlaxoSmithKline (pharmaceuticals) spends large sums to develop new drugs in its laboratories. It depends on innovation, and this is reflected in the systematic organisation of scientific staff, equipment and facilities to find potentially profitable solutions to known medical conditions. It also draws on the expertise of other companies through many joint-venture arrangements – as does Procter & Gamble, the world's largest consumer products company. It is an acknowledged leader in product innovation, and its chief executive, Bob McDonald, believes that they should increasingly embrace other people's good ideas. The company embraces the idea of 'open innovation', by working with outside partners to increase the speed at which it brings new products to market – Tide Total Care was developed with external research from the University of Lund in Sweden, and from two smaller chemical companies.

Need pull

No matter how innovative a new product, it will not make money (add value) unless it has a market, so before investing in development, managers assess the likely demand. This is difficult, as it is hard to assess human needs in isolation. Before the technology arrived, sportsmen and women trained without equipment to combat boredom, and, if asked, would have been unable to express a need for a product. Yet lightweight digital music players and headphones are now an essential part of a runner's or cyclist's training kit. Many products, especially in the area of consumer electronics, were inconceivable a few years ago. While it is logical that the typewriter could pave the way for a product such as Microsoft Word, it is less conceivable that it would lead to Powerpoint. While the link between the home phone and the mobile phone is clear, the jump from the basic mobile to the functionality embodied in the iPhone would have been difficult to envisage.

Regulation changes

Changes to the external context – new laws and regulations – are another source of innovation. Measures to limit climate change and environmental pollution are current examples, which encourage entrepreneurs to search for commercially viable solutions in solar, wind, wave or biomass technologies. Regulations to improve road safety led to the development of speed cameras and air bags. Potential innovators seek opportunities in relevant regulations.

Staff as innovators

Staff (part of the internal context) are a valuable source of innovation, even if it is not expected as a major part of their job. Employee participation became fashionable when people publicised the 'Quality Miracle' of Japanese manufacturers, enabled by the system of 'Kaizen' or 'continuous improvement' (Imai, 1986). Under this method, employees were encouraged to question work processes and look for incremental improvements in all that they did, leading to a better production process, better product quality and organisational efficiency.

While suggestion schemes are not new, the more systematic and proactive approach of the Japanese encouraged 'continuous improvement'. This is now joined by other systems such as 'total quality management' and 'lean manufacturing'. While differing in emphasis, all aim to involve employees in thinking behind the product and process, and encouraging them to generate ideas that lead to value-adding innovations.

Users as innovators

Users are sometimes the source of ideas for innovation, three categories being particularly important:

- **Lead users** – people who not only use the product but also help in its development. Ivor Tiefenbrun, the founder of hi-fi maker Linn Products (Chapter 16, p. 324), developed his model when he became dissatisfied with products then available.
- **User communities** – are groups of users who congregate around a product or product platform, such as early personal computer users, and find new and innovative ways to use the systems.
- **Extreme users** – push products to their limit creating a need for improved performance. The bicycle is an example, with the relentless drive for more durable and higher performing machines.

> ### 11.7 Organisational factors in innovation

The process of innovation

Organisations which depend on innovation implement deliberate systems to ensure an adequate flow. Figure 11.3 shows the innovation process as a filter through which ideas are gathered, channelled and focused before selecting those believed to have most potential. The model appears to be a linear process, but in reality there is continual 're-cycling' back to

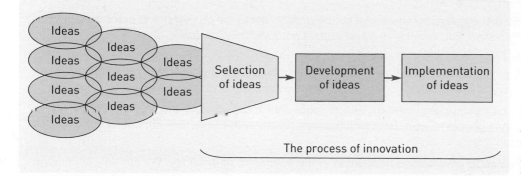

Figure 11.3
A model of the innovation process
Source: Based on Tidd and Bessant (2009).

earlier stages for revisions and to incorporate new ideas. Generating the initial idea is necessarily random – but thereafter firms try to create order as quickly as possible. They apply resources to develop promising ideas into something they can use. The steps are sequential but their duration and complexity will vary – some requiring significant research and development, others merely a change in the focus of the sales effort.

Organisational factors in managing innovation

Organisations who depend on innovation (like Asos – Chapter 10 case study) encourage all staff to help create and implement a strong flow of successful new things. Smith *et al.* (2008) developed a prescriptive model of the organisational features shaping the effectiveness of innovation – 'the four Ss' of innovation.

- **Strategy** – the organisational strategy must communicate a shared vision and goals, indicating that innovation is central to its competitive advantage.
- **Style** – the strategy must be enacted by the management style of the senior team to reinforce the strategic intention. A 'facilitate and empower' style is more likely to foster innovation than a 'command and control' style. For this to work, staff will need resources and time for ideas to emerge.
- **Structure** – a highly specialised division of tasks is detrimental to innovation, while enriched jobs (Chapter 13) and easy horizontal communication will support it. While lone employees can be innovative, teams of employees working together are more likely to succeed.
- **Support** – technology can facilitate the transfer of knowledge by creating a knowledge repository, enabling staff to access information easily.

Pixar – with a unique record of technological and artistic innovation – illustrates some of these points: see the Management in Practice feature below.

Management in practice   Behind Pixar's magic   www.pixar.com

Ed Catmull (co-founder of Pixar, and president of Pixar and Disney Animation Studios) has written about the 'collective creativity' at the company: many of its methods are relevant to other organisations. He emphasises the uncertainty of the innovative process – the idea which starts the process may not work – by definition it is new, and the innovator cannot know at the start if it will lead to a worthwhile result:

> at the start of making [*Ratatouille*] we simply didn't know if [it] would work. However, since we're supposed to offer something that isn't obvious, we bought into somebody's initial vision and took a chance. (2008, p. 66)

'Taking chances' that consistently succeed is not due to luck, but to the principles and practices that Pixar uses to support the people who turn the idea into a useful product. These include:

Getting talented people to work effectively with each other... [by constructing] an environment that nurtures trusting relationships and unleashes everyone's creativity. If we get that right, the result is a vibrant community where talented people are loyal to one another and their collective work. (p. 66)

Everyone must be free to communicate with anyone ...the most efficient way to deal with numerous problems is to trust people to work out the difficulties directly with each other without having to check for permission. (p. 71)

We must **stay close to innovations happening in the academic community.** We strongly encourage our technical artists to publish their research and participate in industry conferences. Publication may give away ideas ... but the connection is worth far more than any ideas we may have revealed: it helps us attract exceptional talent and reinforces the belief throughout the company that people are more important than ideas. (p. 71)

[Measure progress]. Because we're a creative organization, people [think that what we do can't be measured]. That's wrong. Most of our processes involve activities and deliverables that can be quantified. We keep track of the rates at which things happen, how often something had to be reworked, whether a piece of work was completely finished or not when it was sent to another department ... Data can show things in a neutral way, which can stimulate discussion. (Catmull, 2008, p. 72)

Source: Catmull (2008).

Activity 11.2 **What does 'managing change and innovation' mean?**

Having read the chapter, make brief notes summarising the change and innovation issues evident in the organisation you chose for this activity.

- Compare the type of change or innovation you have studied with the frameworks outlined in the chapter. (See Section 11.2, especially Table 11.1.)
- How closely did the way people managed the change correspond to one or more of the four models of change in Section 11.5. If it did not, what model (theory) guided practice?
- What was the main sources of the innovation? (Refer to Section 11.6.)
- Which organisational factors helped or hindered the innovation? (Refer to Section 11.7.)

Compare what you have found with other students on your course.

Summary

1 **Outline the links between creativity, innovation, change and strategy**
   - Many organisations increasingly depend on creativity and innovation as they respond to external demands. If innovation is at the centre of their strategy, they need to create an organisation that supports innovation.

2 **Describe types of innovation, with examples**
   - Product – what the organisation offers for sale.
   - Process – how it creates the product.

- Position – changes in target market.
- Paradigm – how a company frames what it does.

3 **Explain the links between innovation and context**

- A change programme is an attempt to change one or more aspects of the internal context, which then provides the context of future actions. The prevailing context can itself help or hinder change efforts.

4 **Compare life-cycle, emergent, participative and political theories of change**

- Life-cycle: change projects can be planned, monitored and controlled towards achieving their objectives.
- Emergent: reflecting the uncertainties of the environment, change is hard to plan in detail, but emerges incrementally from events and actions.
- Participative: successful change depends on human commitment, which is best obtained by involving participants in planning and implementation.
- Political: change threatens some of those affected, who will use their power to block progress, or to direct the change in ways that suit local objectives.

5 **Illustrate the sources of innovation**

- Eureka moments – capturing the unexpected.
- Knowledge push.
- Need pull.
- External changes – such as regulations.
- Staff.
- Users.

6 **Illustrate the organisational factors believed to support innovation**

- Strategy – innovation is explicitly called for in the corporate strategy.
- Structure – roles and jobs are defined to aid in innovative behaviour.
- Style – management empowers the workforce to behave innovatively.
- Support – IT systems are available to support innovative behaviour.

Review questions

1 What does the term 'performance gap' mean, and what is its significance for change?
2 What are the implications for management of the systemic nature of innovation?
3 Give examples of three types of innovation mentioned in the chapter.
4 How could a manager alter the receptiveness of an organisation to change?
5 Outline the life-cycle perspective on innovation and explain when it is most likely to be useful.
6 How does it differ from the 'emergent' perspective?
7 Describe three sources of innovation, preferably with a new example.

Further reading

Tidd, J. and Bessant, J. (2009), *Managing Innovation: Integrating technological, market and organisational change*, Wiley, Chichester.

An easy to read text combining a comprehensive account of innovation theories with many contemporary examples.

Weblinks

These websites have appeared in, or are relevant to, the chapter:

www.magnamole.co.uk
www.pixar.com
www.google.com
www.apple.com
www.nokia.com
www.inamo-restaurant.com
www.pret.com
www.co-operative.coop
www.asos.com

Visit two of the business sites in the list, or others that interest you, and navigate to the pages dealing with corporate news, investor relations or 'our company'.

* What signs of major innovations can you find?
* Does the site give you a sense of an organisation that is receptive or non-receptive to change?
* What factors appear designed to encourage innovation in the company?

 Annotated weblinks, multiple choice questions and other useful resources can be found on **www.pearsoned.co.uk/boddy**

Case study   Google   www.google.com

Sergey Brin and Larry Page founded Google in 1999 and by 2011 it was the world's largest search engine, with the mission: 'to organise the world's information and make it universally accessible and useful'. The need for search services arose as the World Wide Web expanded, making it progressively more difficult for users to find relevant information. The company's initial success was built on the founders' new approach to online searching: their PageRank algorithm (with 500 million variables and 3 billion terms) identifies material relevant to a search by favouring pages that have been linked to other pages. These links were called 'votes', because they signalled that another page's webmaster had decided that the focal page deserved attention. The importance of the focal page is determined by counting the number of votes it has received.

As a business Google generates revenue by providing advertisers with the opportunity to deliver online advertising that is relevant to the search results on a page. The advertisements are displayed as sponsored links, with the message appearing alongside search results for appropriate keywords. They are priced on a cost-per-impression basis, whereby advertisers pay a fixed amount each time their ad is viewed. The charge depends on what the advertiser has bid for the keywords, and the more they bid the nearer the top of the page their advertisement will be.

A feature of Google is the speed with which it returns search results – usually within a second. From the start its focus has been on developing 'the perfect search engine', defined by Page as something that 'understands what you mean and gives you back what you want'. Rather than use a small number of large servers that tend to run slowly at peak times, Google invested in thousands of linked PCs that quickly find the answer to each query.

Beyond its core search and advertising capabilities, the company has embarked on many new ventures. It's Android mobile phone operating system is capturing a large share of the market, outselling Apple by the end of 2010. It is also involved in blogging, radio and television advertising, online payments and social networks: in 2010 it opened an online book store, known as eBookstore. It often acquires technology from other companies such as Picasa for photo management; YouTube for online videos; DoubleClick for web ads and Keyhole for satellite photos (now Google Earth).

Photo courtesy Google UK.

Google simultaneously tests and markets new applications to the user community – testing and marketing are virtually indistinguishable from one another. This creates a unique relationship with consumers, who become an essential part of the development team – moving seamlessly from testing to using products as they would any other commercial offering.

The company allows independent developers to share access and create new applications that incorporate elements of the Google system. They can easily test and launch applications and have them hosted in the Google world, where there is a large target audience – and a practically unlimited capacity for customer interactions.

Google has a distinctive technocratic culture, in that individuals prosper based on the quality of their ideas and their technological acumen. Engineers are expected to spend 20 per cent of their time working on their own creative projects. The company provides plenty of intellectual stimulation which, for a company founded on technology, can be the opportunity to learn from the best and brightest technologists.

There are regular talks by distinguished researchers from around the world. Google's founders and executives have thought through many aspects of the knowledge work environment, including the design and occupancy of offices (jam-packed for better communication); the frequency of all-hands meetings (every Friday); and the approach to interviewing and hiring new employees (rigorous, with many interviews). None of these principles is particularly novel, but in combination they suggest an unusually high level of recognition for the human dimensions of innovation. Brin, Page and Schmidt (the company's CEO) have taken ideas from other organisations – such as the software firm SAS Institute – that are celebrated for how they treat their knowledge workers.

The company has rapidly extended the range of services it offers, while remaining rigorously focused on search. Although the headquarters is in California, their mission is to facilitate access to information across the world – more than half of their searches are delivered to users living outside the US, in more than 35 languages. The company offers volunteers the opportunity to help in translating the site into additional languages.

The company acquired YouTube, the video-sharing site, in 2006, as a further extension of its services. Such acquisitions can be seen as a way of growing the business in a way that stays focused on Google's distinctive competence (developing superior search solutions) and earning revenue from these through targeted advertising. In 2011, it was hiring many more staff, and was also changing the recruitment process to encourage more entrepreneurial people to join the company.

Sources: Based on Harvard Business School case 9-806-105, *Google Inc.*, prepared by Thomas R. Eisenmann and Kerry Herman; Iyer and Davenport (2008); company website; *Financial Times*, 25 February 2010, 7 December 2010, 7 February 2011; *Independent*, 23 October 2010.

Questions

1 The chapter mentions the 4Ps of innovation (refer to Section 11.3). What examples of these can you find in the case?

2 What examples are there in the case of the sources of innovation mentioned in the chapter? (Refer to Section 11.6.)

3 List specific examples from the case of the organisational factors encouraging innovation. (Refer to Section 11.7.)

PART 5
LEADING

Introduction

Generating the effort and commitment to work towards objectives is central to managing any human activity. One person working alone, in private life or in business, has only themselves to motivate. As an organisation grows, management activities become, in varying degrees, separated from the core work activities. The problem of generating effort changes, as now one person, or one occupational group, has to secure the willing co-operation of other people and their commitment to the task. Those other people may be subordinates, peers or superiors whose support, and perhaps approval, needs to be generated and maintained.

The quality of that commitment is as important as whether or not it is secured. Staff are often in direct contact with customers. They are aware of their unique and changing requirements, and have a significant effect on the view the customer forms of the organisation. Others are in creative roles, with a direct impact on the quality of the service delivered to the final customer, whether they are contributing to a core R&D project or a TV show. Others must work reliably and flexibly to meet changing external or internal customer needs. Unwilling or grudging commitment damages the service offered and eventually the business itself.

How does management secure the motivation it needs from others? This Part offers perspectives on the dilemma. Chapter 12 examines ideas on influencing others, while Chapter 13 presents a range of theories about what those others may want from work. Communication is central to all management tasks, so Chapter 14 examines this topic. Teams are an increasingly prominent aspect of organisations, and the motivation and commitment generated within them is often central to performance: Chapter 15 introduces ideas on teams.

CHAPTER 12
INFLUENCING

Learning outcomes

When you have read this chapter you should be able to:

1 Explain why leading and managing both depend on being able to influence others
2 Compare trait, behavioural and contingency perspectives on influencing
3 Outline theories that focus on power (personal and organisational) as the source of influence
4 Explain why sharing power may increase it
5 Describe the value of networking as a tactic to influence others
6 Use ideas from the chapter to comment on the management issues in the Apple case study

Activity 12.1   What does 'influencing' mean in management?

Before reading the chapter, write some notes on what you think 'influencing' means in management.

Choose the organisation or people who may be able to help you learn about the topic. You may find it helpful to discuss the topic with a manager you know, or reflect on an activity you have managed.

- Identify a situation in which someone tried to influence others, and describe it briefly.
- How did those involved try to persuade others to act in a particular way?
- Did they consciously alter their approach to suit the situation?
- What sources of power did they use?

Keep these notes as you will be able to use them later.

12.1   Introduction

When the late Steve Jobs and Steve Wozniak founded Apple they faced more than technical challenges. They also had to persuade staff to leave good jobs to work for an unknown company, investors to risk their money, suppliers to deliver components – and above all the public to buy the new machines. Clearly they did all of this – but not by accident: they did it by successfully influencing other people to support the business and ensure it survived, while many others failed.

That pattern has continued, though with interruptions – notably when other senior managers opposed what Jobs was doing, and persuaded the board to dismiss him in 1986. Events took another turn, and Jobs returned to the company in 1997, since when it has had many successes – due to the way Jobs and others influenced staff, competitors, customers and suppliers.

All managers have to influence others. Crossrail managers (Chapter 6) successfully influenced many interest groups – local and national politicians, business leaders, financial institutions, Network Rail – to secure approval for the project in 2009. As construction began the following year, they continued to exert influence – now focused on contractors, financiers, residents affected by construction work – to deliver the new line. Those in charge of Mid Staffordsire NHS Trust (Chapter 17 case study) will have had to influence staff to work in different ways after the revelations of poor patient care.

Whatever their role, people add value to resources by influencing others. The tasks of planning, organising, leading and controlling depend on other people agreeing to co-operate within a web of mutual **influence**. Senior managers influence big investors to retain their support, sales staff influence customers, someone designing a new product influences others to back it. Everyone's performance depends on how well they do this, and the targets of their influence are often in more senior positions.

In that sense, the work of the manager is not that of the careful analyst, working out the ideal solution. It is closer to that of an entrepreneur who is determined to get things done in a hostile or indifferent setting. Managers typically operate across functional or departmental boundaries, working with people with other priorities and interests.

This chapter begins by clarifying the purposes of influencing in organisations, and the targets of influence: it also shows four possible outcomes of influence, some of which are better for the influencer than others. It then summarises three 'interpersonal' perspectives – trait, behavioural and contingency theories. A different perspective shows how people use power to influence others, drawing on both personal and organisational sources. In deciding how to influence others, people draw on their (perhaps implicit) knowledge of these theories, and their personal preferences, to devise both interpersonal and power-based methods. The organisational context also affects (and is affected by) the outcomes of an influence attempt. Figure 12.1 shows these themes.

Influence is the process by which one party attempts to modify the behaviour of others by mobilising power resources.

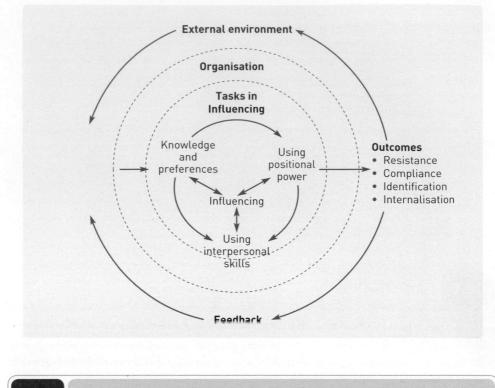

Figure 12.1
Themes of the
chapter

12.2   Purposes, targets and outcomes

Managing and leading

Research and commentary on influencing use the terms 'manager' and 'leader' (and their derivatives) interchangeably, as there is no definitive distinction. It is worth briefly clarifying the meanings which some attach to them.

Chapter 1 defined a manager as someone who gets things done with the support of others. Most commentators view an 'effective manager' as one who 'gets things done' to ensure order and continuity. They maintain the steady state – keeping established systems in good shape and making incremental improvements. People generally use the term 'effective leader' to denote someone who brings innovation, moves an activity out of trouble into success, makes a worthwhile difference. They (like Julian Metcalf at Pret A Manger – see the Management in Practice feature) see opportunities to do new things, take initiatives, inspire people.

Management in practice   **Julian Metcalf, founder of Pret A Manger**   www.pret.com

Commenting on the leadership of Julian Metcalf, who founded Pret A Manger in 1986 (it now has about 225 shops), one of his directors said:

> Pret has always been very innovative because our founder, Julian Metcalf, is a true entrepreneur: he is here most days and he is really the spirit for all things entrepreneurial here and that is fantastic. The benefit of that is that we don't spend months and months and months developing new products, we're very quick to turn things around and it's very fast paced here. We have lots of new products and upgrades to our ingredients going on month in month out. And people comment when they come here, in terms of the pace of change, sometimes it can be hard to keep up with, but it's exciting, and makes us feel like a small organisation when, in fact, we're not.   (Interview with the director)

Peter Drucker (1999) writes of the leader's ability to generate unusual or exceptional commitment to a vision, and of **leadership** being 'the lifting of people's vision to a higher sight, the raising of their performance to a higher standard, the building of their personality beyond its normal limitations'. The late Anita Roddick (founder of the Body Shop) wrote:

> [People] are looking for leadership that has vision . . . You have to look at leadership through the eyes of the followers and you have to live the message. What I have learned is that people become motivated when you guide them to the source of their own power and when you make heroes out of employees who best personify what you want to see in the organization. (Roddick, 1991, p. 223)

Kotter (1990) distinguishes between the terms leadership and management – while stressing that organisations need both, and that one person will often provide both. He regards good management as bringing order and consistency to an activity – through the tasks of planning, organising and controlling. He observed that modern management developed to support the large companies which developed from the middle of the nineteenth century. These complex enterprises tended to become chaotic, unless they developed good management practices to bring order and consistency. The pioneers of management (such as Robert Owen, Chapter 2 case study) created the discipline

> to help keep a complex organization on time and on budget. That has been, and still is, its primary function. Leadership is very different. It does not produce consistency and order . . . it produces movement. (p. 4)

Individuals whom people recognise as leaders have created change – whether for the better or not. Good leadership is that which

> moves people to a place in which they and those who depend on them are genuinely better off, and when it does so without trampling on the rights of others. (p. 5)

Leaders succeed by establishing direction and strategy, communicating it to those whose co-operation is needed, and motivating and inspiring people. Managing and leading are closely related, but differ in their primary functions – the one to create order, the other to create change. Organisations need both if they are to prosper.

People work to create change and to create order in varying degrees, so there is no value in a sharp distinction between managing and leading: John Adair quotes a Chinese proverb:

> What does it matter if the cat is black or white, as long as it catches mice? (Adair, 1997, p. 2)

Managing and leading both depend on influencing others to put effort and commitment into the task – whether to create order or to create change.

Targets of influence

People at all levels who want to get something done need to influence others. The effectiveness of senior managers in influencing others has the most visible effect on performance, shaping the overall direction of the business or changing the way it operates. Yet they depend on people lower down the organisation also being able and willing to exercise influence – whether to bring stability or to initiate change in their area of responsibility.

Managers (and leaders) often influence people who are equally powerful – as the first woman to take the top management job at a leading City of London legal practice observed:

> The hardest things in management . . . are complicated people issues. Sometimes you realise you can't solve everything. Our assets are the brains and personalities of some highly intelligent people, so there are a huge number of relationship issues. Most of these 250 people are very driven. If you get it right, the commitment is already sorted out. But you've got to take a lot of people with you a lot of the time. (*Financial Times*, 15 February 2001, p. 17)

So managing and leading require people to influence colleagues on the same level, those above them in the hierarchy and people outside the organisation.

Sidebar:

Leadership refers to the process of influencing the activities of others toward high levels of goal setting and achievement.

Outcomes of influence

Someone attempting to influence another can consider possible outcomes, and plan accordingly. Kelman (1961) identified three outcomes – compliance, identification and internalisation – to which this section adds a fourth, resistance: see Table 12.1.

- **Resistant** staff will have no commitment to the work. They will either refuse to do what is asked, or do what is required grudgingly and without enthusiasm.
- **Compliance** occurs when 'an individual accepts influence from another person or [group because they hope] to achieve a favorable reaction from the other' (p. 62). They do what is asked of them, not because they believe in it, or agree with it, but because in that way they will avoid further trouble and interference – 'I'll do it to keep the peace.'
- **Identification** occurs when someone acts in the way requested because the person feels that by doing so they are identifying with the person making the request. It is a way of maintaining a desired relationship with the influencer. They do what they are asked, but not because they find it intrinsically satisfying or worthwhile. Identification differs from compliance in that here the individual believes in their actions – but only when they are conscious of their relationship with the person making the request: 'I'll do it – but only because it's you who's asking.'
- **Internalisation** occurs when a person accepts influence – does what they are asked to do – because it is consistent with their values and beliefs. They accept the request because they fundamentally agree that it is the right thing to do – they see that it will solve the problem, be a congenial thing to do, or bring other valuable rewards: 'sure, that should work' could be a typical response indicating that a person has internalised the request.

Resistance or grudging compliance show there may be trouble ahead. Complex work processes require people to work with imagination and flexibility: in service industries customers immediately see that staff are merely complying rather than working with care and enthusiasm. An influencer can repeat their request more forcefully, but this will often bring little improvement. Alternatively (and more wisely) they can pause to consider why people reacted this way. That may give useful information about either what they asked for, or how they did it: either way, it should enable them to use a different approach next time.

How do managers and leaders try to ensure that others do what they want them to do? The sections which follow present answers to that question, beginning with trait theories.

Table 12.1 Four outcomes of influence attempts

Outcome	Description	Commentary
Resistance	Target opposed to the request and actively tries to avoid carrying it out	May try to dissuade the influencer from persisting. May seek support from others to block the influence attempt
Compliance	Target does what is asked, but no more. No enthusiasm, minimal effort	May deliberately let things go wrong, leading to 'I told you so....' May be enough in some situations
Identification	Target does as requested to maintain valued relationship with influencer	Only agreeing because request comes from that person – no wider commitment
Internalisation	Target internally agrees with a request and commits effort to make it work	The most successful outcome for the influencer, especially when task requires high levels of commitment

12.3 Traits models

Researchers have tried to identify the personal characteristics of effective influencers. They observed the personalities of prominent figures, and distinguished what they believed were enduring aspects of their personality, which they displayed in a variety of settings, and which appeared to influence them to behave in a particular way. Early work on personality and leadership identified numerous such **traits** – which hindered the development of a practically useful theory, as the lists of potentially valuable traits grew longer.

A **trait** is a relatively stable aspect of an individual's personality which influences behaviour in a particular direction.

The big five

A major advance came when researchers noted that they could group the many observed traits into five clusters (McRae and John, 1992). These are known as the **big five**: the left-hand column in Table 12.2 shows the label for each cluster, and the other columns show adjectives describing their extreme positions.

McCrae and John (1992) show that each cluster contains six traits. Using these in personality assessments enables researchers to identify the pattern of traits an individual displays, and predict how this pattern will affect performance. Colbert and Witt (2009) note that conscientiousness is the most consistent predictor of work outcomes, probably because such people tend to be dutiful, take care, deal with tasks accurately and persist in overcoming difficulties. They also found that supervisors could influence such workers to perform well by emphasising the value of achieving goals and helping them to do so.

The **big five** refers to trait clusters that appear consistently to capture main personality traits: Openness, Conscientiousness, Extraversion, Agreeableness and Neuroticism.

James Burns: transactional and transformational leaders

James Burns (1978) distinguished between **transactional** and **transformational leaders**. Transactional leaders influence subordinates' behaviour through a bargain. The leader enables followers to reach their goals, while at the same time contributing to the goals of the organisation. If subordinates behave in the way desired by the leader they receive rewards – transactional leaders tend to support the status quo by rewarding subordinates' efforts and commitment.

Burns contrasted this approach with that of transformational (sometimes called charismatic) leaders. They are thought to change the status quo by infusing work with a meaning which encourages subordinates to change their goals, needs and aspirations. Transformational leaders raise the consciousness of followers by appealing to higher ideals and moral values. They

A **transactional leader** is one who treats leadership as an exchange, giving followers what they want if they do what the leader desires.

A **transformational leader** is one who treats leadership as a matter of motivation and commitment, inspiring followers by appealing to higher ideals and moral values.

Table 12.2 The big five trait clusters

Label	Descriptions	
Openness	Explorer (O+): creative, open-minded, intellectual	Preserver (O−): unimaginative, disinterested, narrow-minded
Conscientiousness	Focused (C+): dutiful, achievement-oriented, self-disciplined	Flexible (C−): frivolous, irresponsible, disorganised
Extraversion	Extravert (E+): gregarious, warm, positive	Introvert (E−): quiet, reserved, shy
Agreeableness	Adapter (A+): straightforward, compliant, sympathetic	Challenger (A−): quarrelsome, oppositional, unfeeling
Neuroticism	Reactive (N+): anxious, depressed, self-conscious	Resilient (N−): calm, contented, self-assured

energise people by, for example, articulating an attractive vision for the organisation, reinforcing the values in that vision, and empowering subordinates to come up with new and creative ideas. They also articulate

> transcendent goals, demonstration of self-confidence and confidence in others, setting a personal example for followers, showing high expectations of followers' performance, and the ability to communicate one's faith in one's goals. (Fiedler and House, 1994, p. 112)

A limitation of the traits model is that a trait that is valuable in one situation is not necessarily valuable in another. Whatever traits Fred Goodwin had during his early (successful) years as chief executive at the Royal Bank of Scotland were still there when he resigned from the almost bankrupt company in 2009. Certain traits are probably necessary for effective leadership, but will not be sufficient for all conditions – their effect depends on the situation.

Despite these limitations, the traits model may explain why some people get to positions of great influence and others do not. When people specify desirable traits or personal qualities as part of a selection process, they are implicitly assuming that they enhance performance. As two leading scholars of leadership concluded:

> There is no one ideal leader personality. However, effective leaders tend to have a high need to influence others, to achieve; and they tend to be bright, competent and socially adept, rather than stupid, incompetent and social disasters. (Fiedler and House, 1994, p. 111)

12.4   Behavioural models

Another set of theories sought to identify the behavioural styles of effective managers. What did they do to influence subordinates that less effective managers did not? Scholars at the Universities of Ohio State and Michigan respectively identified two categories of **behaviour**: one concerned with interpersonal relations, the other with accomplishing tasks.

Behaviour is something a person does that can be directly observed.

Ohio State University model

Researchers at Ohio State University (Fleishman, 1953) developed questionnaires that subordinates used to describe the behaviour of their supervisor, and identified two dimensions – 'initiating structure' and 'consideration'.

Initiating structure refers to the degree to which a leader defines peoples' roles, focuses on goal attainment and establishes clear channels of communication. Those using this approach focused on getting the work done – they expected subordinates to follow the rules and made sure they were working to full capacity. Typical behaviours included:

Initiating structure is a pattern of leadership behaviour that emphasises the performance of the work in hand and the achievement of production or service goals.

- allocating subordinates to specific tasks;
- establishing standards of job performance;
- informing subordinates of the requirements of the job;
- scheduling work to be done by subordinates; and
- encouraging the use of uniform procedures.

Consideration refers to the degree to which a leader shows concern and respect for followers, looks after them and expresses appreciation. Such leaders assume that subordinates want to work well and try to make it easier for them to do so. They place little reliance on formal position, typical behaviours including:

Consideration is a pattern of leadership behaviour that demonstrates sensitivity to relationships and to the social needs of employees.

- expressing appreciation for a job well done;
- not expecting more from subordinates than they can reasonably do;
- helping subordinates with personal problems;

- being approachable and available for help; and
- rewarding high performance.

Surveys showed that supervisors displayed distinctive patterns – some scored high on initiating structure and low on consideration, while others were high on consideration and low on initiating structure. Some were high on both, others low on both.

University of Michigan model

Researchers at the University of Michigan (Likert, 1961) conducted similar studies and found that two types of behaviour distinguished effective from ineffective managers: job-centred and employee-centred behaviour.

- **Job-centred supervisors** ensured that they worked on different tasks from their subordinates, concentrating especially on planning, co-ordinating and supplying a range of support activities. These correspond to the initiating structure measures at Ohio.
- **Employee-centred supervisors** combined the task-oriented behaviour with human values. They were considerate, helpful and friendly to subordinates, and engaged in broad supervision rather than detailed observation. These behaviours were similar to what the Ohio group referred to as considerate.

From numerous studies, Likert (1961) concluded that:

Supervisors with the best records of performance focus their primary attention on the human aspects of their subordinates' problems and on endeavouring to build effective work groups with high performance goals. (p. 7)

Managerial grid model

Blake and Mouton (1979) developed the managerial grid model to extend and apply the Ohio State research. Figure 12.2 shows various combinations of concern for production (initiating structure) and concern for people (consideration).

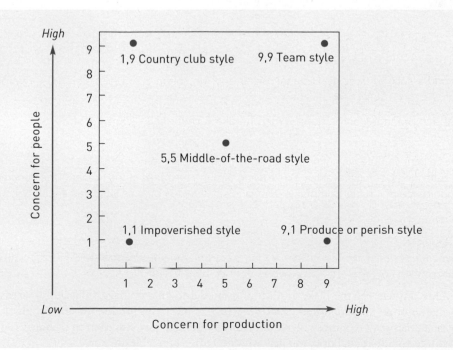

Figure 12.2
The managerial grid

The horizontal scale relates to concern for production, which ranges from 1 (low concern) to 9 (high concern). The vertical scale relates to concern for people, also ranging from 1 (low concern) to 9 (high concern). At the lower left-hand corner (1,1) is the impoverished style: low concern for both production and people. The primary objective of such managers is to stay out of trouble. They merely pass instructions to subordinates, follow the established system, and make sure that no one can blame them if something goes wrong. They do only as much as is consistent with keeping their job.

At the upper left-hand corner (1,9) is the country club style: managers who use this style try to create a secure and comfortable family atmosphere. They assume that their subordinates will respond productively. Thoughtful attention to the need for satisfying relationships leads to a friendly atmosphere and work tempo.

High concern for production and low concern for people is found in the lower right-hand corner (9,1) – the 'produce or perish' style. These managers do not consider subordinates' needs – only the perceived needs of the organisation. They use their formal authority to pressure subordinates into meeting production quotas, believing that efficiency comes from arranging the work so that employees who follow instructions will complete it satisfactorily.

In the centre (5,5) is the middle-of-the-road style. These managers obtain adequate performance by balancing the need to get the work done with reasonable attention to the interests of employees. In the upper right hand corner (9,9) is the team style which, according to Blake and Mouton, is the most effective approach, aiming for both high performance and high job satisfaction. The manager improves performance by building relationships of trust and respect.

Management in practice   Two leaders' styles   FT

Jeroen Van der Veer, CEO of Shell

Good leadership...means being clear about what is weak and what is strong, and where you want to go in the longer term, and having the ability to put it into clear words. The best way for a leader to take a company forward is to have some very simple words about how you would like to change it and the culture of the company.

Source: *Financial Times*, 2 February 2007, p. 19.

Kwon Young-Soo, chief executive of LG Philips LCD

The company is the world's second largest flat panel maker and Mr Young-Soo believes it will thrive on argument:

The era for authoritarian management is gone. When I make a proposal, I want my staff to say 'no' when it does not make sense.

Although the company is a joint venture, its culture, like that of many Korean companies, was based on strict hierarchical structures, reflecting Confucian values. While rising through the ranks of the company he became acutely aware of the importance of internal communication, and since taking over as CEO has encouraged a more open exchange of ideas.

Source: *Financial Times*, 10 September 2007.

Many trainers use the Blake and Mouton model to help managers develop towards the '9,9' style. Others question whether showing a high concern for production and people always works: a crisis may require swift action with little time to pay attention to personal feelings and interests. Situational or contingency models offer a possible answer.

12.5   Situational (or contingency) models

Situational (or **contingency**) **models** present the idea that managers influence others by adapting their style to the circumstances. Two such models are set out below (a third, developed by Vroom and Yetton (1973) featured in Chapter 7).

Situational (or **contingency**) **models** of leadership attempt to identify the contextual factors that affect when one style will be more effective than another.

Tannenbaum and Schmidt's continuum of leader behaviour

Unlike the 'one best way' model implied by the behavioural models, Robert Tannenbaum and Warren Schmidt (1973) saw that leaders worked in different ways, which they presented as a continuum of styles, ranging from autocratic to democratic. Figure 12.3 illustrates these extremes and the positions in between. Which of these the leader uses should reflect three forces:

- **Forces in the manager:** personality, values, preferences, beliefs about participation and confidence in subordinates.
- **Forces in subordinates:** need for independence, tolerance of ambiguity, knowledge of the problem, expectations of involvement.
- **Forces in the situation:** organisational norms, size and location of work groups, effectiveness of team working, nature of the problem.

House's path–goal model

House (House and Mitchell, 1974; House, 1996) believed that effective leaders clarify subordinates' path towards achieving rewards which they value – by, for example, helping them identify and learn behaviours that will help them perform well, and so secure the rewards.

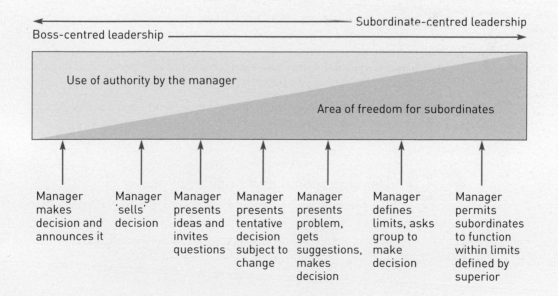

Figure 12.3 The Tannenbaum–Schmidt continuum of leadership behaviour

Table 12.3 Conditions favouring participative or directive styles

Participative style most likely to work when:	Directive style most likely to work when:
Subordinates' acceptance of the decision is important	Subordinates do not share the manager's objectives
The manager lacks information	Time is short
The problem is unclear	Subordinates accept top-down decisions

House identifies four styles of leader behaviour:

- **Directive:** letting subordinates know what the leader expects; giving specific guidance; asking subordinates to follow rules and procedures; scheduling and coordinating their work.
- **Supportive:** treating them as equals; showing concern for their needs and welfare; creating a friendly climate in the work unit.
- **Achievement-oriented:** setting challenging goals and targets; seeking performance improvements; emphasising excellence in performance; expecting subordinates to succeed.
- **Participative:** consulting subordinates; taking their opinions into account.

House suggested that the appropriate style would depend on the situation – the characteristics of the subordinate and the work environment. For example, if a subordinate has little confidence or skill then the leader needs to provide coaching and other support. If the subordinate likes clear direction they will respond best to a leader who gives it. Most skilled professionals expect to use their initiative and resent a directive style: they will respond best to a participative or achievement-oriented leader. The work environment includes the degree of task structure (routine or non-routine), the formal authority system (extent of rules and procedures) and the work group characteristics (quality of teamwork).

The model predicts that:

- a directive style works best when the task is ambiguous and the subordinates lack flexibility – the leader absorbs the uncertainty and shows them how to do the task;
- a supportive style works best in repetitive, frustrating or physically unpleasant tasks – subordinates respect the leader who joins in and helps;
- an achievement-oriented style works best when the group faces non-repetitive ambiguous tasks, which will challenge their ability – they need encouragement and pressure to raise their ambitions;
- a participative approach works best when the task is non-repetitive and the subordinate(s) are confident that they can do the work.

Contingency models indicate that participative leadership is not always effective and that, as Table 12.3 shows, a directive style is sometimes appropriate.

12.6   Using personal and positional power

Earlier sections have shown that people use personal skills to influence others, including their ability to adapt their methods to the situation. Another perspective is that people use **power** to influence others.

Power is 'the capacity of individuals to exert their will over others'. (Buchanan and Badham, 1999)

Sources of power

What are the bases of one person's power over another? Building on French and Raven's (1959) theory of power, Hales (2001) proposed the model shown in Table 12.4. This shows that each type of power can have both a personal and a positional source.

Table 12.4 Personal and positional sources of power

Type of power	Personal sources	Positional sources
Coercive	Forcefulness, insistence, determination	Authority to give instructions, with the threat of sanctions or punishment available
Reward	Credit for previous or future favours in daily exchanges	Authority to use organisational resources, including the support of senior people
Expertise:		
Administrative	Experience of the business, whom to contact, how to get things done	Authority to use or create organisational policies or rules
Technical	Skill or expertise relevant to the task	Authority to access expertise, information and ideas across the business
Referent	Individual beliefs, values, ideas, personal qualities	Authority to invoke norms and values of the organisational culture

Source: Based on Hales (2001).

Coercive

Coercive power is the ability to obtain compliance through fear of punishment or harm. It includes reprimands, demotions, threats, bullying language or a powerful physical presence. It also derives from someone's position in the formal hierarchy which enables them to give instructions or threaten penalties. Kramer (2006) observed how 'Great Intimidators' work – often achieving great success, at other times failing badly. Their tactics include:

> **Coercive power** is the ability to obtain compliance through fear of punishment or harm.

- getting up close and personal – being directly confrontational, often using aggressive behaviour and language;
- being angry – often using a calculated loss of temper to strike fear into their opponent;
- keeping them guessing – revealing as little as possible about their plans, to increase opponents' anxiety;
- know it all – extensive preparation to be able to dominate any discussion. This includes being aware of weaknesses in the opponent's history or character.

Reward

Reward power is the ability to reward another if they comply with a request or instruction. The reward can take many forms – pay, time off or interesting work. Someone's position in the hierarchy enables them to use the financial and other resources of the organisation in return for support. Managers with large budgets and valuable networks of contacts use these resources, or the promise of them, to exert influence. Managers who choose to be remote and isolated in back-room work will not have that power – and so will have little influence on people or events.

> **Reward power** is the ability to reward another if they comply with a request or instruction.

Expertise

Expertise power is when people acknowledge someone's knowledge and are therefore willing to follow their suggestions. This knowledge or skill may be *administrative* (how an organisation operates) or *technical* (how to do a task).

> **Expertise power** is when people acknowledge someone's knowledge and are therefore willing to follow their suggestions.

Administrative expertise

This is the power that the holder of a position has to create formal policies which support their influence attempts. They can create rules, procedures or positions that sustain their power – especially if they can also appoint loyal supporters, or those in their debt, to those positions. In this way they encourage others to act in the way they prefer.

Management in practice   **Too much internal focus**

A department of a local authority consisted of a director, two senior officers, three officers and 14 staff. The director's style was to involve himself in operational matters, and he rarely worked with other senior managers. He normally met only the senior officers in his department and rarely involved others, believing that officers should not be involved in policy. He saw himself as the only competent person in the department and was comfortable in this operational role.

Staff consider themselves to be capable and professional. They expect to be involved more fully and are used to taking initiatives. The director's involvement in operational detail annoyed staff as it showed that he did not trust their abilities. They were even more annoyed at the low status of their department, due to the director not being active externally and so lacking influence outside the department.

Source: Private communication with the manager.

Technical expertise

This is the power a person gains from holding a position that gives them access to information, of being in the know, aware of what is happening and of opportunities which are emerging. They can use their position, and the contacts that go with it, to build their image as a competent person. This credibility adds to their power to influence others. It is a contentious area, since people compete for access to information and the power that goes with it.

Referent

Referent power, sometimes called *charismatic* power, or *personality*, is when some characteristics in a person are attractive to others: they identify with them, which gives the charismatic person power.

Referent power, sometimes called *charismatic* power, or *personality*, is when some characteristics in a person are attractive to others: they identify with them, which gives the charismatic person power. Hales (2001) suggests that managers can also develop and use this power source in an organisational sense when they show that what they propose is consistent with the accepted values and culture of the organisation. They invoke wider values in support of their proposal. Chapter 3 showed how organisations develop distinctive cultures and subcultures. When people refer to the prevailing culture to influence behaviour ('what I'm asking fits the culture') they are drawing on a positional form of referent power.

The more of these sources of power the manager has, the more others will co-operate. They do so because they believe that the manager has the power to make things happen. Such a manager has weight or political influence, which encourages others to co-operate. Someone who has little access to these sources of power will have little influence.

Perceptions of power

Power is only effective if the target of an influence attempt recognises the power source as legitimate and acceptable. If they dispute the knowledge base of a manager, or challenge their positional authority over a matter, the influence attempt is likely to fail. A project manager in an IT company reported how in one project she was leading a team of 40 change agents, who worked for about one day a week on her project, and for their line manager for the rest of the time. Some line managers did not agree with their staff being used on this project, and influenced some of them by using coercive and reward power to keep them full-time on their line job. The project manager retaliated by using her influencing skills to persuade senior managers to alter the pay system slightly, so that the annual review for each employee now included an item related to the contribution they had made to the change project. This reduced the reward power of line managers, who caused less trouble. (personal communication)

Management in practice   Marketing brand Me

People should manage their reputation like a brand. The most effective candidates [for promotion] do not leave their image to chance. They work at it and massage its growth. They know that the best publicists they can have are their immediate staff. They are aware that team members talk about them more than anyone else. So they provide evidence to feed that grapevine . . . Staff need stories about their leader.

Another way to manage your reputation is to manage your boss . . . People keen to manage their reputation should find out what motivates the boss and try to satisfy those goals. If your boss likes punctuality and conscientiousness, turn up on time and work hard. If he or she needs reassurance, give it. If it is power, respond as someone who is less powerful. Why irritate a person who can influence your career path?

Source: Marketing brand Me (John Hunt), *Financial Times*, 22 December 2000.

Managers who are successful influencers ensure they sustain their power sources and take every opportunity to enhance them – see the Management in Practice feature above. Most managers engage in political behaviour at work. In a questionnaire study of 250 middle and senior managers Buchanan (2008) found that they used, or saw, five frequent behaviours:

- building a network of useful contacts;
- using 'key players' to support initiatives;
- making friends with power brokers;
- bending the rules to fit the situation; and
- self-promotion.

They were also asked if they saw politics as a useful tool to improve organisational effectiveness: 60 per cent agreed that 'politics becomes more important as organisational change becomes more complex'; 79 per cent agreed that 'politics can be used to initiate and drive useful change initiatives'; and 81 per cent agreed that 'political tactics can be effective in dealing with resistance to change'. They believed that political skills helped careers: 90 per cent agreed that 'managers who play organisation politics well can improve their career prospects'.

'To increase power, share it'

Perhaps paradoxically, managers can increase their power by delegating some of it to subordinates. As they perform tasks previously done by the manager, he or she has more time to build the external and senior contacts – which further boost power. By delegating not only tasks, but also giving subordinates authority over part of the budget, inviting them to high-level meetings and giving them visible encouragement, managers develop subordinates' confidence. In doing so, they enhance their own power as they can spend more time on external matters, making contacts, keeping in touch with what is happening, engaging in **political behaviour** and generally building their visibility and reputation. Subordinates will respond positively if they believe the manager has status and influence in the organisation. A manager who fails to delegate, and who looks inward rather outward, becomes increasingly isolated.

Political behaviour is 'the practical domain of power in action, worked out through the use of techniques of influence and other (more or less extreme) tactics'. (Buchanan and Badham, 1999)

| **12.7** | Using interpersonal skills and networks |

An important way to influence others is the ability to draw on a network of personal relationships. Table 12.5 shows several types of network.

The ability to influence can be greatly enhanced by being connected to many such networks, giving access to contacts and information. They help people to know what is happening in their business and to extend their range of contacts in other organisations. Strong anecdotal evidence that networking influences career progression was supported by Luthans' (1988) research described in Chapter 1, which showed that people who spent a relatively large amount of time networking received more rapid promotion than those who did not. As Thomas (2003) observed:

> in management what you know and what you have achieved will seldom be sufficient for getting ahead. Knowing and being known in the networks of influence, both for what you have achieved and for who you are may be essential.

Kotter (1982) observed that general managers rely heavily on informal networks of contacts to get things done. This is especially necessary to influence those in other organisations – to make a sale, to gain access to a country's market or to set up a joint venture – such as by appointing ex-politicians to their boards of directors – see the Management in Practice feature below.

| **Management in practice** | Influence in China and Taiwan |

Star TV (a subsidiary of Rupert Murdoch's News Corporation) developed close links with the Chinese authorities, in the hope of expanding the delivery of its entertainment channel on Chinese TV. This paid off in 2003, when it became the first foreign-owned company to receive permission for a limited nationwide service.

> 'Everything in China is about relationships and mutual benefit', said Jamie Davis, head of Star TV in China. 'I think Rupert Murdoch has a very good relationship with the Chinese Government . . . and we work hard at it.'

Source: Adapted from News corp's wooing of Beijing pays off (James Kynge), *Financial Times*, 9 January 2003.

The sudden elevation of Ho-chen Tan to the top job at Chunghwa Telecom last month was demonstration of the value of having friends in high places. He was in charge of transport in Taipei in the mid-1990s, when the Taiwanese President, Chen Shui-bian, was mayor of the city. Mr Ho-chen says his contacts in the administration will help Chunghwa to win a voice in how the government handles the company's privatization:

> I hope our company can win the right to make suggestions. Perhaps my network in the current government and the faith put in me will help the company to get more opportunities.

Source: Adapted from Chairman knows the value of a little help from his friends (Mure Dickie and Kathrin Hille), *Financial Times*, 21 February 2003.

Table 12.5 Types of network

Types	Descriptions
Practitioners	Joined by people with a common training or professional interest, and may be formal or informal
Privileged power	Joined by people in powerful positions (usually by invitation only)
Ideological	Consisting of people keen to promote political objectives or values
People-oriented	Formed around shared feelings of personal warmth and familiarity – friendship groups which people join on the basis of identity with existing participants
Strategic	Often built to help develop links with people in other organisations

Sparrowe and Liden (2005) note that informal networks are probably becoming more important as a means of influencing others:

> As traditional hierarchical structures have given way to flatter and more flexible forms, informal networks have become even more important in gaining access to valuable information, resources, and opportunities. The structure and composition of an individual's network allows him or her to identify strategic opportunities, marshal resources, assemble teams and win support for innovative projects . . . Individuals who hold central positions in informal advice networks enjoy greater influence than those in peripheral positions . . . and receive more favorable performance ratings. (p. 505)

Whichever methods are used, the outcome of an influence attempt will depend not only on the tactics used but on how well the influencer is able to meet the needs of the person they are influencing – see Chapter 13.

Activity 12.2   What does 'influence and power' mean in management?

Having read the chapter, make brief notes summarising the influence and power issues evident in the organisation you chose for this activity.

- What effects did the influence attempts you studied have on the behaviour of the targets? (See Section 12.2.)
- To what extent did the traits or behavioural models appear to affect the outcomes? (See Sections 12.3 and 12.4.)
- Were the attempts at influence affected by the situational models? (See Section 12.5.)
- Can you give examples of the power sources people used? (See Section 12.6.)
- Can you give examples of how networking has helped people exert influence? (See Section 12.7.)

Compare what you have found with other students on your course.

Summary

1 **Distinguish leading from managing, and explain why each is essential to performance**
- Although both are essential and the difference can be overstated, leading is usually seen as referring to activities that bring change, whereas managing brings stability and order. Many people both lead and manage in the course of their work.

2 **Explain why leading and managing both depend on being able to influence others**
- Achieving objectives usually depends on the willing commitment of other people. How management seeks to influence others affects people's reaction to being managed. Dominant use of power may ensure compliance, but such an approach is unlikely to produce the commitment required to meet innovative objectives.

3 **Compare trait, behavioural and contingency perspectives on styles of influence**
- Trait theories seek to identify the personal characteristics associated with effective influencing.
- Behavioural theories distinguish managers' behaviours on two dimensions, such as initiating structure and consideration.
- Contingency perspectives argue that the traits or behaviours required for effective influence depend on factors in the situation, such as the characteristics of the employee, the boss and the task.

4　Outline theories that focus on power (both personal and organisational) as the source of influence

- The more power a person has, the more they will be able to influence others. Table 12.4 identified sources of power as coercion, reward, expertise (administrative and technical) and referent – all of which can have both personal and organisational dimensions.

5　Contrast the style and power perspectives, and explain why sharing power may increase it

- Sharing power with subordinates may not only enable them to have more satisfying and rewarding work, but by enabling the manager to have more time to develop senior and external contacts, that can then enhance their power more than if they focused on internal matters.

Review questions

1　Why is the ability to influence others so central to the management role?

2　What evidence is there that traits theories continue to influence management practice?

3　What are the strengths and weaknesses of the behavioural approaches to leadership?

4　What is meant by the phrase a '9,9 manager'?

5　Discuss with someone how they try to influence people (or reflect on your own practice). Compare this experience with one of the contingency approaches.

6　Evaluate that theory in the light of the evidence acquired in review question 5 and other considerations.

7　Explain in your own words the main sources of power available to managers. Give examples of both personal and positional forms of each.

8　What does the network perspective imply for someone wishing to be a successful influencer?

Further reading

Yukl, G. A. (2009), *Leadership in Organizations* (7th edn), Prentice Hall, Upper Saddle River, NJ.

Combines a comprehensive review of academic research on all aspects of organisational leadership with clear guidance on the implications for practitioners.

Huczynski, A. A. (2004), *Influencing Within Organizations* (2nd edn), Routledge, London.

Draws on a wide range of academic research to provide a practical guide to being an effective influencer – from how to conduct yourself at a job interview to coping with organisational politics.

Pedler, M., Burgoyne, J. and Boydell, T. (2004), *A Manager's Guide to Leadership*, McGraw-Hill, Maidenhead.

A practical book, based on the philosophy that leadership is defined by what people do when faced with challenging situations. The authors use their well-established self-development approach to encourage readers to act on situations requiring leadership, and then to reflect and learn from the experience.

Weblinks

These websites have appeared in, or are relevant to, the chapter:

www.pret.com
www.apple.com
www.google.com
www.gore.com
www.bmw.com
www.co-operative.coop
www.johnlewispartnership.co.uk
www.edenproject.com.

Each of these organisations has tried to develop new approaches to managing and influencing staff and have, despite some difficult circumstances, survived and prospered.

● Use the 'contingency' perspectives (see Section 12.5) to analyse what circumstances may explain their success.

 Annotated weblinks, multiple choice questions and other useful resources can be found on **www.pearsoned.co.uk/boddy**

Case study   Apple Inc.   www.apple.com

When Apple launched the iPad in 2010 it added a further product to a range that already included Mac computers, iPods, iPhones and the Apple stores. Some saw it as a bold attempt by Apple to merge the netbook, phone and mobile entertainment sectors, with the iPad bridging the gap between laptops and smartphones. The full-colour, touch-screen enables users to watch movies, surf the internet, listen to music, view photos and read digital versions of books and newspapers.

The company had signed deals with several major publishers, including Penguin and HarperCollins, and hoped other publishers would make their content available on the platform. As an example, a *New York Times* application allows readers to view videos embedded within online articles, which look and feel like the print edition. Applications and games available in the App Store can be used on the iPad, and developers will be encouraged to build software specifically for the larger-screen device.

With successive products Apple's influence has grown – the iPod represents more than 70 per cent of the mp3 market, and the device has helped to reshape the music publishing industry. The similar success of the iPhone meant that every manufacturer has followed Apple's lead, and now offers a touch-screen smartphone. Apple has the power to reshape markets and influence competitors.

The company has a tradition of innovations, going back to the first Apple computers in 1976, followed by the Macintosh in 1984 – the first commercially successful PC that allowed users to point and click with a mouse. Steve Jobs (the company's co-founder, who died in 2011) saw that this technology would make computers easier to use.

Mr Jobs' success with the Macintosh was soon followed by a major difficulty. He was chairman of the business he had founded with Steve Wozniak in 1976, and Mike Markkula, who had joined the company at the start, was chief executive. Markkula had never intended to stay as CEO, and now wished to leave. The board (including Jobs) decided to appoint John Sculley, an executive from Pepsi-Cola, to the post. The two men frequently disagreed and in 1987 Sculley persuaded the board to dismiss Jobs (then aged 30).

He then entered what he regards as one of the most creative periods of his life – typified by his purchase of Pixar. The company struggled until Mr Jobs

© KIMBERLY WHITE/Reuters/Corbis.

struck a deal with Walt Disney in the 1990s. Using Pixar's creative flair and Disney's marketing and distribution power, Mr Jobs oversaw an uninterrupted string of blockbusters, starting with 'Toy Story' in 1995.

Jobs returned to Apple in 1997 since when the company has continued to grow. His management style was distinctive – but the company stressed that he had built a strong executive team to ensure the continuity of the business.

Apple is credited with putting Silicon Valley on the map, and creating Silicon Valley's hard-working yet corporate-casual environment. Even as the company grew, Jobs worked hard to maintain Apple's rebel spirit.

Apple's corporate culture is characterised by its intense work ethic and casual dress code. Staff surveys regularly refer to a 'relaxed', 'casual', 'collegial' environment with 'long hours, weekends included' and 'no end to challenges and cool projects'.

Michael Moritz, who had observed Jobs for many years noted in 2009:

> Steve is a founder of the company [and the best founders] are unstoppable, irrepressible forces of nature. . . Steve has always possessed the soul of the questioning poet – someone a little removed from the rest of us who, from an early age, beat his own path. [He has a sharp] sense of the aesthetic – that influence is still apparent in all Apple products and advertising. Jobs's critics will say he can be wilfull, obdurate, irascible, temperamental and stubborn [which is true, but he is also a perfectionist]. There is also . . . an insistent, persuasive and mesmerising salesman.

In the early years of John Sculley's time as CEO, Apple appeared to perform well, since the existing products were being sold into the rapidly growing personal computer market. But there were no significant innovations and the company gradually fell victim to stronger competitors like IBM and Microsoft, which made its successful operating system available to any computer company. This weakness eventually became clear, and Sculley left the company in 1993.

In 1997 Jobs re-joined, initially as acting CEO, and then took over as CEO. He found that much of the creativity had gone, and set about re-building it:

> He forced the company to act differently, cutting costs, making many staff redundant, and scrapping product lines he deemed worthless or undistinguished. He brought in new senior managers whom he had worked with, and replaced the increasingly dysfunctional board – which Sculley and his successors had built – with practical members whom he could trust.

The clearest example of the rejuvenation of the company came in 2001 when Apple launched iPod – which went from conception to being on the shelves in eight months. The device contained an operating system which meant that it had as much computing power as many laptops at the time. Moritz (2009) writes:

> Jobs' achievement . . . was to ensure that a technology company employing tens of thousands of people could make and sell millions of immensely complicated yet exquisite products that were powerful and reliable, while also containing a lightness of being. . . [the achievement] is to steer, coax, nudge, prod, cajole, inspire, berate, organise and praise – on weekdays and at weekends – the thousands of people all around the world required to produce something that drops into pockets and handbags or . . . rests on a lap or sits on a desk. (pp. 339–40)

The company has tight control over the retailing end of the business – the Apple network of dealers and its own Apple Stores ensure that the image of the brand is closely dovetailed with the products themselves. The App Store has exceeded expectations, with thousands of software developers offering their products on the site. The iPad, launched in 2010, continues the stream of successful innovations from the company.

Sources: Moritz (2009); *Economist*, 1 October 2009; and other published material.

Questions

1 What examples are there of managers influencing others? (See Section 12.2.)

2 What examples of the Big 5 traits can you identify in Jobs' personality from the case study? (See Section 12.3.)

3 What features of the transaction and transformational leader did Jobs display? (See Section 12.3.)

4 Which of the sources of power in Table 12.4 did Steve Jobs use?

CHAPTER 13
MOTIVATING

Learning outcomes

When you have read this chapter you should be able to:

1 Explain why managers need to understand and use theories of motivation

2 Give examples showing how the context, including the psychological contract, affects motivation

3 Compare behaviour modification, content and process theories

4 Show how ideas on motivation link to those on strategy

5 Use ideas from the chapter to comment on the management issues in the Eden Project case study

Activity 13.1   What does 'motivating' mean in management?

Before reading the chapter, write some notes on what you think 'motivating' means in management. Choose the organisation or people who may be able to help you learn about the topic. You may find it helpful to discuss the topic with a manager you know, or reflect on an activity you have managed.

- Identify a situation in which someone needed to motivate others, and describe it briefly.
- How did those involved try to motivate others to act in a particular way?
- Did they consciously try to understand the needs and interests of their targets?

Keep these notes as you will be able to use them later.

13.1   Introduction

The Eden Project has captured the public imagination, rapidly becoming one of Europe's most successful visitor attractions, with a thriving educational charity running alongside. Tim Smit and his colleagues secured the help of talented architects, the support of local agencies and significant funding bodies – and then of staff, visitors and partner institutions. In good times as well as in bad, charities must raise income and recruit staff to survive: like any business, Eden's management have been thinking up new ways to **motivate** people to continue to support the project as enthusiastically as they have done so far.

Motivation refers to the forces within or beyond a person that arouse and sustain their commitment to a course of action.

All businesses need enthusiastic and committed employees who work in a way that supports organisational goals. This is clearest in service organisations like Eden where staff interact with customers (so their satisfaction or otherwise directly affects quality), but matters just as much in manufacturing or administrative operations. Microsoft and Apple depend on their engineers being motivated to develop a constant flow of innovative products. Hospital patients depend on medical and nursing staff being willing to provide good care.

Managers want people to work well and occasionally to 'go the extra mile' – doing more than usual to fix a problem or to help a colleague. The problem is how to achieve this: surveys regularly show that while some staff engage fully with their work, others do not. The manager's task is to create a context in which people commit to their work, and willingly add value – because they see work as a way to satisfy their needs.

Money is evidently a major motivator for many people, especially those on low incomes. Others find deep satisfaction in the work itself – like Theresa Marshall, who is a classroom assistant in a city primary school:

> I've found my niche and couldn't be happier – it's no exaggeration to say that I absolutely love my job. My favourite part is helping the children with their reading skills and seeing the pleasure that they can get out of books. (private communication)

Some enjoy working with physical things or the challenge of designing an innovative product – while others enjoy working directly with people in sales or customer service jobs.

With people having such diverse needs and interests, how can managers motivate them to work in ways that meet the needs of the organisation? Managers interpret the wider business context, and this shapes what they expect from people – who also have needs and expectations of the organisation. This leads to the idea of a psychological contract that expresses these mutual expectations. Many theories have developed which provide partial answers to

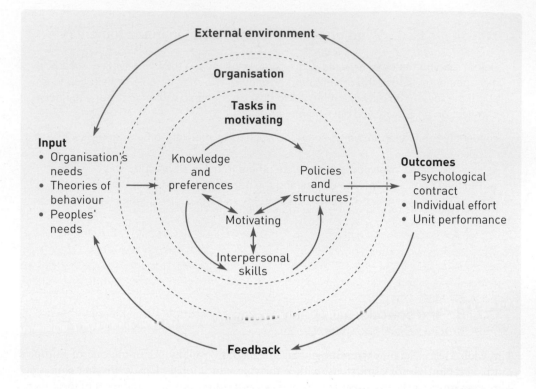

Figure 13.1
Themes of the chapter

the question of how best to create a mutually satisfactory psychological contract: the chapter outlines these content, process and work design theories. Managers draw on their implicit knowledge of these theories, and their personal preferences, to shape policies and structures to motivate others. They also use their interpersonal skills for the same purpose. How they do so affects outcomes such as the state of the psychological contract, individual effort and unit performance. Figure 13.1 shows these themes.

13.2   Perspectives on motivation – targets and the psychological contract

Much behaviour is routine, based on habit, precedent and unconscious scripts. This chapter is concerned with the larger, precedent-setting choices people make about behaviour at work. For some people, work is an occasion for hard, enthusiastic and imaginative activity, a source of rich satisfaction. They are motivated, in the sense that they put effort (arousal) into their work (direction and persistence). For others it is something they do grudgingly – work does not arouse their enthusiasm, or merely passes the time until they find something more interesting. Managers try to understand why such differences occur, and seek to encourage the former attitude rather than the latter. Theories of motivation, which try to identify and explain the factors that energise, channel and sustain behaviour, can inform that consideration.

Targets of attempts to motivate

Managers aim to motivate many other people – not only subordinates but also colleagues, their own senior managers and people in other organisations. They also motivate consumers to buy their products, by using theories of human motivation. In all of these cases, people try

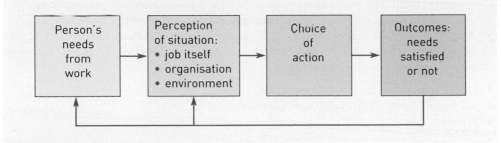

Figure 13.2
Human needs in context – the situational perspective

to understand human needs in the belief that doing so accurately makes it easier to influence what they do.

Figure 13.2 illustrates a simple model of human motivation. We all have needs for food, social contact or a sense of achievement, which motivate behaviour to satisfy that need. If the action leads to a satisfactory outcome we experience a sense of reward. The feedback loop shows that we then decide whether the behaviour was appropriate and worth repeating.

The figure also shows that individuals do not act in isolation, but within a context that includes both immediate and wider elements:

- **the job itself** – e.g. how interesting, varied or responsible it is
- **the organisation** – e.g. supervision, career and promotion prospects, pay systems
- **the environment** – e.g. career threats and opportunities.

These contextual factors affect how people see their job. When jobs are hard to get in a recession, they lower their expectations and take an acceptable job that pays the mortgage. In more affluent times, they can be more choosey. In considering this model, remember that:

- we can only infer, or make reasonable assumptions about, the needs that matter to someone;
- needs change with age, experience and responsibilities;
- we face choices, when we can only satisfy one at the expense of another; and
- the effect of satisfying a need on the future strength of that need is uncertain.

The psychological contract

The **psychological contract** expresses the idea that each side to an employment relationship has expectations of the other – of what they will give and what they will receive in return. Employers (or their agents, managers) offer rewards in the expectation of receiving some level of performance. Employees contribute a level of performance in the expectation that they will receive rewards in return. The parties modify these expectations (usually informally) as the relationship develops, reflecting the influence of changing contexts or individual circumstances. There is a constant risk that a contract which satisfied both parties at one time may, perhaps inadvertently, cease do so – which will have consequences for attitudes and behaviour.

Rousseau and Schalk (2000) refer to psychological contracts as

> the belief systems of individual workers and their employers regarding their mutual obligations. (p. 1)

Some elements in the contract are written, but most are implicit, or at least not written down. A consequence of this is that both parties may have different understandings of what obligations have been promised and whether they have been delivered. If both parties are content with the current balance, this is likely to lead to a positive relationship: if either side believes the other has breached the contract, the relationship is likely to suffer.

A **psychological contract** is the set of understandings people have regarding the commitments made between themselves and their organisation.

Perception is the active psychological process in which stimuli are selected and organised into meaningful patterns.

In times of rapid economic change researchers have studied employees' **perceptions** of the state of the psychological contract with their employer, since competitive business conditions may lead employers to make changes which employees see as breaking the contract. If they do, what are the effects? Deery *et al.* (2006) studied employees in a call centre who perceived their employer had breached the contract by:

- failing to implement a pay-for-performance system;
- not respecting staff knowledge and skills; and
- not asking for their opinions.

These breaches of the psychological contract led employees to have lower trust in management, to experience less co-operative employment relations and to have higher rates of absence. As Kolb *et al.* (1991) remarked:

> a company staffed by 'cheated' individuals, who expect far more than they get, is headed for trouble. (p. 6)

From the employee's point of view, research by Gallup has shown that staff are motivated if they:

- have a manager who shows care, interest and concern for each of them;
- know what is expected of them;
- have a role that fits their abilities;
- receive positive feedback and recognition regularly for work well done.

In a study of performance at unit level, covering more than 200,000 employees across many industries, teams that rated managers highly on these four factors were more productive and more profitable. They also had lower staff turnover and higher customer satisfaction ratings. (*People Management*, 17 February 2000, p. 45.)

At a time of great change in the business world, previously stable psychological contracts are easily broken. Technological changes and increased competition lead senior management to change employment policies and working conditions, or put staff under great pressure to meet demanding performance targets.

Management in practice   What IKEA expects and offers www.IKEA.com

On the website, the company explains that working for the company is a matter of give and take: 'IKEA co-workers enjoy many advantages and opportunities from working in such a free and open environment – but all freedoms are counter-balanced with expectations. For example, the expectation that each co-worker is able to assume responsibility for his or her actions.'

What do we expect from you?

- You have the ambition to do a good job and the desire to take on responsibility and to take the consequences that this entails
- You do your best on the basis of your abilities and experience
- You are service-oriented and have the customers' best interests at heart
- You are not status minded, but rather open in your approach to others

What do we offer you?

- The chance to work in a growing company with a viable business idea
- The opportunity to further develop your professional skills
- The opportunity to choose between many different jobs in the company
- A job with fair and reasonable conditions
- The chance to assume responsibility following recognised good results, regardless of age.

Source: Company website.

The next section outlines an early theory of motivation which some companies use to influence the actions of staff.

13.3   Behaviour modification

Behaviour modification refers to a range of techniques developed to treat psychological conditions such as eating disorders and heavy smoking: managers have used them to deal with issues such as lateness and absenteeism. The techniques developed from Skinner's (1971) theory that people learn to see relationships between actions and their consequences, and that this learning guides behaviour. If we receive a reward for doing something, we tend to do it again: if the consequences are unpleasant, we do not.

Behaviour modification techniques focus on specific, observable behaviours rather than on attitudes and feelings.

> In promoting safety . . . we did not dwell on accident-prone workers or probe for personality or demographic factors, none of which can be changed. Instead we focused on the organization and what it can do to rearrange the work environment. (Komaki, 2003, p. 96)

This includes specifying what people should do, measuring actual behaviour and identifying the consequences that people experience. If the influencer sees the behaviour as undesirable, they try to influence the person by changing the consequences – rewarding or punishing them.

Komaki (2003) explains how she and her colleagues used the method in a bakery to encourage safe working practices. They worked with management to design these steps:

- **Specify desired behaviour.** This included defining very precisely the safe working practices that were required – such as walking round conveyor belts, how to sharpen knives and using precise terms when giving instructions.
- **Measure desired performance.** Trained observers visited the site and recorded whether workers were performing safely by following the specified behaviours.
- **Provide frequent, contingent, positive consequences.** In this case, the positive consequence was feedback, in the form of charts showing current accident figures, which were much lower than previous levels.
- **Evaluate effectiveness.** Collecting data on accident levels and comparing these with earlier data. In this case, people were now working more safely, and the number of injuries had fallen from 53 a year to 10.

Practitioners emphasise that several principles must be used for the method to be effective (Komaki *et al.*, 2000).

- payoffs (benefits) must be given only when the desired behaviour occurs;
- payoffs must be given as soon as possible after the behaviour, to strengthen the link between behaviour and reward;
- desirable behaviour is likely to be repeated if reinforced by rewards;
- reinforcement is more effective than punishment, as punishment only temporarily suppresses behaviour;
- repeated reinforcement can lead to permanent change in behaviour in the desired direction.

> **Behaviour modification** is a general label for attempts to change behaviour by using appropriate and timely reinforcement.

Management in practice   Behaviour modification in a call centre

In our call centre staff are rewarded when behaviour delivers results in line with business requirements. Each month, staff performance is reviewed against a number of objectives such as average call length, sales of each product and attention to detail. This is known as Effective Level Review and agents can move through levels of effectiveness ranging from 1 to 4, and gain an increase in salary after six months of successful reviews. Moving through effective levels means that they have performed well and can mean being given other tasks instead of answering the phone. The role can become mundane and repetitive so the opportunity to do other tasks is seen as a reward for good performance. Thus it reinforces acceptable behaviour.

Conversely, staff who display behaviour that is not desirable cannot move through these levels and repeated failure to do so can lead to disciplinary action. This can be seen as punishment rather than behaviour modification. People can become resentful at having their performance graded every month, particularly in those areas where it is their line manager's perception of whether or not they have achieved the desired results.

Source: Private communication from the call centre manager.

Above all, advocates stress the need to *reward* desirable behaviours rather than treat them with indifference. These rewards can result from individual action (a word of praise or thanks) or from organisational practices (shopping vouchers for consistently good time-keeping). Supporters believe the approach encourages management to look directly at what makes a particular person act in a desirable way, and to ensure those rewards are available. It depends on identifying rewards the person will value (or punishments they will try to avoid). Theories that attempt to understand these are known as content theories of motivation.

13.4   Content theories of motivation

Most writers on this topic have tried to identify human needs so that they can use this knowledge to influence their actions. Frederick Taylor (Chapter 2) believed that people worked for money and that they would follow strict working methods if management rewarded them financially. Chapter 2 also showed how Mary Parker Follett and Elton Mayo identified other human needs, such as being accepted by a group: if people value this more than the financial incentive, they will conform with what the group expects. Maslow developed a theory which incorporates these and other needs.

Abraham Maslow – a hierarchy of needs

Maslow was a clinical psychologist who developed a theory of human motivation to help him understand the needs of his patients. He stressed the clinical sources of the theory and that it lacked experimental verification, though he was aware that Douglas McGregor (see below) had used the theory to interpret his observations of people at work.

Maslow proposed that individuals experience a range of needs, and will be motivated to fulfil whichever need is most powerful at the time (Maslow, 1970). What he termed the lower-order needs are dominant until they are at least partially satisfied. Normal individuals would then turn their attention to satisfying needs at the next level, so that higher-order needs would gradually become dominant. He suggested these needs formed a hierarchy: the middle column of Table 13.1 shows this, while the others indicate how they can be satisfied at work and away from it.

Physiological needs are those which must be satisfied to survive – food and water particularly. Maslow proposed that if all the needs in the hierarchy are unsatisfied then the physiological needs will dominate. People will concentrate on obtaining the necessities of life and ignore higher needs.

Once the physiological needs were sufficiently gratified a new set of needs would emerge, which he termed *safety needs* – the search for

security; stability; dependency; protection; freedom from fear, anxiety and chaos; need for structure, order, law, limits . . . and so on. (Maslow, 1970, p. 39)

Table 13.1 How Maslow's needs can be satisfied on and off the job

Ways to satisfy on the job	Hierarchy of needs	Ways to satisfy off the job
Opportunities for personal growth, wider challenges	Self-actualisation	Education, hobbies, community activities
Recognition, thanks, more responsibilities	Esteem	Approval of family, friends and community
Relations with fellow workers, customers, supervisors	Belongingness	Acceptance by family, friends, social groups
Safe work, well-designed facilities, job security	Safety	Freedom from violence, disturbance, pollution
Basic salary, warmth	Physiological	Food, oxygen, water

People then concentrate on satisfying these to the exclusion of others. If this need is domi-nant for a person, they can satisfy it by seeking a stable, regular job with secure working con-ditions and access to insurance for ill-health and retirement. They resent sudden or random changes in job prospects.

Belongingness needs would follow the satisfaction of safety needs:

> [If] both the physiological and the safety needs are fairly well gratified, there will emerge the love and affection and belongingness needs . . . now the person will feel keenly the absence of friends . . . and will hunger for affectionate relations with people in general. (p. 43)

These needs include a place in the group or family, and at work they would include wanting to be part of a congenial team. People object when management changes work patterns or locations if this disrupts established working relationships. They welcome change that brings them closer to people they know and like.

Maslow observed that most people have *esteem needs* – self-respect and the respect of others. Self-respect is the need for a sense of achievement, competence, adequacy and confi-dence. People also seek the respect of others, what he called a desire for reputation in the eyes of other people – prestige, status, recognition, attention. They can satisfy this by taking on challenging or difficult tasks to show they are good at their job and can accomplish something worthwhile. If others recognise this, they earn status and respect.

Lastly, Maslow used the term *self-actualisation* needs to refer to the desire for self-fulfilment and for realising potential:

> At this level, individual differences are greatest. The clear emergence of these needs usually rests upon some prior satisfaction of the physiological, safety, love, and esteem needs. (pp. 46–47)

People seeking self-actualisation look for personal relevance in their work, doing things that matter deeply to them, or which help them discover new talents.

Management in practice   A new manager at a nursing home

Jean Parker was appointed manager of a nursing home for the elderly. Recent reports by the Health Authority and Environmental Health inspectors had been so critical that they threatened to close the home. Jean recalls what she did in the first eight months:

> My task was to make sweeping changes, stabilise the workforce and improve the reputation of the home. I had no influence on pay, and low pay was one of the problems. To motivate staff I had to use

other methods. Staff facilities were appalling – the dining areas were filthy, showers and some toilets were not working, there were no changing rooms and petty theft was rife. Given the lack of care and respect shown to staff it is little wonder that care given to residents was poor, and staff were demotivated. They turned up to work, carried out tasks and went home. There had been little communication between management and staff. My approach was to work alongside the staff, listen to their grievances, gain their trust and set out an action plan.

The first steps were easy. The staff room was cleaned and decorated, changing rooms and working showers and toilets were provided. Refreshments were provided at meal breaks. Police advice was sought to combat petty theft and lockers were installed in each area. The effect of these changes on staff commitment was astounding. They felt somebody cared for them and listened. In turn, quality of care improved and staff started to take pride in the home, and bring in ornaments and plants to brighten it.

I then started to hold monthly meetings to give management and staff an opportunity to discuss expectations. Policies and procedures were explained. Noticeboards displaying 'news and views' were put up. A monthly newsletter to residents and relations was issued. Staff took part enthusiastically in fund-raising activities to pay for outings and entertainment. This gave them the chance to get to know residents in a social setting, and was a break from routine. A training programme was introduced.

Some staff did not respond and tried to undermine my intentions. Persistent unreported absence was quickly followed by disciplinary action. By the end of the year, absenteesim was at a more acceptable level, many working problems were alleviated, and the business started to recover.

Source: Private communication and discussions with the manager.

Maslow did *not* claim that the hierarchy was a fixed or rigid scheme. His clinical experience suggested that most people had these needs in about this order, but he had seen exceptions – people for whom self-esteem was more important than love. For others creativity took precedence, in that they did not seek self-actualisation *after* satisfying basic needs, but did so even when they were *not* being satisfied. Others had such low aspirations that they experienced life at a very basic level.

Nor did he claim that as people satisfy one need completely, another emerges. Rather he proposed that most normal people are partially satisfied and partially unsatisfied in their needs. A more accurate description of the hierarchy would be in terms of decreasing percentages of satisfaction at successive levels. So a person could think of themselves as being, say, 85 per cent satisfied at the physiological level and 70 per cent at the safety level (the percentages are meaningless). A higher-level need does not emerge suddenly – a person gradually becomes aware that they could now attain a higher need.

In summary, Maslow believed that people are motivated to satisfy needs that are important to them at that point in their life, and offered a description of those needs. The strength of a particular need would depend on the extent to which lower needs had been met. He believed that most people would seek to satisfy physiological needs first, before the others became operative. Self-actualisation was fulfilled last and least often, although he had observed exceptions.

How does Maslow's approach compare with Skinner's? Skinner believed that by providing positive reinforcement (or punishment) people would be motivated to act in a particular way. The rewards they obtained would satisfy their needs. Maslow took the slightly different position that people would seek to satisfy their needs by acting in a particular way. Both believed that to change behaviour it would be necessary to change the situation. Skinner emphasised that this would take the form of positive reinforcement to satisfy needs after an activity. Maslow implied that influencers should provide conditions that enable people to satisfy their needs from the activity.

Clayton Alderfer – ERG theory

Doubtful about the empirical support for the hierarchy of motives proposed by Maslow, Alderfer developed another approach (Alderfer, 1972). His work built on Maslow's ideas and presented an alternative. He developed and tested his theory by questionnaires and interviews in five organisations – a manufacturing firm, a bank, two colleges and a school. He aimed to identify the primary needs – those that an organism possesses by the nature of being the creature it is. Satisfaction refers to the internal state of someone who has obtained what they are seeking. Frustration is the opposite – when someone seeks something but does not find it.

Existence needs include all the physiological and material desires – hunger and thirst represent deficiencies in existence needs; pay and benefits represent ways of satisfying material requirements.

Existence needs reflect a person's requirement for material and energy.

Relatedness needs involve relationships with significant other people – family members, colleagues, bosses, subordinates, team members or regular customers. People satisfy relatedness needs by sharing thoughts and feelings. Acceptance, confirmation and understanding help to satisfy relatedness needs.

Relatedness needs involve a desire for relationships with significant other people.

Growth needs impel a person to be creative or to have an effect on themselves and their surroundings. People satisfy them by engaging with problems that use their skills or require them to develop new ones: being able to exercise talents fully brings a greater sense of completeness.

Growth needs are those which impel people to be creative or to produce an effect on themselves or their environment.

Alderfer proposed that his three categories of need are active in everyone, although in varying degrees of strength. Unlike Maslow, he found no evidence of a hierarchicy of needs, though he did find that if higher needs are frustrated, lower needs become prominent again, even if they have already been satisfied. Both theories are hard to test empirically, as it is difficult to establish whether a person has satisfied a need.

David McClelland

McClelland (1961) and his colleagues examined how people think and react in a wide range of situations. This work led them to identify three categories of human need, which individuals possess in different amounts:

- need for affiliation – to develop and maintain interpersonal relationships;
- need for power – to have control over one's environment; and
- need for achievement – to set and meet standards of excellence.

McClelland believed that, rather than being arranged in a hierarchy, individuals possess each of these possibly conflicting needs, which motivate their behaviour when activated. McClelland used the Thematic Apperception Test to assess how significant these categories were to people. The research team showed people pictures with a neutral subject and asked them to write a story about it. The researchers coded the stories and claimed these indicated the relative importance to the person of the affiliation, power and achievement motives.

Douglas McGregor – Theory X and Theory Y

Managers' attempts to motivate people reflect their assumptions about how they will react. Douglas McGregor (1960) developed this idea in his book *The Human Side of Enterprise*:

> every managerial act rests on assumptions, generalisations and hypotheses – that is to say, on theory. (p. 6)

McGregor presented two sets of assumptions underlying management practice. *Theory X*, which he called the traditional view of direction and control, expresses these assumptions:

- the average human being has an inherent dislike of work;
- because of this, most people must be coerced, controlled or threatened with punishment to get them to work;

- the average human being prefers to be directed, avoids responsibility, has little ambition and wants security above all.

McGregor believed that these assumptions led to a management strategy which ignored the full range of human needs. Theory X assumptions concentrated on the lower-level needs that Maslow had identified. Managers who acted on Theory X would fail to discover, let alone use, the potential of the average human being.

He observed that accumulating knowledge about human behaviour suggested an alternative, *Theory Y*, which expressed a different set of assumptions:

- the expenditure of physical and mental effort in work is as natural as play or rest;
- people will exercise self-direction and self-control in the service of objectives to which they are committed;
- commitment to objectives is a function of the rewards associated with their achievement;
- the average human being learns, under proper conditions, not only to accept, but also to seek, responsibility;
- the capacity to exercise a relatively high degree of imagination, ingenuity and creativity in the solution of organisational problems is widely, not narrowly, distributed in the population.

The practical implications of the assumptions are clear. Those who hold Theory X will use time-recording systems, close supervision, external quality checks, narrowly defined jobs and precise job descriptions. The central principle of Theory X is that of external control by systems, procedures or supervision.

Managers who hold to Theory Y create conditions in which people accept responsibility, and apply imagination, ingenuity and creativity to organisational problems. The central principle of Theory Y is that managers, and the organisation, will benefit if they enable employees to use their talents. They should be less prescriptive and directive and create the conditions that integrate individual and organisational goals.

Frederick Herzberg – two-factor theory

While Maslow and McClelland focused on individual differences in motivation, Herzberg (1959) related motivation to the nature of a person's work. He developed his theory following interviews with 200 engineers and accountants about their experience of work. The researchers first asked them to recall a time when they had felt exceptionally good about their job, and then asked about the events that had preceded those feelings. The research team then asked respondents to recall a time when they had felt particularly bad about their work, and the background to that. Analysis showed that when respondents recalled good times they frequently mentioned one or more of these factors:

- achievement
- recognition
- work itself
- responsibility
- advancement.

They mentioned these much less frequently when describing the bad times. When talking about the bad times they most frequently recalled these factors:

- company policy and administration
- supervision
- salary
- interpersonal relations
- working conditions.

They mentioned these much less frequently when describing the good times.

Herzberg concluded that factors associated with satisfaction describe people's relationship to what they were doing – the nature of the task, the responsibility or recognition received. He named these '**motivator factors**', as they seemed to influence people to superior performance and effort. The factors associated with dissatisfaction described conditions surrounding the work – like supervision or company policy. He named these **hygiene or (maintenance) factors** as they served mainly to prevent dissatisfaction, not to encourage high performance.

Herzberg concluded that satisfaction can only come from within, through the satisfaction of doing a task which provides a sense of achievement, recognition and so on. Managers cannot require motivation, though they can certainly destroy it by some thoughtless act. In his *Harvard Business Review* article (Herzberg, 1968) he wrote about what he termed 'Kick in the Ass' management:

> If I kick my dog . . . he will move. And when I want him to move again what must I do? I must kick him again. Similarly, I can change a person's battery, and then recharge it, and recharge it again. But it is only when one has a generator of one's own that we can talk about motivation. One then needs no outside stimulation. One wants to do it. (p. 55)

Motivator factors are those aspects of the work itself that Herzberg found influenced people to superior performance and effort.

Hygiene (or maintenance) factors are those aspects surrounding the task which can prevent discontent and dissatisfaction, but will not in themselves contribute to psychological growth and hence motivation.

Management in practice   Gamma Chemical (part 1) – a focus on hygiene factors

Gamma Chemical purchased another chemical company that had recently failed, and re-employed 30 of the 40 employees. While there was no overt dissatisfaction, management found it hard to motivate staff. They showed no initiative or creativity, and no commitment to the new company or its goals. Yet the company had:

- increased the salaries of the re-employed staff;
- improved working conditions and provided better equipment;
- placed people in positions of equal status to their previous jobs;
- operated an 'Open Door' policy, with supervisors easily approachable; and
- offered security of employment and a no-redundancy policy.

Other aspects of practice included:

- no structured training or development programmes;
- the small unit restricted opportunities for career advancement;
- people had little responsibility as management made decisions; and
- there was no clear connection between individual work and company performance.

Source: Private communication and discussions with the manager.

Herzberg believed that motivation depends on whether a job is intrinsically challenging and provides opportunities for recognition. He linked thinking about motivation with ideas about job design, and especially the motivational effects of job enrichment. There are many examples where management has redesigned people's jobs with positive effects. Few, if any, of these experiments were the result of knowing about Herzberg's theory, but their effects are often consistent with its predictions.

13.5   Process theories of motivation

Process theories try to explain why people choose one course of action towards satisfying a need rather than another. A person who needs a higher income could satisfy it by, say, moving to another company, applying for promotion or investing in training. What factors will influence their choice?

Expectancy theory

Vroom (1964) developed one attempt to answer that question with what he termed the **expectancy theory** of motivation. It focuses on the thinking processes people use to achieve rewards. Stuart Roberts is studying a degree course in Chemistry and has to submit a last assignment. He wants an A for the course, and so far has an average of B+. His motivation to put effort into the assignment will be affected by (a) his expectation that hard work will produce a good piece of work, and (b) his expectation that it will receive a grade of at least an A. If he believes he cannot do a good job, or that the grading system is unclear, then his motivation will be low.

The theory assumes that individuals:

- have different needs and so value outcomes differently;
- make conscious choices about which course of action to follow; and
- choose between alternative actions based on the likelihood of an action resulting in an outcome they value.

There are, then, three main components in expectancy theory. First, the person's expectation (or **subjective probability**) that effort (E) will result in some level of performance (P):

$$(E \rightarrow P)$$

This will be affected by how clear they are about their roles, the training available, whether the necessary support will be provided and similar factors. If Stuart Roberts understands what the assignment requires and is confident in his ability to do a good job, his $(E \rightarrow P)$ expectancy will be high.

The second component is the person's expectation that performance will be **instrumental** in leading to a particular outcome (O):

$$(P \rightarrow O)$$

This will be affected by how confident the person is that achieving a target will produce a reward. This reflects factors such as the clarity of the organisation's appraisal and payment systems and previous experience of them. A clear grading system, which Stuart understands and knows that staff apply consistently, will mean he has a high $(P \rightarrow O)$ expectancy. If he has found the system unpredictable this expectancy would be lower.

The third component is the **valence** that the individual attaches to a particular outcome:

$$(V)$$

This term is best understood as the power of the outcome to motivate that individual – how keen Roberts is to get a good degree. It introduces the belief that people differ in the value they place on different kinds of reward. So the value of V varies between individuals, reflecting their unique pattern of motivational needs (as suggested by the content theories). Someone who values money and achievement would place a high valence on an outcome that was a promotion to a distant head office. They would try to work in a way which led to that. Such an outcome would be much less welcome (have a much lower valence) to a manager who values an established pattern of relationships or quality of life in the present location.

In summary:

$$F = (E \rightarrow P) \times (P \rightarrow O) \times V$$

in which F represents the force exerted, or degree of motivation a person has towards an activity. Two beliefs will influence that motivation, namely the expectation that:

- making the effort will lead to performance $(E \rightarrow P)$
- that level of performance will lead to an outcome they value $(P \rightarrow O)$

Adjusting these beliefs for valence – how desirable the outcome is to the person – gives a measure of their motivation. The beliefs that people hold reflect their personality and their experience of organisational practices.

Expectancy theory proposes that motivation depends on a person's belief in the probability that effort will lead to good performance, and that good performance will lead to them receiving an outcome they value (valence).

Subjective probability (in expectancy theory) is a person's estimate of the likelihood that a certain level of effort (E) will produce a level of performance (P) which will then lead to an expected outcome (O).

Instrumentality is the perceived probability that good performance will lead to valued rewards, measured on a scale from 0 (no chance) to 1 (certainty).

Valence is the perceived value or preference that an individual has for a particular outcome.

Using the multiplication sign in the equation signifies that both beliefs influence motivation. If a person believes that however hard they try they will be unable to perform well, they will not be motivated to do so (so E → P = 0). The same applies for (P → O). A low score in either of these two parts of the equation, or in V, will lead to low effort, regardless of beliefs about the other part.

A criticism of the theory is that it implies a high level of rational calculation, as people weigh the probabilities of various courses of action. It also implies that managers estimate what each employee values, and try to ensure that motivational practices meet them. Neither calculation is likely to be made that rationally, which may diminish the model's practical value.

However, it is useful in recognising that people vary in their beliefs (or probabilities) about the components in the equation, and show how managers can affect these beliefs by redesigning work. If people are unclear about their role, or receive weak feedback, the theory predicts that this will reduce their motivation.

The theory predicts that managers can influence motivation by practical actions such as:

- establishing the rewards people value;
- identifying and communicating performance requirements;
- ensuring that reasonable effort can meet those requirements;
- providing facilities to support the person's effort;
- ensuring a clear link between performance and reward; and
- providing feedback to staff on how well they are meeting performance requirements.

The theory links insights from the content theories of motivation with organisational practice.

J. Stacey Adams – equity theory

Equity theory is usually associated with J. Stacy Adams (a behavioural scientist working at the General Electric Company) who put forward the first systematic account (Adams, 1963) of the idea that fairness in comparison with others influences motivation. People like to be treated fairly and compare what they put into a job (effort, skill, knowledge etc.) with the rewards they receive (pay, recognition, satisfaction etc.). They express this as a ratio of their input to their reward. They also compare their ratio with the input-to-reward ratio of others whom they consider their equals. They expect management to reward others in the same way, so expect the ratios to be roughly equal. The formula below sums up the comparison:

Equity theory states that perception of unfairness leads to tension, which then motivates the individual to resolve that unfairness.

$$\frac{\text{Input (A)}}{\text{Reward (A)}} : \frac{\text{Input (B)}}{\text{Reward (B)}}$$

Person A compares the ratio of her input to her reward to that of B. If the ratios are similar she will be satisfied with the treatment received. If she believes the ratio is lower than that of other people she will feel inequitably treated and be dissatisfied.

The theory predicts that if people feel unfairly treated they will experience tension and dissatisfaction. They will try to reduce this by one or more of these means:

- reducing their inputs, by putting in less effort or withholding good ideas and suggestions;
- attempting to increase their outcomes, by pressing for increased pay or other benefits;
- attempting to decrease other people's outcomes by generating conflict or withholding information and help;
- changing the basis of their comparison, by making it against someone else where the inequity is less pronounced;
- increasing their evaluation of the other person's output so the ratios are in balance.

As individuals differ, so will their way of reducing inequity. Some will try to rationalise the situation, suggesting that their efforts were greater or lesser than they originally thought them to be, or that the rewards are reasonable. For example, a person denied a promotion may decide that the previously desired job would not have been so advantageous after all. Members may put pressure on other members of the team whom they feel are not pulling their weight. Some may choose to do less, so bringing their ratio into line with that of other staff.

Clearly the focus and the components of the comparisons are highly subjective, although the theory has an intuitive appeal. The subjective nature of the comparison makes it difficult to test empirically, and there has been little formal research on the theory in recent years (though see Mowday and Colwell, 2003). There is, however, abundant anecdotal evidence that people compare their effort/reward ratio with that of other people or groups.

Edwin A. Locke – goal-setting theory

Goal-setting theory
states that motivation is
influenced by goal diffi-
culty, goal specificity and
knowledge of results.

Goal-setting theory refers to a series of propositions designed to help explain and predict work behaviour. Its best-known advocate is Edwin Locke (Locke, 1968; Locke and Latham, 2002) and the theory has four main propositions:

1 *Challenging goals* lead to higher levels of performance than a vague goal, such as 'do your best'. Difficult goals are sometimes called 'stretch' goals because they encourage us to try harder, to stretch ourselves. However, beyond a point this effect fades – if people see a goal as being impossible, their motivation declines.

2 *Specific goals* lead to higher levels of performance than vague goals (such as 'do your best'). We find it easier to adjust behaviour when we know exactly what the objective is, and what is expected of us.

3 *Participation* in goal setting can improve commitment to those goals, since people have a sense of ownership and are motivated to achieve the goals. However, if management explains and justifies the goals, without inviting participation, that can also increase motivation.

4 *Knowledge of results* of past performance – receiving feedback – is necessary to motivation. It is motivational in itself, and contains information that may help people attain the goals.

The main attraction of goal theory is the directness of the practical implications, including:

- *Goal difficulty*: set goals that are hard enough to stretch employees, but not so difficult as to be impossible to achieve.
- *Goal specificity*: set goals in clear, precise and if possible quantifiable terms.
- *Participation*: allow employees to take part in setting goals, to increase ownership and commitment.
- *Acceptance*: if goals are set by management, ensure they are adequately explained and justified, so that people understand and accept them.
- *Feedback*: provide information on past performance to allow employees to use it in adjusting their performance.

While goal theory has many implications for appraisal schemes and other performance management techniques, several variables have been shown to moderate the relationship between goal difficulty and performance – such as ability, task complexity and situational constraints. Another major question is whether personality traits moderate the relationship – someone with a high need for achievement may be more likely to respond positively to a challenging goal than someone with a lower need for achievement.

The context may affect the motivational quality of challenging goals. In some careers, entry to, or advancement within, the high status aspects of the job depends on spending months or years, on less challenging assignments. People may be willing to work diligently at less challenging tasks, if they see them as a stepping stone to a future with more challenging work. A person's career stage will also affect the motivational effect of challenging goals – in late career they may be less inclined to seek challenge than they were when young.

13.6 Designing work to be motivating

People value both **extrinsic** and **intrinsic rewards**. Extrinsic rewards are those that are separate from the task, such as pay, security and promotion. Intrinsic rewards are those that people receive as they do the task itself – using skills, sensing achievement, doing satisfying work. Recall that a central element in scientific management was the careful design of the 'one best way' of doing a piece of manual work. Experts analysed how people did the job and identified the most efficient method, usually breaking the job into many small parts. Such work provided few if any intrinsic rewards – and Taylor's system concentrated on providing clear extrinsic rewards.

Working on a small element of a task is boring to many people, making them dissatisfied, careless and frequently absent. As these limitations became clear managers looked for ways to make jobs more intrinsically rewarding – so that the work itself brought a reward of interest or challenge. The ideas from Maslow, Herzberg and McGregor prompted attempts to increase the opportunity for people to satisfy higher-level needs at work. The assumption was that staff would work more productively if management offered intrinsic rewards (motivators in Herzberg's terms) as well as extrinsic ones (Herzberg's hygiene factors), leading to ideas about job enrichment.

Intrinsic rewards are valued outcomes or benefits that come from the individual, such as feelings of satisfaction, achievement and competence.

Extrinsic rewards are valued outcomes or benefits provided by others, such as promotion, a pay increase or a bigger car.

Job characteristics theory

Hackman and Oldham (1980) built on these ideas to develop and test empirically an approach to the design of work which focused on the objective characteristics of employees' jobs. Their basic idea was to build into those jobs the attributes which are likely to offer intrinsic motivation to staff, and so encourage them to perform well. Their **job characteristics theory** predicts that the design of a job will affect internal motivation and work outcomes, with the effects being mediated by individual and contextual factors. Figure 13.3 shows the model, with the addition of implementing concepts in the left-hand column. The model provides guidance on how to design enriched jobs which satisfy employees' higher-level needs.

The model identifies three *psychological states* that must be present to achieve high motivation. If any are low, motivation will be low. The three states are:

Job characteristics theory predicts that the design of a job will affect internal motivation and work outcomes, with the effects being mediated by individual and contextual factors.

- **Experienced meaningfulness** The degree to which employees perceive their work as valuable and worthwhile. If workers regard a job as trivial and pointless, their motivation will be low.
- **Experienced responsibility** How responsible people feel for the quantity and quality of work performed.
- **Knowledge of results** The amount of feedback employees receive about how well they are doing. Those who do not receive feedback will care less about the quality of their performance.

These psychological states are influenced by five *job characteristics* that contribute to experienced meaningfulness of work:

- **Skill variety** The extent to which a job makes use of a range of skills and experience. A routine administrative job is low in variety, whereas that of a marketing analyst may require a wide variety of statistical and interpersonal skills.
- **Task identity** Whether a job involves a complete operation, with a recognisable beginning and end. A nurse who organises and oversees all the treatments for a hospital patient will have more task identity than one who provides a single treatment to many different patients.
- **Task significance** How much the job matters to others in the organisation or to the wider society. People who can see that their job contributes directly to performance, or that it is a major help to others, will feel they have a significant task.

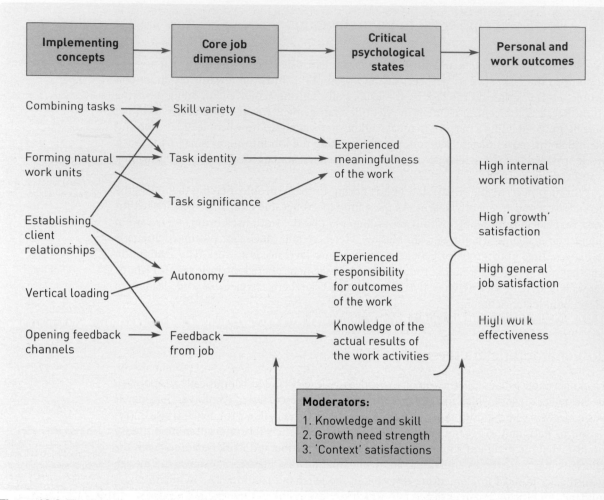

Figure 13.3 The job characteristics model

Source: Adapted from Hackman and Oldham (1980).

- **Autonomy** How much freedom and independence a person has in deciding how to go about doing the work. A sales agent in a call centre following a tightly scripted (and recorded) conversation has less autonomy than a sales agent talking face to face to a customer.
- **Feedback** The extent to which a person receives feedback on relevant dimensions of performance. Modern manufacturing systems can provide operators with very rapid information on quality, scrap, material use and costs. Operators can then receive a high level of feedback on the results of their work.

The extent to which a job contains these elements can be calculated using a tested instrument, and then using the scores to calculate the *motivating potential* score for the job.

The model also shows how to increase the motivating potential of a job, by using one or more of five 'implementing concepts':

- **Combine tasks** Rather than divide the work into small pieces, as Taylor recommended, staff can combine them so they use more skills and complete more of the whole task. An order clerk could receive orders from a customer and arrange transport and invoicing instead of having these done by different people.
- **Form natural workgroups** In order to give more responsibility and enable sharing of skills, groups could be created that carry out a complete operation. Instead of a product passing down an assembly line, with each worker performing one operation, a group may assemble the whole product, sharing out the tasks among themselves.

- **Establish customer relations** This would bring home to employees the expectations of the people to whom their work goes, whether inside or outside the organisation, enabling them to see how their job fits into the larger picture. Instead of people doing part of the job for all customers, they can look after all the requirements of some customers. They establish closer relationships and gain a better understanding of their customers' needs.
- **Vertical loading** This involves workers taking on some responsibilities of supervisors to solve problems and develop workable solutions, thus adding to their autonomy. Operators may be given responsibility for checking the quantity and quality of incoming materials and reporting any problems. They may use more discretion over the order in which they arrange a week's work.
- **Open feedback channels** This would ensure that people receive feedback on their performance from internal or external customers. Operators can attend meetings at which customers give their views on the service provided as a basis for improving performance and building client relationships.

The last feature of the Hackman–Oldham model is the specification of three moderating influences:

- **knowledge and skill** – a person's ability to do the work;
- **growth need strength** – the extent to which an individual desires personal challenges, accomplishment and learning on the job – which clearly varies; and
- **'context' satisfaction** – pay and other conditions surrounding the job.

Many managers, such as those at Gamma Chemical (see the Management in Practice feature below), have changed the kind of work they expect employees to do. This has not usually been to provide more interesting jobs, but as a response to business conditions. Nevertheless, the results of such changes often support what the theory predicts. Another approach is to give staff more responsibility to make decisions without referring to their supervisors: this is usually called empowerment.

Management in practice   Gamma Chemical (part 2) – a focus on motivating factors

After taking control, Gamma Chemical made these changes to working arrangements:

- introduced a cross-training programme to improve job diversity and individual growth;
- created problem-solving teams from natural work units to give operators a sense of ownership and achievement;
- expected operators to make more decisions, increasing individual authority and accountability;
- introduced an appraisal system that shows operators how their function affects company performance.

Management believed these changes had resulted in 20 per cent more output and 50 per cent less wastage.

Source: Private communication and discussions with the manager.

Activity 13.2   What does 'motivation' mean in management?

Having read the chapter, make brief notes summarising the motivational issues evident in the organisation you chose for this activity.

- What effects did the motivational attempts you studied have on the behaviour of the targets? (See Section 13.2.)

- To what extent did they strengthen or weaken the psychological contract? (See Section 13.2.)
- To what extent did the evidence of these attempts support any ONE of the content theories of motivation described in the chapter? (See Section 13.4.)
- To what extent did the evidence of these attempts support any ONE of the process theories of motivation described in the chapter, including work design? (See Sections 13.5 and 13.6.)

Compare what you have found with other students on your course.

Summary

1 Explain why managers need to understand and use theories of motivation

- People depend on others within and beyond the organisation to act in a particular way, and understanding what motivates them is critical to this. Motivation includes understanding the goals which people pursue (content), the choices they make to secure them (process) and how this knowledge can be applied to influence others (including through work design).

2 Show how the context, including the psychological contract, affect motivation

- Social changes affect the people managers try to motivate, so they may need to adapt their approach to suit.
- The relationship between employer and employee is expressed in the psychological contract, which needs to be in acceptable balance for effective performance.

3 Understand behaviour modification, content and process theories of motivation

- Behaviour modification theories attempt to explain that people can influence the behaviour of others by using appropriate and timely reinforcement.
- Content theories seek to understand the needs which human beings may seek to satisfy at work and include the work of Maslow, Alderfer and Herzberg as well as of earlier observers such as Taylor and Mayo.
- Expectancy theory explains motivation in terms of valued outcomes and the subjective probability of achieving those outcomes.
- Equity theory explains motivation in terms of perceptions of fairness by comparison with others.
- Goal-setting theory believes that motivation depends on the degree of difficulty and specificity of goals.

4 Use work design theories to diagnose motivational problems and recommend actions

- Most of the models can be used to analyse the likely effects of organisational practices on motivation, and to indicate areas for possible management action.
- People are only motivated if the job meets a need which they value – providing appropriate content factors leads to satisfaction and performance.
- Herzberg suggests that motivation depends on paying attention to motivating as well as hygiene factors.
- Jobs can be enriched by increasing skill variety, task identity, task significance, autonomy and feedback.

Review questions

1 Outline the basic assumptions of McGregor's Theory X and Theory Y.

2 Describe the psychological contract. What are you expecting (a) from an employer in your career; (b) from an employer who provides you with part-time work while you are studying?

3 Which three things are pinpointed when using behaviour modification?

4 How does Maslow's theory of human needs relate to the ideas of Frederick Taylor?

5 How does Alderfer's theory differ from Maslow's? What research lay behind the two theories?

6 Explain the difference between Herzberg's hygiene and motivating factors. Give three examples of each.

7 Explain the difference between E → P and P → O in expectancy theory.

8 What are the five job design elements that are expected to affect a person's satisfaction with their work?

9 Give an example of an implementing concept associated with each element.

Further reading

Herzberg, F. (1959), *The Motivation to Work*, Wiley, New York.

McGregor, D. (1960), *The Human Side of Enterprise*, McGraw-Hill, New York.

Maslow, A. (1970), *Motivation and Personality* (2nd edn), Harper & Row, New York.

The original accounts of these influential works are readable books showing organisations and research in action.

Heil, G., Bennis, W. and Stephens, D. C. (2000), *Douglas McGregor Revisited*, Wiley, New York.

A review of McGregor's ideas, which the authors argue are more in tune with modern organisational needs than when he wrote *The Human Side of Enterprise* in 1960.

Weblinks

Visit the websites of companies that interest you, perhaps as possible places to work. Or you could visit the websites of some of these sites:

www.ikea.com
www.edenproject.com
www.childbase.co.uk
www.greatplacetowork.co.uk
www.timpson.co.uk

Navigate to the pages dealing with 'about the company' or 'careers'.

● What do they tell you about working there? What seem to be the most prominent features?

● What needs do they seem to be aiming to meet? Would they meet your needs?

 Annotated weblinks, multiple choice questions and other useful resources can be found on **www.pearsoned.co.uk/boddy**

Case study   The Eden Project   www.edenproject.com

The Eden Project is one of the most visited attractions in Europe: over 10 million people have visited it since it opened in 2002. Tim Smit (who had earlier been responsible for re-opening The Lost Gardens of Heligan to the public, which have become the most visited gardens in Britain) co-founded the project, which developed from his Heligan experience. This had convinced him that people (even those who did not initially like gardens) could be attracted by anecdotes – accessible stories about what they were looking at. He also noticed that people felt very positive about being in well-made, abundant gardens.

This led him to develop the idea of creating a place that looked good, was technically sophisticated, and which was dedicated to explaining how all life on earth depends on plants. More that that, it could become:

> a place where you started to think about your connection with nature, and whether you might want to get closer to nature again and whether some lessons of life might not be buried in there.

From this initial vision, Eden has, in only nine years, become one of the 50 most recognised brands (alongside established businesses like Nokia and Pepsi-Cola); has generated over £900m in revenues for other businesses in Cornwall; and employs some 300 staff.

The first task in turning the idea into reality was to persuade people to invest in the project – which would cost about £76 million to build. Smit approached one of the leading architects of the time: who, after consulting with his colleagues agreed to work on the project: Smit says:

> So for the next 18 months we had possibly the best design team in the world working for us for nothing. I think the reason Eden came into being was that we formed an enormous gang. There was a bunch of people that were really interested in the idea and we would meet in motorway service stations and in pubs and in people's houses and this just grew as people heard about it. People started leaving their jobs because they became so obsessed with it. And it suddenly had an inevitability, when we realised we were saying 'when' not 'if'. . . and the dice rolled unbelievably well for us.

Eden Project.

> The environment became a big thing, plants are good, people can imagine the Crystal Palace and this is bigger than the Crystal Palace. We said we wanted the biggest in the world, to contain a full-size rainforest, we don't just want some namby-pamby greenhouse. I said we wanted to build a global must-see like the Guggenheim. The tourism people thought we might get 500,000 visitors in the first year: we actually had 1.8 million.
>
> And in the middle of all that there was a huge fund-raising effort to raise the money for what we called the eighth wonder of the world.

Gaynor Coley is Managing Director at the Eden Project, and her financial background was crucial in raising the money which the project needed.

> I spent the first three years raising the money: a really exciting period, using all those skills you learn in the City about having a robust business plan, together with skills you may use in fringe theatre, which are about how to get something off the ground when nothing exists.
>
> To get the finance we had to identify people with a similar purpose to us. For example, the Millennium Commission wanted to put really landmark architecture into the landscape and it was obvious that there was nothing else in the south west that would meet this brief. So it was research around what agendas a portfolio of stakeholders had, understanding them and actually making a pitch relevant to that particular stakeholder.

Tim Smit on the reasons for Eden:

> Of course, we have to give people a good day out, a cup of tea they enjoy, and all that. But

I think we have actually struck a vein which has got deeper and more important to us as a society, which is people are not just looking for leisure: what many are looking for is a purpose in their lives, and I think the combination of a great day out, with something meaningful, learning about your environment, learning about your relationship with nature, was a killer proposition. That's why I think we get the numbers we do.

The mission of Eden has changed and developed over the years, but I think there's a seed of an idea that's never gone away and that is about how important it is for us as human beings to understand our relationship with nature. We aren't independent of it: we are dependent on it and part of it. We think about how we operate, how we do business, and we believe that what you do is really, really important. So the authenticity of the welcome that you get when you come here, the authenticity of how we treat our suppliers, is what I think lies behind the strength of the Eden brand.

To work at Eden you've got to be interested in a lot of stuff. You've got to be prepared to catch people when they fall, because people are trying stuff all the time, and you've got to be prepared for the unexpected because part of the way we work is almost deliberately creating chaos by doing more stuff than we've possibly got time to do, which means more junior members have more chance to become leaders because the senior ones can't do it all.

One of the things I think is very special about Eden is that the letters after your name don't make any difference. It's what you can do . . . Sure the Finance Director's got to be an accountant and all that sort of stuff, but in the wider scheme of things, to be an Eden person you've got to be optimistic and smiley and damned hard working.

Gayle Conley adds:

We try not to be prescriptive about defining talent and we try to encourage people to take individual responsibility for their own career path here as much as we can help them to a career path.

Jess Ratty speaks about her work:

I began at Eden as a waitress when I was 18 years old with no qualifications: I'm now 24 and the Press Officer. So I've worked in about eight departments and worked my way up through the company. I think Eden's been a fantastic opportunity for me – the ethos and the way you don't have to have a degree – you know they'll give people a chance . . . after working as a waitress I moved to the Stewards team where I learnt a lot about dealing with people. I worked in plant sales, learning a lot about different plants, which was great to learn at 18. Then I worked in retail, the product side of things, and was then picked up by the design team . . . and after a few more jobs one of the managers said 'do you want to go for the job of communications assistant?' And I thought, 'people actually believe in me, they want me to do a job they think I'll be good at!'

Sources: Interviews with Tim Smit, Gaynor Coley and Jess Ratty; Eden Project website.

Questions

1 Which groups of people does Eden need to motivate, and what clues are there in the case about what motivates different people to give their support? (See Sections 13.1 and 13.2.)

2 What human needs is Eden seeking to satisfy? (See Section 13.4.)

3 Which of Herzberg's 'motivating factors' do staff refer to in their comments? (See Section 13.4.)

4 How has the company tried to generate positive attitudes amongst its staff? (Refer to Sections 13.5 and 13.6.)

CHAPTER 14
COMMUNICATING

Learning outcomes

When you have read this chapter you should be able to:

1 Explain the role of communicating in managing
2 Identify and illustrate the elements and stages in the communication process
3 Use the concept of information richness to select a communication channel
4 Compare the benefits of different communication networks
5 Outline some essential interpersonal communication skills
6 Use ideas from the chapter to comment on the management issues in the Facebook case study

Activity 14.1 What does 'communicating' mean in management?

Before reading the chapter, write some notes on what you think 'communicating' means in management. Choose the organisation or people who may be able to help you learn about the topic. You may find it helpful to discuss the topic with a manager you know, or reflect on an activity you have managed.

- Identify a significant situation in which someone needed to communicate with others, and describe it briefly.
- How did those involved try to communicate their message?
- Did they consciously vary the way they communicated, depending on the circumstances?
- What communication skills did they use?

Keep these notes as you will be able to use them later.

14.1 Introduction

Facebook (and similar sites) are widely accepted tools for mass communication, representing a dramatic and permanent change in our ability to communicate with others. The site makes people's personal relationships more visible and quantifiable than ever before. They are also becoming useful vehicles for news and channels of influence. Some companies doubt the benefits of online social networking in the office, and try to block access – concerned about security and staff wasting time. Others see many potential benefits in these new communication tools, as they enable people to enhance connections and spread ideas and innovations around the world at unprecedented speed.

Managers at Facebook themselves face communication challenges – they need (among other things) to communicate the attractions of working at the company to potential staff, ensure rapid and accurate communication among software developers, and to understand what users expect from Facebook. They also watch for information on developments at Twitter and MySpace, two competitors.

Most managers experience similar communication issues, though in less challenging circumstances. The success of GSK depends on intense communication between research teams, clinical trial staff, regulators and marketers as they develop new drugs. Those in service organisations such as HMV want staff to communicate ideas and suggestions – and to understand company policy. Professionals providing care for the sick and vulnerable need to communicate accurate and timely information, often in stressful conditions: spectacular failures often originate in poor communication.

Even with the technologies now available, people continue to experience ineffective communication. Computer-based systems are useful tools, but do not replace the need for human communication. Company-wide information systems make it easy for geographically separated people to exchange messages – but how they interpret those messages depends on their relationship:

> Technology won't make messages more useful unless we build personal relationships first. The message will get through more easily if the recipient has some pre-existing relationship with the sender. (Rosen, 1998)

Until people meet they cannot develop the mutual trust and shared knowledge essential for true communication.

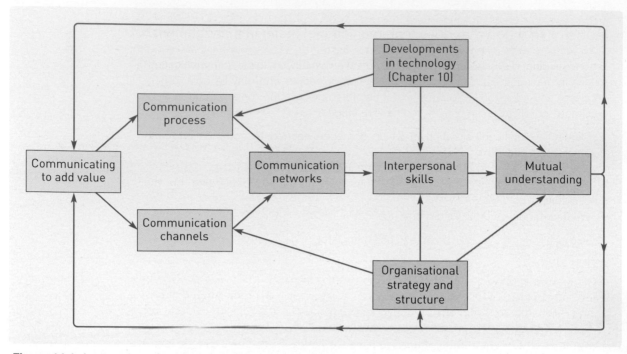

Figure 14.1 An overview of communicating in organisations

Some managers underestimate communication problems. Someone who works with a major utility business wrote to the author:

> The majority of managers within [the business] consider themselves to be effective commu-nicators. Staff have a different perspective, and a recent staff survey rated communications as being very poor, with information being top down, no form of two-way communications and managers only hearing what they want to hear. (private communication)

This chapter begins by showing how communication is essential to managing. People send and receive messages through one or more distinct channels (or media), passing along formal and informal organisational networks. While technology can help, communication remains a human activity which depends on identifiable skills. People also communicate within a con-text, which affects what methods they use and whether they achieve mutual understanding. Figure 14.1 provides an overview.

14.2   Communicating to add value

We base our understanding of the world on information and feelings that we receive and send. People at all levels of an organisation need to communicate with others about:

- **inputs** – e.g. the availability of materials or equipment;
- **transformation** – e.g. about capacity or quality; and
- **outputs** – e.g. customer complaints or advertising policy.

Information about a customer's order needs to flow accurately to all the departments that will help to deliver it – and then between departments as the task progresses. People communicate up and down the vertical hierarchy, and horizontally between functions, departments and other organisations.

Formal and informal communication is central to the management job. This is most evident in the informational role – but equally, managers can only perform their interpersonal and decisional roles by communicating. Computer-based information systems communicate structured, explicit data and information very efficiently – but are less good at transmitting unstructured, tacit information and knowledge.

What is communication?

Communication happens when people share information to reach a common understanding. Managing depends on conveying and interpreting messages clearly so that people can work together. Speaking and writing clearly are easy: achieving a common understanding is not. Background and personal needs affect our ability to absorb messages from those with different histories, but until people reach a common understanding, they have not communicated.

> **Communication** is the exchange of information through written or spoken words, symbols and actions to reach a common understanding.

How communicating adds value

Communication features in some way in every chapter – making a plan, communicating a decision, influencing people or working in a team. It is through communication that people add value through innovation, quality, delivery and cost. *Innovation* depends on good information about customer needs and relevant discoveries – which comes from communication with the scientific community. Efforts to enhance *quality* depend on everyone involved understanding what quality means to the customer. Without communication there is no quality.

Another measure of performance is *delivery* – supplying the customer with what they expect, when they expect it. That is only possible if people communicate accurate, reliable and timely information up and down the supply chain. Competition adds to pressure to continually reduce the *cost* of goods and services – so people need information about current performance and ways of removing waste.

Management in practice   Twitter and Facebook as marketing tools

Social networking sites offer small businesses a quick and free way to promote their wares to a large audience. Two sisters who opened a bakery in 2008 use Twitter and Facebook as a marketing tool: one said:

> Together they work like a virtual focus group, a bulletin board and a marketing campaign rolled into one.

As well as posting details of new flavours, specials and events, they use the social networking sites to promote their new nationwide delivery service together with a new store.

Many small business owners find traditional advertising channels such as television, radio and newspapers too expensive. For others, the web is a medium more in tune with their potential customers. Someone who runs a pizza business in a university town:

> They're not a good fit for everyone, but if you're a small business with a customer base who uses social media, you can't afford not to use them. It's a great way to interact one on one and build a relationship with our customers.

She recently asked her Twitter and Facebook followers to vote on which company she should use to supply soft drinks.

Facebook offers businesses special pages, and the option to show advertisements to users who like similar companies.

Source: *BBC News*, 15 October 2009.

Chapter 10 showed how modern information systems transform how people receive, use and distribute information. It also showed that when managers implement such systems, they need to ensure that the context (structure, culture and so on) and the system are compatible. Technically sophisticated systems only add value if the people responsible for them also manage organisational issues well. A similar lesson applies to communicating. Modern technology only improves communication if people pay attention to familiar issues in the communication process: human barriers to communication endanger hi-tech interactions just as much as they do low-tech ones.

14.3 Communication processes

> The **message** is what the sender communicates.

We communicate whenever we send a **message** to someone and as we think about what they say in return. This is a subtle and complex process, through which people easily send and receive the wrong message. Whenever someone says: 'That's not what I meant' or 'I explained it clearly, and they still got it wrong' there has been a communication failure. We waste time when we misunderstand directions, or cause offence by saying something that the listener misinterprets.

We infer meaning from words and gestures and then from the person's reply to our message. We continually interpret their messages and create our own. As colleagues have a conversation, each listens to the other's words, sees their gestures, reads the relevant documents or looks over the equipment to understand what the other means. When they achieve a mutual understanding about what to do they have communicated effectively. Figure 14.2 shows a model of the process (Berlo, 1960) which enables someone to analyse the sources of communication success or failure.

Communication requires at least two people – a sender and a receiver. The *sender* initiates the communication when they try to transfer ideas, facts or feelings to the *receiver* – the person to whom they send the message. The sender **encodes** the idea they wish to convey into a message by using symbols such as words, actions or expressions. Deciding how to encode the message is an important choice, and depends in part on the purpose:

> **Encoding** is translating information into symbols for communication.

- Is it to convey specific and unambiguous information?
- Is it to raise an open and unfamiliar problem, and a request for creative ideas?
- Is it to pass routine data, or to inspire people?

The message is the tangible expression of the sender's idea. The sender chooses one or more channels (the communication medium) – such as an email, a face-to-face meeting or

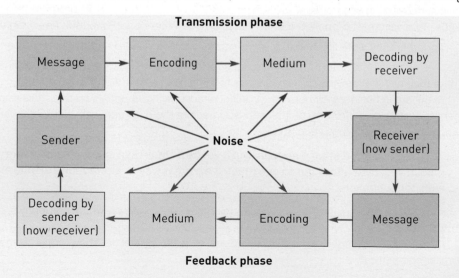

Figure 14.2 The communication process

a letter – to transmit the coded message. The receiver **decodes** the symbols contained in the message, and tries to reconstruct the sender's original thought. Coding and decoding are sources of communication failure as the sender and receiver have different knowledge, experience and interests. Receivers also evaluate a message by their knowledge of the sender, which affects whether they regard the information to be valuable. These 'filters' interfere with the conversion of meaning to symbols and *vice versa*: like other distractions and interruptions, they are called **noise**.

The final stage in the episode is when the receiver responds to the message by giving **feedback** to the sender. This turns one-way communication into two-way. Without feedback the sender cannot know whether the receiver has the message or whether they have interpreted it as the sender intended. The flow of information between parties is continuous and reciprocal, each responding by giving feedback to the other, and is only completed when the sender knows that the receiver has received and understood the message as intended.

Effective communicators understand it is a two-way process, and positively check for feedback. They do not rely only on making their message as clear as possible, but also encourage the receiver to provide feedback. Without some response – a nod, a question that implies understanding, a quick email acknowledgement – the sender has not communicated successfully.

Assume that communication is going to fail, and put time and effort into preventing that.

Non-verbal communication

Interpersonal communication includes **non-verbal communication**, sometimes called body language, which can have more impact on the receiver than the words in the message. Signals include the tone of voice, facial expression, posture and appearance, and provide most of the impact in face-to-face communication.

Small changes in eye contact, raising eyebrows or a directed glance while making a statement, add to the meaning that the sender conveys. A stifled yawn, an eager nod, a thoughtful flicker of anxiety gives the sender a signal about the receiver's reaction. Gestures and body position give strong signals: leaning forward attentively, moving about in the chair, hands moving nervously, gathering papers or looking at the clock – all send a message. A skilful manager will use non-verbal cues to detect that something is worrying an employee even if they are hesitant to speak out.

Positive non-verbal feedback helps to build relations within a team. A smile or wave to someone at least acknowledges that they exist. Related to a task it indicates approval in an informal, rapid way that sustains confidence. Negative feedback can be correspondingly damaging. A boss who looks irritated by what the staff member sees as a reasonable enquiry is giving a negative signal, as is one who looks bored during a presentation.

Decoding is the interpretation of a message into a form with meaning.

Noise is anything that confuses, diminishes or interferes with communication.

Feedback (in communication) occurs as the receiver expresses their reaction to the sender's message.

Non-verbal communication is the process of coding meaning through behaviours such as facial expression, gestures and body postures.

Management in practice   Virtual teams at Cisco   www.cisco.com

Cisco Systems supplies much of the physical equipment which supports the internet, and most design teams contain staff working in facilities across the world. One team member said:

> It means you have to be a bit more careful when it comes to communication. Most of the time you have to use email and instant messaging to discuss issues, which means there can be misunderstandings if you're not careful. When you interact in person you use things like facial expression and hand gestures – none of these are available when emailing so you have to state your arguments more clearly.

Source: Private communication.

As with any interpersonal skill, some people are better at interpreting non-verbal behaviour than others. The sender of a spoken message can benefit by noting the non-verbal responses to what they say. If they do not seem appropriate (raised eyebrows, an anxious look), the speaker should pause and check that the receiver has received the message that the sender intended.

Perception

Perception is the process by which individuals make sense of their environment by selecting and interpreting information. We receive a stream of information beyond our capacity to absorb, and **selective attention** keeps us sane. We actively notice and attend to a small fraction of the available information, filtering out what we do not need, based in part on the strength of the signal and our evaluation of the sender.

When people observe information they interpret it, and react to it, uniquely. This 'perceptual organisation' arranges incoming signals into patterns that give meaning to data – relating it to our interest, the status of the sender or the benefits of attending to it. Experience, social class and education affect the meanings people attach to information.

A common form of perceptual organisation is **stereotyping**. 'They always complain' or 'You would expect people from marketing to say that' are signs that someone is judging a message not by its content but by the group to which the sender belongs. It leads us to misinterpret a message because we are making inaccurate assumptions about the sender. Perceptual differences are natural, but interfere with communication. Our unique personalities and perceptual styles affect how we interpret a message, so senders cannot assume that receivers attach the same meaning to a message as they intended.

Selective attention is the ability, often unconscious, to choose from the stream of signals in the environment, concentrating on some and ignoring others.

Stereotyping is the practice of consigning a person to a category or personality type on the basis of their membership of some known group.

14.4 Selecting communication channels

The model of communication in Figure 14.2 shows the steps that people take to communicate effectively. The process fails if either sender or receiver does not encode or decode the symbols of the message in the same way. Selecting the wrong communication **channel** also leads to difficulty: sending a message that requires subtle interpretation as a written instruction with no chance for feedback is not good practice.

Lengel and Daft (1988) developed the idea of **information richness** to compare the capacity of channels to promote common understanding between sender and receiver: see Figure 14.3.

The richness of a medium (or channel) depends on its ability to:

- handle many cues at the same time;
- support rapid two-way feedback; and
- establish a personal focus for the communication.

A **channel** is the medium of communication between a sender and a receiver.

Information richness refers to the amount of information that a communication channel can carry, and the extent to which it enables sender and receiver to achieve common understanding.

Face-to-face communication

Face-to-face discussion is the richest medium, as both parties can pick up many information cues (concentration, eye contact, body movements, facial expression) in addition to the spoken words. This enables them to gain a deep understanding of the nuances of meaning.

Managers spend most of their time in face-to-face contact with others. Oral communication is quick, spontaneous and enriched by non-verbal signals. It takes place in one-to-one conversation (face-to-face), through meetings of several people or when someone addresses

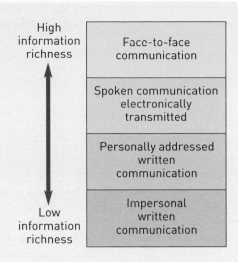

Figure 14.3 The Lengel–Daft media richness hierarchy

Source: Lengel and Daft (1988).

an audience at a conference. Management by wandering around is a widely used and effective communication technique, when managers go into the work areas and talk to employees about the issues that concern them. They gain insights into what is happening, which reports from supervisors may filter. Jim Goodnight, co-founder and chief executive of SAS, the world's largest privately held software business, with revenues in 2009 of £1.4 billion, and about 11,000 employees worldwide:

> I think it's extremely important for the chief executive to talk to anybody in the company . . . If you're surrounded by just your group of managers and that's the only people you talk to, then you [end up hearing what you want to hear] not what the truth is. You've got to have people that you know, that you can speak to in the lunch line, speak to in the elevator. (*Financial Times*, 1 February 2010).

Despite the benefits of face-to-face communication, few managers rely on it entirely. It takes time and becomes less practical as managers and staff become geographically dispersed. There is also no written record, so some prefer to combine it with a written communication confirming what was agreed. Advances in technology are helping in this area. Videoconferencing allows people to communicate face to face (and so see each others' facial expressions and gestures) without the time and cost of travel, though in many situations (such as a discussion between colleagues who know each other well), a voice-only teleconference is just as satisfactory at a fraction of the cost.

Spoken communication electronically transmitted

This is the second highest form of communication in terms of media richness. Although when we use a telephone or mobile we cannot see the non-verbal expressions or body language, we can pick up the tone of voice, the sense of urgency or the general manner of the message, as well as the words themselves. Feedback is quick so both parties can check for understanding.

Voicemail systems and answering machines can supplement telephone systems, by allowing people to record messages by both the sender and the intended receiver. Many companies use message recording systems to pass customers to the right department, by offering options to which they respond by pressing the buttons on their keypads. These systems reduce costs but often annoy customers, especially when they want to speak to a human being. Teleconference systems allow several people who are physically distant to take part in a discussion using their telephones.

Personally addressed written communication

Personally addressed written communication has the advantage of face-to-face communication in that, being addressed personally to the recipient, it tends to demand their attention. It also enables the sender to phrase the message in a way that they think best suits the reader. If both parties express their meanings accurately and seek and offer feedback, a high level of mutual understanding can be reached, which is also recorded. Even if people reach their understanding by communicating face to face, they will often follow it up with a written email, fax or letter.

Email and, more recently, social networking (more messages are now sent through social networking sites than by email) have grown rapidly to communicate within and between organisations and between individuals. They have the 'permanent record' advantage of the letter, while instant delivery allows people to complete an exchange in minutes that could have taken days. Sending them from mobiles enables people to stay in touch from wherever they are. Some disadvantages are:

- lack of body language;
- adding many recipients to the 'copy' box, leading to email overload; and
- using the technology to send unsolicited messages.

A careless email can cause conflict. An email communicates emotions as well as content (intentionally or not), and the nature of the medium (lacking the visual and verbal cues of face-to-face transactions) makes it more likely that the receiver will misunderstand these. Conversely, being able to revise a possibly inflammatory comment before sending the email might balance this.

Impersonal written communication

This is the least information rich medium – but is suitable for sending a message to many people. Newsletters and routine computer reports are lean media because they provide a single cue, are impersonal and do not encourage response.

Managers use them to send a simple message about the company and developments in it to widely dispersed employees and customers. They also use them to disseminate rules, procedures, product information and news about the company, such as new appointments. The medium also ensures that instructions are communicated in a standard form to people in different places, and that a record of the message is available. Electronic means such as emails and company websites supplement paper as a way of transmitting impersonal information. The ease with which electronic messages can be sent to large numbers of people leads to **information overload**, when people receive more information than they can read, let alone deal with adequately.

Information overload arises when the amount of information a person has to deal with exceeds their capacity to process it.

Each channel has advantages and disadvantages. If the message is to go to many people and there is a significant possibility of misunderstanding, some relatively structured written or electronic medium is likely to work best. If it is an unusual problem which needs the opinion of several other people, then a face-to-face discussion will be more effective.

In a study of 95 executives in a petrochemical company Lengel and Daft (1988) found that the preferred medium depended on how routine the topic was:

> Managers used face-to-face [communication] 88 per cent of the time for non-routine communication. The reverse was true for written media. When they considered the topics [were] routine and well understood, 68 per cent of the managers preferred . . . written modes. *(p. 227)*

Blogs and social network sites

A blog is a frequently updated, interactive website through which people can communicate (by blogging) with anyone who has access to the medium. There are at least five types:

- individual/personal – set up by individuals to share personal and family news and ideas;
- news/commentary – report, comment and interpret current events;
- advertising/promotional/customer service – communicate with potential customers;
- business/professional – insight and commentary on business and professional issues, including company practices;
- internal/knowledge management – used within companies to share information about products and projects.

Managers in many companies are actively considering how best to engage with social network sites. They represent a shift from vertical to horizontal communication on the web. Where until now most organisational communication has been transmitted downward from sender to receiver, the receivers – individual web users – now have many tools they can use to talk to each other. These consumer-focused devices hold threats and opportunities for business. Technical concerns centre on employees' use of the sites, since this can mean a loss of time and of network capacity. Employees may also post inappropriate comments about customers, or the company, on the website, which in extreme cases leads to further bad publicity. The biggest danger, however, is that managers ignore the trend, rather than thinking out how to use it positively.

Companies that want to make use of the medium take several paths. Some feature positive stories which they hope will be picked up by other sites: if they are, this makes the site more visible. Others (Dell – **www.dell.com** – is one) ask customers for ideas upon which they can then vote: Dell receives some free market research and some good publicity. Innocent Drinks (**www.innocentdrinks.com**) encourages staff and customers to share information and ideas about current projects or marketing ideas, as well as to chat socially. They can also highlight articles or other information, enabling instant access across the company. Other companies use social network sites for recruitment, identifying suitable candidates and keeping in touch with former employees. Some, like Pepsi, are starting to use Facebook to interact with customers, hoping to gain their interest and loyalty to the brand.

14.5 Communication networks

The grapevine

The grapevine is the spontaneous, informal system through which people pass information and gossip. It happens throughout the organisation and across all hierarchical levels as people meet in the corridor, by the photocopier, at lunch, on the way home. The information that passes along the grapevine is usually well ahead of the information in the formal system. It is about who said what at a meeting, who has applied for another job, who has been summoned to explain their poor results to the directors, or what orders the company has won.

The grapevine does not replace the formal system, but passes a different kind of information around – qualitative rather than quantitative, current ideas and proposals rather than agreed policies. As it is uncensored and reflects the views of people as a whole rather than of those in charge of the formal communications media, it probably gives a truer picture of the diversity of opinions within the company than the formal policies will. Nevertheless, the rumours and information on the grapevine might be wrong or incomplete. Those passing gossip and good stories of spectacular disasters in department X may also have their own interests and agendas, such as promoting the interests of department Y. The grapevine is as likely to be a vehicle for political intrigue as any of the formal systems.

The grapevine can be a source of early information about what is happening elsewhere in the organisation. This allows those affected, but not yet formally consulted, to prepare their position. Put the other way round, someone preparing proposals or plans can be quite sure that information about them will be travelling round the grapevine sooner than they expect. Sometimes it is useful to deliberately let the matter slip out and begin circulating information to be able to gauge reaction before going too far with a plan.

Communicating in groups and teams

To understand how people in a group communicate, members need to have some tools to analyse the patterns of interaction. Different tasks require different communication and Figure 14.4 illustrates two patterns. In a centralised network, information flows to and from the person at the centre, while in the decentralised pattern more of the messages pass between those in the network. If the task is simple, the centralised pattern will work adequately. An example would be to prepare next year's staff budget for the library when there are to be no major changes. The person at the centre can give and receive familiar, structured information from section heads.

If the task is uncertain the centralised structure will obstruct performance. Imagine a team is developing a new product rapidly in conjunction with suppliers and customers. Because of the novelty of the task, unfamiliar questions will arise, and the group members can only deal with these by exchanging information rapidly. If all information has to pass through a person at the centre they will not cope with the volume of queries, leading to delays.

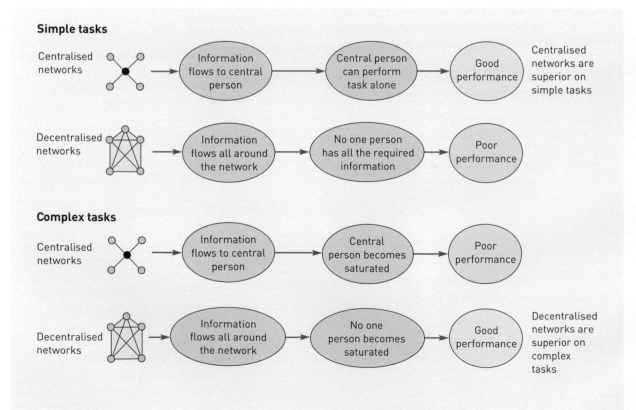

Figure 14.4 Communication structure and type of task

Source: Based on Baron and Greenberg (1997).

Communicating downwards

Managers communicate downwards when they try to co-ordinate activities of separate units. They may issue instructions or procedures about, for example:

- new policies, products or services;
- budget changes or any changes in financial reporting and control systems;
- new systems and procedures;
- new appointments and reorganisations;
- hear the views of staff.

If the downward communication inhibits comments or responses, the sender will be unclear how receivers reacted to the message. If it is unclear, people will interpret it in ways that suit them, perhaps making things worse. Managers can avoid this by checking a draft with one or two colleagues, to ensure that what it says is what they mean.

Team briefings

Team briefings are a popular way of passing information rapidly and consistently throughout the organisation – Blakstad and Cooper (1995) quote the results of a survey of 915 companies in which 57 per cent of respondents rated team briefings as the most common method of communicating with employees. Under this method senior management provides a standard message and format, and briefs the next level in the hierarchy. Those managers then brief their subordinates following the same format, and this continues down the organisation. Addressing small groups with a common structure enables managers to:

- deliver a consistent message;
- involve line managers personally in delivering the message;
- deliver the message to many people quickly;
- reduce the possible distortions by 'the grapevine';
- hear the views of staff.

Communicating upwards

Companies can install systems which encourage employees to pass on views and ideas to managers. In small organisations this is usually fairly easy as the owner-manager is likely to be close to the action and so aware of employees' ideas. As the business grows the layers of the hierarchy can easily break the flow. Unless they create mechanisms to allow information to move upwards, their boards may be acting on the wrong information.

| Management in practice | Communication failures at BP   www.bp.com   FT |

In March 2005 an explosion at BP's Texas City refinery killed 15 and injured 500 people. A US Chemical Safety Board report showed that the oil group was so intent on improving the big picture on safety – its statistics – that it missed the pointers to deeper problems. The company focused on improving compliance with procedures and reducing occupational injury rates, while leaving 'unsafe and antiquated equipment designs and unacceptable deficiencies in preventive maintenance'. Supervisors knew that key instruments did not work, or were unreliable.

Yet Don Holmstrom, the CSB investigator leading the investigation, said the poor state of the refinery was hidden in the statistics. Indeed, in 2004 the refinery had the lowest injury rate in its history, but that did not take account of catastrophic hazards or distinguish between injuries and fatalities. 'When personal safety statistics improved, the refinery leadership thought it had turned the corner', he said. 'However, existing process safety metrics and the results of a safety culture survey indicated continuing problems with safety systems and concerns about another major accident.'

Source: Adapted from Catastrophic safety risks (Sheila McNulty), *Financial Times*, 31 October 2006.

Employee opinion surveys

Some companies conduct regular surveys among their employees to gauge their attitudes and feelings towards company policy and practice. They may also seek views on current issues, or about possible changes in policy or practice. The surveys can be valuable both as a general indicator of attitudes and as a way to identify issues that need attention. Many specialists offer to conduct such surveys for companies, usually through an online, web-based system – see for example *Personnel Today* (**www.personneltoday.com**).

Suggestion schemes

These are devices by which companies encourage employees to suggest improvements to their job or other aspects of the organisation. Employees usually receive a cash reward if management accepts their idea.

Formal grievance procedures

These set out the steps to be followed when an individual or group is in dispute with the company. For example, an employee who has been penalised by a supervisor for poor time-keeping may disagree with the facts as presented or with the penalty imposed. The grievance procedure states how the employee should set about pursuing a claim for a review of the case. Similar procedures now exist in colleges and universities, setting out how a student with a grievance about their assessment can appeal against their results to successively higher levels of the institution.

Horizontal communication

Horizontal communication crosses departmental or functional boundaries, usually connecting people at broadly similar levels within the organisation. Computer-based information systems have greatly increased the speed and accuracy with which routine information can pass between departments. As a customer places an order, modern systems can quickly pass the relevant information to all the departments that will play a part in meeting it, making production a much smoother and more predictable process.

Management in practice   An online tyre service   www.blackcircles.com

Michael Welch founded Blackcircles when he was 22. Customers order their tyres online or by phone, then drive to a garage where the tyres will have been delivered ready for fitting. He claims to sell tyres for about 40 per cent less than high street retailers – being able, among other things, to stock a greater range of tyres ready for delivery than would be possible for any single garage. He has also cut his cost of acquiring a new customer from £12 in 2006 to about 12p now – mainly through alliances with bigger brands such as Tesco, the AA and Barclaycard:

> Two years ago we communicated with 400,000 potential customers through partnerships. Last year it was 4m and this year it will be 22m . . . the more communication with potential customers, the more sales we make, and the lower our cost of acquisition is – and therefore we can invest that back in the price.

Source: *Financial Times*, 8 April 2009; company website.

Much horizontal communication is about less routine, less structured problems: when different parts of the organisation co-operate on projects to introduce new products or systems, people communicate frequently. They need to pass information to each other on the current state of affairs so that each distinct unit can be ready to contribute to the project as required.

This also includes communication with other organisations – especially suppliers, customers or partners in collaborative projects. Modern technology makes it technically much easier to pass information between people irrespective of where they are – and this can be used to improve the quality of service. Organisational factors are sometimes a barrier to implementing such systems, especially functional, structural and professional boundaries.

14.6   Interpersonal skills for communication

If communication was perfect the receiver would always understand the message as the sender intended. That rarely happens, as people interpret information from their perspectives, and their words fail to express feelings or emotions adequately. Power games affect how people send and receive information, so we can never be sure that the message sent is the message received. Breakdowns and barriers can disrupt any communication chain.

Communication skills for senders

The ideas presented in this section suggest some practices which are likely to help improve anyone's interpersonal communication skill.

Send clear and complete messages

The subject, and how the sender views it, is as much part of the communication process as the message itself. The sender needs to compose a message that will be clear to the receiver, and complete enough to enable both to reach a mutual understanding. This implies anticipating how others will interpret the message, and eliminating potential sources of confusion.

Encode messages in symbols the receiver understands

Senders need to compose messages in terms that the receiver will understand – such as avoiding the specialised language (or jargon) of a professional group when writing to an outsider. Similarly, something which may be read by someone whose native language is different should be written in commonplace language, and avoid the clichés or local sayings that mean nothing to a non-native speaker.

Select a medium appropriate for the message

The sender should consider how much information richness a message requires, and then choose the most appropriate of the alternatives (such as face to face, telephone, individual letter or newsletter), taking into account any time constraints. The main factor in making that choice is the nature of the message, such as how personal it is or how likely it is to be misunderstood.

Select a medium that the receiver monitors

The medium we use greatly affects what we convey. Receivers prefer certain media and pay more attention to messages that come by a preferred route. Some dislike over-formal language, while others dislike using casual terms in written documents. Putting a message in writing may help understanding, but others may see it as a sign of distrust. Some communicate readily by email, others are reluctant to switch on their system.

Avoid noise

Noise refers to anything that interferes with the intended flow of communication, which includes multiple – sometimes conflicting – messages being sent and received at the same time. If non-verbal signals are inconsistent with the words, the receiver may see a different meaning in your message from what was intended. Noise also refers to the inclusion in a message of distracting or minor information that diverts attention from the main business. Communication suffers from interruptions that distract both parties and prevent the concentration essential to mutual understanding.

Communication skills for receivers

Pay attention

Busy people are often overloaded and have to think about several things at once. Thinking about their next meeting or a forthcoming visit from a customer, they become distracted and do not attend to messages they receive. In face-to face communication the sender will probably notice this, and that will affect how they respond.

Be a good listener

Communication experts stress the importance of listening. While the person sending the message is responsible for expressing the ideas they want to convey as accurately as they can, the receiver also has responsibilities for the success of the exchange. Listening involves the active skill of attending to what is said, and gaining as accurate a picture as possible of the meaning the sender wished to convey.

Many people are poor listeners. They concentrate not on what the speaker is saying but on what they will say as soon as there is a pause. Six practices for effective listening are:

1 **Stop talking**, especially internal, mental, silent chatter. Let the speaker finish. It is tempting in a familiar situation to complete the speaker's sentence and work out a reply. This assumes you know what they are going to say: you should instead listen to what they are actually saying.
2 **Put the speaker at ease** by showing that you are listening. The good listener does not look over someone's shoulder or write while the speaker is talking. If you must take notes, explain what you are doing. Take care, because the speaker will be put off if you look away or concentrate on your notes instead of nodding reassuringly.
3 **Remember that your aim is to understand** what the speaker is saying, not to win an argument.
4 **Be aware of your personal prejudices** and make a conscious effort to stop them influencing your judgement.
5 **Be alert to what the speaker is not saying** as well as what they are. Very often what is missing is more important than what is there.
6 **Ask questions.** This shows that you have been listening and encourages the speaker to develop the points you have raised. It is an active process, never more important than when you are meeting someone for the first time – when your objective should be to say as little and learn as much as possible in the shortest time.

Be empathetic

Receivers are empathetic when they try to understand how the sender feels, and to interpret the message from the sender's perspective, rather than from their own position.

A junior member of staff may raise a problem with a more senior colleague, which perhaps reflects their inexperience. The senior could be dismissive of the request, indicating that the subordinate ought to know how to deal with the situation. An empathetic response would take account of the inexperience, and treat the request with a greater understanding.

Activity 14.2 — What does 'communication' mean in management?

Having read the chapter, make brief notes summarising the communication issues evident in the organisation you chose for this activity.

- What effects (if any) did the communication practices you studied have on the behaviour of their targets? (See Section 14.2.)
- How did those involved try to communicate with others? (See Section 14.3.)
- Did they consciously vary the way they communicated, depending on the circumstances? (See Section 14.4.)
- Which examples did you find of the communication practices described in Sections 14.5 and 14.6?

Compare what you have found with other students on your course.

Summary

1 **Explain the role of communication in managing**

- People at all levels of an organisation need to add value to the resources they use, and to do that they need to communicate with others – about inputs, the transformation process and the outputs. It enables the tasks of planning, organising, leading and controlling.
- It also enables managers to perform their informational, decisional and interpersonal roles.

2 **Identify and illustrate the elements and stages in the communication process**

- Sender, message, encoding, medium, decoding receiver and noise.

3 **Use the concept of information richness to select a communication channel**

- In descending order of information richness, the channels are
  - face-to-face communication
  - spoken communication electronically transmitted
  - personally addressed written communication
  - impersonal written communication.

4 **Compare the benefits of different communication networks**

- Centralised networks work well on structured, simple tasks, but are less suitable for complex tasks as the centre becomes overloaded.
- Decentralised networks work well on complex tasks, as information flows between those best able to contribute. On simple tasks this is likely to cause confusion.

5 **Outline some essential interpersonal communication skills**

- Send clear and complete messages.
- Encode messages in symbols the receiver understands.

- Select a medium appropriate for the message.
- Include a feedback mechanism in the message.
- Pay attention.
- Be a good listener.

Review questions

1 Explain why communication is central to managing.
2 Draw a diagram of the communication process, showing each of the stages and elements. Then illustrate it with a communication episode you have experienced.
3 How does feedback help or hinder communication?
4 What is non-verbal communication, and why is it important to effective communication?
5 What do you understand by the term 'information richness', and how does it affect the choice of communication method?
6 What is team briefing?
7 Name three practices that can improve interpersonal communication skill.

Further reading

Whetten, D. A. and Cameron, K. S. (2010), *Developing Management Skills* (8th edn), Prentice Hall International, Upper Saddle River, NJ.

Extended discussion of interpersonal communication skills, with useful exercises.

Dimbleby, R. and Burton, G. (2006), *More Than Words: An introduction to communication* (4th edn), Routledge, London.

Accessible introduction to all aspects of communication.

Finkelstein, S. (2003), *Why Smart Executives Fail: and what you can learn from their mistakes*, Penguin, New York.

Fascinating account of the sources of communication failure in public and private organisations.

Weblinks

These websites have appeared in, or are relevant to, the chapter:

www.cisco.com
www.dell.com
www.innocentdrinks.com
www.bp.com
www.personneltoday.com
www.blackcircles.com
www.facebook.com/facebook

Visit two of the sites, or others which interest you, and navigate to the pages dealing with recent news, press or investor relations.

- In what ways is the company using the website to communicate information about inputs, outputs and transformation processes?
- Is it providing a one-way or a two-way communication process?

 **WWW** Annotated weblinks, multiple choice questions and other useful resources can be found on **www.pearsoned.co.uk/boddy**

Case study   Facebook www.facebook.com/facebook

In early 2011 Facebook was the world's largest online social network with over 600 million users, who post over 65 million updates a day and share more than 4.0 billion pieces of content every week. It has expanded far beyond its American roots, with 70 per cent of users being outside the United States. In 2010, a survey reported that more than 100 million people were actively using the site from their mobile devices – up from 65 million only six months previously.

Mark Zuckerburg founded the site which allows users to create a profile page and make links with friends and acquaintances. Other students at Harvard claim the original idea, and that they hired Zuckerburg to write the programs: lawyers are on the case.

About 800 employees work at the main Facebook campus at Palo Alto, California, but in May 2007 it introduced Facebook Platform, which allows independent software developers to create applications for Facebook. Over 1 million now do so, creating an online directory with over 500,000 apps (games, music, photo-sharing tools and many more), which serve to attract further users to the site. That leaves the company's developers free to concentrate on innovations that encourage even more sharing.

Like other social network sites, Facebook has benefited from a continuing fall in the cost of hardware needed to store and process data. They have also been able to use free, open-source software to build systems that scale quickly and easily. And they have built some unique solutions to cope with rapid growth. The firm's software engineers built a system called MultiFeed that searches databases near-instantly for relevant news from a person's friends. This has allowed the network to add many millions of new users without damaging its ability to provide a constant stream of up-to-date news to people's pages.

Paying attention to the quality of the site's technology is believed to be one of the reasons why Facebook had, by 2010, become the dominant global social network (available in 70 languages, and also as Facebook Lite, a stripped-down version that is popular in countries without fast broadband connections).

This popularity is such that some smartphone makers (such as HTC) now feature Facebook as an integral feature of their handsets. The handsets have a dedicated button that takes users straight to the Facebook site, where they can see video and photo

© Kim Komenich/San Francisco Chronicle/Corbis

alerts, and 'live' home screens that update as friends post messages and pictures on the site. One smartphone manufacturer said:

> **Facebook is now much bigger than a social network – it's a communication platform.**

Mr Zuckerberg's goal is to connect as much of the world's population as possible via the network and then to persuade them to use it as their main way into the internet. He is so keen to realise his vision that he is said to have turned down offers to buy the company which would have made him an instant billionaire.

In May 2009 a Russian investment firm, Digital Sky technologies invested $200 million in return for a 1.96 per cent shareholding in the business. Microsoft had earlier bought a 1.6 per cent stake. In 2011, Facebook raised a further $500 million from enthusiastic private investors. It plans to sell shares in the business to the public in 2012, and many financial analysts expect that this will value the company at $50 billion – though others are more cautious.

Facebook developers pay much more attention to the 'plumbing' that connects people with each other than to the content that flows through it. Matt Cohler, a former employee explains:

> The people at Facebook are essentially utilitarians. They want to give people the very best technology for sharing and then get out of their way.

That technology is so good that people are willing to continue using the site as it grows. The firm has what some have called a hacker-type culture which has produced the innovations that have made the service so addictive. Mike Schroepfer, Facebook's head of engineering, says that one of its mottos is 'move fast and break stuff'. What matters is getting fresh products out to users quickly, even if they do not always work as intended. To help generate new ideas it gives staff plenty of freedom to try out their ideas on Facebook's site.

The company competes fiercely with Google for talented staff (it employs many former 'Googlers') and offering free food encourages employees to work long hours. Many are in their early 20s, new from college where they were often up all night. Facebook continues this tradition with its 'hack-athons', where employees are invited to work all night on programs and other tasks that are not part of their normal assignments. The kitchen staff participate by creating new dishes that are available throughout the night.

Food is a lubricant that keeps the innovation machine running. A Facebook spokeswoman said:

> The thinking for us is, what can we do to make our employees' lives easier so they can focus on the job? They come into work and don't have to worry about packing lunch.

Sources: *New York Times*, 27 May 2009, 25 December 2009, *Economist*, 30 January 2010; *Financial Times*, 10 February 2011; *Independent*, 21 May 2011.

Questions

1 What examples are there here of people communicating to (directly or indirectly) build Facebook?

2 If you use Facebook (or similar), what changes, if any, has it made to the way you communicate? (Refer to Sections 14.1 and 14.2.)

3 What evidence is there in the case about the communication channels which Facebook developers use? How does the company encourage this? (Refer to Section 14.4.)

4 Section 14.4 describes communication channels: into which of these categories does a message on Facebook fit?

5 How might Facebook affect the way people use communication networks? (Refer to Section 14.5.)

CHAPTER 15
WORKING IN TEAMS

Learning outcomes

When you have read this chapter you should be able to:

1 Distinguish the types of teams used by organisations
2 Use a model to analyse the composition of a team
3 Identify the stages of team development and explain how they move between them
4 Identify specific team processes and explain how they affect performance
5 Evaluate the outcomes of a team for the members and the organisation
6 Outline contextual factors that influence team performance
7 Use ideas from the chapter to comment on the management issues in the Cisco case study

Activity 15.1   What does 'working in teams' mean in management?

Before reading the chapter, write some notes on what you think 'working in teams' means in management.

Choose the organisation or people who may be able to help you learn about the topic. You may find it helpful to discuss the topic with a manager you know, or reflect on an activity you have managed.

- Identify a situation where someone has created a team to do a task, and describe it briefly.
- How did those involved try to ensure team members had a suitable balance of skills?
- Did the team members change the way they worked together as the task progressed?
- What did team members do or say which helped or hindered them in the task?

Keep these notes as you will be able to use them later.

15.1   Introduction

Managers at Cisco use teams extensively to deliver products and services to customers. The people with the skills it needs for a particular project are widely dispersed around the organisation but need to work together to meet customer needs. Teams bring them together during a project – they then disperse and re-form in different combinations to work on other projects. The company also uses teams for internal development projects, where staff from several functions and countries work together to deal with pressing management problems, such as improving a financial or marketing system.

People at work have always developed loyalties among small groups of fellow workers, especially in some industries where work was formally organised in small, self-managing teams (Trist and Bamforth, 1951). This continues in organisations where teams, rather than isolated individuals, do the work. This is most evident in research-based organisations such as Microsoft or GlaxoSmithKline, where scientists or engineers from different disciplines come together to work on a common project and disband when it is complete. There are many cross-organisational teams – such as when BAA (**www.baa.com**) created integrated teams from suppliers, consultants, contractors and their own staff during the construction of Terminal 5 at London's Heathrow Airport. Teams bring people from relevant disciples and backgrounds to solve difficult problems.

Forming a team does not mean it will work well. Despite their popularity with managers and team members, the evidence about teams and performance is mixed. Some, such as those at Cisco, work to very high standards and levels of achievement: others fail to add value, wasting time and other resources. Figure 15.1 helps to explain this variation, by showing teams as an open system. The inputs are mainly the team members – so one factor in performance is its composition. Members need to learn to work together collaboratively to deliver their task: the processes they use will help or hinder them in that. They also work within a context of internal and external factors – which also help or hinder the outcomes of the team's work.

The chapter begins by outlining the types of team you may encounter, which leads to a definition. You will then learn about the composition of teams, their stages of development and internal processes and how context affects performance. A final section examines the outcomes of teams for members and the organisation.

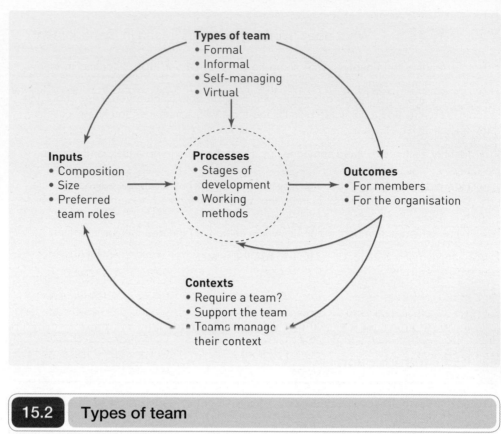

Figure 15.1
A model of team
performance

15.2   Types of team

A team's function affects the risks and opportunities which the members will encounter, so it is useful to be aware of these.

Functions of teams

Hackman (1990) identified seven team functions, and Table 15.1 summarises the risks and opportunities associated with each.

Formal teams

A **formal team** is one that management has deliberately created to perform specific tasks to help meet organisational goals.

Managers often create **formal teams** as they shape the organisation's basic structure, and allocate specific tasks to them. Vertical 'teams' consist of a manager and their subordinates within a single department or function. The manager and staff in the treasury department of a bank, or the senior nurse, nursing staff and support staff in a unit of the Western General Hospital, are formally constituted into (possibly several) vertical teams. So is a team leader and their staff in a BT call centre. In each case, senior managers created them to support their goals.

Horizontal teams consist of staff from roughly the same level, but from different functions. The Cisco EMF team is an example, being brought together to release the new software. In Hackman's typology, task forces would be an example: often called cross-functional teams, these deal with non-routine problems (such as to develop a new product) that require several types of professional knowledge.

Informal groups

An **informal group** is one that emerges when people come together and interact regularly.

Informal groups are a powerful feature of organisational life. They develop as day-to-day activities bring people into contact with each other – who then discover common sporting or social interests. Work-related, informal groups arise when people in different formal groups

Table 15.1 Hackman's classification of team types and their associated risks and opportunities

Type	Risks	Opportunities
Top management teams – to set organisational directions	Underbounded; absence of organisational context	Self-designing; influence over key organisational conditions
Task forces – for a single unique project	Team and work both new	Clear purpose and deadline
Professional support groups – providing expert assistance	Dependency on others for work	Using and honing professional expertise
Performing groups – playing to audiences	Skimpy organisational supports	Play that is fuelled by competition and/or audiences
Human service teams – taking care of people	Emotional drain; struggle for control	Inherent significance of helping people
Customer service teams – selling products and services	Loss of involvement with parent organisation	Bridging between parent organisation and customers
Production teams – turning out the product	Retreat into technology; insulation from end users	Continuity of work; able to hone team design and product

Source: Hackman (1990), p. 489.

exchange information and ideas: staff using a software package may begin to pass around problems or tips. Staff in separate departments dealing with a customer may start passing information to each other to avoid misunderstandings, even though this is not part of the specified job. Sometimes people use their initiative and volunteer to work together on an organisational problem which they believe is affecting performance – and then suggest their proposed solution to managers.

Informal groups sometimes develop in opposition to management – as when people believe they are being unfairly treated, and come together from across groups to express a common dissatisfaction with current policy.

Self-managing teams

Self-managing teams are responsible for a complete area of work and operate without close supervision. Members are responsible for getting the work done, but have a high degree of autonomy in how they do it: they manage themselves, including planning and scheduling tasks and assigning tasks among the members. They are also likely to establish the pace of work, make operating decisions, work out how to overcome problems and manage quality. Sometimes they play a big role in selecting new employees to work in the team.

A **self-managing team** operates without an internal manager and is responsible for a complete area of work.

Virtual teams

Modern communications technologies enable and encourage people to create teams in which the members are physically distant for most of the time, even though they are expected to deliver high-quality collective outcomes. Many of the teams in Cisco are like this. The growing internationalisation of management means that people frequently work in **virtual teams** drawn from different nations and cultures, as well as working remotely, raising new teamwork challenges.

Virtual teams are those in which the members are physically separated, using communications technologies to collaborate across space and time to accomplish their common task.

Virtual teams use computer technology to link members together, communicating via technologies such as email, videoconferencing and online discussion through a website. They can perform all the functions of a team that is located in the same place, but lack the face-to-face interaction and discussion which helps to smooth working relationships. While virtual teams can sometimes use the fact that they are in different time zones to their advantage, Saunders *et al.* (2004) examine some of the challenges. At a superficial level, differences of time zone create problems of managing different working hours, lunch breaks and holiday times. More fundamental difficulties arise from contrasting visions of time between cultures and nations – such as whether it is an objective or subjective notion, or differences in the meaning of words such as 'soon' or 'urgent'.

While virtual teams bring expertise together without the expense of travel, they require careful management to ensure the benefits of team working are retained. Practices include ensuring that some regular (or at least initial) face-to-face contact occurs, and that members resolve issues of roles, working methods and conflict management.

15.3 Crowds, groups and teams

The types of team described in the previous section were not just random collections of people. A crowd in the street is not usually a team: they are there by chance, and will have little if any further contact. What about the staff in a supermarket or in the same section of a factory? They are not a crowd: they have some things in common, and people may refer to them as a team. Compare them with five people designing some software for a bank, each of whom brings distinct professional skills to their collective discussions of the most suitable design, or with seven students working together on a group assignment. They have a **structure** to handle the whole process, work largely on their initiative, and move easily between all the tasks, helping each other as needed.

In normal conversation, people typically use the words 'group' and 'team' as if they mean the same thing, and this book follows that usage. Katzenbach and Smith (1993) define a **team** as 'A small number of people with complementary skills who are committed to a common purpose, performance goals, and working approach for which they hold themselves mutually accountable' (p. 45). This suggests some criteria against which to evaluate features of a team.

> **Structure** is the regularity in the way a unit or group is organised, such as the roles that are specified.

> A **team** is 'a small number of people with complementary skills who are committed to a common purpose, performance goals, and approach for which they hold themselves mutually accountable' (Katzenbach and Smith, 1993).

Small number

Groups of more than about 12 people find it hard to operate as a coherent team. It becomes harder to agree on a common purpose and the practicalities of where and when to meet become tricky. Most teams have between two and ten people – with between four and eight probably being the most common range. Larger groups usually divide into subgroups.

Complementary skills

Teams benefit from having members who, between them, share *technical*, *functional* or *professional skills* relevant to the work. A team implementing a networked computer system will require at least some members with appropriate technical skills, while one developing a new strategy for a retailer will contain people with strategic or marketing skills.

Second, a team needs people with *problem-solving* and *decision-making skills*. These enable members to approach a task systematically, using appropriate techniques such as SWOT or five forces analysis. Finally, a team needs people with *interpersonal skills* to hold it together. Members' attitudes and feelings towards each other and to the task change as work continues.

This may generate irritation and conflict, so someone needs the skill to manage these disagreements constructively.

Common purpose

Teams cannot work to a common purpose unless members spend time and effort to clarify and understand it. They need to express it in clear performance goals upon which members can focus their time and energy. A common purpose helps members to communicate, since they can interpret and understand their contributions more easily.

Common approach

Teams need to decide how they will work together to accomplish their purpose. This includes deciding who does what, how the group should make and modify decisions and how to deal with conflict. The common approach includes integrating new members into the team, and generally working to promote mutual trust necessary to team success.

Mutual accountability

A team cannot work as one until its members willingly hold themselves to be collectively and mutually accountable for the results of the work. As members do real work together towards a common objective, commitment and trust usually follow. If one or more members are unwilling to accept this collective responsibility, the team will not become fully effective.

15.4 Team composition

Figure 15.1 shows that teams depend first on inputs – especially their composition. In a mechanical sense, team composition includes size and membership. Is there an acceptable balance of part-time and full-time members? Are the relevant functions represented? Equally important is whether members have the right skills and ways of working to form an effective team – Uhl-Bien and Graen (1998) warn:

> Although cross-functional teams may be highly effective if implemented correctly (for instance, staffed with strong team players), if implemented incorrectly (staffed with independently focused self-managing professionals) they may . . . harm organizational functioning. (p. 348)

As people work in a team they behave in ways that reflect diverse perspectives, skills and interests, which lead them to take on distinctive roles. A group needs a balance of these, so a task for the team leader is to do what they can to shape its composition. Two useful ideas are the distinction between task and maintenance roles, and Belbin's research on team roles.

Task and maintenance roles

Some people focus on the task, on getting the job done, on meeting deadlines. Others put their energy into keeping the peace and holding the group together. Table 15.2 summarises the two.

Teams need both roles, and skilful project managers try to ensure this happens.

Table 15.2 Summary of task and maintenance roles

Emphasis on task	Emphasis on maintenance
Initiator	Encourager
Information seeker	Compromiser
Diagnoser	Peacekeeper
Opinion seeker	Clarifier
Evaluator	Summariser
Decision manager	Standard setter

Meredith Belbin – team roles

Meredith Belbin and his colleagues systematically observed several hundred small groups while they performed a task, and concluded that each person in a group tends to behave in a way that corresponds to one of nine distinct roles. Some people were creative, full of ideas and suggestions. Others were concerned with detail, ensuring that the team dealt with all aspects and that quality was right. Others spent their time keeping the group together. Table 15.3 lists the nine roles identified in Belbin (1993). Belbin observed that winning teams had members who fulfilled a balance of roles that was different from the less successful ones.

Table 15.3 Belbin's team roles

Role	Typical features
Implementer	Disciplined, reliable, conservative and efficient. Turns ideas into practical actions
Co-ordinator	Mature, confident, a good chairperson. Clarifies goals, promotes decision-making, delegates well
Shaper	Challenging, dynamic, thrives on pressure. Has the drive and courage to overcome obstacles – likes to win
Plant	Creative, imaginative, unorthodox – the 'ideas' person who solves difficult problems
Resource investigator	Extrovert, enthusiastic, communicative – explores opportunities, develops contacts, a natural networker
Monitor–evaluator	Sober, strategic and discerning. Sees all options, judges accurately – the inspector
Teamworker	Co-operative, mild, perceptive and diplomatic. Listens, builds, averts friction, calms things – sensitive to people and situations
Completer	Painstaking, conscientious, anxious. Searches out errors and omissions. Delivers on time
Specialist	Single-minded, self-starting, dedicated. Provides scarce knowledge and skill

Source: Based on Belbin (1993).

Winning teams had an appropriate balance, such as:

- a capable co-ordinator;
- a strong plant – a creative and clever source of ideas;
- at least one other clever person to act as a stimulus to the plant;
- a monitor–evaluator – someone to find flaws in proposals before it was too late.

Ineffective teams usually had a severe imbalance, such as:

- a co-ordinator with two dominant shapers – since the co-ordinator will almost certainly not be allowed to take that role;
- two resource investigators and two plants – since no one listens or turns ideas into action;
- a completer with monitor–evaluators and implementers – probably slow to progress, and stuck in detail.

Belbin did *not* suggest that all teams should have nine people, each with a different **preferred team role**. His point was that team composition should reflect the task:

> The useful people to have in a team are those who possess strengths or characteristics that serve a need without duplicating those that are already there. Teams are a question of balance; what is needed is not well-balanced individuals but individuals who balance well with one another. In that way human frailties can be underpinned and strengths used to full advantage. (Belbin, 1981, p. 77)

Trainers use the model widely to enable members to evaluate their preferred roles. They also consider how the balance of roles within a team affects performance. Some managers use it when filling vacancies. A personnel director joined a new organisation and concluded that it employed few 'completer–finishers'. Management started initiatives and programmes but left them unfinished as they switched to something else. She resolved that in recruiting new staff she would try to bring at least one more 'completer–finisher' to the senior team.

Preferred team roles are the types of behaviour that people display relatively frequently when they are part of a team.

Management in practice	Using Belbin's roles in film-making teams

Hollywood had experienced a shift from long-term jobs to short-term project teams. With their highly skilled, freelance staff who come together for a brief period to carry out specific tasks and then disband, film making offers a model for the future of work in the wider world. Angus Strachan has been using Belbin's model to help film directors manage expensive production teams more effectively:

> Managing film teams requires a mature coordinator who can handle creative people with delicate egos and strong opinions . . . A good unit production manager is a strong monitor–evaluator, someone who can carefully analyse the overall situation and make the big calls. The second assistant director needs to be a strong completer–finisher, passing on accurate information that enables the unit production manager to keep abreast of the situation . . . A successful assistant director also needs to be a good communicator and organizer who has the flexibility to adjust schedules – in Belbin's terms to take on the resource investigator role.

Source: Angus Strachan, 'Lights, camera, action', *Personnel Management*, 16 September 2004, pp. 44–46.

However, there is little evidence that managers deliberately use the model when forming teams from existing staff – they typically choose members on criteria of technical expertise, departmental representation, or who is available. How the team processes will work is a secondary consideration. This is understandable, but in doing so, managers make the implicit assumption that people will be able and willing to cover roles if one seems to be lacking. Whether managers use the theory or not, it implies that anyone responsible for a team may find the work goes better if they put effort into securing the most suitable mix of members.

Team performance is affected by how they progress through distinct stages of development, and by the team processes they establish.

15.5   Stages of team development

Putting people into a team does not mean they perform well immediately, and some never perform well. Members of a team need to trust each other, which develops as they do their work, learn about each other and how they can work well together. This develops their mutual trust. Tuckman and Jensen (1977) developed a theory that groups potentially pass through five stages of development. Figure 15.2 shows these.

Forming

Forming is the stage at which members choose, or are told, to join a team. They come together and begin to find out who the other members are, exchanging fairly superficial information about themselves, and beginning to offer ideas about how the group should work. People are trying to make an impression on the group and to establish their identity with the other members.

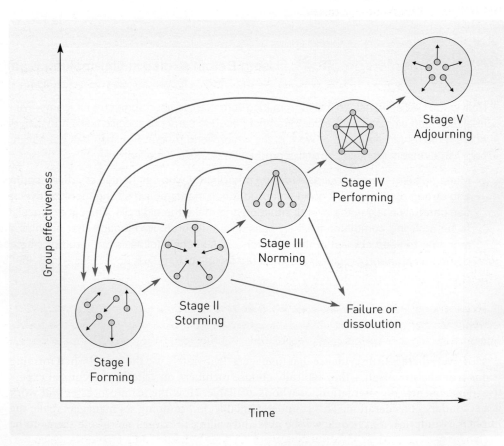

Figure 15.2
Modified model of the stages of team development

Storming

Conflicts may occur at the storming stage, so it can be an uncomfortable time for the group. As the group begins the actual work members begin to express differences of interest that they withheld, or did not recognise, at the forming stage. People realise that others want different things from the group, have other priorities and, perhaps, have hidden agendas. Different personalities emerge, with contrasting attitudes towards the group and how it should work. Some experience conflicts between the time they are spending with the group and other duties. Differences in values become clear.

Some groups never pass this stage. There may be little open conflict and members may believe the group is performing well – but may be deluding themselves. If the group does not confront disagreements it will remain at the forming or storming stage and will do no significant work. Performance depends on someone doing or saying something to move the group to the next stage.

Norming

Here the members are beginning to accommodate differences constructively and to establish adequate ways of working together (see Section 15.6). They develop a set of shared norms – expected ways of behaving – about how they should interact with each other, how they should approach the task, how they should deal with differences. People create or accept roles so that responsibilities are clear. The leader may set those roles formally or members may accept them implicitly during early meetings. Members may establish a common language to guide the group and allow members to work together effectively.

Performing

Here the group is working well, gets on with the job to the required standard and achieves its objectives. Not all groups get this far.

Adjourning

The team completes its task and disbands. Members may reflect on how the group performed and identify lessons for future tasks. Some groups disband because they are clearly not able to do the job, and agree to stop meeting.

A team that survives will go through these stages many times. As new members join, as others leave, as circumstances change, new tensions arise that take the group back to an earlier stage. A new member implies that the team needs to revisit, however briefly, the forming and norming stages to ensure the new member is part of the team and understands how they are expected to behave. A change in task or a conflict over priorities can take a team back to the storming stage, from which it needs to work forward again. Figure 15.2 develops Tuckman and Jensen's original (linear) progression through the stages to show this more iterative progress.

15.6   Team processes

Effective teams, often with the help of skilled team coaches (Hackman and Wageman, 2005), develop working methods, or team processes, that help them to accomplish their tasks. These include developing a common approach, understanding categories of communication, and observing team practices.

Common approach

A primary outcome of an effective 'norming' stage is that members agree both the administrative and social aspects of working together. This includes deciding who does which jobs,

Table 15.4 Five tips for effective meetings

Meetings are likely to succeed if:	Meetings are likely to fail if:
• they are scheduled well in advance	• they are fixed at short notice (some members will be absent)
• they have an agenda, with relevant papers distributed in advance and invite additions at the start	• they have no agenda or papers (no preparation, lack of focus, discussion longer)
• they have a starting and finishing time and follow prearranged time limits on each item	• they are of indefinite length (discussion drifts), time is lost and important items are not dealt with (delay, and require a further meeting)
• decisions and responsibilities for action are recorded and circulated within 24 hours	• decisions lack clarity (misunderstanding what was agreed, delay, reopening issues)
• they keep subgroups or members of related teams informed of progress	• the team is not aware of work going on in other teams that is relevant to its work

what skills members need to develop, and how the group should make and modify decisions. In other words the group needs to agree the work required and how it will fit together. It needs to decide how to integrate the skills of the group and use them co-operatively to advance performance.

The common approach includes supporting and integrating new members into the team. It also includes practices of remembering and summarising agreements. If a group works together on these tasks it promotes mutual trust and constructive debate. Groups need to spend as much time on developing a common approach as they do on developing a shared purpose.

Team members need to control their meetings effectively – whether face to face or at a distance. That involves ensuring they are conducted in a way that suits the purpose of the task, without participants feeling they are being manipulated. Table 15.4 is an example of the advice widely available to managers about effective and ineffective meetings.

Categories of communication

Group members depend on information and ideas from others to help them perform the group task; a useful skill is to be able to identify the kind of contribution that people make (Chapter 14 illustrated patterns of group communication), and whether this helps the group to manage the task. To study and learn how people behave in groups we need a precise and reliable way to describe events. There are many such models, each suited to a purpose: Table 15.5 illustrates one such list, implying that how members divide their time between these categories will affect performance. A group that devotes most of its time to proposing ideas and disagreeing with them will not progress far. A more effective group will spend more time proposing and building – probably because members have developed better listening skills.

Observing the team

Observation is the activity of concentrating on how a team works rather than taking part in the activity itself.

Members can develop the skill of assessing how well a team is performing a task. There are many guides to help them do this, and anyone can develop their ability to **observe** groups

Table 15.5 Categories of communication within a group

Category	Explanation
Proposing	Putting forward a suggestion, idea or course of action
Supporting	Declaring agreement or support for an individual or their idea
Building	Developing or extending an idea or suggestion from someone else
Disagreeing	Criticising another person's statement
Giving information	Giving or clarifying facts, ideas or opinions
Seeking information	Seeking facts, ideas or opinions from others

by concentrating on this aspect rather than on the **content** of the immediate task. They work slightly apart from the team for a short time and keep a careful record of what members say or do. They also note how other members react, and how that affects the performance of the team. At the very least, members can reflect on these questions at the end of a task:

Content is the specific substantive task that the group is undertaking.

- What did people do or say that helped or hindered the group's performance?
- What went well during that task, which we should try to repeat?
- What did not go well, which we could improve?

With practice, skilled members of a team are able to observe what is happening as they work on the task. They can do this more easily and powerfully if they focus their observations on certain behaviour categories, such as those shown in Table 15.5 – but suited to the purpose of the observation.

Teams have outcomes that can benefit the members, the organisation – and perhaps both.

15.7   Outcomes of teams (1) – for the members

The Hawthorne studies described in Chapter 2 showed that a supportive work group had more influence on performance than physical conditions. People have social needs that they seek to satisfy by being acknowledged and accepted by other people. This can be done person to person (mutual acknowledgement or courteous small-talk on the train), but most people are also members of several relatively permanent co-operative groups. These provide an opportunity to express and receive ideas and to reshape one's views by interacting with others. Acceptance by a group meets a widely held human need.

Mary Parker Follett observed the social nature of people and the benefits of co-operative action. She saw the group as an intermediate institution between the solitary individual and the abstract society, and believed that it was through the group that people organised co-operative action:

> Early psychology was based on the study of the individual; early sociology was based on the study of society. But there is no such thing as the 'individual', there is no such thing as 'society'; there is only the group and the group-unit – the social individual. Social psychology must begin with an intensive study of the group, of the selective processes which go on within it, the differentiated reactions, the likenesses and the unlikenesses, and the spiritual energy which unites them. (Quoted in Graham, 1995, p. 230)

Likert (1961) developed this theme of organising work in groups. He observed that effective managers encouraged participation by group members in all aspects of the job, including

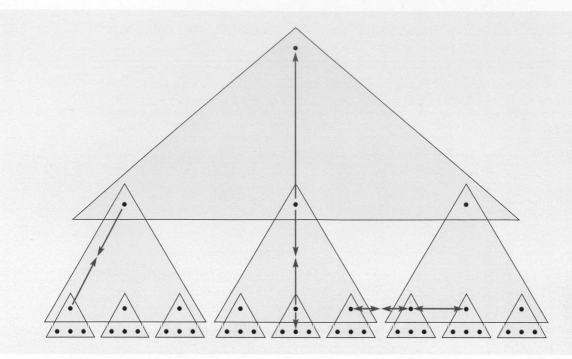

Figure 15.3 Likert's principle of supporting relationships

Note: The arrows indicate the linking-pin functions, both vertical and horizontal – as in cross-functional teams.

Source: Adapted from Likert (1967), p. 50.

setting goals and budgets, controlling costs and organising work. Individuals became members of a team who were loyal to each other and who had high levels of team-working skills. Likert maintained that these groups were effective because of the *principle of supportive relationships*. He agreed with Maslow that people value a positive response from others, which helps to build and maintain their self-esteem. Social relationships at work serve the same purpose, especially when people spend much of their time in a group. Managers in effective organisations had deliberately linked such groups to ensure people had overlapping membership of more than one group: 'each person . . . is a member of one or more functioning workgroups that have a high degree of group loyalty, effective skills of interaction and high performance goals' (Likert, 1961, p. 104). Figure 15.3 shows the principle.

These ideas continue to influence practice. Katzenbach and Smith (1993) observed that members of a team who surmount problems together build trust and confidence in each other. They benefit from the buzz of being in a team, and of 'being part of something bigger than myself'.

On the other side, some teams subject their members to what Barker (1993) refers to as a system of **concertive control**, which arose as workers negotiated a consensus among themselves.

Concertive control is when workers reach a negotiated consensus on how to shape their behaviour according to a set of core values.

Barker studied an electronics company whose founders decided to organise the 90 manufacturing staff into self-managing teams, each being responsible for part of the product range and able to decide how they would work together. An example of concertive control occurred when the late delivery of components meant that a team would miss a delivery target. To recover the position the team agreed to work late and also to accommodate the external commitments of some members. This set a precedent for the way members would behave:

> I work my best at trying to help our team to get stuff out the door. If it requires overtime, coming in at five o'clock and spending your weekend here, that's what I do. (Barker, 1993, p. 422)

Members rewarded those who conformed by making them feel part of the team. They punished those who had 'bad' attitudes. The norms evolved from a loose system that workers 'knew' to a tighter system of objective rules. One explained:

> Well we had some disciplinary thing. We had a few certain people who didn't show up on time and made a habit of coming in late. So the team got together and kind of set some guidelines and we told them, you know, 'If you come in late the third time and you don't do anything to correct it, you're gone.' That was a team decision that this was a guideline that we follow. (p. 426)

Barker concludes that creating autonomous or self-managed teams does not free workers from the obligation to follow rules. Instead:

> They must invest a part of themselves in the team: they must identify strongly with their team's values and goals, its norms and rules. (pp. 435–36)

15.8	Outcomes of teams (2) – for the organisation

Teams can bring together various professional and technical skills beyond those of any individual. In health and social care there is a growing interest in team working to deliver care, since patients frequently have conditions which require inputs from several professions – health, social work, and housing, for example. More generally, the ability to deal with customer requirements requires the exchange of ideas among those from different professions, which is made easier if they are part of a recognised team:

> When representatives from all of the relevant areas of expertise are brought together, team decisions and actions are more likely to encompass the full range of perspectives and issues that might affect the success of a collective venture. Multidisciplinary teams are therefore an attractive option when individuals possess different information, knowledge, and expertise that bear on a complex problem. (Van der Vegt and Bunderson, 2005, p. 532)

Management in practice   Teamwork pays off at Louis Vuitton   www.vuitton.com

The French company, Louis Vuitton, is the world's most profitable luxury brand. The success of the company is attributed to a relentless focus on quality, a rigidly controlled distribution system and ever-increasing productivity in design and manufacture. Eleven of the 13 Vuitton factories are in France: although they could move to cheaper locations, management feels more confident about quality control in France.

Employees in all Vuitton factories work in teams of between 20 and 30 people. Each team, such as the ones at the Ducey plant in Normandy, works on one product, and members are encouraged to suggest improvements in manufacturing. They are also briefed on the product, such as its retail price and how well it is selling, says Stephane Fallon, who runs the Ducey factory. 'Our goal is to make everyone as multi-skilled and autonomous as possible', says team leader Thierry Nogues.

The teamwork pays off. When the Boulogne Multicolour (a new shoulder bag) prototype arrived at Ducey, workers who were asked to make a production run discovered that the decorative metal studs caused the zipper to bunch up, adding time and effort to assembly. The team alerted factory managers, and technicians quickly moved the studs a few millimetres away from the zipper. Problem solved.

Source: *Business Week*, 22 March 2004.

Teams can bring both high efficiency and high quality jobs by:

- providing a structure within which people work together;
- providing a forum in which issues can be raised and dealt with – rather than being ignored;
- enabling people to extend their roles, perhaps increasing responsiveness and reducing costs;
- encouraging acceptance and understanding by staff of a problem and the solution proposed; and
- promoting wider learning by encouraging reflection, and spreading lessons widely.

Teams can also obstruct performance. The discussion which generates new perspectives takes longer than it would take for an individual to make a decision. If a team strays onto unrelated issues or repeats a debate it loses time. Opponents of a decision can prolong discussion to block progress. Some teams allow one member to dominate, such as the formal leader in a hierarchical organisation, where people do not challenge those in authority. It may also be a technical expert who takes over, when others hesitate to show their lack of knowledge or to ask for explanations. In either case, the group will probably be a dissatisfying and unproductive experience. It may produce a worse result, and be more costly, than if one person had dealt with the issue.

Some research has shown the effects of teams on organisational-level variables like output or profitability. For example, Glassop (2002) found that companies with self-managing work groups and quality circles (another form of team work) reported higher productivity and lower staff turnover than those with no team structures.

Others analyse the performance of the team itself – Hackman (1990) proposed three criteria against which to evaluate this, shown in Table 15.6.

Research with 27 teams of different types led Hackman to propose that to perform well a group must surmount three hurdles. Members must:

- be willing to exert sufficient effort to accomplish the task to an acceptable level;
- bring adequate knowledge and skill to the task;
- use group processes that are appropriate to the work and the setting.

To overcome them, Hackman suggested that a team needs both internal and external support, as the manager cannot rely only on internal team practices or personal enthusiasm. He or she should also attend to wider organisational conditions such as the availability of **team-based rewards**. If both are in place it is more likely that the group will put in the effort, have the skill and use good team processes. Table 15.7 summarises these points.

Hackman's work is especially valuable as it makes specific reference to the context within which teams work, and to the way these contextual factors affect team performance.

Team-based rewards are payments or non-financial incentives provided to members of a formally established team and linked to the performance of the group.

Table 15.6 Criteria for evaluating team effectiveness

Criteria	Description
Has it met performance expectations?	Is the group completing the task managers gave to it – not only the project performance criteria, but also measures of cost and timeliness?
Have members experienced an effective team?	Is it enhancing their ability to work together as a group? Have they created such a winning team that it represents a valuable resource for future projects?
Have members developed transferable teamwork skills	Are members developing teamwork skills that they will take to future projects?

Source: Based on Hackman (1990).

Table 15.7 Points of leverage for enhancing group performance

Requirements for effectiveness	Internal conditions	Organisational context
Effort (see Chapter 13)	Motivational structure of task	Remedying co-ordination problems and rewarding team commitment
Knowledge and skill	Team composition	Available education and training, including coaching and guidance
Group processes	Working processes that foster review and learning	Information system to support task and provide feedback on progress

Source: Based on Hackman (1990), p. 13.

Activity 15.2   What do 'teams' mean in management?

Having read the chapter, make brief notes summarising the team issues in the organisation you chose for this activity.

- What was the main function of the team? (Refer to Section 15.2.)
- How closely did it correspond to the definition in the chapter? (Refer to Section 15.3.)
- Did members have the right balance of roles and skills? (Refer to Section 15.4.)
- Comment on the teams development – can you identify the stages in the Tuckman and Jensen model? (Refer to Section 15.5.)
- Did anything that team members did or said help or hinder the completion of the task? (Refer to Section 15.6.)

Compare what you have found with other students on your course.

Summary

1 **Distinguish the types of teams used by organisations**
   - As management faces new expectations about cost and quality many see teams as a way of using the talents and experience of the organisation more fully to meet these tougher objectives.
   - Hackman's typology shows the opportunities and challenges faced by top teams, task forces, professional support, performing, human service, customer service and production teams respectively.

2 **Use a model to analyse the composition of a team**
   - Belbin identified nine distinct roles within a team and found that the balance of these roles within a team affected performance. The roles are: implementer, co-ordinator, shaper, plant, resource investigator, monitor–evaluator, teamworker, completer, specialist.

3 **Identify the stages of team development and explain how they move between them**
   - Forming, storming, norming, performing and adjourning. Note also that these stages occur iteratively as new members join or circumstances change.

4 **Identify specific team processes and explain how they affect performance**

- Effective teams develop a common approach and working methods, develop skills in several types of communications and are skilled in observation and review, enabling them to learn from their experience.

5 **Evaluate the outcomes of a team for the members and the organisation**

- Members benefit from being part of a social group, from meeting performance expectations, from experiencing an effective team, and developing transferable teamwork skills.
- The organisation can benefit from the combination of skills and professions, though the evidence of the links to organisational success are mixed.

Review questions

1 What are the potential benefits of teamwork to people and performance?

2 What types of team have you experienced?

3 Compare the meaning of the terms 'task' and 'maintenance' roles.

4 Reflect on Belbin's model of team roles, and explain how the balance of these affects the effectiveness of a team. What is your preferred role?

5 How many stages of development do teams go through? Use this model to compare two teams.

6 List the main categories of behaviour that someone observing a group may identify.

Further reading

Belbin, R.M. (1993), *Team Roles at Work*, Butterworth/Heinemann, Oxford.

An account of the experiments that led Belbin to develop his model of team roles.

Hayes, N. (2002), *Managing Teams*, Thomson Learning, London.

A lively and well-referenced account of many of the issues covered here.

Weblinks

These websites have appeared in, or are relevant to, the chapter:

www.baa.com
www.vuitton.com
www.cisco.com
www.microsoft.com
www.asos.com
www.gsk.com
www.gore.com

Each has tried to develop new approaches to using teams – encouraging staff to share ideas and experience, as well as gaining personal satisfaction from them. Try to gain an impression from the site (perhaps under the careers/working for us section) of what it would be like to work in an organisation in which teams are a prominent feature of working.

Annotated weblinks, multiple choice questions and other useful resources can be found on **www.pearsoned.co.uk/boddy**

Case study   Cisco Systems   www.cisco.com

Cisco Systems is a company at the heart of the internet. It is a leading developer and supplier of the physical equipment and software that allow digital data to travel around the world over the internet, and also provides various support services that enable companies to improve their use of the network. It was founded in 1984 by a group of scientists from Stanford University, and its engineers have focused on developing internet Protocol (IP)-based networking technologies. The core areas of the business remain the supply of routing and switching equipment, but it is also working in areas such as home networking, network security and storage networking.

Courtesy of Cisco Systems, Inc. Unauthorised use not permitted.

The company employs 34,000 staff working from 70 offices around the world, developing new systems and working with customers to implement and enhance their network infrastructure. Most projects are implemented by staff from several sites working as virtual teams, in the sense that they are responsible for a collective product but work in physically separate places.

The company created a team to co-ordinate the testing and release of a new version of Cisco's Element Management Framework (EMF), a highly complex piece of software that monitors the performance of large numbers of elements in a network. When the product was released a few months later, the members of the team were free to work on other projects. The team had eight members, drawn from four sites and three countries:

Name	Location	Role
Steve	Raleigh, North Carolina	Project co-ordinator
Richard	Cumbernauld, Scotland	Development manager
Graham	Cumbernauld, Scotland	Development engineer
Eddie	Cumbernauld, Scotland	Development engineer
Rai	Austin, Texas	Test engineer
Silvio	Austin, Texas	Test engineer
Jim	Raleigh, North Carolina	Network architect
Gunzal	Bangalore, India	Release support engineer

The role of the co-ordinator was to ensure the smooth operation of the team and to monitor actual progress against the challenging delivery schedule. The software was developed in Cumbernauld, by engineers writing the code and revising it as necessary after testing by the test engineers. They were responsible for rigorously testing all software and reporting all problems concisely and accurately to the development engineers.

The network architect has extensive knowledge of the network hardware that the software would manage, and supervised the development and testing of the software to ensure that it worked as efficiently as possible with the hardware. The release support engineer dealt with the logistics of software release, such as defining each version and ensuring deliverables are available to the manufacturing departments at the appropriate times.

Each member worked full-time on the project, though they never met physically during its lifetime. All members took part in a weekly conference call, and also a daily call attended by the co-ordinator, development manager and a member of the test team. Communication throughout the team was mainly by electronic mail, together with instant messaging.

Recalling the roles within the team, Steve said:

My job was mainly to ensure that everything in the virtual team runs smoothly – often just a matter of arranging and co-ordinating meetings, but also encouraging some kind of creative spark that'll help discussion along. Gunzal takes his time to make decisions, but when he does, he's usually correct. Eddie is very systematic in his work, and very hard working.

Another commented:

> I'd say Graham is often the one who comes up with original ideas, while Jim has an incredible range of contacts within the company, and can usually find the right person to go to. Rai is very precise in everything he does and it's very important that he receives the correct information from the engineers. If they don't explain something properly he's good at going back to ask for more information.

Members of the team commented on the way the team developed. A common issue was the problem of scheduling meetings:

> I've always found in virtual teams that when the team is first formed it isn't really getting any serious work done (unless we're under severe time pressure), it's about getting everyone together so they at least have some knowledge of the others in the team. (Steve)

Another said:

> It was strange when we first started working together, because we didn't push on and get any testing or fixing done straight away. Steve was really pushing for us all to spend a few hours in conference calls getting to know each other and how we were all going to work together. We took our time to get into the actual work that was required. (Graham)

Other reflections included:

> I had a few discussions with Steve . . . he wanted us to spend most of our time in conference meetings with the rest of the team, while my engineers already had a good understanding of the work that was needed and just wanted to get on with it. But Steve is the team lead so we had to go along with his approach. (Richard)

> It's weird having to form such a close relationship with someone [when] you don't even know what they look like. But as we're using IM [Instant Messaging] just about every day you get used to it. I think you sometimes have to make an extra effort to talk directly to people, just to keep the relationship going. Sometimes it'd be easier for me to email Rai, but I phone him, just so we can have a bit of a chat. (Eddie)

> It means you have to be a bit more careful when it comes to communication. Most of the time you have to use email and IM to discuss issues, which means there can be misunderstandings if you're not careful. When you interact in person you use things like facial expression and hand gestures – none of these are available when e-mailing so you have to state your arguments more clearly. (Jim)

Source: Communication from members of the project team

Questions

1 What challenges would you expect a team that never meets will face during its work?

2 In what ways may it need to work differently from a conventional team? (See Section 15.2.)

3 What kinds of team does Cisco use, in Hackman's typology? (See Section 15.2.)

4 Which of the Belbin roles can you identify among the members of the team? (See Section 15.4.)

5 Are any of the roles missing, and how may that have affected team performance? (See Section 15.4.)

6 Relate this account to the stages of team development – what examples of forming, storming and norming does it contain? (See Section 15.5.)

PART 6
CONTROLLING

Introduction

Any purposeful human activity needs some degree of control if it is to achieve what is intended. From time to time you check where you are in relation to your destination. The sooner you do this, the more confident you are of being on track. Frequent checks ensure you take corrective action quickly to avoid wasting effort and resources.

An owner-manager can often exercise control by making a personal observation then using experience to decide on corrective action. As the organisation grows, and work activities become dispersed, it becomes progressively more difficult for managers to understand whether progress is on track.

They therefore use a range of systems and techniques to monitor progress and maintain direction towards their objectives. Chapter 16 introduces operations management as a source of control and discusses the concept of controlling the quality of products and services. Chapter 17 explores control in more detail by investigating how organisational performance is monitored and adjusted to ensure the enterprise meets its objectives.

CHAPTER 16
MANAGING OPERATIONS AND QUALITY

Learning outcomes

When you have read this chapter you should be able to:

1 Define the term 'operations management'
2 Describe the transformation process model of operations management
3 Show how operations can contribute to the competitiveness of the organisation
4 Identify different forms of operational activity
5 Explain the meaning of quality and how operations can enhance it
6 Use ideas from the chapter to comment on the management issues in the Zara case study

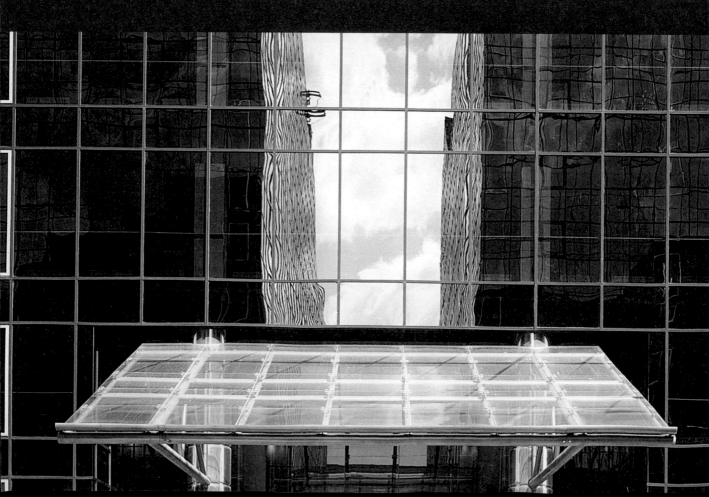

Activity 16.1	What does 'operations and quality' mean in management?

Before reading the chapter, write some notes on what you think 'operations and quality' means.

Choose the organisation or people who may be able to help you learn about the topic. You may find it helpful to discuss the topic with a manager you know, or reflect on an activity you have managed.

- Identify a situation in which someone was dealing with an operations or quality issue, and describe it briefly.
- Did it concern a physical product or an intangible service?
- Can you describe briefly how production was organised?
- How did they try to measure, and improve, the quality required?

Keep these notes as you will be able to use them later.

16.1 Introduction

Zara is a fashion company that relies heavily on good operational systems. It is an integrated business in that it does most of the work itself to design, manufacture, distribute and sell the products. It relies on quick turnaround times on most products, which it sells in relatively large quantities. Its garments must be available on time to catch the latest fashion trend and must also be of a consistent quality to ensure customers return to buy again. Two factors are critical to Zara's success – the creative ability to catch the mood of the customer with interesting and exciting designs; and the operational capability to design, manufacture and distribute goods quickly and efficiently. Neither factor can exist alone – it needs creative, novel design AND reliable operational processes.

Any organisation hoping to add value to resources depends on good operations to deliver what the customer expects, at the quality they expect. When Apple launched the iPad in 2010, and sold hundreds of thousands of them in the first few weeks, it was only able to do so because of the robust operational system which it has built. Many factors contribute to Ryanair's success – and one of these is the operations systems that enable the rapidly growing fleet to fly more flights each day than longer-established airlines are able to do. If you receive hospital treatment, the outcomes depend not only on skilled staff, but on processes that ensure that facilities, equipment, staff and supplies are available when required.

Good process and practice have always been important in production and manufacturing areas, but service organisation also use operations management. The chapter begins by introducing the basic concepts and language of operations management, which you can use in any sector of the economy. It will then explain what a 'product' is in manufacturing and services respectively. It will show what operations managers do, and concludes by exploring the meaning of quality and how to manage it.

16.2 What is operations management?

System and process

We live in a world of systems, which shape our personal lives, our transport, our security, our work. Our lives are continually 'managed' within the system that is our society. Such systems bring safety and economy by removing many random events and allowing better use of time and energy. Organisations also benefit from consistency and predictability. Creating effective systems is the central challenge of operations management.

The operations challenge

operations management is all of the activities, decisions and responsibilities of managing the production and delivery of products and services.

Slack *et al.* (2010) define **operations management** as the activities, decisions and responsibilities of managing the production and delivery of products and services.

The way to do this is to implement systems and processes that are:

- repeatable – can be done over and over again;
- consistent – produce the same result every time;
- reliable – do not break down randomly.

The standard of performance required against each criterion is growing because of:

- increased competition in cost and quality as a result of globalisation and the development of new technologies, especially in information and communications;
- more complex activities as more sophisticated customers expect more differentiated products with higher functionality;
- tighter environmental regulation to control pollution; and
- legislation on employment and working conditions.

Processes therefore need also to be:

- efficient – producing most output for least input;
- competitive – at least as good as others who are doing similar things; and
- compliant with the legislation that governs the industrial environment.

The transformation process

The **transformation process** refers to the operational system that takes all of the inputs; raw materials, information, facilities, capital and people and converts them into an output product to be delivered to the market.

The first step in achieving an efficient, process-based organisation is to understand the work of the organisation as a **transformation process** which turns inputs (or resources) into the outputs that are the product.

Figure 16.1 (which builds on Figure 1.1) models the transformation process. It shows inputs entering the operational processes of the organisation which transform them into an output – the product or service to be sold. There are two types of input:

Transforming resources, that do the transformation:

- facilities – buildings, equipment/tools and process technology;
- staff – people involved in the transformation process working to complete activities, operate machinery or maintain the equipment; and
- capital which is needed to buy materials and pay for the facilities and staff.

Transformable resources, that become the product:

- materials such as metal, wood or plastic, which become parts such as nuts and bolts, structures, or printed circuit boards, which can be built into the final product such as cars, buildings or phones. In moving through the transformation process the physical form of input materials changes to create the final product.
- information such as design specifications, assembly instructions, scientific concepts or market intelligence. Information is used in two ways. First, it can be used to inform the transformation process – such as design specifications or diagrams. Second, the information itself can become part of the output – such as turning raw financial data into published accounts.

The transformation process includes a feedback system which monitors performance and notes deviations from normal. There are bound to be variations in (for example) material

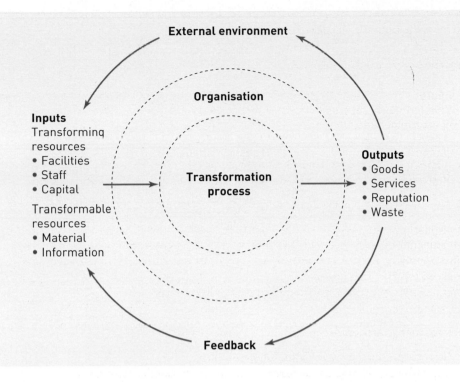

Figure 16.1
The transformation process

quality and the condition of equipment, so this monitoring is essential to ensure the process performs in a repeatable, reliable and consistent manner. There are two broad types of process feedback:

- Feedback that is internal to the transformation process ensures that it results in a consistent product. This feedback is generally quantitative in nature and monitors key aspects of the product or process, e.g. the number of units produced, dimensions such as weight of a chocolate bar or measurements such as temperature of an oven. Any deviation in the measurements indicates that the process is not performing correctly and requires some remedial action.
- Feedback that is external to the transformation process ensures the product is accepted by the market and satisfies the customer. This type of feedback can be either qualitative – how the customer enjoyed the product, or quantitative – how many people buy it.

The nature of products

It is common to associate the term 'product' with something tangible such as a physical artefact that can be seen, held and used. The term is often applied to intangibles such as financial services, holidays or healthcare – a mortgage is as much a product as a car or a watch. It is designed for a purpose, sold, paid for and used. Operations managers see the 'production' process of these intangible products in the same way as the production process of tangible products – inputs, processes, outputs and feedback loops.

In restaurants, the product we buy is the experience of the meal. Although we think of eating-out as a service, it is a combination of the physical product that is the meal and the service experience that attentive staff and the ambience of the surroundings provided (or not).

The distinction between physical product and service delivered is, therefore, becoming blurred. Few physical products are sold without some form of service package. For operations managers this means that the transformation process model applies as much to restaurants,

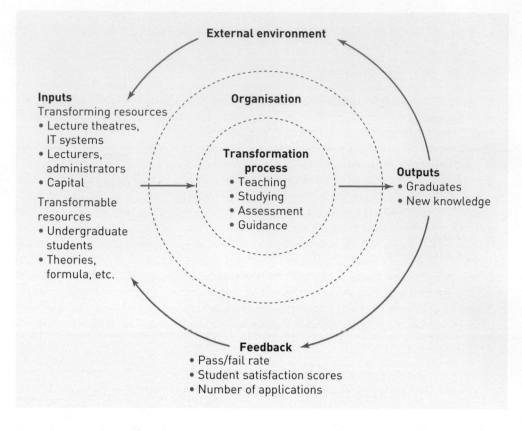

Figure 16.2
An educational
transformation

banks, schools and hospitals as it does to factories. Figure 16.2 illustrates the transformation process in education.

Service delivery and the customer

While the transformation process takes place in producing goods and delivering services, there are some differences. The main one is that in service delivery the customer is present during the process, and is, indeed, one of the raw materials that is transformed – a student from non-graduate to graduate, a customer with untidy hair to one with styled hair, a patient with a disease to one who is cured. The presence of the customer has these consequences:

- Randomness – in manufacturing most of the work is done in a factory closed to interference by the customer. The presence of the customer in services means the process needs to be able to handle the randomness caused by the customer's unpredictable behaviour.
- Heterogeneity – randomness leads to inconsistencies in the service delivered, as each customer will have a slightly different experience: a dining experience will be affected by the atmosphere created by other customers.
- Intangibility – the nature of the service experience makes it difficult to ensure that a process is delivering a quality service. The experience combines tangible, objective features of a physical product and the intangible, subjective dimensions of a service.
- Perishability – services are difficult to store. If a hotel room is empty this revenue is permanently lost, as the next night is a different revenue generating opportunity. The experience of going to a concert cannot be wrapped and mass produced. The CD of the concert cannot match the actual experience.

16.3   The practice of operations management

The birth of process management

When we walk into a McDonald's we enter a process for queuing, are served by someone who is not a trained waiter, and purchase a meal cooked by someone who is not a skilled chef. It has been designed to particular standards of quality; is the product of a process of manufacture; and the presentation of the items we choose will be exactly the same regardless of where or when it is bought. McDonald's is the ultimate in systemisation.

Process design is associated with Fredrick Winslow Taylor (see Chapter 2) and his five principles of management. In the late nineteenth and early twentieth centuries the United States was experiencing rapid industrialisation. Entrepreneurs were creating complex organisations and many of the world's best-known companies were taking shape – like ESSO, General Motors and Ford. Skilled workers were scarce, even basic language skills were difficult to find. Taylor and his idea of scientific management solved this problem by making the attributes of the worker mostly irrelevant. Taylor and his supporters believed in 'rationalism' – the view that if one understands something, one should be able to state it explicitly and write a rule for it. Taylor's objective in applying rules and procedures to work was to replace uncertainty with predictability. Applying this thinking to manufacturing would lead to reliability, consistency and repeatability.

> The **craft system** refers to a system in which the craft producers do everything. With or without customer involvement they design, source materials, manufacture, sell and perhaps service. The craft system is based on workers with the embodied knowledge, skill and experience to carry out all necessary activity.

Management in practice   Disney's 'production' of cartoons

At the age of 21, Walter Elias 'Walt' Disney left the midwest, moved to Hollywood and opened his own movie studio. In *The Magic Kingdom*, Steven Watts describes Walt Disney's attempts to apply the techniques of mass production to the art of making cartoons. Disney had great admiration for Henry Ford and his achievments and introduced an assembly line at the Disney studio. Like all production lines this system employed a rigorous division of labour. Instead of drawing entire scenes, artists were given narrowly defined tasks, meticulously sketching and inking characters while supervisors looked on with stopwatches timing how long it took to complete each activity.

During the 1930s this 'production' system resembled that of an automobile plant. Hundreds of young people were trained and fitted into the machine for 'manufacturing' entertainment. While this was labelled the 'Fun Factory' the working conditions on the assembly line often led to employee dissatisfaction and strikes.

Source: Watts (2001).

Before Taylor, work was based on the **craft system** where individuals controlled the work process because their skill and knowledge told them what to do and how to do it. This left managers and owners who were trying to implement **factory production** with a level of control over the process of manufacture similar to that which a beekeeper has over the productive capacity of a hive of bees. To take full advantage of the possibilities of mechanisation and the factory system, all of the activities within a particular transformation process had to be fully understood by those who controlled the organisation.

Although Taylor conducted the experiments almost exclusively in the steel industry, his ideas have endured to become the basis of operations management today. Henry Ford developed the ideas to create the production line system that came to dominate manufacturing, and have since spread to many parts of the service sector all over the world.

While Taylor's principles had a profound and positive effect on efficiency, they also had negative effects, especially by deskilling workers and disrupting the craft system (see Chapters 2 and 13 for more on this). It meant that the worker no longer had the knowledge

> **Factory production** is a process-based system that breaks down the integrated nature of the craft worker's approach and makes it possible to increase the supply of goods by dividing tasks into simple and repetitive processes and sequences which could be done by unskilled workers and machinery on a single site.

or skill to ensure the manufacture of a quality product. This depended more on the quality of the process of manufacture than on the skill of the workman: this meant that the design of the process was vital, as a poorly designed process would lead to a poor product.

Management in practice   **Seeking the best** www.sunseeker.com

From modest beginnings in a shed, to a workforce of 2500, modern shipyards and world-beating technology, Sunseeker is the iconic brand supplying yachts to the very rich. While the products are at the cutting edge of quailty and technology, the company remains committed to craftsmanship. Although much of the work in design and manufacturing is done by computers and machinery, Sunseeker claims the basis of their success is the skill of the artisans who form and polish the woods, metals and glass that produce the work of art that is a Sunseeker yacht.

The production process is a subtle blend of machine-produced fabrication using the best that process management can offer, and hand-assembly and detail finishing where the human influence on product quality cannot be matched.

Sunseeker admit that you can build a quality boat without the traditonal craftsmanship they rely on – but, they say, 'it wouldn't be Sunseeker'.

Source: Company website.

Operations strategy

operations strategy is
the pattern of decisions
that shapes the long-
term capability of the
operation.

Chapter 8 looked at managing strategy as the process of setting an organisation's direction. As operations is the means of delivering the products which represent that direction, the enterprise also needs an **operations strategy**. Slack *et al.* (2010) define operations strategy as the pattern of decisions which shape the long-term capability of an operation – so that it supports the corporate strategy. It clarifies the primary purposes and characteristics of the operations processes and designs the systems to achieve these.

Management in practice   **Linn Products** www.linn.co.uk

Linn Products was established in 1972 by Ivor Tiefenbrun. Born in Glasgow, he was passionate about two things – engineering and listening to music. When he couldn't buy a hi-fi good enough to satisfy his needs he decided to make one himself.

In 1972, Linn introduced the Sondek LP12 turntable, the longest-lived hi-fi product still in production anywhere in the world and still the benchmark by which all turntables are judged. The Linn Sondek LP12 turntable revolutionised the hi-fi industry, proving categorically that the source of the music is the most important component in the hi-fi chain. Linn then set out to make the other components in the hi-fi chain as revolutionary as the first, setting new standards for performance over the years with each new product.

Today, Linn is an independent, precision-engineering company uniquely focused on the design, manufacture and sale of complete music and home theatre systems for customers who want the best. Linn systems can be found throughout the world in royal residences and on-board super-yachts.

At Linn operations is an integrated process, from product development through to after-sales service. All aspects of Linn's products are designed in-house and all the key processes are controlled by Linn people. Linn believe everything can be improved by human interest and attention to detail. So the same person builds tests and packs a complete product from start to finish. They take all the time necessary to ensure every detail is correct.

Only then will the person responsible for building the product sign their name and pack it for despatch. Every product can be tracked all the way from that individual to the customer, anywhere in the world. Linn systems are sold only by selected specialist retailers who have a similar commitment to quality products and service.

Source: Company website

The 4 Vs of operations

Although all operations systems transform inputs into outputs, they differ on four dimensions:

- Volume: how many units are produced of a given type of product. Consumer goods are examples of high-volume production, supported by investment in specialised facilities, equipment and process planning.
- Variety: how many types (or versions) of a product have to be manufactured by the same facility. Fashion houses and custom car makers use more hand tools and highly skilled staff to enable the flexibility required to make a variety of unique products.
- Variation in demand: how the volume of production varies with time. Facilities at holiday resorts have to cope with vast differences in throughput depending on the time of year.
- Visibility: the extent to which customers see manufacturing or delivery process. This applies mainly to the service sector where the presence of the customer is vital to the process.

16.4   Operations processes

The 4 Vs define an operations strategy – managers must decide on the type of operation it will be – what volume, how much variation, how will volume vary with time, and how visible? Only then can they begin to design the detailed processes.

Production systems

For production operations, these decisions translate into two main considerations: volume of production and flexibility of the operations system – its ability to cope with changes in volume and/or variety. Hayes and Wheelwright (1979) propose that a single manufacturing system cannot efficiently produce different volumes of a variety of products. If a high volume is required consistently and reliably, then the manufacturing system must be arranged to produce only one product. If several products are required then a more flexible system is required to cope with their multiple requirements. Hayes and Wheelwright categorise four types of production operation – see Figure 16.3.

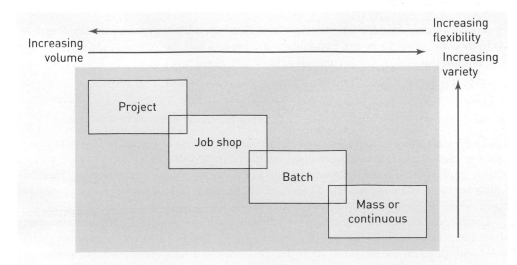

Figure 16.3
The product–process matrix

Source: Adapted and reprinted by permission of Harvard Business Review. Based on Hayes and Wheelwright (1979). © 1979 Harvard Business School Publishing Corporation; all rights reserved.

Project systems

These exist at the low-volume end of the spectrum often making only single units. This entails many interdependent parallel operations of long duration to achieve an output. Examples include construction projects such as oil rigs, dams and skyscrapers, in which thousands of operations accumulate to complete one product over several years. The defining feature of this system is that the product is built in one place with all the resources brought to it and all the activities going on around it. The product will not move until it is complete, and sometimes not at all. Examples are Crossrail or the Google website and algorithm.

Job-shop systems

These are also relatively low-volume producing special products or services to customer specifications with little likelihood that any product will be repeated often. In a manufacturing context a tool room that makes special tools and fixtures is a classic example, as is a tailor who makes made-to-measure clothes to customer requirements. Such low-volume systems tend to use general-purpose equipment manned by highly skilled personnel. They exhibit a high degree of flexibility but have high unit costs. Examples would be Sunseeker Yachts or a Cisco network infrastructure for a client.

Batch operations

These are possibly the most common systems in use today. Many different products are produced at regular or irregular intervals. One of the distinctive features of such systems in comparison to job-shop systems is that, since orders are repeated from time to time, it becomes worthwhile to spend time planning and documenting the sequence of processing operations, employing work study techniques, providing special tooling and perhaps some automation. There will be a mix of skilled, semi-skilled and unskilled labour in this type of system. Nokia's assembly plants are an example of this.

Mass production and continuous flow manufacturing

This type is used where demand for a single product is sufficiently high to warrant the installation of specialised automatic production lines. With their high rates of output and low manning levels, unit costs are typically very low. Such systems generally have little flexibility. Where the entities produced are discrete items such as cars or mobile phones, the term 'mass production' is used, where the entity is not discrete such as chemicals like petroleum or other substances such as cement then the term 'continuous production' is used. BP is an example.

Service systems

In service systems the product–process matrix does not adequately cater for the fourth V: visibility – the presence of the customer in the process and the potential for diversity and randomness this brings. Three concepts help to distinguish types of service delivery:

- **contact time** – how long the customer is present;
- **customer interaction** – how much the customer can intervene in the process; and
- **customisation** – how much the service can vary to suit the needs of the customer.

Customer interaction is not the same as contact time. A lecture to a large class is high in 'contact' but comparatively low in 'interaction': so high duration of contact does not always mean a more interactive service. Organisations with a high degree of both interaction and customisation are categorised as professional services. Those which have a low degree of interaction and customisation are categorised as mass services.

The purpose of such a classification is to allow operations managers to decide how systems should be set up to deliver the type of service required. This will also vary between organisations with different markets and strategies: processes in a fee-paying school, for example, would look different from those in a state school, as they differ in class sizes, available support staff and the amount of extra-curricular activities.

Professional services

These are high contact operations where customers spend a lot of time in the process. They provide high levels of customisation and are adaptable to individual customer's needs. As a result the operational system relies on skilled and knowledgeable people rather than high levels of automation. Typical examples of these are Hiscox Insurance or the NHS.

Service shops

These offer lower levels of customer contact and less customisation to deal with larger volumes of customers with similar needs. Examples include most restaurants and hotels, high street banks and many public services. Essentially, the customer is buying a standard service which may be slightly adapted to individual needs. Staff are part of the process, often having limited skills and knowledge, with less discretion as they work within a defined process. Examples would be Starbucks, HMV or IKEA.

Mass services

These provide standardised customer transactions, very limited contact time and little or no customisation: the emphasis on automation and repetition. Staff will be low skilled and follow set procedures much like the staff on a production line, and the processes may be highly automated. Typical mass services include supermarkets, call centres and mass transport systems. Staff in a railway station sell tickets, but have no discretion to offer customised journeys or make decisions beyond that specified process. Examples would be Ryanair or Tesco.

16.5   The main activities of operations

Providing goods and services to a customer depends on five key operations activities, and these provide a useful way of describing and analysing an organisation's operations system (Sprague, 2007). These activities are:

- capacity
- standards
- materials
- scheduling
- control.

None of these activities operates alone, but they combine to form an operations system.

Capacity

Capacity is the ability to yield an output – it is a statement of the ability of the numerous resources within an organisation to deliver to the customer. Defining capacity depends on identifying the main resources required to deliver a saleable output – staff, machinery, materials and finance. Capacity is limited by whichever resource is in shortest supply – a hospital's capacity to conduct an operation will be determined by some minimum number of specifically competent surgeons, nurses and related professionals. In service organisations, all aspects of capacity may be visible to the customer – they can see the quality of staff and the state of the physical equipment and resources.

Standards

Standards relate to either quality or work performance. Quality standards are embedded in the specification of the product or service delivered to the customer. Work performance standards enable managers to estimate and plan capacity by providing information on the time it takes to do something. One of the advantages which low-cost airlines have established is that the time it takes them to turn round an aircraft between landing and take-off is much lower than for conventional airlines. This enables them to fly more journeys with each aircraft – significantly increasing capacity at little cost.

Materials

A vital aspect of the operations function is to ensure an adequate supply of the many material resources needed to deliver an output. Holding stocks of materials, called inventory, is expensive – it ties up working capital, incurs storage costs and in changing markets there is a risk that stocks become outdated because of a change in model. Too much material can be as problematic as too little. Materials management is particularly important in manufacturing systems where all labour costs are invested in the product itself. In service settings, most material is simple and is usually consumed by the customer during the service process.

Scheduling

This is the function of co-ordinating the available resources by time or place – specifying which resources need to be available and when in order to meet demand. It begins with incoming information about demand and its likely impact on capacity. Service, productivity and profitability depend on matching supply with demand. Capacity management generates supply; scheduling links demand with capacity. It can be carried out over several time periods. Aggregate scheduling is done for the medium term, and is closely associated with planned levels of capacity: as airlines plan their fleets, which they do several years ahead, they make judgements about both their capacity and the likely demand (translated into frequency of flights on particular routes). Master scheduling deals with likely demand (firm or prospective orders) over the next few months, while dispatching is concerned with immediate decisions, for example about which rooms to allocate to which guests in a hotel.

Control

Control is intended to check whether the plans for capacity, scheduling and inventory are actually working. Without control, there is little point in planning, as there is no mechanism then to learn from the experience. There are generally four steps in the control process:

- setting objectives – setting direction and standards;
- measuring – seeing what is happening;
- comparing – relating what is happening to what was expected to happen; and
- acting – taking short-term or long-term actions to correct significant deviations.

Only through control can immediate operations be kept moving towards objectives, and lessons learned for future improvements.

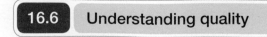

16.6 Understanding quality

What is quality?

In addition to the factors that govern the design of effective and efficient operations systems, features of the product or service that is being delivered must also be considered – especially the attention to pay to quality.

In some sectors of a market, consumers pay little attention to quality – such as local transport, basic household cleaning products or services such as fast food. To them the price will be paramount, and many will regard the cheapest as being the best. The price the customer is charged is governed largely by the cost of production, which in turn is largely driven by the efficiency of the operation. Therefore if low cost is important the operational processes – how they are sequenced, the automation and tooling and the people who work within them – must all be designed with low cost in mind. This may mean compromising on the quality of the product by offering a basic service or product as opposed to a more comprehensive or functional one.

In many other areas, quality is a much more significant factor in a customer's purchase decision. The challenge is that **quality** appears difficult to quantify as it depends on the product, the application and the subjective views of the person making the assessment. As Crosby (1979) wrote:

> The first erroneous assumption is that quality means goodness, or luxury or shine, or weight. The word 'quality' is used to signify the relative worth of things in such phrases as 'good quality', bad quality … 'Each listener assumes the speaker means what he or she, the listener, means by the phrase' … This is precisely the reason we must define quality as conformance to requirements if we are to manage it. If a Cadillac conforms to the requirements of a Cadillac then it is a quality car, if a Pinto conforms to the requirements of a Pinto then it is a quality car. Don't talk about poor quality or high quality talk about conformance and non-conformance. (p. 14)

Quality is conformance to customer requirements.

Crosby's proposal moves the definition of quality from a term that is nebulous and difficult to define to a set of more tangible measures. Six generic features (applying to goods and services) help to define quality in terms of what customers expect:

- **Functionality** – what the product does. Where price is less of a consideration, products that do more may be more attractive. This is especially true with technology-based products such as the iPhone where functionality is the prime consideration in choice: users see a product that does more as being of higher quality than one that does less.
- **Performance** – how well it does what it is meant to do. This element will feature more strongly in higher value 'statement' products such as a Porsche car where top speed and acceleration are considered important. A product that is faster, more economical, stronger or easier to use will be seen as higher quality than others which are not. A higher performance product is seen as a higher quality product.
- **Reliability** – the consistency of performance over time. Are the promises made to the customer honoured correctly and in the same way over many occasions? A more reliable product is seen as a higher quality product.
- **Durability** – how robust it is. This may feature more on products that are used a lot such as tools and equipment or products that operate in a harsh environment. Climbing equipment needs to be resistant to breakage. A more durable product is seen as a higher quality product.
- **Customisation** – how well the product fits the need. This is more relevant in products where additional features may be added to the core functions in products such as a mobile phone, or in financial services. The more a product or service fits exactly to a customer's need the higher quality it is seen to be.
- **Appearance** – how the product looks. This is important not only to convey the correct image such as a well-decorated house or a highly polished car, but also where appearance affects the utility of the product such as a website: a clear layout will be a major factor in how easy it is to use. A product that looks good is considered a higher quality product.

The customer's perception of quality will combine some or all of these factors: each contributes (or detracts from) the customer's view of the product.

Additional dimensions of service quality

All of the elements mentioned apply to both products and services and are commonly labelled the 'tangibles'. In service operations intangible features affect perceptions of quality:

- **Responsiveness** – willingness to help a customer and provide prompt service. While applicable to all service encounters, this element is most powerful in a less structured service environment where there is more opportunity for the customer to request something beyond the normal scope of the operation. A high-class restaurant may be expected to be more responsive than a fast-food outlet where the customer would not think to request an alteration to the meal on offer.
- **Assurance** – ability of the operation to inspire confidence. This element is most easily illustrated in provision of professional services: in a dental surgery the ambience of the surroundings, the equipment and the knowledge and expertise of the staff make the customer feel secure.
- **Empathy** – understanding and attentiveness shown to customers. Here the focus is mainly on the skills of the staff, their awareness of others and ability to communicate effectively. This is most easily seen in relation to the emergency services where empathising with the victim is both a key feature of the service experience and a critical factor in the effective performance of the task.

Order-winning and order-qualifying criteria

A good way to determine the relative importance of each quality element is to distinguish between order-winning criteria and order-qualifying criteria (Hill, 1993).

- Order-winning criteria are features that the customer regards as the reason to buy the product or service. Improving these will win business.
- Order-qualifying criteria will not win business, but may lose it – if they are not met they will disqualify the product or service from consideration.

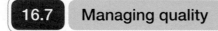

16.7   Managing quality

Quality depends on operational systems in place. Theory and techniques about managing quality were developed first in the manufacturing sector, but are now also used in the service sector.

In manufacturing, craftspeople tend to have pride in their work and continuously strive to improve their mastery of the craft. During the evolution of the factory system the craft system suffered as management subdivided the work process into smaller tasks performed by different people. This had two detrimental effects on quality. First, no single person was responsible for the whole process, so the pride in work that was evident in the craft system and was the basis of quality was removed. Second, craft skills were eroded and the consequence of this was that the capability of the individual to build quality into a product was lost. In essence, process management removed quality assurance from the remit of production staff, in effect taking the responsibility for producing quality products away from manufacturing workers. To remedy this situation attempts were made to 'build' quality into the process with more and more detailed and comprehensive processes used for the manufacture of each product. This, however, had only limited success.

The problem of production quality was not fully grasped until the mid to late twentieth century with pioneers such as Juran (1974), Deming (1988) and Feigenbaum (1993), working to develop philosophies and methods. Although developed in the West, it was the Japanese who had most success as they applied the lessons widely and conscientiously. They recognised the fundamental truth of craft production, which is that the person who performs the transformation is the best person to ensure quality. The Japanese quality revolution was therefore based on placing the responsibility for quality with the worker. History has thus come full circle, with individuals taking pride in doing quality work and striving to make regular improvements in the production process.

Although there were many people involved in the search for quality and many systems developed, the principles are best encapsulated in the system of **Total Quality Management (TQM)**. This advocates that a constant effort to remove waste adds value. Some of these wastes are obvious – scrapped material and lost time through equipment failure – but other wastes come through bad systems or poor communications and may be more difficult to find and measure. Progressive, small improvements reduce costs as the operational process uses resources more effectively. Crosby (1979) introduced the idea that 'quality is free': it is getting it wrong that costs money.

In contrast to the scientific management approach, modern writers propose that quality management should not be separated from production: everyone is responsible for contributing to quality. Methods used include team working, brainstorming techniques and simple statistical process controls (Oakland, 1994).

Thinking about quality at the design stage brings important benefits. Choices here should incorporate ideas and information from as many insiders, customers and suppliers as is sensible. Such processes capture the prevention and 'right first time' ideals and create opportunities to save cost and time. Waste minimisation is the goal – waste being the use of resources that do not add value for the customer. Note that customers are not the only stakeholders. Management may be able to justify an activity not directly required by a direct customer – such as environmental and legal obligations.

> **Total Quality Management (TQM)** is a philosophy of management that is driven by customer needs and expectations and focuses on continually improving work processes.

Quality systems and procedures

While it is relatively simple to understand the elements that make up quality and the philosophy behind it, operationalising it by implementing a system to embed quality into all that the organisation does is a different matter. A quality management system consists of the organisational structure, responsibilities, procedures, processes and resources for implementing quality management. Dale (2007) proposes that:

> The purpose of a quality management system is to establish a framework of reference points to ensure every time a process is performed the same information, methods, skills and controls are used and applied in consistent manner. (p. 280)

The documentation which makes up the quality system has three levels:

1 Company quality manual – a basic document that provides a concise summary of the quality management policy, strategy and system together with how it supports the company objectives and organisational structure.
2 Procedures manual that describes the function, structure and responsibilities of each department.
3 Detail work instructions, specifications, standards and methods which support the processes.

While setting up a quality system is relatively straightforward, achieving its effective implementation requires some additional elements.

- A clear quality strategy that supports the company strategic objectives – this is necessary to provide the direction that keeps the company quality programme in line with operational strategy.
- Top management support – the top management must understand and believe in the benefits of doing things right, promote these at all times, communicate the principles of quality development and maintain a clear idea of what quality means for the operation.
- Team-based approach – these days everyone must work together to achieve the quality goals.
- Investment in training – changes in attitudes, work practice and skills are key, therefore the achievement of quality throughout the organisation is very much reliant on the development of quality people.

> ### Activity 16.2   What does 'operations and quality' mean in management?
>
> Having read the chapter, make brief notes summarising the operational and quality issues evident in the organisation you chose for this activity.
>
> - Which of the production system outlined in Section 16.4 did it use?
> - Can you give examples of each of the operations activities? (Refer to Section 16.5.)
> - Which dimensions of quality did they pay particular attention to? (Refer to Section 16.6.)
> - How did they attempt to manage quality? (Refer to Section 16.7.)
>
> Keep these notes as you will be able to use them later.

Summary

1 **Define the term operations management**

- Operations management is the activities, decisions and responsibilities of managing the production and delivery of products and services.
- This includes responsibility for people and process and product.

2 **Describe the transformation process model of operations management**

- Transformation process is the organisational system that takes inputs:
  - Facilities
  - Staff
  - Finance
  - Raw materials
  - Information
  and transforms these into output products – either tangible goods or intangible services that can be sold in the market.

3 **Show how operations management can contribute to the competitiveness of the organisation**

- By designing and implementing systems and processes that are repeatable, consistent, reliable, efficient and compliant with the legislation that governs the overall environment.
- By creating an operations system that is aligned with the goals of the organisation in terms of volume of output, variety of product, variation in demand and visibility of process.

4 **Identify different forms of operational activity**

- Managing the capacity of the transformation process.
- Setting process and product standards to be adhered to within the transformation process.
- Managing the materials pipeline into and through the transformation process.
- Scheduling of the required resources to be used in the transformation process.
- Controlling the activities within the transformation process.

5 **Define the term quality and describe features that can be used to quantify it**

- Quality means conformance to the requirements of the customer.
- Product or service quality can be described in relation to functionality, performance, reliability, durability, customisation and appearance.

Review questions

1 Review some consumer goods such as mobile phones, cars and kitchen appliances. Identify the service elements attached to the purchase of these products.

2 Discuss why variation in the inputs to the transformation process is a bad thing. Which of the five inputs is likely to be subject to most variation and which to least?

3 Why is control over quality at source so important?

4 How does service quality differ from manufacturing quality?

5 Why is delivery reliability more important than delivery speed?

6 Discuss the concepts of order winners and order qualifiers.

Further reading

Crosby, P. (1979) *Quality is Free*, McGraw-Hill, New York.

A classic text detailing the basics of quality management and showing how it all started.

Slack, N., Chambers, S. and Johnston, R. (2010) *Operations Management* (6th edn), Prentice Hall, Harlow.

Covers all of the main topics in operations management.

Sprague, L. (2007) 'Evolution of the field of operations management', *Journal of Operations Management,* vol. 25, pp. 219–38.

A brief but comprehensive summary of the field of operations management from a historical perspective.

Weblinks

These websites have appeared in, or are relevant to, the chapter:

www.sunseeker.com
www.linn.co.uk
www.zara.com

Visit two of the websites in the list (or any other company that interests you) and navigate to the pages dealing with the products and services they offer.

● What messages do they give about the nature of the goods and services they offer? What challenges are they likely to raise for operations in terms of their emphasis on, for example, quality, delivery or cost? What implications might that have for people working in the company?

● See if you can find any information on the site about the operating systems, or how they link with their suppliers.

 Annotated weblinks, multiple choice questions and other useful resources can be found on **www.pearsoned.co.uk/boddy**

Case study   Zara   www.zara.com

Zara had six stores by 1979 and established retail operations in all the major Spanish cities during the 1980s. In 1988 the first international Zara store opened in Porto, Portugal, followed shortly by New York in 1989 and Paris in 1990. But foreign expansion was rapid during the 1990s when Zara entered Europe, the Americas and Asia.

The company is now present across the world, with a network of over 1500 stores. Its international presence shows that national frontiers are no impediment to sharing a single fashion culture. Zara claims to move with society, dressing the ideas, trends and tastes that society itself creates. It is claimed that Zara needs just two weeks to develop a product and get it into stores in comparison to the industry average of nearly six months. Zara has a large design team and the design process is closely linked to the public. Information travels from the stores to the design teams, transmitting the demands and concerns of the market. The vertical integration of activities – design, production, logistics and sales in the company's own stores – means Zara is flexible and fast in adapting to the market. Its model is characterised by continuous product renovation. Zara pays special attention to the design of its stores, its shop windows and interior decor, and locates them in the best sites of major shopping districts.

What sets Zara apart from many of its competitors is what it has done with its business information and operations processes. Rather than trying to forecast demand and producing to meet that (possible) demand, it concentrates on reacting swiftly to (actual) demand. A typical clothes supplier may take three months to develop the styles for a season's range and the same again to set up the supply chain and manufacturing processes: six months pass before the garments are in the stores. Zara does this in weeks by:

- making decisions faster with better information;
- running design and production processes concurrently;
- holding stocks of fabric that can be used in several lines;
- distributing products more efficiently.

Zara designs all its products in-house – about 40,000 items per year from which 10,000 are selected for production. The firm encourages a collegial atmosphere among its designers, who seek inspiration

Copyright © Inditex.

from many sources such as trade fairs, discotheques, catwalks and magazines. Extensive feedback from the stores also contributes to the design process.

The designers for women's, men's and children's wear sit in different halls in a modern building attached to the headquarters. In each of these open spaces the designers occupy one side, the market specialists the middle, and the buyers (procurement and production planners) occupy the other side. Designers first draw out design sketches by hand and then discuss them with colleagues – not just other designers but also the market specialists and planning and procurement staff. This process is crucial in retaining an overall 'Zara style'.

The sketches are then redrawn where further changes and adjustments, for better matching of weaves, textures and colours are made. Critical decisions are made at this stage, especially regarding selection of the fabric. Before moving further through the process, it is necessary to determine whether the new design could be produced and sold at a profit. The next step is to make a sample, a step often completed manually by skilled tailors located in the small pattern and sample-making shops co-located with the designers. If there are any questions or problems, the tailors can just walk over to the designers and discuss and resolve them on the spot.

The final decision on what, when and how much to produce is normally made by agreement between the relevant designer, market specialist and procurement and production planner.

Zara manufactures approximately 50 per cent of its products in its own network of Spanish factories and uses subcontractors for all sewing operations. The other half of its products are procured from outside suppliers. With its relatively large and stable orders, Zara is a preferred customer for almost all its suppliers, this is important as suppliers will give priority to Zara orders and generally be more responsive.

The purchased fabric is then cut by machine. A typical factory has 3 or 4 cutting machines with long tables where typically 30 to 50 layers of fabric are laid out under a top paper layer. The cutting pattern is generated by the Computer Aided Design system (which automatically minimises fabric waste), checked by skilled operators, and then drawn by the machine onto the top layer (so that cut pieces can be identified later). After a final visual check by the operator, the machine then cuts the multiple layers into hundreds of different small pieces. Operators pack each piece into a separate clear plastic bag to be sent to one of some 500 sewing sub-contractors. They bring back the sewn items to the same factory, where each piece is inspected. Finished products are then placed in plastic bags, labelled and sent to the distribution centre.

Completed products procured from outside suppliers are also sent directly to the distribution centre and Zara control their quality by sampling batches of these. The middle-aged mother buys clothes at Zara because they are cheap while her teenage daughter buys there because they are in fashion. The matching of both low cost and acceptable quality is a winning combination. Like any other industry, low cost in the clothing industry is obtained by having efficient and streamlined operational processes. Quality is more subjective; with garments, quality is defined more by the design or 'look' that the customer wants to be seen wearing rather than the quality of the construction. Most of these garments are destined to have a short life as they will be discarded or relegated to the back of the cupboard when fashion changes. This means aspects of manufacturing quality such as durability and robustness will be of little importance to the customer so long as a certain standard is reached.

Questions

1 What do you think are the major managerial challenges in setting up an operations system to serve a fast-moving and fickle market such as fashion? (Refer to Section 16.2.)

2 Is Zara a craft or a factory system? (Refer to Section 16.3.)

3 Which operations systems do they use in the company? (Refer to Section 16.4.)

4 Which aspects of quality does the company emphasise? (Refer to Section 16.6.)

5 What features of the quality management can you observe in the case? (Refer to Section 16.7.)

CHAPTER 17
CONTROLLING AND MEASURING PERFORMANCE

Learning outcomes

When you have read this chapter you should be able to:

1 Define control and explain why it is an essential activity in managing
2 Describe and give examples of the generic control activities
3 Explain how the choice of suitable measures affects performance
4 Outline the significance of human perspectives on control
5 Use ideas from the chapter to comment on the management issues in the Foundation Hospital case study

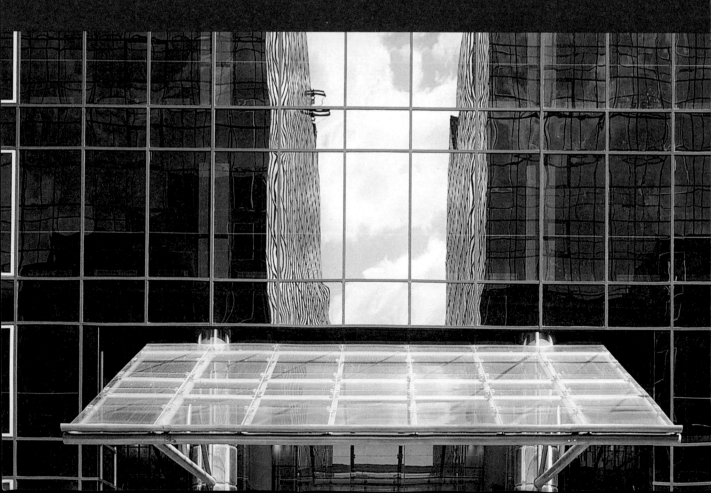

Activity 17.1   What does 'control' mean in management?

Before reading the chapter, write some notes on what you think 'control' means in management.

Choose the organisation or people who may be able to help you learn about the topic. You may find it helpful to discuss the topic with a manager you know, or reflect on an activity you have managed.

- Identify a situation in which an issue of control arose and describe it briefly.
- How did those involved try to exercise control?
- What methods did they use?
- Did they consciously take account of human perspectives on control?

Keep these notes as you will be able to use them later.

17.1   Introduction

The problems at the Foundation Hospital (see chapter case study) illustrate what happens when those responsible for an activity work with inadequate systems of control. There is evidence in the case that this happened at all levels of the organisation. Those at the top were responsible for ensuring the trust met stringent financial and performance targets, and to do that they would need to have systems to monitor performance against these measures, in time to take corrective action. These seem to have failed, since the trust had severely overspent the budget – which led to staff cuts and to some of the problems highlighted in the case. Those responsible for managing the operating units or departments, such as A&E, need control systems to measure performance within their area – and whatever systems they had were clearly inadequate.

Controlling a hospital starts at the top with those to whom hospital managers are responsible. They face strategic issues – how to balance central and local control and whether to adopt a mechanistic or organic approach. Operational control is devolved through the management of the hospital and, as discussed in Chapter 9, is visible in the structure – which shows the reporting responsibilities of each manager. Decisions on how to staff the hospital, who is responsible for what, how to design processes and what equipment to buy – these are all part of the management task of ensuring the hospital operates correctly. This **control** system must then be embodied in a system measuring whether the hospital is performing in the way it should and achieving the quality standards set for it.

Control is the process of monitoring activities to ensure that results are in line with the plan and acting to correct significant deviations.

All managers exercise control as they transform inputs (resources) into outputs (products and services). No matter how thoroughly they plan their objectives and how to meet them, unforeseen internal and external events will occur. Apple monitors very closely the actual and potential demand for each new product, so that it knows very quickly if it needs to increase or reduce production. Fashion retailers like Asos or Zara do the same – they need to know very quickly which designs are selling well so that they can produce more and re-stock the shops before the popular models go out of fashion. Facebook monitors the growth of new users, and how they are using the site, to gain clues about what features to build in to make it more attractive.

Managers at all levels supplement the activity of planning with that of controlling – checking that work is going to plan, and if necessary taking corrective action. The sooner they note deviations, the easier it is to bring performance into line. In this sense, control has positive meanings, standing for order, predictability or reliability. If things are under control, employees are clear about what others expect them to do, and customers know what standard of product they will receive. Control is an essential part of organisational life, helping to ensure that the co-operative work of many resources adds value. An absence of control implies uncertainty, chaos, inefficiency and waste. However, control depends on influencing people, so designing a control system is not a technical, rational process, but one that needs to take account of human factors and the context in which it operates.

The chapter begins by describing control and the strategies and tactics people can use to achieve it. It then outlines how to measure an organisation's performance, and the types of control system suitable for different circumstances. Finally, it introduces a human perspective on control and shows how control systems and people interact.

17.2 What is control and how to achieve it?

The control process

The **control process**
is the generic activity
of setting performance
standards, measuring
actual performance,
comparing actual
performance with the
standards, and acting
to correct deviations or
modify standards.

A **control system** is
the way the elements in
the control process are
designed and combined
in a specific situation.

Standard of performance is the defined
level of performance
to be achieved against
which an operation's
actual performance is
compared.

The **control process** is intended to support the achievement of objectives. Managers design specific **control systems** for different organisational activities, all of which incorporate the elements shown in Figure 17.1 – setting targets, measuring performance, comparing this with target, and acting to correct any significant gap between the two.

Targetting

Targets provide direction and a **standard of performance** to aim for. The standard will itself affect achievement – people will ignore standards that are too high as being unattainable, or too low as not being worthwhile. Some measures are generic – employee satisfaction, costs against budget, or sales against target – and are relevant to most management situations. Managers also use measures that are unique to their activity and area of responsibility – pages of advertising booked or number of students recruited.

Some measures are objective and quantifiable – such as sales, profit or return on invesmtent. Equally important aspects of performance (product innovation, flexibility, company reputation or service quality) are more subjective and here managers seek acceptable qualitative measures.

Measuring

Control depends on measuring performance against a target. Table 17.1 shows the sources of information people can use to do this, and their advantages and disadvantages: combining them gives a more reliable picture than any one method.

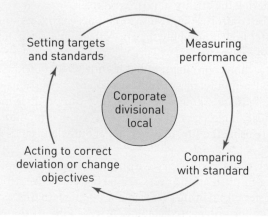

Figure 17.1
The control
process

Table 17.1 Common sources of information for measuring performance

	Advantages	Disadvantages
Personal observation	Gives first-hand knowledge, information is not filtered, shows the manager is interested	Subject to personal bias, time consuming, obtrusive – people see what is happening
Oral reports	Quick way to get information, allows for verbal and non-verbal feedback	Information is filtered, no permanent record
Written reports	Comprehensive, and can show trends and relationships, easy to store and retrieve	Time to prepare, may ignore subjective factors
Online information systems	Rapid feedback, often during the process	Information overload, may be stressful to staff

Comparing

This step shows the variation between actual and planned performance. There is bound to be some variation from the plan, so before taking action a manager needs to know the acceptable **range of variation** – the acceptable limits of variation between actual and planned performance. Acceptable range of variation is illustrated in Figure 17.2 As long as the variation falls within this range, the manager need take no action – but as it goes beyond that range, the case for action becomes stronger, especially if the trend is continuing. This stage also implies searching for the causes of a significant variation, to increase the chances of an appropriate response.

> The **range of variation** sets the acceptable limits within which performance can vary from standard without requiring remedial action.

Correcting

The final step is to act on significant variations from plan – either to correct future performance or to revise the standard. Bringing performance up to the required standard could require acting on any or all aspects of the transformation process. **Corrective action** could

> **Corrective action** aims to correct problems to get performance back on track.

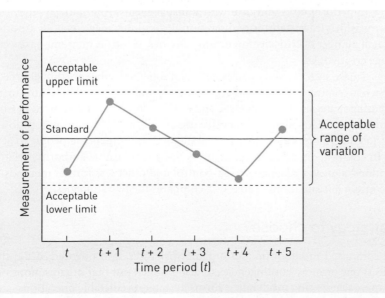

Figure 17.2
Defining the acceptable range of variation

involve taking on more staff, redesigning a process, resetting a machine, cutting prices to sell excess stocks – and many more. It may also mean dealing with longer-term issues of product design, quality or staff skills.

| Management in practice | Enron – the opposite of control |

The Enron scandal, revealed in October 2001, eventually led to the bankruptcy of the Enron Corporation, an energy company based in Texas, and the dissolution of its auditor, Arthur Andersen, one of the world's largest accountancy partnerships.

Enron was formed in 1985 after the merger of Houston Natural Gas and InterNorth. By 1992, it was the largest natural gas merchant in North America, and to achieve further growth, pursued a diversification strategy. It grew into a conglomerate that owned and operated gas pipelines, paper mills and electricity plants. The corporation also traded in financial markets for products and services.

When Chief executive Jeffrey Skilling was hired, he developed a staff of executives who were able, by exploiting accounting loopholes and poor financial control, to hide billions of dollars in debt from failed deals and projects. The roots of the scandal lay in the accumulation over several years of inappropriate habits and values, which finally spiralled out of control.

From late 1997 until its collapse, the primary motivations for Enron's accounting and financial transactions seem to have been to keep reported income and reported cash flow high, inflate asset values and hide liabilities. These criminal practices meant that, in addition to the bankruptcy, many executives at Enron were sentenced to prison.

The loss of control was not limited to accounting. By the mid 1990s Enron had developed a culture that encouraged innovation and risk-taking: short-term performance goals were generously rewarded to the detriment of longer-term sustainability. There were few organisational control mechanisms in place to ensure that managers were performing in a sensible and professional manner.

Source: McLean and Elkind (2003).

Strategies for control – mechanistic or organic?

Managers design a control system using their assumptions about how it will affect behaviour. They can set rules and procedures which give people precise and unambiguous direction on how to perform tasks and deal with unusual events. Alternatively, they set them in broader terms which leave staff more discretion. Procedures may cover all aspects of work, or only a small number of critically important activities. Controls may emphasise conformity or encourage creativity.

If managers make such decisions consistently and coherently, they are probably taking a strategic approach to control, in the sense that they understand its purposes and how to implement it. Two opposing strategies are mechanistic and organic, terms first introduced in Chapter 9.

Mechanistic control involves the extensive use of rules and procedures, top-down authority, written job descriptions and other formal methods of influencing people to act in desirable ways. In contrast, organic control involves the use of flexible authority, relatively loose job descriptions, a greater reliance on self-control and other less formal methods. Both will be effective in suitable situations. Table 17.2 compares the two strategies.

Which strategy to choose?

Chapter 9 contrasted mechanistic and organic structures, and introduced the theory that choice reflects one or more contingencies. It also pointed out that organisations often combine both approaches, using mechanistic forms in stable, predictable operations, and organic

Table 17.2 Examples of mechanistic and organic controls

Tools	Mechanistic control	Organic control
Supervision	Stress on following procedures and plans	Stress on encouraging learning and creativity
Organisation structure	Top-down authority, emphasis on position power, detailed job descriptions	Dispersed authority, emphasis on expert power, flexible job descriptions
Rules and procedures	Detailed, on many topics	Broad, on as few topics as practicable
Machinery	Information on performance used by supervisors to check on staff	Information on performance used by staff to learn and improve
Cultural	Encourages conformity, focus is on controlling individuals	Encourages creativity, innovation and self control

Table 17.3 Contingencies and choice of control strategies

Contingency	When	Control strategy likely to be appropriate
Competitive strategy	Cost leadership	Mechanistic, use of rules and procedures, and machinery to measure quantitative output
	Differentiation	Organic, use of HRM and cultural controls stressing self-managing teams and qualitative output measures
Importance of innovation	Low	Mechanistic, use of rules and procedures, and machinery to measure quantitative output
	High	Organic, use of HRM and cultural controls stressing self-managing teams and qualitative output measures
Employee expertise	Low	Mechanistic, use of rules and procedures, and machinery to measure quantitative output
	High	Organic, use of HRM and cultural controls stressing self-managing teams and qualitative output measures

ones in volatile, uncertain parts of the business. The same approach can shape the choice of control systems. Table 17.3 shows how three 'contingencies' are likely to guide decisions on whether to move towards a mechanistic or an organic form.

Being aware of these alternative approaches enables managers to choose an appropriate approach to control that is suitable for the context.

Tactics for control

Setting control strategy is the first step in creating a coherent system, which is then supported by specific control methods or tactics that encourage the desired behaviour. Each of the following control mechanisms can contribute in the right circumstances. Some, such as management by objectives, are more suited to organic control strategies where workers are given more autonomy in how to do their work than to mechanistic strategies where autonomy is discouraged.

Direct supervision

In small organisations, most control is by process and supervision as the owner or the management team can see directly what is happening. They can personally inspect and report on progress, quickly see whether or not it is in line with the plan, and act if necessary. Done with enthusiasm and sensitivity this method is very effective – if people use it clumsily staff will find it intrusive and overbearing.

Organisation structure

Most organisations set out what people are expected to do by giving them job descriptions that allocate the person's tasks and responsibilities. These can be very narrowly and specifically defined, or they can be broad and defined in general terms. They may also establish with whom the job holder is expected to communicate, and the boundaries of their responsibility. This is a form of control as it constrains people – by specifying what they can or cannot do, and what output standards they should achieve. Similarly, organisations can be centralised, with control being held at the top, or decentralised with control spread throughout the structure.

Rules and procedures

As organisations become too large for personal control, managers develop rules and procedures to control activities and alert senior people to significant deviations. Rules establish acceptable behaviour and levels of performance and so are a way of controlling the workforce. They can guide people on how to conduct the business, how to perform the tasks, how to apply for equipment or what to do when a customer places an order.

Management by objectives

Management by objectives is a system in which managers and staff agree their objectives, and then measure progress towards them periodically.

Some organisations use a system of **management by objectives** to exercise control, requiring people throughout the hierarchy to agree their goals for the following period. The approach applies goal-setting theory (Chapter 13), which predicts that the level of difficulty of a goal will affect the effort people put into achieving it. If staff are expected to focus on the goals, this implies they have considerable latitude in deciding how to achieve them.

Control through machinery

In this method, machines or information systems are designed to control, directly or indirectly, what people do. Direct technological controls occur where the machine directs what people do or say. Assembly lines transport the object being made along a moving conveyor, with operators performing a short task to add another piece to the product, with almost no scope to alter the way they work. The speed of work is paced by the machine, the time spent on the task is very short, and there is limited scope for worker interaction. The scripts in a call centre, which specify the questions to ask, how to respond to customer questions and how to close the conversation, have a similar controlling effect on the way a person works. In process industries such as brewing, computer sensors capture information on process performance, compare it with set criteria and, if needed, automatically adjust the equipment to keep the process in line with the plan.

Human resource management control

Human resource management practices can support the control process. Selection and training procedures ensure that the number and type of recruits fit the profile of attitudes, social skills and technical competence that support wider objectives, and that new staff are trained to follow the company's ways of working. The appraisal and reward system can encourage behaviour that supports business objectives. The behaviour of employees can be controlled by offers of rewards if people comply with management policies and of penalty if they do not.

Values and beliefs

Another approach to control aims to ensure that members of the organisation meet management requirements by encouraging internal compliance rather than relying on external constraint. To the extent that a unit develops a strong culture with which staff can identify, this will help to control their actions. Extensive socialisation and other practices encourage them to act in ways that are consistent with the dominant values and beliefs. This may be positive, but can sometimes be oppressive and constraining.

Management in practice **Control at Apple**   www.apple.com

All organisations use a mix of control tactics, many combining mechanistic and organic strategies. A simple example of this can be seen in organisations that both design and manufacture products. The Apple iPad was lanched on 27 January 2010, the latest in a long line of innovative high-tech products from Apple. The company has a creative and flexible culture that allows innovation to flourish. The success of the company is built on the excellence of this design and development capability. Ideas cannot be 'manufactured' by process or thought of 'to order': the control strategy used in R&D is organic, with staff working within a flexible and supportive environment.

However, the products are manufactured using a mechanistic approach. Each unit must be exactly the same with each manufacturing process designed to be completely consistent and reliable. Control of quality is critical with manufacturing tolerences sometimes specified in microns (millionths of a meter) and process defect rates of less than one in a million. Cleanliness is vital with clean rooms set up to ensure contaminants are eliminated. To achieve this workers must fit into the process with no deviation tolerated, as any unplanned activity will lead to a process failure.

Control of cost in volume manufacturing is also critical, with companies like Apple manufacturing their products in low-wage countries, using many of the principles of scientific management, within a strict control system where reducing cost is the critical target. People doing exactly what they are told is the key to production efficiency in this system.

Sources: Gamble *et al.* (2004); company website.

17.3   How do you know you are in control?

Once the strategy for guiding the control system has been decided and the tactics selected, some mechanism for setting standards and monitoring performance must be implemented. This depends on measuring key variables regularly.

Types of performance measurement

In the last chapter we discussed the processes of the organisation and how feedback must be gathered to ensure they are consistently reliable. Feedback is a control mechanism based on measuring defined parameters at the beginning, during or at the end of the process. A car journey illustrates the steps in the process.

Input measures

An **input measure** is an element of resource that is measured as it is put in to the transformation process.

Think of the journey as a 'process' of travelling from one place to another. The driver can refuel the car before the journey. If they then measure what they put in and what is left at the end, doing some arithmetic, they can calculate the fuel efficiency of the car. In organisational terms this may mean measuring the amount of material that is input to the process then working to reduce the waste so that less is needed. A more sophisticated **input measure** may be the skill of the workers, since a better worker may result in a more efficient process.

Process measures

A **process measure** is a measurement taken during an operational process that provides data on how the process is performing.

Instruments can measure speed during the journey to tell us whether we are moving fast enough to arrive as planned. Moving too quickly means arriving too soon with the associated reduction in fuel efficiency, moving too slowly means the danger of being late. In organisational terms, **process measures** may be the heat of an oven, the flow rate of liquid in a pipe or the speed of rotation of a machine. In all cases, deviation from the norm will indicate possible sub-optimal performance. Another process measure is health and safety – the number and type of accidents occurring during a process, against a target of zero.

Output measures

An **output measure** is a measurement taken after an operational process is complete

This is the activity of measuring the quantity of output for a definable area of work – whether for a unit or the business as a whole. In relation to our car journey, this may be the arrival time or total fuel used. In an operational process this may simply be the number of units produced: is it on target or not? It may be a dimension: is a 100 gram bar of chocolate actually 100 grams; if more, then too much chocolate has been given and profit reduced; if less, the customer is receiving less than the advertised amount and the company is in trouble. Other popular **output measures** are financial metrics such as labour and materials cost.

The measures taken in our car journey should show us how to alter the process the next time to improve either fuel consumption or on-time performance. The same is true in operational processes. The measures taken should provide information that allows the control system to be adjusted to achieve a better outcome and so optimise efficiency.

Performance measures are required to calculate how efficiently or effectively our organisation is operating. While both these terms are sometimes used interchangeably, they have very different meanings.

Efficiency

Efficiency is a measure of the inputs required for each unit of output.

Efficiency is often thought of as 'doing things right'. It is a measure of output divided by the inputs needed to produce the output. It is widely used to show how productively a process is working, and how well people have managed it – more output for fewer inputs is better, since that implies that value is being added to the resources. A simple measure of output is sales revenue (number sold × price), while input can be measured by the cost of acquiring and transforming resources into the output. An increase in the ratio of output to input indicates an increase in efficiency. Managers are under constant pressure from shareholders or taxpayers to produce their output more efficiently, by using fewer resources.

Effectiveness

Effectiveness is a measure of how well an activity contributes to achieving organisational goals.

Effectiveness is often thought of as 'doing the right things'. It is a measure of how well the outcomes of a process relate to the broader objectives of the unit – that is, how well the process supports the achievement of broader goals. A library can measure the efficiency of its cataloguers by recording the number of volumes catalogued by each employee. That would not measure effectiveness, which would require measures of accuracy, consistency, timeliness or maintenance of the catalogue. A delivery service can measure efficiency (cost of the service) or effectiveness (predictability, frequency of collections or accuracy of deliveries).

17.4 How to measure performance

Alternative measures of performance

There are five generic performance measures – quality, speed, dependability, flexibility and cost. These can be broken down into more detailed measures such as product produced or materials used or aggregated into composite measures such as customer satisfaction scores.

Composite or detailed?

The five indicators are composites of many smaller measures. For example, quality is a composite of many process measures which ensure that the product is exactly as it should be. In the same way, speed is an aggregate of how quickly materials are moved between processes and how effectively machines and staff work to complete each process. The composite measures usually have more strategic relevance indicating such things as how a product is performing in the market.

Detailed measures tend to have more operational relevance, such as how a process or a person is performing. Detailed measures are usually taken close to the action, and very frequently – sensors can monitor mechanised processes hundreds of times a second. In practice, companies use a range of measures to assess performance – much as a doctor will check blood pressure, heart rate and cholesterol rather than relying on any single one for a diagnosis. Table 17.4 shows how detail measures can be aggregated into composite ones.

Too many or too few?

One problem in devising useful performance measures is to achieve a balance between having a few measures (straightforward and simple but comprehensive enough to be useful) and having too many detailed measures (complex and difficult to manage). People usually compromise by making sure that there is a clear link between the measures chosen and the strategic objectives of the operation – quality, speed, dependability, flexibility and cost. If high quality is the main reason that customers buy the product, then managers should put more emphasis on measures that ensure the quality, rather than the cheapness, of the product. The most important measures are called **key performance indicators (KPIs)**.

Intended and unintended consequences

A second problem is that setting performance targets may encourage unintended behaviour as staff try to find ways around them – perhaps meeting the target, but to the detriment of the overall operation. Here, common sense must be applied and the consequences of each

Key performance indicators (KPIs) are a summarised set of the most important measures that inform managers how well an operation is achieving organisational goals.

Table 17.4 Aggregating performance measures

Composite measure	Customer satisfaction		Agility		Resilience
Generic measure	Quality	Dependability	Speed	Flexibility	Cost
Detail measure	– Defects per unit	– Mean time between failures	– Delivery time	– Range of functionality	– Raw material cost
	– Customer returns	– Lateness	– Throughput	– Number of options	– Labour cost
	– Scrap rate				

Source: Adapted from Slack et al. (2010).

target must be thoroughly considered in tandem with the overall control strategy that is in place. In the Foundation Hospital case, the key to the successful operation of the A&E department is in the skill of the staff, the quality of the support infrastructure and equipment and providing the front-line doctors and nurses with the flexibility to do their job the best way that they see fit. Instead of using an output measure such as a 4-hour waiting time, implementing input measures such as skills matrices combined with process measures such as equipment availability should ensure the best people are supported by the best equipment. This should lead to reduced waiting times and improved quality of care.

Easy or useful measures?

A third problem in measuring performance is the tendency to focus on the 'easy to measure' things such as finance and units of output, while avoiding more useful, but more complex, ones such as customer satisfaction and quality of employee. The more 'difficult to measure' aspects are sometimes the most useful. In design and development work, ensuring that employees have the skills and knowledge to do their jobs will do more for effectiveness than measuring the output of a deficient employee. Likewise, measuring customer satisfaction and loyalty will be more useful than measuring revenue, since a satisfied customer will return and thus generate more revenue.

The balanced scorecard

Addressing the problem of measures at the 'composite' level, Kaplan and Norton (1992) noted that while

> traditional financial performance measures worked well for the industrial era . . . they are out of step with the skills and competencies companies are trying to master today.   (p.71)

Financial measures are essential, but carry the hazard that short-term targets may encourage practices that damage long-run performance – for example by postponing investment in equipment or customer service. They found that senior executives recognised that no single measure could provide a clear performance target or focus attention on the critical areas of the business. Rather, they wanted a balanced presentation of both financial and operational measures. Their research enabled them to devise a **balanced scorecard** – a set of measures that gives a fast but comprehensive view of the business. It includes financial measures that tell the results of actions taken, and complements these with measures of customer satisfaction, internal processes and innovation – measures which drive future financial performance.

The **balanced scorecard** is a performance measurement tool that looks at four areas: financial, customer, internal processes and innovation and learning, which contribute to organisational performance.

It allows managers to view performance comprehensively, by answering these questions:

- How do customers see us? (customer perspective);
- What must we excel at? (internal perspective);
- Can we continue to improve and create value? (innovation and learning perspective);
- How do we look to shareholders? (financial perspective).

The scorecard shown in Figure 17.3 brings together in a single management report many elements of a company's agenda, such as the need to be customer oriented, to shorten response time, improve quality or cut the time taken to launch a new product. It also guards against the dangers of working in isolation, as it requires senior managers to consider all the important operational measures together. They can then judge whether improvement in one area may have been achieved at the expense of another.

Kaplan and Norton (1993) advocate that companies spend time identifying, for each of the four measures, the external and internal factors which are important and developing suitable measures of performance. For example, under the customer heading, they may believe that customers are concerned about time, quality, performance, service and cost. They should therefore articulate goals for each factor, and then translate these goals into specific measures.

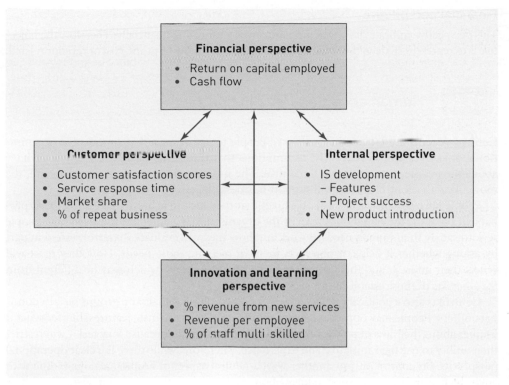

Figure 17.3
The balanced
scorecard

The approach has been widely adopted (Neely and Al Najjar, 2006) but Akkermanns and van Oorschot (2005) warn managers to apply it critically by asking:

- Are the selected measures the right ones?
- Should there be more, or fewer?
- At what levels should performance targets be set?

Perspectives in detail

Each perspective of the balanced scorecard can in itself be considered a composite measure in terms of Table 17.4. It is important to understand what each perspective is there to represent and the detailed measures that could be used in each to provide meaningful information.

Innovation and learning perspective

This set of measures should indicate how intangible assets such as people and information are supporting the organisation. The objective is to ensure the company is managing its intangibles in the correct way and it should describe people performance such as skills, talent and know-how with measures such as training logs and attendance, and information performance with measures such as data accuracy and IT fault logging.

Internal perspective

This perspective indicates whether the company is doing the right things in the right way. The objective here is to ensure the correct processes are being used effectively and efficiently. Measures here may be productivity, machine down-time or part scrap-rates.

Customer perspective

This perspective indicates whether the customer is getting what they want. The objective is to ensure the customer is happy with the product or service. The measures therefore represent customer satisfaction such as product in-service performance or number of customer complaints.

Financial perspective

This perspective indicates how well the company is performing financially. Therefore the objective is to represent shareholder value. Here measures can simply be profit, cost or revenue related.

17.5 Human considerations in control

Control systems are intended to influence people to act in ways that support the organisational objectives and so reflect the assumptions that those who designed the systems have about the people they are trying to control. The more accurate these assumptions are, the more likely the control system will support business objectives.

People have personal and local objectives that they seek to achieve in addition to, or perhaps in place of, the stated objectives of the organisation. Chapter 13 discussed how people seek to satisfy their human needs at work and how they will evaluate a control system in part by asking whether it helps or obstructs them in meeting those needs. How they react will reflect their interests and their interpretation of the situation – which may be different from the interests of those establishing the controls.

Control is also a political process in which powerful individuals and groups seek to dominate others. People may oppose a control system not for its intrinsic features, but for what it implies about their loss of power relative to another group, or because they feel it will restrict their ability to use their initiative and experience. Therefore, while there is a clear operational perspective on control or, put another way, a neutral aspect of keeping actions in line with goals, control is also closely tied to ideas about motivation, influence and power.

While effective control depends on suitable control and performance measurement systems, these systems in turn depend on how people see them. Control is only effective when it influences people to act in the way intended by those designing the system, who therefore need to take into account the likely reactions of those being controlled. People may resist a system that they feel threatens their satisfaction or in some way undermines their ability to meet their psychological needs from work.

Table 17.5 illustrates this by showing how a control system can have either positive or negative effects on a person's ability to satisfy each of the human needs identified in Chapter 13. Controls can encourage both positive and negative behaviour – positive by encouraging commitment and enthusiasm, negative if they lead people to be fearful and defensive.

Table 17.5 Possible effects of control systems on human needs

Maslow's categories of human needs	Controls may support satisfaction	Controls may hinder satisfaction
Self-actualisation	Feedback encourages higher performance, accepting new challenges	Controls may limit initiative, autonomy, ability to experiment and discover
Esteem	Publishing successes builds recognition, self-confidence; reputation with colleagues and senior managers	Publishing failure damages esteem, undermines reputation; inaccurate information also damaging
Belongingness	Team-based assessments can support bonding and team development	Individual rewards may breed competition and damage co-operation
Security	Knowledge of how performance is assessed gives certainty	Controls that leave expectations unclear undermine security; information seen as threat
Physiological	Help focus effort and meet performance requirements	Controls highlight poor performance and threaten job

Activity 17.2   What does 'control' mean in management?

Having read the chapter, make brief notes summarising the control issues evident in the organisation you chose for this activity.

- What were the outcomes of the attempts at control? (Refer to Section 17.1.)
- On balance, did they adopt a mechanistic or an organic approach? Was this suitable for the circumstances? (Refer to Section 17.2.)
- What tactics did those involved use to exercise control? (Refer to Sections 17.2 and 17.3.)
- What was their approach to measuring wider organisational performance? Did they use any methods similar to the balanced scorecard? (Refer to Section 17.4.)
- What effects did human factors have on the design and/or the results of the control system? (Refer to Section 17.5.)

Compare what you have found with other students on your course.

Summary

1 **Define control and explain why it is an essential activity in managing**
   - Control is the counterpart of planning and is the process of monitoring activities to ensure that results are in line with the plan and taking corrective action if required.
   - Organisational control ensures that operational processes remain consistent, repeatable and reliable.

2 **Describe and give examples of the generic control activities of setting targets, measuring, comparing and correcting**
   - Setting targets gives direction to an activity and sets standards of acceptable performance.
   - Measuring involves deciding what measures to use, and how frequently.
   - Comparing involves selecting suitable objects for comparison, and the time period over which to do it.
   - Correcting aims to rectify a deviation from plan either by altering activities or changing the objectives.

3 **Discuss strategies and tactics used to gain and maintain control**
   - Control systems exist on a spectrum where the extremes are mechanistic and organic.
   - Mechanistic approaches are likely to be suitable in stable environments or in support of cost leadership strategies.
   - Organic approaches are likely to be suitable in unstable environments or in support of differentiation strategies.
   - Organisations can use a combination of direct supervision, organisational structure, rules and procedures, management by objectives, machinery, HRM practice and values and beliefs to maintain control.

4 **Explain how the choice of suitable measures of performance can help in managing the organisation**
   - Managers can use either input, process or output measures.
   - The balanced scorecard supplements financial measures with those of customer satisfaction, internal process and innovation, and growth – which all play a part in an overall assessment of performance.
   - Control systems must be matched to the overall model of management within the organisation – which can be indicated by the competing values framework.

5 Explain why those designing performance measurement and control systems need to take account of human reactions

   - Control depends on influencing people, so is only effective if it takes account of human needs.
   - Controls can encourage behaviour that is not in the best interests of the organisation.
   - Controls can encourage people to supply the system with inaccurate information.
   - People will resist controls that they feel threaten their ability to satisfy their needs from work.

Review questions

1 Explain why control is important.

2 Is planning part of the control process?

3 Describe the four steps in the control process.

4 Explain how the balanced scorecard was an improvement on earlier performance measurement systems.

5 Give an original example of a measure in each quadrant of the balanced scorecard.

6 Explain how input, process and output measures differ.

7 Explain why the competing values framework can help in designing a control and performance management system.

Further reading

Kaplan, R. S. and Norton, D. P. (2008) *The Execution Premium: Linking strategy to operations for competitive advantage,* Harvard, Boston, MA.

> Brings balanced scorecards, performance measurement and management control right up to date, linking them all to show how they can be used to create competitive advantage.

Weblinks

These websites feature in, or are relevant to, the chapter,

   www.apple.com
   www.tesco.com
   www.crossrail.co.uk
   www.hmv.com
   www.gsk.com
   www.bp.com

Visit any company website and go to the section in which the company reports on its performance:

   - What financial measures do they report on most prominently?
   - From the chairman's and/or chief executive's reports, what other measures have they been using to assess their performance?

   Annotated weblinks, multiple choice questions and other useful resources can be found on **www.pearsoned.co.uk/boddy**

Case study   A Foundation Hospital

Foundation Hospitals were introduced in 2002, and by 2009 there were 122 in the National Health Service in England (NHS). They were created to devolve decision-making from central government to enable health service providers to be more responsive to the needs of local communities. They were an important part of the government's agenda to create a patient-led NHS in England. Achieving Foundation status brings a significant change to the way a hospital is controlled.

> **NHS foundation trusts (often called Foundation Hospitals) are at the cutting edge of the Government's commitment to devolution and decentralisation of public services and are at the heart of a patient-led NHS. They are not subject to direction from Whitehall. Instead local managers and staff working with local people have the freedom to develop services tailored to the particular needs of their patients and local communities.** (*A Short Guide to NHS Foundation Trusts*)

Although Foundation Trusts are still part of the NHS and work to NHS care standards, hospitals that gain Foundation status are accountable to a board of governors and nationally to Monitor (the independent regulator of NHS Foundation Trusts). This form of control should allow each hospital more autonomy to use the income it receives from the local Primary Care Trust to provide care in the area.

Hospitals are among the most complex organisations in existence. They employ highly skilled staff, use sophisticated technology, operate complex processes, and often manage life-threatening situations. Their performance has been at the forefront of the government's agenda for many years and control is central to improving performance.

Creating Foundation hospitals represents a shift in philosophy between centralised, one size fits all, directive control by government to a more decentralised, customised and empowered form of control. This means hospitals are responsible for managing their own income in an attempt to create a market-like environment in the hope that empowered managers will be better able to intelligently allocate resources to areas of most need and behave more efficiently.

The introduction of Foundation Trusts has not been without its critics. Some pointed out that they go against the NHS principles. Others doubt whether the Foundation members will be able to control

Getty Images.

hospital management, which is heavily influenced by powerful medical professionals with a tradition of autonomy and resistance to outside interference.

These potential difficulties were highlighted when a major scandal developed at Stafford Hospital, part of Mid Staffordshire NHS Foundation Trust. A routine inspection in the Accident and Emergency department found examples of poor care and inadequate hygiene standards. Publication of these led to many other deficiencies coming to light, which eventually led to several inquiries into performance at this and other hospitals in the area.

The inquiry reports placed some of the blame on the performance measurement system. One performance metric that was criticised was the Accident and Emergency 4-hour waiting-time target. Staff told the Healthcare Commission that there was a lot of pressure on them to meet this target. Several recounted occasions where managers had asked them to leave seriously ill patients to treat minor ailments, so that the target could be met. One had been asked to leave a heart-attack patient being given life-saving treatment.

Nurses reported leaving meetings in tears after being told their jobs were at risk after breaching the target. And the report concluded patients were sometimes 'dumped' into wards near A&E with little nursing care so the targets could be met.

The 4-hour target, which in simple terms aims to ensure that patients are treated and either admitted or sent home within four hours, at first seems straightforward. However on further consideration it is much more complicated to enforce. Patients have different requirements: medical staff suggest that some groups – such as those with chest pains, recovering from alcohol or drug overdoses, and those too vulnerable to be discharged in the middle of the night – should be exempt from the target. Some hospitals were able to meet the 4-hour target by placing observation wards beside A&E to which patients could be admitted. Others refused to accept patients into their A&E departments from the ambulance so that the 'four hour clock' would not start ticking.

Unthinkingly trying to meet this simple but ultimately misconceived target seriously damaged patient care. An inquiry into the Foundation Hospital by Monitor found failings in a number of areas. From a performance measurement and control perspective the two most relevant were:

- a lack of clarity on the standards that should be achieved as the threshold for gaining Foundation status; and
- that Monitor itself – the regulatory body – must revise its view of what information is required as evidence that performance standards are being achieved.

A separate inquiry also noted that 'figures were preferred to people' – in the sense that managers gave more weight to performance data than to the opinions of those involved. Moreover, the performance measurement systems did not bring to light the serious and systemic failures in the hospital – even though that was the main purpose of the system.

Second, it found that there was a 'focus on systems not outcomes' – in the sense that staff were focusing too much on the process and not enough on the care that resulted from the process – even though the main purpose of the systems was to ensure they encourage good quality care.

Sources: Monitor (2009), *Learning and Implications from the Mid Staffordshire NHS Foundation Trust*, Monitor-Independent Regulator of NHS Foundation Trusts Final Report; Francis, R (2010), *Independent Inquiry into care provided by Mid Staffordshire Foundation Trust*; Department of Health (2005), *A Short Guide to NHS Foundation Trusts*; *The Times*, 18 March 2009.

Questions

1 Why does control matter in a hospital? What will be the main issues in developing control systems in a hospital? (Refer to Sections 17.1 and 17.2.)

2 Does the control system appear to be mechanistic or organic? (Refer to Section 17.2.)

3 What variables does the control system mainly measure? (Refer to Section 17.3.)

4 Which performance measures seem suitable in this setting? Do they use them? (Refer to Section 17.4.)

5 To what extent did the hospital management show awareness of the human considerations in control? (Refer to Section 17.5.)

GLOSSARY

Administrative management is the use of institutions and order rather than relying on personal qualities to get things done.

The **administrative model of decision-making** describes how people make decisions in uncertain, ambiguous situations.

Ambiguity is when people are uncertain about their goals and how best to achieve them.

The **balanced scorecard** is a performance measurement tool that looks at four areas: financial, customer, internal processes and innovation and learning, which contribute to organisational performance.

Behaviour is something a person does that can be directly observed.

Behaviour modification is a general label for attempts to change behaviour by using appropriate and timely reinforcement.

The **big five** refers to trait clusters that appear consistently to capture main personality traits: Openness, Conscientiousness, Extraversion, Agreeableness and Neuroticism.

A **blog** is a web log that allows individuals to post opinions and ideas.

Bounded rationality is behaviour that is rational within a decision process which is limited (bounded) by an individual's ability to process information.

Bureaucracy is a system in which people are expected to follow precisely defined rules and procedures rather than to use personal judgement.

A **business plan** is a document which sets out the markets the business intends to serve, how it will do so and what finance they require.

Centralisation is when a relatively large number of decisions are taken by management at the top of the organisation.

Certainty describes the situation when all the information the decision-maker needs is available.

A **channel** is the medium of communication between a sender and a receiver.

Co-creation is product or service development that makes intensive use of the contributions of customers.

Coercive power is the ability to obtain compliance through fear of punishment or harm.

Collectivism 'describes societies in which people, from birth onwards, are integrated into strong, cohesive ingroups which . . . protect them in exchange for unquestioning loyalty' (Hofstede, 1991, p. 51).

Communication is the exchange of information through written or spoken words, symbols and actions to reach a common understanding.

Competences are the skills and abilities by which resources are deployed effectively – systems, procedures and ways of working.

A **competitive environment (or context)** is the industry-specific environment comprising the organisation's customers, suppliers and competitors.

Competitive strategy explains how an organisation (or unit within it) intends to achieve competitive advantage in its market.

Concertive control is when workers reach a negotiated consensus on how to shape their behaviour according to a set of core values.

Consideration is a pattern of leadership behaviour that demonstrates sensitivity to relationships and to the social needs of employees.

Content is the specific substantive task that the group is undertaking.

Contingencies are factors such as uncertainty, interdependence and size that reflect the situation of the organisation.

Contingency approaches to organisational structure propose that the performance of an organisation depends on having a structure that is appropriate to its environment.

Control is the process of monitoring activities to ensure that results are in line with the plan and acting to correct significant deviations.

The **control process** is the generic activity of setting performance standards, measuring actual performance, comparing actual performance with the standards, and acting to correct deviations or modify standards.

A **control system** is the way the elements in the control process are designed and combined in a specific situation.

Corporate governance refers to the rules and processes intended to control those responsible for managing an organisation.

Corporate responsibility refers to the awareness, acceptance and management of the wider implications of corporate decisions.

Corrective action aims to correct problems to get performance back on track.

A **cost leadership strategy** is one in which a firm uses low price as the main competitive weapon.

The **craft system** refers to a system in which the craft producers do everything. With or without customer involvement they design, source materials, manufacture, sell and perhaps service.

Creativity is the ability to combine ideas in a unique way, or to make unusual associations between ideas.

Critical success factors are those aspects of a strategy that *must* be achieved to secure competitive advantage.

Critical thinking identifies the assumptions behind ideas, relates them to their context, imagines alternatives and recognises limitations.

Culture is a pattern of shared basic assumptions that was learned by a group as it solved its problems of external adaptation and internal integration, that has worked well enough to be considered valid and transmitted to new members (Schein, 2004, p. 17).

Customer relationship management (CRM) is a process of creating and maintaining long-term relationships with customers.

Data are raw, unanalysed facts, figures and events.

Decentralisation is when a relatively large number of decisions are taken lower down the organisation in the operating units.

A **decision** is a specific commitment to action (usually a commitment of resources).

Decision criteria define the factors that are relevant in making a decision.

Decision-making is the process of identifying problems and opportunities and then resolving them.

Decision support systems help people to calculate the consequences of alternatives before they decide which to choose.

A **decision tree** helps someone to make a choice by progressively eliminating options as additional criteria or events are added to the tree.

Decoding is the interpretation of a message into a form with meaning.

Delegation occurs when one person gives another the authority to undertake specific activities or decisions.

Determinism is the view that the business environment determines an organisation's structure.

Differentiation strategy consists of offering a product or service that is perceived as unique or distinctive on a basis other than price.

A **divisional structure** is when tasks are grouped in relation to their outputs, such as products or the needs of different types of customer.

e-business refers to the integration, through the internet, of all an organisation's processes from its suppliers through to its customers.

e-commerce refers to the activity of selling goods or service over the internet.

Economies of scale are achieved when producing something in large quantities reduces the cost of each unit.

Effectiveness is a measure of how well an activity contributes to achieving organisational goals.

Efficiency is a measure of the inputs required for each unit of output.

Emergent models of change emphasise that in uncertain conditions a project will be affected by unknown factors, and that planning has little effect on the outcome.

Emergent strategies are those that result from actions taken one by one that converge in time in some sort of consistent pattern.

Encoding is translating information into symbols for communication.

Enlightened self-interest is the practice of acting in a way that is costly or inconvenient at present, but which is believed to be in one's best interest in the long-term.

Enterprise resource planning (ERP) is a computer-based planning system which links separate databases to plan the use of all resources within the enterprise.

Entrepreneurs are people who see opportunities in a market, and quickly mobilise resources to deliver the product or service profitably.

Equity theory argues that perception of unfairness leads to tension, which then motivates the individual to resolve that unfairness.

Escalating commitment is a bias which leads to increased commitment to a previous decision despite evidence that it may have been wrong.

Ethical audits are the practice of systematically reviewing the extent to which an organisation's actions are consistent with its stated ethical intentions.

Ethical consumers are those who take ethical issues into account in deciding what to purchase.

Ethical decision-making models examine the influence of individual characteristics and organisational policies on ethical decisions.

Ethical investors are people who only invest in businesses that meet specified criteria of ethical behaviour.

Ethical relativism is the principle that ethical judgements cannot be made independently of the culture in which the issue arises.

An **executive information system** provides those at the top of the organisation with easy access to timely and relevant information.

Existence needs reflect a person's requirement for material and energy.

Expectancy theory argues that motivation depends on a person's belief in the probability that effort will lead to good performance, and that good performance will lead to them receiving an outcome they value (valence).

Expertise power is when people acknowledge someone's knowledge and are therefore willing to follow their suggestions.

The **external environment (or context)** consists of elements beyond the organisation – it combines the competitive and general environments.

An **extranet** is a version of the internet that is restricted to specified people in specified companies – usually customers or suppliers.

Extrinsic rewards are valued outcomes or benefits provided by others, such as promotion, a pay increase or a bigger car.

Factory production is a process-based system that breaks down the integrated nature of the craft worker's approach and makes it possible to increase the supply of goods by dividing tasks into simple and repetitive processes and sequences which could be done by unskilled workers and machinery on a single site.

Feedback (in systems theory) refers to the provision of information about the effects of an activity.

Feedback (in communication) occurs as the receiver expresses their reaction to the sender's message.

Femininity pertains to societies in which social gender roles overlap.

Five forces analysis is a technique for identifying and listing those aspects of the five forces most relevant to the profitability of an organisation at that time.

A **focus strategy** is when a company competes by targeting very specific segments of the market.

Foreign direct investment (FDI) is the practice of investing shareholder funds directly in another country, by building or buying physical facilities, or by buying a company.

Formal authority is the right that a person in a specified role has to make decisions, allocate resources or give instructions.

Formal structure consists of guidelines, documents or procedures setting out how the organisation's activities are divided and co-ordinated.

A **formal team** is one that management has deliberately created to perform specific tasks to help meet organisational goals.

Formalisation is the practice of using written or electronic documents to direct and control employees.

Franchising is the practice of extending a business by giving other organisations, in return for a fee, the right to use your brand name, technology or product specifications.

Functional managers are responsible for the performance of an area of technical or professional work.

A **functional structure** is when tasks are grouped into departments based on similar skills and expertise.

The **general environment (or context)** (sometimes known as the macro-environment) includes political, economic, social, technological, (natural) environmental and legal factors that affect all organisations.

General managers are responsible for the performance of a distinct unit of the organisation.

Global companies work in many countries, securing resources and finding markets in whichever country is most suitable.

Globalisation refers to the increasing integration of internationally dispersed economic activities.

A **goal (or objective)** is a desired future state for an activity or organisational unit.

Goal-setting theory argues that motivation is influenced by goal difficulty, goal specificity and knowledge of results.

Groupthink is 'a mode of thinking that people engage in when they are deeply involved in a cohesive in-group, when the members' striving for unanimity overrides their motivation to realistically appraise alternative courses of action' (Janis, 1972).

Growth needs are those which impel people to be creative or to produce an effect on themselves or their environment.

Heuristics are simple rules or mental short cuts that simplify making decisions.

High-context cultures are those in which information is implicit and can only be fully understood by those with shared experiences in the culture.

Horizontal specialisation is the degree to which tasks are divided among separate people or departments.

Human relations approach is a school of management which emphasises the importance of social processes at work.

Hygiene (or maintenance) factors are those aspects surrounding the task which can prevent discontent and dissatisfaction, but will not in themselves contribute to psychological growth and hence motivation.

An **ideology** is a set of integrated beliefs, theories and doctrines that helps to direct the actions of a society.

The **illusion of control** is a source of bias resulting from the tendency to overestimate one's ability to control activities and events.

Incremental innovations are small changes in a current product or process which brings a minor improvement.

People use an **incremental model** of decision-making when they are uncertain about the consequences. They search for a limited range of options, and policy unfolds from a series of cumulative small decisions.

Individualism pertains to societies in which the ties between individuals are loose.

Influence is the process by which one party attempts to modify the behaviour of others by mobilising power resources.

An **informal group** is one that emerges when people come together and interact regularly.

Informal structure is the undocumented relationships between members of the organisation that emerge as people adapt systems to new conditions and satisfy personal and group needs.

Information comes from data that have been processed so that it has meaning for the person receiving it.

Information overload arises when the amount of information a person has to deal with exceeds their capacity to process it.

Information richness refers to the amount of information that a communication channel can carry, and the extent to which it enables sender and receiver to achieve common understanding.

Information systems management is the planning, acquisition, development and use of these systems.

Initiating structure is a pattern of leadership behaviour that emphasises the performance of the work in hand and the achievement of production or service goals.

Innovation is the process through which new ideas, objects, behaviours and practices are created, developed and implemented into a product or service that can be sold for profit.

An **input measure** is an element of resource that is measured as it is put in to the transformation process.

Instrumentality is the perceived probability that good performance will lead to valued rewards, measured on a scale from 0 (no chance) to 1 (certainty).

Intangible resources are non-physical assets such as information, reputation and knowledge.

The **interaction model** is a theory of change that stresses the continuing interaction between the internal and external contexts of an organisation, making the outcomes of change hard to predict.

The **internal environment (or context)** consists of elements which make up the organisation – such as its structure, culture, people and technologies.

International management is the practice of managing business operations in more than one country.

The **internet** is a web of hundreds of thousands of computer networks linked together by telephone lines and satellite links through which data can be carried.

An **intranet** is a version of the internet that only specified people within an organisation can use.

Intrinsic rewards are valued outcomes or benefits that come from the individual, such as feelings of satisfaction, achievement and competence.

Job characteristics theory predicts that the design of a job will affect internal motivation and work outcomes, with the effects being mediated by individual and contextual factors.

A **joint venture** is an alliance in which the partners agree to form a separate, independent organisation for a specific business purpose.

Key performance indicators are a summarised set of the most important measures that inform managers how well an operation is achieving organisational goals.

Leadership refers to the process of influencing the activities of others toward high levels of goal setting and achievement.

Licensing is when one firm gives another firm the right to use assets such as patents or technology in exchange for a fee.

Life-cycle models of change are those that view change as an activity which follows a logical, orderly sequence of activities that can be planned in advance.

Line managers are responsible for the performance of activities that directly meet customers' needs.

Management is the activity of getting things done with the aid of people and other resources.

Management as a distinct role develops when activities previously embedded in the work itself become the responsibility not of the employee, but of owners or their agents.

Management as a universal human activity occurs whenever people take responsibility for an activity and consciously try to shape its progress and outcome.

Management by objectives is a system in which managers and staff agree their objectives, and then measure progress towards them periodically.

A **management information system** provides information and support for managerial decision-making.

Management tasks are those of planning, organising, leading and controlling the use of resources to add value to them.

A **manager** is someone who gets things done with the aid of people and other resources.

Masculinity pertains to societies in which social gender roles are clearly distinct.

A **matrix structure** is when those doing a task report both to a functional and a project or divisional boss.

A **mechanistic structure** means there is a high degree of task specialisation, people's responsibility and authority are closely defined and decision-making is centralised.

The **message** is what the sender communicates.

Metcalfe's law states that the value of a network increases with the square of the number of users connected to the network.

A **mission statement** is a broad statement of an organisation's scope and purpose, aiming to distinguish it from similar organisations.

Motivation refers to the forces within or beyond a person that arouse and sustain their commitment to a course of action.

Motivator factors are those aspects of the work itself that Herzberg found influenced people to superior performance and effort.

Multinational companies are managed from one country, but have significant production and marketing operations in many others.

Needs are states of felt deprivation, reflecting biological and social influences.

A **network structure** is when tasks required by one company are performed by other companies with expertise in those areas.

Networking refers to behaviours that aim to build, maintain and use informal relationships (internal and external) that may help work-related activities.

Noise is anything that confuses, diminishes or interferes with communication.

A **non-programmed (unstructured) decision** is a unique decision that requires a custom-made solution when information is lacking or unclear.

Non-receptive contexts are those where the combined effects of features of the organisation (such as culture or technology) appear likely to hinder change.

Non-verbal communication is the process of coding meaning through behaviours such as facial expression, gestures and body postures.

Observation is the activity of concentrating on how a team works rather than taking part in the activity itself.

An **office automation system** uses several systems to create, process, store and distribute information.

Online communities are groups of people loosely joined together by a common interest who exchange information using web tools.

An **open system** is one that interacts with its environment.

Operational plans detail how the overall objectives are to be achieved, by specifying what senior management expects from specific departments or functions.

Operational research is a scientific method of providing managers with a quantitative basis for decisions regarding the operations under their control.

Operations management is the activities, decisions and responsibilities of managing the production and delivery of products and services.

Operations strategy is the pattern of decisions that shapes the long-term capability of the operation.

An **opportunity** is the chance to do something not previously expected.

Optimism bias is a human tendency to see the future in a more positive light than is warranted by experience.

An **organic structure** is one where people are expected to work together and to use their initiative to solve problems; job descriptions and rules are few and imprecise.

An **organisation** is a social arrangement for achieving controlled performance towards goals that create value.

An **organisation chart** shows the main departments and senior positions in an organisation and the reporting relations between them.

Organisation structure 'The structure of an organisation [is] the sum total of the ways in which it divides its labour into distinct tasks and then achieves co-ordination among them' (Mintzberg, 1979).

Organisational change is a deliberate attempt to improve organisational performance by changing one or more aspects of the organisation, such as its technology, structure or business processes.

Organisational performance is the accumulated results of all the organisation's work processes and activities.

Organisational readiness refers to the extent to which staff are able to specify objectives, tasks and resource requirements of a plan appropriately, leading to acceptance.

An **output measure** is a measurement taken after an operational process is complete.

Outsourcing is the practice of contracting out defined functions or activities to companies in other countries who can do the work more cost-effectively.

The **participative model** is the belief that if people are able to take part in planning a change they will be more willing to accept and implement the change.

A **perceived performance gap** arises when people believe that the actual performance of a unit or business is out of line with the level they desire.

Perception is the active psychological process in which stimuli are selected and organised into meaningful patterns.

Performance imperatives are aspects of performance that are especially important for an organisation to do well, such as flexibility and innovation.

A **person culture** is one in which activity is strongly influenced by the wishes of the individuals who are part of the organisation.

PESTEL analysis is a technique for identifying and listing the political, economic, social, technological, environmental and legal factors in the general environment most relevant to an organisation.

Philanthropy is the practice of contributing personal wealth to charitable or similar causes.

Planning is the iterative task of setting goals, specifying how to achieve them, implementing the plan and evaluating the results.

A **planning system** refers to the processes by which the members of an organisation produce plans, including their frequency and who takes part in the process.

A **policy** is a guideline that establishes some general principles for making a decision.

Political behaviour is 'the practical domain of power in action, worked out through the use of techniques of influence and other (more or less extreme) tactics' (Buchanan and Badham, 1999).

The **political model** is a model of decision-making that reflects the view that an organisation consists of groups with different interests, goals and values.

Political models of change reflect the view that organisations are made up of groups with separate interests, goals and values, and that these affect how they respond to change.

Political risk is the risk of losing assets, earning power or managerial control due to political events or the actions of host governments.

Power is 'the capacity of individuals to exert their will over others' (Buchanan and Badham, 1999).

A **power culture** is one in which people's activities are strongly influenced by a dominant central figure.

Power distance is the extent to which the less powerful members of organisations within a country expect and accept that power is distributed unevenly.

Preferred team roles are the types of behaviour that people display relatively frequently when they are part of a team.

Prior hypothesis bias results from a tendency to base decisions on strong prior beliefs, even if the evidence shows that they are wrong.

A **problem** is a gap between an existing and a desired state of affairs.

A **process control system** monitors and controls variables describing the state of a physical process.

A **process measure** is a measurement taken during an operational process that provides data on how the process is performing.

A **procedure** is a series of related steps to deal with a structured problem.

A **programmed (or structured) decision** is a repetitive decision that can be handled by a routine approach.

Project managers are responsible for managing a project, usually intended to change some element of an organisation or its context.

A **psychological contract** is the set of understandings people have regarding the commitments made between themselves and their organisation.

Quality is conformance to customer requirements.

Radical innovations are large game changing developments that alter the competitive landscape.

The **range of variation** sets the acceptable limits within which performance can vary from standard without requiring remedial action.

The **rational model of decision-making** assumes that people make consistent choices to maximise economic value within specified constraints.

Real goals are those to which people pay most attention.

Receptive contexts are those where features of the organisation (such as culture or technology) appear likely to help change.

Referent power, sometimes called *charismatic* power, or *personality*, is when some characteristics in a person are attractive to others: they identify with them, which gives the charismatic person power.

Relatedness needs involve a desire for relationships with significant other people.

Representativeness bias results from a tendency to generalise inappropriately from a small sample or a single vivid event.

Responsibility refers to a person's duty to meet the expectations others have of them in their role.

Reward power is the ability to reward another if they comply with a request or instruction.

Risk refers to situations in which the decision-maker is able to estimate the likelihood of the alternative outcomes.

A **role** is the sum of the expectations that other people have of a person occupying a position.

A **role culture** is one in which people's activities are strongly influenced by clear and detailed job descriptions and other formal signals as to what is expected of them.

A **rule** sets out what someone can or cannot do in a given situation.

Satisficing is the acceptance by decision-makers of the first solution that is 'good enough'.

Scenario planning is an attempt to create coherent and credible alternative stories about the future.

Scientific management the school of management called 'scientific' attempted to create a science of factory production.

Selective attention is the ability, often unconscious, to choose from the stream of signals in the environment, concentrating on some and ignoring others.

A **self-managing team** operates without an internal manager and is responsible for a complete area of work.

A **sensitivity analysis** tests the effect on a plan of several alternative values of the key variables.

Situational (contingency) models of leadership attempt to identify the contextual factors that affect when one style will be more effective than another.

The **social contract** consists of the mutual obligations that society and business recognise they have to each other.

Social networking sites use internet technologies which enable people to interact within an online community to share information and ideas.

A **socio-technical system** is one in which outcomes depend on the interaction of both the technical and social subsystems.

A **span of control** is the number of subordinates reporting directly to the person above them in the hierarchy.

Staff managers are responsible for the performance of activities that support line managers.

Stakeholders are individuals, groups or organisations with an interest in, or who are affected by, what the organisation does.

Standard of performance is the defined level of performance to be achieved against which an operation's actual performance is compared.

Stated goals are those which are prominent in company publications and websites.

Stereotyping is the practice of consigning a person to a category or personality type on the basis of their membership of some known group.

A **strategic business unit** consists of a number of closely related products for which it is meaningful to formulate a separate strategy.

A **strategic plan** sets out the overall direction for the business, is broad in scope and covers all the major activities.

Strategy is about how people decide to organise major resources to enhance performance of an enterprise.

Structural choice emphasises the scope which management has to decide the form of structure, irrespective of environmental conditions.

Structure is the regularity in the way a unit or group is organised, such as the roles that are specified.

Subjective probability (in expectancy theory) is a person's estimate of the likelihood that a certain level of effort (E) will produce a level of performance (P) which will then lead to an expected outcome (O).

Subsystems are the separate but related parts that make up the total system.

Sustainable performance refers to economic activities that meet the needs of the present population while preserving the environment for the needs of future generations.

A **SWOT analysis** is a way of summarising the organisation's strengths and weaknesses relative to external opportunities and threats.

A **system** is a set of interrelated parts designed to achieve a purpose.

A **system boundary** separates the system from its environment.

Tangible resources are the physical assets of an organisation such as plant, people and finance.

A **task culture** is one in which the focus of activity is towards completing a task or project using whatever means are appropriate.

A **team** is 'a small number of people with complementary skills who are committed to a common purpose, performance goals, and approach for which they hold themselves mutually accountable' (Katzenbach and Smith, 1993).

Team-based rewards are payments or non-financial incentives provided to members of a formally established team and linked to the performance of the group.

Technology is the knowledge, equipment and activities used to transform inputs into outputs.

The **theory of absolute advantage** is a trade theory which proposes that by specialising in the production of goods and services which they can produce more efficiently than others, nations will increase their economic well-being.

A **theory (or model)** represents a complex phenomenon by identifying the major elements and relationships.

Total Quality Management (TQM) is a philosophy of management that is driven by customer needs and expectations and focuses on continually improving work processes.

A **trait** is a relatively stable aspect of an individual's personality which influences behaviour in a particular direction.

The **transformation process** refers to the operational system that takes all of the inputs; raw materials, information, facilities, capital and people and converts them into an output product to be delivered to the market.

A **transaction processing system (TPS)** records and processes data from routine transactions such as payroll, sales or purchases.

A **transactional leader** is one who treats leadership as an exchange, giving followers what they want if they do what the leader desires.

A **transformational leader** is a leader who treats leadership as a matter of motivation and commitment, inspiring followers by appealing to higher ideals and moral values.

Transnational companies operate in many countries and delegate many decisions to local managers.

Uncertainty is when people are clear about their goals, but have little information about which course of action is most likely to succeed.

Uncertainty avoidance is the extent to which members of a culture feel threatened by uncertain or unknown situations.

A **unique competence** is an activity or process through which resources are deployed to give competitive advantage in ways that others cannot imitate or obtain.

Unique resources are those which are vital to competitive advantage and which others cannot obtain.

User-generated content (UGC) is text, visual or audio material which users create and place on a website for others to view.

Valence is the perceived value or preference that an individual has for a particular outcome.

Value is added to resources when they are transformed into goods or services that are worth more than their original cost plus the cost of transformation.

A **value chain** 'divides a firm into the discrete activities it performs in designing, producing, marketing and distributing its product. It is the basic tool for diagnosing competitive advantage and finding ways to enhance it' (Porter, 1985).

Vertical specialisation refers to the extent to which responsibilities at different levels are defined.

Virtual teams are those in which the members are physically separated, using communications technologies to collaborate across space and time to accomplish their common task.

Wikinomics describes a business culture in which customers are no longer only consumers but also co-creators and co-producers of the service.

REFERENCES

Adair, J. (1997), *Leadership Skills*, Chartered Institute of Personnel and Development, London.

Adams, J. S. (1963), 'Towards an understanding of inequity', *Journal of Abnormal and Social Psychology*, vol. 67, no. 4, pp. 422–36.

Akkermanns, H. A. and van Oorschot, K. E. (2005), 'Relevance assumed: a case study of balanced scorecard development using system dynamics', *Journal of the Operational Research Society*, vol. 56, no. 8, pp. 931–41.

Alderfer, C. (1972), *Existence, Relatedness and Growth: Human needs in organizational settings*, Free Press, New York.

Ambec, S. and Lanoie, P. (2008), 'Does it pay to be green? A systematic overview', *Academy of Management Perspectives*, vol. 22, no. 4, pp. 45–62.

Ansoff, H. I. (1968), *Corporate Strategy*, Penguin, London.

Argenti, P. A. (2004), 'Collaborating with activists: How Starbucks works with NGOs', *California Management Review*, vol. 47, no. 1, pp. 91–116.

Barker, J. R. (1993), 'Tightening the iron cage: concertive control in self-managing teams', *Administrative Science Quarterly*, vol. 38, no. 3, pp. 408–37.

Baron, R. A. and Greenberg, J. (1997) *Behaviour in Organizations* (6th edn), Pearson Education, Upper Saddle River, NJ.

Barrett, S. D. (2009), 'EU/US Open Skies – Competition and change in the world aviation market: the implications for the Irish aviation market', *Journal of Air Transport Management,* vol. 15, no. 2, pp. 78–82.

Barthélemy, J. (2006), 'The experimental roots of revolutionary vision', *MIT Sloan Management Review*, vol. 48, no. 1, pp. 81–84.

Belbin, R. M. (1981), *Management Teams: Why they succeed or fail*, Butterworth/Heinemann, Oxford.

Belbin, R. M. (1993), *Team Roles at Work*, Butterworth/Heinemann, Oxford.

Berle, A. A. and Means, G. C. (1932), *The Modern Corporation and Private Property*, Macmillan Company, New York.

Berlo, D. K. (1960), *The Process of Communication: An Introduction to Theory and Practice*, Holt, Rinehart & Winston, New York.

Berners-Lee, T. (1999), *Weaving the Web*, Orion, London.

Bernoff, J. and Li, C. (2008), 'Harnessing the power of the oh-so-social web', *MIT Sloan Management Review*, vol. 49, no. 3, pp. 36–42.

Biggs, L. (1996), *The Rational Factory*, The Johns Hopkins University Press, Baltimore, MD.

Birkinshaw, J. (2010), *Reinventing Management: Smarter Choices for Getting Work Done,* Jossey-Bass, San Francisco, CA.

Blake, R. R. and Mouton, J. S. (1979), *The New Managerial Grid*, Gulf Publishing, Houston, TX.

Blakstad, M. and Cooper, A. (1995), *The Communicating Organization*, Institute of Personnel and Development, London.

Blau, P. M. (1970), 'A formal theory of differentiation in organizations', *American Sociological Review*, vol. 35, no. 2, pp. 201–18.

Blowfield, M. and Murray, A. (2008), *Corporate Responsibility: A critical introduction*, Oxford University Press, Oxford.

Boddy, D. (2002), *Managing Projects: Building and leading the team*, Financial Times/Prentice Hall, Harlow.

Boddy, D., Macbeth, D. K. and Wagner, B. (2000), 'Implementing collaboration between organisations: an empirical study of supply chain partnering', *Journal of Management Studies*, vol. 37, no. 7, pp. 1003–17.

Boddy, D., Boonstra, A. and Kennedy, G. (2009a), *Managing Information Systems: Strategy and organisation* (3rd edn), Financial Times/Prentice Hall, Harlow.

Boddy, D., King, G., Clark, J. S., Heaney, D. and Mair, F. (2009b), 'The influence of context and process when implementing e-health', *BMC Medical Informatics and Decision Making*, vol. 9, no. 9.

Brookfield, S. D. (1987), *Developing Critical Thinkers*, Open University Press, Milton Keynes.

Buchanan, D. (2001), *The Lived Experience of Strategic Change: A hospital case study*, Leicester Business School Occasional Paper 64.

Buchanan, D. A. (2008), 'You stab my back, I'll stab yours: management experience and perceptions of organization political behaviour', *British Journal of Management*, vol. 19, no. 1, pp. 49–64.

Buchanan, D. and Badham, R. (1999), *Power, Politics and Organizational Change: Winning the turf game*, Sage, London.

Buchanan, L. and O'Connell, A. (2006), 'A brief history of decision making', *Harvard Business Review*, vol. 84, no. 1, pp. 32–41.

Burns, J. M. (1978), *Leadership*, Harper & Row, New York.

Burns, T. and Stalker, G. M. (1961), *The Management of Innovation*, Tavistock, London.

Butt, J. (ed.) (1971), *Robert Owen: Prince of cotton spinners*, David & Charles, Newton Abbott.

Carroll, A. B. (1989), *Business and Society: Ethics and stakeholder management*, South Western, Mason, OH.

Carroll, A. B. (1999), 'Corporate social responsibility', *Business and Society*, vol. 38, no. 3, pp. 268–95.

Catmull, E. (2008), 'How Pixar fosters collective creativity', *Harvard Business Review*, vol. 86, no. 9, pp. 64–72.

Chaffey, D. (ed.) (2003), *Business Information Systems* (2nd edn), Financial Times/Prentice Hall, Harlow.

Chandler, A. D. (1962), *Strategy and Structure*, MIT Press, Cambridge, MA.

Child, J. (2005), *Organization: Contemporary principles and practice*, Blackwell Publishing, Oxford.

Colbert, A. E. and Witt, L. A. (2009), 'The role of goal-focused leadership in enabling the expression of conscientiousness', *Journal of Applied Psychology*, vol. 94, no. 3 , pp. 790–96

Colville, I. D. and Murphy, A. J. (2006), 'Leadership as the enabler of strategizing and organizing', *Long Range Planning*, vol. 39, no. 6, pp. 663–77.

Crosby, P. (1979), *Quality is Free*, McGraw-Hill, New York.

Currie, G. and Proctor, S. J. (2005), 'The antecedents of middle managers' strategic contribution: the case of a professional bureaucracy', *Journal of Management Studies*, vol. 42, no. 7, pp. 1325–56.

Cyert, R. and March, J. G. (1963), *A Behavioral Theory of the Firm*, Prentice Hall, Englewood Cliffs, NJ.

Czarniawska, B. (2004), *Narratives in Social Science Research*, Sage, London.

Dale, B. G. (2007), 'Quality management systems', in Dale, B. G. (ed.), *Managing Quality*, Prentice Hall, Harlow.

Davenport, T. H. (1998), 'Putting the enterprise into enterprise systems', *Harvard Business Review*, vol. 76, no. 4, pp. 121–32.

Davenport, T. H. and Harris, J. G. (2005), 'Automated decision making comes of age', *MIT Sloan Management Review*, vol. 46, no. 4, pp. 83–89.

Deal, T. E. and Kennedy, A. A. (1982), *Corporate Culture: The rites and rituals of corporate life*, Addison-Wesley, Reading, MA.

Deery, S., Iverson, R. D. and Walsh, J. T. (2006), 'Towards a better understanding of psychological contract breach: a study of customer service employees', *Journal of Applied Psychology*, vol. 91, no. 1, pp. 166–75.

Deming, W. E. (1988), *Out of the Crisis*, Cambridge University Press, Cambridge.

Dimbleby, R. and Burton, G. (2006), *More Than Words: An introduction to communication* (4th edn), Routledge, London.

Doganis, R. (2006), *The Airline Business* (2nd edn), Routledge, London.

Donachie, I. (2000), *Robert Owen: Owen of New Lanark and New Harmony*, Tuckwell Press, East Linton.

Donaldson, L. (1996), *For Positive Organization Theory*, Sage, London.

Donaldson, L. (2001), *The Contingency Theory of Organizations*, Sage, London.

Doz, Y. and Kosonen, M. (2008), 'The dynamics of strategic agility: Nokia's rollercoaster experience', *California Management Review*, vol. 50, no 3, pp. 95–118.

Drucker, P. F. (1999), *Management Challenges for the 21st Century,* Butterworth-Heinemann, Oxford.

Edvardsson, B. and Enquist, B. (2002), 'The IKEA saga: how service culture drives service strategy', *Services Industries Journal, vol 22, no, 4, pp. 153–86.

Fayol, H. (1949), *General and Industrial Management*, Pitman, London.

Feigenbaum, A. V. (1993), *Total Quality Control*, McGraw-Hill, New York.

Fiedler, F. E. and House, R. J. (1994), 'Leadership theory and research: a report of progress', in C. L. Cooper and I. T. Robertson (eds), *Key Reviews of Managerial Psychology*, Wiley, Chichester.

Finkelstein, S. (2003), *Why Smart Executives Fail: and what you can learn from their mistakes*, Penguin, New York.

Finkelstein, S., Whitehead, J. and Campbell, A. (2009a), 'How inappropriate attachments can drive good leaders to make bad decisions', *Organizational Dynamics*, vol. 38, no. 2, pp. 83–92.

Finkelstein, S., Whitehead, J. and Campbell, A. (2009b), *Think Again: Why good leaders make bad decisions and how to keep it from happening to you*, Harvard Business School Press, Boston, MA.

Fleishman, E. A. (1953), 'The description of supervisory behavior', *Journal of Applied Psychology*, vol. 37, no.1, pp. 1–6.

Follett, M. P. (1920), *The New State: Group organization, the solution of popular government*, Longmans Green, London.

French, J. and Raven, B. (1959), 'The bases of social power', in D. Cartwright (ed.), *Studies in Social Power*, Institute for Social Research, Ann Arbor, MI.

Friedman, M. (1962), *Capitalism and Freedom*, University of Chicago Press, Chicago, IL.

Friedman, T. (2005), *The World is Flat: A brief history of the globalized world in the 21st century*, Penguin/Allen Lane, London.

Gamble, J., Morris, J. and Wilkinson, B. (2004), 'Mass production is alive and well: the future of work and organization in east Asia', *International Journal of Human Resource Management*, vol. 15, no. 2, pp. 397–409.

Garnier, J.-P. (2008), 'Rebuilding the R&D engine in big pharma', *Harvard Business Review*, vol. 86, no. 5, pp. 68–76.

Gilbreth, F. B. (1911), *Motion study: A method for increasing the efficiency of the workman*, Van Norstrand, New York.

Gilbreth, L. M. (1914), *The Psychology of Management*, Sturgis & Walton, New York.

Giraudeau, M. (2008), 'The drafts of strategy: opening up plans and their uses', *Long Range Planning*, vol. 41, no. 3, pp. 291–308.

Glassop, L. (2002), 'The organizational benefits of teams', *Human Relations*, vol. 55, no. 2, pp. 225–49.

Grant, R. M. (1991), 'The resource-based theory of competitive advantage: implications for strategy formulation', *California Management Review*, vol. 33, no. 3, pp. 114–35.

Grant, R. M. (2003), 'Strategic planning in a turbulent environment: evidence from the oil majors', *Strategic Management Journal*, vol. 24, no. 6, pp. 491–517.

Grattan, L. and Erickson, T. J. (2007), '8 ways to build collaborative teams', *Harvard Business Review*, vol. 85, no. 11, pp. 100–09.

Guthrie, D. (2006), *China and Globalization: The social, economic and political transformation of Chinese society*, Routledge, London.

Hackman, J. R. (1990), *Groups that Work (and Those that Don't)*, Jossey-Bass, San Francisco, CA.

Hackman, J. R. and Oldham, G. R. (1980), *Work Redesign*, Addison-Wesley, Reading, MA.

Hackman, J. R. and Wageman, R. (2005), 'A theory of team coaching', *Academy of Management Review*, vol. 30, no. 2, pp. 269–87.

Hales, C. (2001), *Managing through Organization*, Routledge, London.

Hales, C. (2006), 'Moving down the line? The shifting boundary between middle and first-line management', *Journal of General Management*, vol. 32, no. 2, pp. 31–55.

Handy, C. (1988), *Understanding Voluntary Organizations*, Penguin, Harmondsworth.

Handy, C. (1993), *Understanding Organizations* (4th edn), Penguin, Harmondsworth.

Harrison, E. F. (1999), *The Managerial Decision-Making Process* (5th edn), Houghton Mifflin, Boston, MA.

Hartley, J. (2008) (ed.), *Managing to Improve Public Services*, Cambridge University Press, Cambridge.

Harvey, J. B. (1988), 'The Abilene paradox: the management of agreement', *Organizational Dynamics*, vol. 17, no. 1, pp. 17–43.

Hawken, P., Lovins, A. B. and Lovins, L. H. (1999), *Natural Capitalism: The next industrial revolution*, Earthscan, London.

Hayes, N. (2002), *Managing Teams*, Thomson Learning, London.

Hayes, R. H. and Wheelwright, S. C. (1979), 'Link manufacturing process and product lifecycles', *Harvard Business Review*, vol. 57, no. 1, pp. 133–40.

Heil, G., Bennis, W. and Stephens, D. C. (2000), *Douglas McGregor Revisited*, Wiley, New York.

Heller, R. (2001), 'Inside Zara', *Forbes Global*, 28 May, pp. 24–25, 28–29.

Herzberg, F. (1959), *The Motivation to Work*, Wiley, New York.

Herzberg, F. (1968), 'One more time: how do you motivate employees?', *Harvard Business Review*, vol. 46, no. 1, pp. 53–62.

Hill, T. (1993), *Manufacturing Strategy Text and Cases*, Macmillan, London.

Hodgkinson, G. P., Sadler-Smith, E., Burke, L. A., Claxton, G. and Sparrow, P. R. (2009), 'Intuition in organizations: implications for strategic management', *Long Range Planning*, vol. 42, no. 3, pp. 277–97.

Hofstede, G. (1991), *Cultures and Organizations: Software of the mind*, McGraw-Hill, London.

Hofstede, G. (2001), *Culture's Consequences: Comparing values, behaviors, institutions and organizations across nations*, Sage, London.

Hofstede, G. and Hofstede, G. J. (2005), *Cultures and Organizations: Software of the mind* (2nd edn), McGraw-Hill, New York.

House, R. J. (1996), 'Path–goal theory of leadership: lessons, legacy and a reformulation', *Leadership Quarterly*, vol. 7, no. 3, pp. 323–52.

House, R. J. and Mitchell, T. R. (1974), 'Path–goal theory of leadership', *Contemporary Business*, vol. 3, no. 2, pp. 81–98.

Huczynski, A. A. (2004), *Influencing Within Organizations* (2nd edn), Routledge, London.

Huczynski, A. A. and Buchanan, D. A. (2007), *Organizational Behaviour* (6th edn), Financial Times/Prentice Hall, Harlow.

Imai, M. (1986), *Kaizen – the Key to Japan's Competitive Success*, McGraw-Hill, New York.

Iyer, B. and Davenport, T. H. (2008), 'Reverse engineering Google's innovation machine', *Harvard Business Review*, vol. 86, no. 4, pp. 58–68.

Janis, I.L. (1972), *Victims of Groupthink*, Houghton-Mifflin, Boston, MA.

Jennings, D. (2000), 'PowerGen: the development of corporate planning in a privatized utility', *Long Range Planning*, vol. 33, no. 2, pp. 201–19.

Johnson, G., Scholes, K. and Whittington, R. (2008), *Exploring Corporate Strategy* (8th edn), Financial Times/ Prentice Hall, Harlow.

Johnson, J. and Tellis, G.J. (2008), 'Drivers of success for market entry into China and India', *Journal of Marketing*, vol. 72, no. 1, pp. 1–13.

Jones, O. (2000), 'Scientific management, culture and control: a first-hand account of Taylorism in practice', *Human Relations*, vol. 53, no. 5, pp. 631–53.

Juran, J. (1974), *Quality Control Handbook*, McGraw-Hill, New York.

Kahneman, D. and Tversky, A. (1974), 'Judgement under uncertainty: heuristics and biases', *Science*, vol. 185, pp. 1124–31.

Kanter, R. M. (2001), 'The ten deadly mistakes of wanna dots', *Harvard Business Review*, vol. 79, no. 1, pp. 91–100.

Kaplan, R. S. and Norton, D. P. (1992), 'The balanced scorecard – measures that drive performance', *Harvard Business Review*, vol, 70, no. 1, pp. 71–79.

Kaplan, R. S. and Norton, D. P. (1993), 'Putting the balanced scorecard to work', *Harvard Business Review*, vol. 71, no. 5, pp. 134–42.

Kaplan, R. S. and Norton, D. P. (2008), *The Execution Premium: Linking strategy to operations for competitive advantage*, Harvard Business School Press, Boston, MA.

Katzenbach, J. R. and Smith, D. K. (1993), *The Wisdom of Teams*, Harvard Business School Press, Boston, MA.

Kelman, H. C. (1961), 'Processes of opinion change', *Public Opinion Quarterly*, vol. 25, no. 1, pp. 57–78.

Kennedy, G., Boddy, D. and Paton, R. (2006), 'Managing the aftermath: lessons from The Royal Bank of Scotland's acquisition of NatWest', *European Management Journal*, vol. 24, no. 5, pp. 368–79.

Kirby, M. W. (2003), *Operational Research in War and Peace: The British experience from the 1930s to the 1970s*, Imperial College Press, London.

Kirkman, B. L., Lowe, K. B. and Gibson, C. B. (2006), 'A quarter century of *Culture's Consequences*: A review of empirical research incorporating Hofstede's cultural values framework', *Journal of International Business Studies*, vol. 37, no. 3, pp. 285–320.

Klein, G. (1997), *Sources of Power: How people make decisions*, MIT Press, Cambridge, MA.

Kolb, D., Rubin, E. and Osland, J. (1991), *Organizational Psychology*, Prentice Hall, Englewood Cliffs, NJ.

Komaki, J. (2003), 'Reinforcement theory at work: enhancing and explaining what workers do', in L. W. Porter, G. A. Bigley and R. M. Steers (eds), *Motivation and Work Behavior* (7th edn), Irwin/McGraw-Hill, Burr Ridge, IL.

Komaki, J. L., Coombs, T., Redding, T. P. and Schepman, S. (2000), 'A rich and rigorous examination of applied behavior analysis research in the world of work', in C. L. Cooper and I. T. Robertson (eds), *International Review of Industrial and Organizational Psychology*, Wiley, Chichester, pp. 265–367.

Kotter, J. P. (1982), *The General Managers*, Free Press, New York.

Kotter, J. P. (1990), *A Force for Change: How leadership differs from management*, The Free Press, New York.

Kramer, R. M. (2006), 'The great intimidators', *Harvard Business Review*, vol. 84, no. 2, pp. 88–96.

Kumar, N. (2006), 'Strategies to fight low-cost rivals', *Harvard Business Review*, vol. 84, no. 12, pp. 104–12.

Lawrence, P. and Lorsch, J.W. (1967), *Organization and Environment*, Harvard Business School Press, Boston, MA.

Laudon, K. C. and Laudon, J. P. (2010), *Essentials of Management Information Systems* (9th edn), Pearson Education, Harlow.

Lengel, R. H. and Daft, R. L. (1988), 'The selection of communication media as an executive skill', *Academy of Management Executive*, vol. 11, no. 3, pp. 225–32.

Likert, R. (1961), *New Patterns of Management*, McGraw-Hill, New York.

Likert, R. (1967), *The Human Organization: Its management and value*, McGraw-Hill, New York.

Lindblom, C. E. (1959), 'The science of muddling through', *Public Administration Review*, vol. 19, no. 2, pp. 79–88.

Lock, D. (2007), *Project Management* (9th edn), Gower, Aldershot.

Locke, E. A. (1968), 'Towards a theory of task motivation and incentives', *Organizational Behavior and Human Performance*, vol. 3, pp. 157–89.

Locke, E. A. and Latham, G. P. (1990), *A Theory of Goal Setting and Task Performance*, Prentice Hall, Englewood Cliffs, NJ.

Locke, E. A. and Latham, G. P. (2002), 'Building a practically useful theory of goal setting and task motivation – A 35-year odyssey', *American Psychologist*, vol. 57, no. 9, pp. 705–17.

Lorsch, J.W. (1986), 'Managing culture: the invisible barrier to strategic change', *California Management Review*, vol. 28, no. 2, pp. 95–109.

Lovallo, D. and Kahneman, D. (2003), 'Delusions of success', *Harvard Business Review*, vol. 81, no. 7, pp. 56–63.

Luthans, F. (1988), 'Successful vs effective real managers', *Academy of Management Executive*, vol. 11, no. 2, pp. 127–32.

Magretta, J. (2002), *What Management Is (and Why it is Everyone's Business)*, Profile Books, London.

Mallin, C. A. (2007), *Corporate Governance* (2nd edn), Oxford University Press, Oxford.

March, J. G. (1988), *Decisions and Organizations*, Blackwell, London.

Martin, J. (2002), *Organizational Culture: Mapping the terrain*, Sage, London.

Maslow, A. (1970), *Motivation and Personality* (2nd edn), Harper & Row, New York.

Mayo, E. (1949), *The Social Problems of an Industrial Civilization,* Routledge and Kegan Paul, London.

McClelland, D. (1961), *The Achieving Society*, Van Nostrand Reinhold, Princeton, NJ.

McCrae, R. R. and John, O. P. (1992), 'An introduction to the five-factor model and its applications', *Journal of Personality*, vol. 60, no. 2, pp. 175–215.

McGregor, D. (1960), *The Human Side of Enterprise*, McGraw-Hill, New York.

McLaren, D. J. (1990), *David Dale of New Lanark*, Heatherbank Press, Milngavie.

McLean, B. and Elkind, P. (2003), *The Smartest Guys in the Room*, Penguin, Harmondsworth.

McMillan, E. and Carlisle, Y. (2007), 'Strategy as order emerging from chaos: A public sector experience', *Long Range Planning*, vol. 40, no. 6, pp. 574–93.

Miller, S., Wilson, D. and Hickson, D. (2004), 'Beyond planning: strategies for successfully implementing strategic decisions', *Long Range Planning*, vol. 37, no. 3, pp. 201–18.

Mintzberg, H. (1973), *The Nature of Managerial Work*, Harper & Row, New York.

Mintzberg, H. (1979), *The Structuring of Organizations*, Prentice Hall, Englewood Cliffs, NJ.

Mintzberg, H. (1994a), *The Rise and Fall of Strategic Planning*, Prentice Hall International, Hemel Hempstead.

Mintzberg, H. (1994b), 'Rethinking strategic planning. Part I: Pitfalls and fallacies', *Long Range Planning*, vol. 27, no. 3, pp. 12–21.

Mintzberg, H., Ahlstrand, B. and Lampel J. (1998), *Strategy Safari*, Financial Times/Prentice Hall, Harlow.

Mitroff, I. I. (1983), *Stakeholders of the Organizational Mind*, Jossey-Bass, San Francisco, CA.

Moritz, M. (2009), *Return to the Little Kingdom*, Duckworth Overlook, London.

Mowday, R. T. and Colwell, K. A. (2003), 'Employee reactions to unfair outcomes in the workplace: the contribution of Adams' equity theory to understanding work motivation', in L. W. Porter, G. A. Bigley and R. M. Steers (eds), *Motivation and Work Behavior* (7th edn), Irwin/McGraw-Hill, Burr Ridge, IL.

Neely, A. and Al Najjar, M. (2006), 'Management learning not management control: the true role of performance measurement', *California Management Review*, vol. 48, no. 3, pp. 101–14.

Nutt, P. C. (2002), *Why Decisions Fail: Avoiding the blunders and traps that lead to debacles*, Berrett-Koehler, San Francisco, CA.

Oakland, J. (1994), *Total Quality Management*, Butterworth/Heinemann, Oxford.

O'Connell, J. F. and Williams, G. (2005), 'Passengers' perceptions of low cost airlines and full service carriers', *Journal of Air Transport Management*, vol. 11, no. 4, pp. 259–72.

Ogbonna, E. and Harris, L. C. (1998), 'Organizational culture: it's not what you think', *Journal of General Management*, vol. 23, no. 3, pp. 35–48.

Ordanini, A., Rubera, G. and Sala, M. (2008), 'Integrating functional knowledge and embedding learning in new product launches: how project forms helped EMI music', *Long Range Planning*, vol. 41, no. 1, pp. 17–32.

Orlitzky, M., Schmidt, F. and Rynes, S. (2003), 'Corporate social and financial performance: a meta-analysis', *Organization Studies*, vol. 24, no. 3, pp. 403–41.

Pascale, R. (1990), *Managing on the Edge*, Penguin, London.

Pedler, M., Burgoyne, J. and Boydell, T. (2004), *A Manager's Guide to Leadership*, McGraw-Hill, Maidenhead.

Peloza, J. (2006), 'Using corporate social responsibility as insurance for financial performance', *California Management Review*, vol. 48, no. 2, pp. 52–72.

Peters, T. J. and Waterman, D. H. (1982), *In Search of Excellence*, Harper & Row, London.

Pettigrew, A. (1985), *The Awakening Giant: Continuity and change in imperial chemical industries*, Blackwell, Oxford.

Pierce, L. and Snyder, J. (2008), 'Ethical spillovers in firms: evidence from vehicle emissions testing', *Management Science*, vol. 54, no. 11, pp. 1891–903.

Porter, M. E. (1980a), *Competitive Strategy*, Free Press, New York.

Porter, M. E. (1980b), *Competitive Advantage*, Free Press, New York.

Porter, M. E. (1985), *Competitive Advantage: Creating and sustaining superior performance*, Free Press, New York.

Porter, M. E. (2008), 'The five competitive forces that shape strategy', *Harvard Business Review*, vol. 86, no. 1, pp. 78–93.

Prastacos, G., Soderquist, K., Spanos, Y. and Van Wassenhove, L. (2002), 'An integrated framework for managing change in the new competitive landscape', *European Management Journal*, vol. 20, no. 1, pp. 55–71.

Pugh, D. S. and Hickson, D. J. (1976), *Organization Structure in its Context: The Aston Programme I*, Gower, Aldershot.

Quinn, R. E., Faerman, S. R., Thompson, M. P. and McGrath, M. R. (2003), *Becoming a Master Manager* (3rd edn), Wiley, New York.

Roddick, A. (1991), *Body and Soul*, Ebury Press, London.

Roethlisberger, F. J. and Dickson, W. J. (1939), *Management and the Worker*, Harvard University Press, Cambridge, MA.

Ronen, S. and Shenkar, O. (1985), 'Clustering countries on attitudinal dimensions: review and synthesis', *Academy of Management Review*, vol. 10, no. 3, pp. 435–54.

Rosen, S. (1998), 'A lump of clay', *Communication World*, vol. 15, no. 7, p. 58.

Rousseau, D. M. and Schalk, R. (2000), *Psychological Contracts in Employment: Cross-national perspectives*, Sage, London.

Royle, E. (1998), *Robert Owen and the Commencement of the Millennium: A study of the Harmony community*, Manchester University Press, Manchester.

Rugman, A. M. (2005), *The Regional Multinationals*, Cambridge University Press, Cambridge.

Sahlman, W. A. (1997), 'How to write a great business plan', *Harvard Business Review*, vol. 75, no. 4, pp. 98–108.

Saunders, C., Van Slyke, C. and Vogel, D. R.. (2004), 'My time or yours? Managing time visions in global virtual teams', *Academy of Management Executive*, vol. 18, no. 1, pp. 19–31.

Schein, E. (2004), *Organization Culture and Leadership* (3rd edn), Jossey-Bass, San Francisco, CA.

Schultz, H. with Gordon, J. (2011), *Onward: How Starbucks fought for its life without losing its soul*, Wiley, Chichester.

Scott, D. M. and Halligan, B. (2010), *Marketing Lessons from the Grateful Dead: What every business can learn from the most iconic band in history*, Wiley, Hoboken, NJ.

Shaw, W. H. (1991), *Business Ethics*, Wadsworth, Belmont, CA.

Simon, H. (1960), *Administrative Behavior*, Macmillan, New York.

Simons, R. (1995), 'Control in an age of empowerment', *Harvard Business Review*, vol. 73, no. 2, pp. 80–88.

Sine, W. D., Mitsuhashi, H. and Kirsch, D. A. (2006), 'Revisiting Burns and Stalker: Formal structure and new venture performance in emerging economic sectors', *Academy of Management Journal*, vol. 49, no. 1, pp. 121–32.

Skinner, B. F. (1971), *Contingencies of Reinforcement*, Appleton-Century-Crofts, East Norwalk, CT.

Slack, N., Chambers, S. and Johnston, R. (2010), *Operations Management* (6th edn), Financial Times/ Prentice Hall, Harlow.

Smith, A. (1776), *The Wealth of Nations*, ed. with an introduction by Andrew Skinner (1974), Penguin, Harmondsworth.

Smith, M., Busi, M., Ball, P. and Van Der Meer, R. (2008), 'Factors influencing an organisation's ability to manage innovation: A structured literature review and conceptual model', *International Journal of Innovation Management*, vol. 12, no. 4, pp. 655–76.

Sparrowe, R. T. and Liden, R. C. (2005), 'Two routes to influence: integrating leader–member exchange and social network perspectives', *Administrative Science Quarterly*, vol. 50, no. 4, pp. 505–35.

Sprague, L. (2007), 'Evolution of the field of operations management', *Journal of Operations Management*, vol. 25, no. 2, pp. 219–38.

Spriegel, W. R. and Myers, C. E. (eds) (1953), *The Writings of the Gilbreths*, Irwin, Homewood, IL.

Stavins, R. N. (1994), 'The challenge of going green', *Harvard Business Review*, vol. 72, no. 4, pp. 38–39.

Steinbock, D. (2001), *The Nokia Revolution*, American Management Association, New York, NY.

Stewart, R. (1967), *Managers and Their Jobs*, Macmillan, London.

Strachan, A. (2004), 'Lights, camera, action', *Personnel Management* (16 September), pp. 44–46.

Sull, D. N. (2007), 'Closing the gap between strategy and execution', *MIT Sloan Management Review*, vol. 48, no. 4, pp. 30–38.

Swartz, M. and Watkins, S. (2002), *Power Failure: The rise and fall of Enron*, Aurum, London.

Tannenbaum, R. and Schmidt, W. H. (1973), 'How to choose a leadership pattern: should a manager be democratic or autocratic – or something in between?', *Harvard Business Review*, vol. 37, no. 2, pp. 95–102.

Tapscott, D. and Williams, A. D. (2006), *Wikinomics: How mass collaboration changes everything*, Viking Penguin, New York.

Taylor, F. W. (1917), *The Principles of Scientific Management*, Harper, New York.

Thomas, A. B. (2003), *Controversies in Management: Issues, debates and answers* (2nd edn), Routledge, London.

Thompson, J. D. (1967), *Organizations in Action*, McGraw-Hill, New York.

Thompson, P. and McHugh, D. (2002), *Work Organizations: A critical introduction*, Palgrave, Basingstoke.

Tidd, J. and Bessant, J. (2009), *Managing Innovation: Integrating technological, market and organisational change*, Wiley, Chichester.

Toffler, B. L. and Reingold, J. (2003), *Final Accounting: Ambition, greed and the fall of Arthur Andersen*, Broadway Books, New York.

Trevino, L. K. (1986), 'Ethical decision-making in organisations: a person–situation interactionist model', *Academy of Management Review*, vol. 11, no. 3, pp. 601–17.

Trevino, L. K. and Weaver, G. R. (2003), *Managing Ethics in Business Organizations: Social scientific perspectives*, Stanford University Press, Stanford, CA.

Trist, E. L. and Bamforth, K. W. (1951), 'Some social and psychological consequences of the Longwall method of coal getting', *Human Relations*, vol. 4, no. 1, pp. 3–38.

Tuckman, B. and Jensen, N. (1977), 'Stages of small group development revisited', *Group and Organizational Studies*, vol. 2, pp. 419–27.

Uhl-Bien, M. and Graen, G.B. (1998), 'Individual self-management: analysis of professionals' self-managing activities in functional and cross-functional teams', *Academy of Management Journal*, vol. 41, no. 3, pp. 340–50.

Van der Heijden, K. (1996), *Scenarios: The art of strategic conversation*, Wiley, Chichester.

Van der Vegt, G. S. and Bunderson, J. S. (2005), 'Learning and performance in multidisciplinary teams: the importance of collective team identification', *Academy of Management Journal*, vol. 48, no. 3, pp. 532–47.

Vogel, D. (2005), *The Market for Virtue: The potential and limits of corporate social responsibility*, Brookings Institution Press, Washington, DC.

Vroom, V. H. (1964), *Work and Motivation*, Wiley, New York.

Vroom, V. H. and Yetton, P. W. (1973), *Leadership and Decision-making*, University of Pittsburgh Press, Pittsburgh, PA.

Watts, S (2001), *The Magic Kingdom: Walt Disney and the American way of life*, Houghton-Mifflin, Boston, MA.

Weber, M. (1947), *The Theory of Social and Economic Organization*, Free Press, Glencoe, IL.

Whetten, D. A. and Cameron, K. S. (2010), *Developing Management Skills* (8th edn), Prentice Hall International, Upper Saddle River, NJ.

Whipp, R., Rosenfeld, R. and Pettigrew, A. (1988), 'Understanding strategic change processes: some preliminary British findings', in A. Pettigrew (ed.), *The Management of Strategic Change*, Blackwell, Oxford.

Whitley, R. (1999), *Divergent Capitalisms: The social structuring and change of business systems*, Oxford University Press, Oxford.

Whitley, R. (2009), 'U.S. Capitalism: A tarnished model?', *Academy of Management Perspectives*, vol. 23, no. 2, pp. 11–22.

Whittington, R., Molloy, E., Mayer, M. and Smith, A. (2006), 'Practices of strategising/organising: broadening strategy work and skills', *Long Range Planning*, vol. 39, no. 6, pp. 615–29.

Wolff, H.-G. and Moser, K. (2009), 'Effects of networking on career success: a longitudinal study', *Journal of Applied Psychology*, vol. 94, no. 1, pp. 196–206.

Woodward, J. (1965), *Industrial Organization: Theory and practice* (2nd edn 1980), Oxford University Press, Oxford.

Yip, G. S. (2003), *Total Global Strategy* II, Pearson Education, Upper Saddle River, NJ.

Yukl, G. A. (2009), *Leadership in Organizations* (7th edn), Prentice Hall, Upper Saddle River, NJ.

INDEX

Note: glossary entries are shown in **bold**.